Integral Advantage

The author of Integral Advantage *manages to facilitate a pathway of appreciation and reason into the complex cosmology surrounding the development of emerging societies within our universe. It also gives a voice to a reality often silent and unrepresented within our global landscape…*

Bennie Anderson, CEO of Da Vinci Institute, South Africa

This remarkable book written by Professor Lessem underlies future hope for the sustainable integral society, exploring the emotional truth of social innovation. He re-visits the 'modern' economic concept of the BRICS, transforming it into the 'ecology of holistic philosophy', re-framing it into the GENE-ius that characterizes the Trans4m Centre for Integral Development in Geneva, and finding unique cultural, social, economic and spiritual paradigms of Brazil, the Russia which I have known so well, India, China and South Africa, reflecting systematic and effective ways of integral advantage, giving birth to new perspectives for the local-global reach.

J. Lapidus, Business strategist of Zerno Consulting, Latvia – South Africa

Ronnie Lessem's insights into the very soul and soil of India provide a rich and fertile ground for an integral model of development; not just for the renewal of Indian society but for the advantage of the world at large.

Sudhanshu Palsule, Indian School of Business, Hyderabad, India

One of the most critical aspects of our times is to find the references that will guide our transition toward a more sustainable and humane civilization. Ronnie Lessem provides such a guidance by offering new examplars and frameworks, inspiring questions that deepen our Brazilian inquiry.

Thais Corral, social innovator, founder of Sinal do Vale and Adapta Sertao

The author has successfully articulated the complicated individual and social systems of the Chinese. An understanding of the Chinese conceptualization of 'Egocentricism', 'Xiaokang' and 'Chinese Pragmatism' is very necessary for gaining the knowledge of how this second largest single economy of the world will impact on the global social and economic development.

Junie Tong, Staffordshire University, UK

Transformation and Innovation Series

Series Editors:
Ronnie Lessem, Trans4m Center for Integral Development, Switzerland
Alexander Schieffer, Trans4m Center for Integral Development, Switzerland

The world's economic and socio-political landscape has changed dramatically and created a now-or-never momentum for transformation and innovation. 'Business as usual' no longer works. The time has come to fundamentally rethink enterprise, economics and development.

The Gower 'Transformation and Innovation Series', with contributions by leading thinkers-and-doers from diverse cultures across the globe, combines theory and practice, informing both decision makers and scholars. It provides cutting-edge, viable approaches to the unprecedented challenges faced by business leaders, management consultants, economic policy makers and development agents.

The pioneering Integral Worlds approach, developed by Lessem and Schieffer, provides a unique and coherent orientation to the wide-ranging volumes in the series. This approach combines individual, organizational and socio-economic development. Drawing on the particularities of each and every culture, it enhances local identity while contributing to global integrity. It activates the potential for a holistic realignment of enterprise and economics with other major dimensions of society, such as nature and community; culture and spirituality; as well as science, systems and technology.

Latest titles in the series

Integral Renewal
A Relational and Renewal Perspective
Ronnie Lessem with Alexander Schieffer
ISBN 978-1-4724-5435-5

Inclusive Organizational Transformation
An African Perspective on Human Niches and Diversity of Thought
Rica Viljoen
ISBN 978-1-4724-2299-6

Integral Polity
Integrating Nature, Culture, Society and Economy
Ronnie Lessem with Ibrahim Abouleish, Marko Pogačnik and Louis Herman
ISBN 978-1-4724-4247-5

Integral Advantage

Revisiting Emerging Markets and Societies

RONNIE LESSEM

Routledge
Taylor & Francis Group
LONDON AND NEW YORK

First published 2015 by Gower Publishing

Published 2016 by Routledge
2 Park Square, Milton Park, Abingdon, Oxon OX14 4RN
711 Third Avenue, New York, NY 10017, USA

Routledge is an imprint of the Taylor & Francis Group, an informa business

Gower Applied Business Research
Our programme provides leaders, practitioners, scholars and researchers with thought provoking, cutting edge books that combine conceptual insights, interdisciplinary rigour and practical relevance in key areas of business and management.

British Library Cataloguing in Publication Data
A catalogue record for this book is available from the British Library

Library of Congress Cataloging-in-Publication Data
Lessem, Ronnie.
Integral advantage : revisiting emerging markets and societies / by Ronnie Lessem.
pages cm. -- (Transformation and innovation)
Includes bibliographical references and index.
ISBN 978-1-4724-7186-4 (hardback) -- ISBN 978-1-4724-7187-1 (ebook) -- ISBN 978-1-4724-7188-8 (epub) 1. Economic development--Developing countries. 2. Developing countries--Economic policy. I. Title.

HC59.7.L385 2016
338.9009172'4--dc23

2015020658

ISBN 13: 978-1-4724-7186-4 (hbk)

Contents

List of Figures

List of Tables

PART I

Orientation

Chapter 1

The Internet is Not the Answer: Fields, Factories and Workshops to Networked Economy

When you're tramping through the jungle. Or up a mountain, or across a field, you've no idea how your progress might look form a bird's eye view, or why it would be useful to see things differently.

Dayo Olopade (1), The Bright Continent: Making Change in Modern Africa

1.1 Introduction

COMPARATIVE TO INTEGRAL ADVANTAGE

The Illusion of Economic Progress

In this book we shall be turning conventional *economic* wisdom on its head, specifically in relation to *emerging* markets, that is the BRICS countries. To that extent, we shall be arguing, that both Smith (capitalism) and Marx (communism) got it wrong. Neither the division of labour (Smith) nor economic determinism (Marx) offers a viable way forward. In fact the whole idea of 'progress', for us, is a misnoma, and we have as much, if not more, to learn from the past than we can learn from the present and future. Hence the title of this chapter: *why the Internet is not the answer.*

Need for Integral Advantage

Moreover, we go on to argue, firstly and paradoxically, that we have as much to learn from an emerging Russia straddling 'east–west' than from the established Anglo-Saxon, capitalist 'west-north', so to speak. Moreover, to the extent that we can learn from America, it is South America, specifically Brazil in the 'south-west', rather than North America, that leads the emerging twenty-first century way. Secondly, perhaps even more surprisingly, we reckon we have as much to learn from an African 'north–south', than from a European 'north-west', the latter aligned with Marxism or socialism hitherto.

That said, our overall contention is not that one society is any better than another, but that all societies – in their nature and their culture, in their technology and their economy – have something *potentially* unique to contribute (which is why our opening quote from Nigerian-American journalist Dayo Olopade is significant), as an *integral* whole.

As such, we totally reject the classical economic notion of 'comparative advantage', because it focuses exclusively on *economic* advantage, in isolation of nature, culture and society, and what we term an all round 'polity' (2) that serves to align each of such altogether. It is that individual and societal all-roundedness to which we will allude, as *integral* advantage, bearing in mind that, on the one hand, *the west needs the east, the north needs the south, and they need each other, altogether;* and on the other hand, *each and every society needs to build on its own local grounds, albeit that thereafter, in order to evolve, the local and the global need to interact.* That is what we mean by integral advantage.

WHAT'S WRONG WITH 'EMERGING' MARKETS

Nothing New Under the Sun

Ironically as such, while our major focus in this work is on the *emerging* markets *and societies*, specifically the BRICS – Brazil, *Russia*, India, China, and *South Africa* – most especially as we shall see on Russia and South Africa – we reject the conventional 'growth map' underlying 'emerging markets' as a partial truth at best. For the very notion of 'emergence', as we shall see later in Chapter 2, implies that something fundamentally new needs to come into being, new life so to speak. This new life is born out of a meeting between different worlds, rather than through competition between one and another. Compare such with what the originator of the notion of BRICs, Jim O'Neill (3), who was a senior executive of Goldman Sachs at the time of writing, had to say in 2011:

> *Tens of millions of people from the BRICs and beyond are being taken out of poverty by the growth of their economies. While it is easy to focus on the fact that China has created so many billionaires, it should not be forgotten that in the past 15 years or so, 300 million or more Chinese have been lifted out of poverty. In India the lives of many tens*

of millions have similarly improved, and perhaps 300 million or more will join them in the next decade or two. Vast swathes of mankind are having their chance to enjoy the fruits of wealth creation. That is the big story.

Little is Truly Emerging

Well it may be a 'big' story, and it is 'new', but only in a merely quantitative sense. There is nothing qualitatively new in there being many more Chinese billionaires or Indians 'lifted out of poverty', economically so to speak. In fact later on, in Chapters 12 and 13, we shall also hear about the downsides of economic 'development', in India and China. Meanwhile what is emerging, in the final analysis, is a further encroachment of 'western-northern' capitalism on the 'south-east' (India) and 'north-east' (China), albeit with some BRIC variations on such an underlying capitalist theme. Moreover, the theme is a singularly economic, not an integral – natural and cultural, societal as well as economic – one. In other words, little substantively and qualitatively new then is emerging from O'Neill's *Growth Map.* That's what, for us, is 'wrong' with such an allegation of *emerging* BRICS economies, in isolation of their societies.

RELEASING A SOCIETY'S GENIUS

Pursuing an Integral Rhythm

What, for us then, is qualitatively new, and thereby truly *emergent,* can only be found if we go beyond economics per se, and, if you like, the comparative *economic* advantage of each BRICS nation. In effect we need to uncover the *integral* advantage within each. In other words, we need to reveal the emerging nature, culture, society and economy of each 'polity' as a whole, that is, for us, the source of its overall integrity. So we argue that *the fate of Greece or Slovenia (4) in Europe today, or indeed Libya or Iraq within the Middle East, is determined, by and large, by the extent to which each can be enabled to pursue what we term its integral rhythm* (5), locally and naturally grounding, locally–globally and culturally emerging, newly globally and socially/scientifically navigating, and thereafter globally-locally economically effecting: altogether then serving to release its genius. That is no easy task, and currently there is no field of study, or agency in society, to integrally promote such. Hence the need for a book such as this, and a developmental agency to follow, one which we have hitherto termed, as above, an *integral university,* to make a start.

The Part Dominates the Whole

What we mean by all that will be elaborated, much more extensively, in Chapter 2 and more especially in Chapter 3. But here is a brief synopsis. For us the pursuit of *integral advantage is not dependent on relative factor costs, and thereby economic specialization that follows* (see below), *but on the overall uniqueness, and authenticity, of each society,* in itself and in relation to the wider world. Most, if not all, societies are inhibited, both internally and externally, from realizing such. Instead, one society tends to dominate over another, and prevent itself, or the other, from realizing itself as a whole. Alternatively, one part of a particular society is dominant over others, whereby development, as a whole, is inhibited. As a result you might have poverty, autocracy, environmental decay, or another such malfunction, as such, a part dominates the whole, both internally and/or externally. In short, the society, altogether, is disintegrating, to some degree or another.

Moreover, because all too often 'western-northern' concepts and institutions – set apart from, but dominating over the world as a whole – like free markets or liberal democracy have become so all pervasive, a particular society, be it Egypt or Ireland, is inhibited from *emerging.* Integral development, centred in middle-up-down-across guise, needs to arise initially and locally from the ground up: naturally and communally as such, and subsequently develop, culturally and spiritually and locally–globally so to speak, outgrowing its prior parochial self. So, on the one hand, once supposedly released from their despotic shackles, Libya or Iraq disintegrate, because each is not enabled to emerge in such integral guise. Greece and Spain, on the other hand, implode, as each has done of late, because austerity may bite, and such austerity does nothing to help each country uncover and release their overall, societally-based integral advantage. Indeed, there is no integral agency – certainly neither, for example, IMF nor EU – to promote such.

INTEGRAL BRICS

East, West, North and South

What we shall be doing in this book then, is to point to such an emerging *integral BRICS advantage,* in relation to each of the five economies *and* societies, generally – Brazil, Russia, India, China and South Africa – and in relation to two of these, Russia and South Africa, more specifically. Why, then, do these two countries assume pride of place in our integral context?

Figure 1.1 Integral advantage

True to our integral realities, spanning east and west, north and south, we chose two countries whose reason for being spans, respectively, those geographical and psychological polarities, that is Russia *spirit*ually and materially (east/west) and South Africa in terms of nature or *wild*erness and humankind (south/north). Moreover, because our concerns are integral, rather than merely economic, these two countries are, for us, of major existential concern: South Africa, not only the place of humankind's origins, but also renowned for its 'long walk to freedom' between the 1960s and 1990s, leading to the fall of 'apartheid', and Russia, because it was, for a long time, the major counter-force, socio-politically, to the all pervasive capitalist 'west', and today, geographically, straddles 'east–west'.

Alongside these Russian and South African two then, and positioned integrally, Brazil 'south-west', India 'south-east', China 'north-east' and the conventional BRICS wisdom as formulated by the US/UK in the 'west-north', will be as shown in Figure 1.1 above.

Google Laden Future to Guild Laden Past

We now turn back to Russian geographer Peter Kropotkin to set a necessary backdrop to take us into the past, when compared and contrasted with the 'age of the Internet', which takes us into the future. Thereby, we are able to recognize that there is no such automatic thing as future 'progress'. To that extent we can learn, for example, from the Russia of the past as from the US of the future. In fact, as the Brazilian polymath Roberto Mangabeira Unger (6), will ultimately reveal (Chapter 14), the *seemingly bright prospects* of, for example, a *Google laden future*, have in fact prevented us from learning from, and developing anew, the *allegedly dim* prospects from a Kropotkin laden, *guild*-edged past.

1.2 Fields, Factories and Workshops

FROM DIVISION TO INTEGRATION OF LABOUR

The Economic Division of Labour

Peter Kropotkin (7), about whom we shall hear much more in Chapter 4, was born and bred in nineteenth-century Russia, before being forced to flee to France, to Switzerland and to Britain, thereafter returning to Russia after the 1917 revolution. In our view, as we shall see, Kropotkin is a key representative of the 'east–west' (spiritual-material) polarity that Russia potentially, if not actually, embodies today. From the outset he lamented the fact that *we were taught, as per Ricardo's theory of comparative (economic) advantage,* for instance, *that Hungary and Russia are predestined by nature to grow corn in order to feed the manufacturing industries,* that Britain had to provide the world market with cottons, iron goods and coal; Belgium with woollen cloth; and so on.

Each region as such has to have its own exclusive economic speciality. Humanity though, for Kropotkin, perceives there is no advantage for the community in riveting a human being for all his life to a given spot, in a workshop nor a mine; no gain in depriving him of such work that would bring him into free intercourse with nature, make of him a conscious part of the grand whole, a partner in the highest enjoyment of art, of free work and creation.

Each Nation is a Compound Aggregate

Nations then as such should refuse to be specialized in purely economic terms. *Each nation is a compound aggregate of states and inclinations, of wants and resources, of capacities and inventive powers.* The territory occupied by each society is in its turn a most varied texture of soils and climates, of hills and valleys, of slopes leading to a still greater variety of territories and races. Political economy has hitherto insisted chiefly upon *division.* Kropotkin proclaims *integration* – and *the ideal towards which society is already marching is one of integrated, combined labour*. Each nation then has her own agriculturalist and manufacturer; each individual working in the field and in some industrial art; each individual combining scientific knowledge with the knowledge of handicraft – such is, he affirms, the present tendency of civilized nations. In that capacity, Kropotkin in his fields, factories and workshops now, as will Evtuov (8) in her integrated Russian province later (see Chapter 7) sows the seeds for our notion of *integral advantage.*

SMALL INDUSTRIES AND INDUSTRIAL VILLAGES CREATED AND DESTROYED

Sister Arts

The two sister arts of *agriculture and industry*, Kropotkin says, were not always so estranged from one another as they are now (in the first decade of the twentieth century). *There was a time, and that time is not so far back, when both were thoroughly combined*; the villages were then the seats of a variety of industries, and the artisans in the cities did not abandon agriculture; many towns were nothing else but industrial villages.

But then came the water-motors, steam, the development of machinery, and they broke the link which formerly connected the farm with the workshop. Factories grew up and they abandoned the fields. Millions of labourers, driven away by sheer force from the land, gathered in the cities in search of jobs – we shall see below how that has affected the Chinese of late – and soon forgot the bonds which formerly attached them to the soil.

False Necessity

And we, in our admiration for the 'progress' achieved under the new factory system, which Brazilian social scientist Mangabeira Unger, under the guise of his 'false necessity', will vigorously later protest, overlooked the advantages of the old system under which the tiller of the soil was the industrial worker at the same time. Of course, today, it is not just a matter of going back, but of going backward and forward at the same time. *We doomed to disappearance all those branches of industry which formerly used to prosper in the villages; we condemned in industry all that was not a big factory.* The present and the future, by way of modernization, took over from, rather than connected with – in the course of transcending – the past.

CREATING UNIMAGINABLE RICHES

Blending Factories and Fields

In the final analysis, Kropotkin goes on to urge all of us to locate factory and workshop at the gates of your fields and gardens. Eliminate those large factory establishments in which huge masses of materials have to be dealt with, in favour of the countless variety of small workshops and factories required to satisfy the infinite variety of tastes amongst people, something characteristic of Europe in the Middle Ages (eleventh and twelfth centuries). Not those factories in which children lose all the appearance of children in the atmosphere of industrial hell, as per Victorian England or 'made in China' below, but those *airy and hygienic, and consequently economical, factories in which human life is of more account than machinery and the making of profits.*

For centuries science and so called practical wisdom have said to man: 'it is good to be rich, to be able to satisfy, at least, your material needs; but the only means to be rich is to train your mind and capacities so as to be able to compel other men and women – slaves, serfs or wage earners – to make these riches for you. But modern knowledge has another issue to offer to thinking men and women. It tells all of us that in order to be rich we need not take bread from the mouths of others; but that *the more rational outcome would be a society in which men, with the work of their own hands and intelligence, and by the aid of machinery invented and to be invented should create unimaginable riches.* In other words, for Russia's Kropotkin, in combining fields and factories, manual and brain work, scientific method and human community, nature and culture, technology and society, such an 'integrated labour' would be far preferable to the division of labour advocated by the classical British economists, and pursued by modern, and indeed post-modern industry.

Fields Factories and Workshops to Silicon Valley

Now let us compare and contrast his position, in the early twentieth century, with that of Silicon Valley in the early part of the twenty-first century. Such a perspective is provided by Internet entrepreneur, and social scientist, Andrew Keen. While the views Keen expresses are not broadly representative, they do touch at least a chord, for many of us concerned with the overall social and economic impact of the Internet. Moreover, while Kropotkin hails from the Russian 'east–west', Keen is firmly lodged in the American 'west-north'.

Where then, and how, if at all, do the two meet?

1.3 Why the Internet is Not the Answer

DIGITAL DISRUPTION

Networked Economy is Making us Poorer

Andrew Keen (10), who is a historian and political scientist, as well as being an Internet entrepreneur, has spent most of his adult life in Northern California (our 'west-north'), and has thereby gained intimate familiarity with its 'workshops and factories', if not also with the 'fields' surrounding Silicon Valley. Overall, then, his view is that:

> *Rather than making us wealthier, the distributed capitalism of the new networked economy is making us poorer. Rather than generating more jobs, this digital disruption is a principal cause of our structural unemployment crisis. Rather than creating more competition, it has created immensely powerful monopolists like Google and Amazon.*

In other words, for him as for us, the quintessential 'west-north', that is Silicon Valley, in the twenty-first century, for all its positive contributions, which of course are legion (how else would I be writing this book on my laptop, and accessing materials for it on the Internet), is making a negative overall contribution to America, if not to the world at large. So the question of whether there has been progress or regression, over the course of the last century, between the times that Russia's Kropotkin and the UK/US's Keen were respectively writing, is a real enough one. Specifically in fact, in today's digital experiment, for Keen, '*the world is being transformed into a winner-take-all, upstairs-downstairs kind of society*'. This networked future is characterized by an astonishingly unequal distribution of economic value and power in almost every industry that the Internet is disrupting. Of course, the Internet – from Wikipedia to Twitter to Google – can be a source of great enlightenment, but that, as he says, is only one side of the overall social and economic coin.

How then has this all come to pass?

MONEY, MONEY, MONEY

Social Overtaken by Technological Innovation

The founding fathers of the Internet, primarily American and British, in the post-war period, were well intentioned technologists, more interested in making a social contribution than in making money. The American polymath Norbert Wiener and his compatriot the engineer Vannevar Bush together with British physicist Tim Berners Lee who invented the World Wide Web, altogether in the post-war period, were motivated by the power of technology to do good for society. For Berners Lee (11), duly inspired by 'nature's web', in his book on *Weaving the Web* written at the end of the twentieth century:

> *The Web is more of a social creation than a technical one. I designed it for a social effect – to help people work together – and not as a technical toy. The ultimate goal of the Web is to support and improve our web-like existence in the world. We clump into families, associations and companies.*

The structure of the Internet-based economy today though, is the reverse of the technological open architecture created by the Internet pioneers. Its top-down system concentrates wealth rather than spreading it. *Rather than producing more jobs or prosperity,* for Keen, *the Internet is dominated by winner-take-all companies like Amazon and Google* that are now monopolizing vast swathes of our information economy.

The First Public-Spirited Story Fed by Civic Purpose

The history of the Internet, overall then, comes in two phases, once again involving, as a whole, more regression rather than progression. *The first story, from World War 11 through to the end of the Cold War into the early 1990s, is a narrative of public-spirited technologists.* As we have indicated, publically funded in the main by institutions like ARPA (Advanced Research Projects Network in America) and CERN (European Organization for Nuclear Research in Europe), each had respectively security oriented and civic objectives. And it is a story, in the first progressive phase, of well-meaning pioneers' relative indifference and occasional hostility to lucrative economic opportunities offered by their creation. Their focus was technological/societal (northern) rather than material/economic (western).

Second Winner Takes All Story Fed by Advertising Revenues

The Internet's second act, a regressive one for Keen, began in the early 1990s when the American government handed over the running of the Internet backbone to commercial Internet Service Providers. This phase of the story, for him then, can be summarized in a single word: money. Just as the end of the Cold War led to the scramble by Russian financial oligarchs, thereby by-passing the Russian nation's potentially integral advantage, as we shall demonstrate (Chapters 4–7), in favour of its comparative economic advantage in the mining and production of oil, so the privatization of the Internet after the end of the Cold War triggered the rush by a new class of technological oligarchs in the United States.

By 2014, Google had joined Amazon as a winner-takes-all company. The Internet leviathan now controls around 65 per cent of search globally, according to Keen, revealing the new power laws of our networked economy. Moreover, and this for us is key, *the Google-type business strategy is to give away their tools and services for free and rely on advertising sales as their main source of revenue.* So such advertising revenues, for soap or sanitary towels, aerosols or automobiles, which have nothing whatsoever to do, directly, with my searching for information or ordering my books or sending e-mails to maintain contact with people in my network, ultimately control the show. In other words, my own nature and culture, individually and communally, is now completely disconnected from the technology and economy which ostensibly makes Google's world go around!

In the process of my 'searching', of course, I am working for Facebook or Google for free, manufacturing the very personal data that makes their company so valuable to the global advertising industry. So, because of my 'free labour', Google, with its market value in 2014 of $400 billion no less, needs to employ only 46,000 people, getting the rest of the work done by me and others for free, whereas a General Motors, with its market value at just over one tenth that of Google, employs 200,000. Moreover, the fate of the world economy is now put in the hands of those few cash hoarders, for Keen, like Google, Amazon and Apple, whose profits are mainly kept offshore.

Idealism to Materialism

Meanwhile, there is a great twist to this 'western' story, which is key to this book. The story of the Internet's pre-eminent company, Google, is indeed laced with irony. Invented by a couple of idealistic computer science graduates, one of whom was in fact an immigrant from Russia, Sergey Brin, they represented, at the outset, the United States' *integral* advantage: *openness to the outside world, tolerance of cultural diversity, innate inventiveness, products of a flourishing higher educational infrastructure, not to mention, also, as per Silicon Valley, the gift for association* that de Tocqueville had originally pointed to in his travels through nineteenth-century America.

In fact, and given their youthful idealism, Sergei Brin and Larry Page, Google's two founders, had originally banned advertisements from their home page. Yet today, pursuing the exclusive economic advantage they have now established, they have become the largest and most powerful advertising industry in the world, thereby fuelling America's consumer-based economy, arguably sustaining its affluent consumer advantage, which is putting more and more individual people, as well as the nation as a whole, into ever more debt!

The New Feudalism

In fact, for Keen, the overall result has been what can be termed a 'new feudalism'. As such the 'oligarch' billionaires, from the likes of Google, Apple and Amazon, are accompanied, at the next economic level, by a 'clerisy' of media commentators, and heaped at the bottom are the 'new serfs' of the working poor and the unemployed. These include the skilled workers from towns like Rochester, New York, the home of Kodak that recently went bankrupt, and 146,000 employees were victims of the new winner-takes-all networked economy. At the same time in Santa Clara County, the geographical heart of Silicon Valley, the poverty rate shot up from 8 per cent in 2001 to 14 per cent in 2013, with the food stamp population jumping from 25,000 in 2001 to 125,000 in 2013. *The sharing economy has ultimately become the selfish economy.*

1.4 Pursuing Integral Advantage

EAST MEETS WEST: SPIRITUAL–MATERIAL

How the Middle Ages Surpassed the Modern Era

Why then have we devoted so much attention, in a book which is supposedly focused on *emerging* markets, in relation to the BRICS, on the emergent networked economy with its headquarters on the 'west-north' coast of Northern California. The reason for this is that *Silicon Valley is supposed to represent the very quintessence of our modern, or indeed post-modern global economy*, building upon America's comparative economic advantage in inventing, developing and commercializing communications technologies. Surely this must be an economic state toward which an 'emerging' market, like a China or an India, must aspire, that is *emerge* towards?! Or should they rather *de-merge* toward fields and workshops?

Factory Workers in the Global Workplace

Of course, a counter response, at this point, is that economic development in the 'west-north' has reached its nadir, and it is from the 'east', that is especially the brIC (Indian 'south-eastern' and Chinese 'north-eastern') countries that we can expect future economic growth. Low costs of production in these two countries, or what has been more irreverently called 'the race to the bottom', in relation to labour costs, today serves to ensure that these 'eastern' tigers are coming up economic trumps. While, on the one hand, we increasingly outsource software production to India, China, on the other hand, has become the manufacturing centre of the world (where would today's most profitable company, Apple, be without its low-cost Chinese manufacturing hub) due to their respective sources of technological (India) and economic (China) comparative advantage.

At the Cost of your Life

Of course Chinese electronics companies, producing computer hardware for the Apples and Googles of this world, are duly pursuing their distinctive source of economic, if not also technical, advantage, primarily located in the cheap, and willing, female workforce. Emigrating from the rural areas in pursuit of more money, and indeed securing a degree of independence from their hitherto socially constrained communal lives, the young women are gaining some economic, if not also social, advantage. But at what cost? The cost of their health, and indeed their very lives (see Chapter 13), so that you and I can purchase our next generation of tablet or smart phone!

Indeed, in contemporary guise, we are revisiting the colonial days, in the eighteenth and nineteenth centuries, when the cheap imports from the 'south' were fuelling the 'northern' economies, also at the cost of indigenous people's lives! Hence, ultimately toward the end of the last century, with the fall of apartheid, as charted in Nelson Mandela's (12) *Long Walk to Freedom*, and the process of social and political reconciliation that ensued thereafter, is of iconic significance for our times. In other words, it is of greater *integral* importance, or at the very least of equal importance, for us, compared with the pursuit of economic growth, as per China, or even the advance of liberal democracy, as per America.

As such, and overall, the two major world polarities, east–west and north–south, which hitherto have been so distorted through the respective orientations towards communism versus capitalism (east–west) and the poor versus the rich (south–north) are now being recast in spiritual–material and natural–societal, more integral guise. Embodied, respectively, by our new look at Russia and South Africa, in the foreground, and by Brazil, India and China, altogether set against the conventional economic wisdom (US/UK) in the still all important background, we shall pursue the BRICS, integrally anew, as emerging societies, as a whole, rather than mere emerging markets. We now turn to the structure of the book as a whole.

1.5 Conclusion: Structure of the Book

PART I: ORIENTATION

1. The Internet is Not the Answer: Fields, Factories and Workshops to Networked Economy

In the opening chapter we set the scene, somewhat dramatically, by illustrating that the so called quintessence of a modern, or post-modern, 'western–northern' economy is not the inevitable way to go. Drawing on the recent work of Internet entrepreneur, and political scientist, Andrew Keen, we focus on the downsides of such a post-modern networked economy, where the 'Internet oligarchs' of Silicon Valley so to speak, have become the equivalent of the Russian oligarchs, in their different pre-modern guise, both in the singular pursuit of economic advantage in the twenty-first century. We compare and contrast such with the more integrally oriented 'Fields, Workshops and Factories for Tomorrow', highlighted by Russian nineteenth-century geographer, Peter Kropotkin, drawing on the heritage of European mutual aid, dating back to the Middle Ages. The overall argument here is that we need to reach backwards and forwards, locally and globally, agriculturally and industrially, at one and the same time.

2. Emerging Markets and Societies: North-Western Conventional Economic Wisdom

In the second orientation chapter we introduce the conventional wisdom on 'Emerging Markets', as embodied in the 'Growth Map' of Goldman Sachs' senior executive, economist Jim O'Neill, who was the first person to come up with the notion of the BRICs countries, with a particular emphasis on Brazil, Russia, India and China. We highlight the fact that, in exclusively focusing on economic growth, in conventional terms, O'Neill was effectively restricting the nature and scope of such BRICs to the conventional economic wisdom that underlay 'western–northern' economies, like the US and UK, in theory if not in practice. In practice, then, as we shall illustrate, there is nothing qualitatively 'new' in the notion of 'emerging' markets, which belies the very idea of 'emergence' in its current systemic sense. This will be compared and contrasted with David Ricardo's conventional economic wisdom, underlying the very concept of international trade that follows from the theory of comparative advantage.

3. Towards Integral Advantage: Integral Realities and Rhythms

The final orientation chapter opens with the argument made by people ranging from pan-Africanist W.E.B. Du Bois, in America, and poet-statesman Leopold Senghor, in the Senegal, that each culture and society has unique gifts to bring to the world. In more recent times the same has been argued by UK-based economist Christopher Houghton Budd, and by Harvard Law School-based Brazilian social scientist and polymath Mangabeira Unger, in his 'Free Trade Re-Imagined'. I then turn to the particular methodology we have developed, in our previous works published in our Transformation and Innovation series, on ways and means of releasing GENE-ius, through Grounding and Emergence, Navigation and Effect. Particular emphasis will be placed on the phase of local–global integral 'Emergence', to counteract the more limited connotation of 'Emerging' Markets. Finally, and aligned with such an integral rhythm, we shall cite the work of Japanese organizational sociologists on the analogous knowledge spiral, spawned 'middle-up-down' by a knowledge creating company, and for us, society. We then turn, most prolifically, to Russia (east–west) and South Africa (north–south).

PART II: AN EAST–WEST RUSSIAN INTEGRAL PERSPECTIVE

4. Mutual Aid to Earth Manifesto: Grounding in Russian Nature and Community

Building on the prior introduction to 'Fields, Workshops and Factories' from Peter Kropotkin, we trace a Russian 'east–west' path, through his work, grounded in mutual aid, drawing first on nature, specifically through the animal world, and then onto community, through the tradition of mutual aid, that reaches back to the European guilds in the Middle Ages, that is in the eleventh and twelfth centuries, most specifically in Russia. In the process Kropotkin argues, like Darwin had done before him, that both individualism and communalism have their place, but the latter is primary and the former secondary, as a grounding for our east–west, spiritual–material economy and society.

5. Cosmism to Anthropoecology: Grounding to Russian Emergence through Culture and Spirituality

At the crucial 'emergent' phase, when something fundamentally new prospectively arises, there needs to be a fusion of horizons, in the Russian case uniquely between east and west, that is specifically between 'Slavophiles', so called, and 'westernizers'. In the twentieth-century event, the westernizers in the form of Marxism won the exclusive day, with disastrous results, as we know today. Arguably equally disastrous has been the twenty-first-century turn toward a mercantilist form of capitalism embodied in the Russian economic oligarchs. What we shall highlight in this chapter is a uniquely Russian form of cosmism, uniting east and west, art and science, economy and society, associated with such illustrious figures as Federov and Soloviev, Berdyaev and Bulgakov, largely unknown is the 'western' canon, but seminal figures in Russia's unique and authentic emergence. As such it is a holistic approach to life as a whole rather than a Marxist economics that comes to the fore, harking back to the prior grounding in mutual aid and the subsequent navigation of the economy as an extended household.

6. Anthropoecology to the World as Household – Russian Navigation: Philosophy of Economy as Social Science

One of the abovementioned Russian cosmist philosophers, Sergey Bugakov, in the twentieth century, whose childhood origins lay in Russian Orthodoxy, and in his youthful idealism turned to Marxism, subsequently evolved his own cosmist 'Philosophy and Economy', which has since been aligned with the work of ISCRA – Institute for Scientific Research into Cosmic Anthropoecology in Siberia. In his spiritualized approach to 'the economics of the household', taking on the form where Aristotle had left off, he illustrates how production and consumption are, in their essence, cosmic forces, rather than mere demand and supply curves, as per neoliberal economics. To that extent economy is a holistic offshoot of philosophy, and thereby of life as a whole, rather than a separate discipline from which comparative economic advantage can be derived.

7. Portrait of a Russian Province: Nizhnii Novgorod Zemstvo Effect

In direct contrast with the approach of modernization theory, underlying globalization, whereby progress is the order of the day, and the Internet-based networked economy represent the quintessence of such, we return to the Russian past to guide our integral future, from an east–west, spiritual–material perspective. Drawing on the seminal work of Georgetown University, Russian-born historian, Catherine Evtuhov, we illustrate through her interpretive work, how such a Russian province functioned in the nineteenth century.

The key to such, drawing on Kropotkin's original ground, is the merging of fields, workshops and factories, in the Russian countryside, on the one hand, and the seminal role played by what Nonaka has termed 'knowledge engineers', and Evtuov terms 'knowledge purveyors' at the heart of provincial society. Moreover, in effecting rural-and-urban development, simultaneously, Niznhii Novgorod, the province in question and the heart of Russia, and specifically the self-governing zemstvo within it, explodes the myth that Russia at the time was an agrarian economy in need of industrialization, but, as an economic and societal household, incorporated both. We then turn 'north–south'.

PART III: NORTH–SOUTH AFRICAN INTEGRAL PERSPECTIVE

8. Wild Law to Earth Jurisprudence: Grounding Southern Africa in Local Nature and Community

In turning now from eastern Europe, albeit as a bridge to the west, given Russia's Eurasian land mass, to Southern Africa, albeit as a bridge to the north, given South Africa's idiosyncratic position in Africa, we ground integral advantage, now, in both so called Earth Jurisprudence, as specifically in the work of environmental lawyer Cormack Cullinan and wilderness champion Ian Player, aligned with that of Afrikaaner writer, adventurer and naturalist, Laurens van der Post. Best known for his book on the 'Lost World of the Kalahari', featuring the ancient African bushmen. For our integral purposes his seminal work, in the 1950s, was on *The Dark Eye of Africa*. In it he emphasizes that if we ignore the 'primitive' natural person within us, and the earth we inhabit as such, we wreak havoc, as supposed 'civilized' people, on the world. This applies as much to 'civilized' Nazis, hitherto, as the Aryan race vis à vis those 'dark peoples', the Jews, as it does today, to those 'highly educated' Muslim women who leave Britain for Syria, to do battle, alongside the Islamic State, with the 'infidels'. Moreover, and more specifically for Van der Post, Africa, from which humankind originated, acts today as a kind of primal mirror of the world as a whole.

9. Future Primal and the Truth Quest: Emerging through Local–Global Culture and Consciousness

In the same way as Africa as a whole is primal territory, and as such humankind's original home, so, for South African political scientist now based in Hawaii, Louis Herman, the so-called *Future Primal*, politically if not also economically speaking, needs to reach back to both indigenous (bushman) and ancient (Greek) peoples, as well as forward to the future. Processes of direct democracy, Socratic dialogue and individuation need thereby to be aligned with a relevant 'big picture' for a particular society, and an overall 'truth quest'. Herman then takes on, politically and socially, from where Player, Cullinan and Van der Post leave off culturally and naturally.

10. Truth and Reconciliation: Navigating Towards Freedom

For South African academic and theologian John de Gruchy, furthermore, in his work on 'Justice and Reconciliation', that the very term reconciliation emerges from prior 'exchange', and that such exchange is intrinsically social as well as economic in its basic nature. To that extent, moreover, and as Archbishop Tutu has pointed out, in his 'No Future without Forgiveness', unless and until the famed process of 'Truth and Reconciliation' in South Africa, reached out from the social and political, to also the economic, there would be no ultimate process of reconciliation in the country.

In that emergent guise the very notion of *ubuntu* – 'I am Because You Are' – needs to be extended into society and economy, as a fusion, if you like, between 'Black Consciousness', as per the late Steve Biko, and Truth and Reconciliation as per the TRC (South African Truth and Reconciliation Commission). Mandela's 'Long Walk to Freedom', pursued over a 30-year period, was ultimately undertaken in pursuit of such, indeed underlying the so-called Reconstruction and Development Program (RDP) inaugurated in the 1990s. Unfortunately, such a powerful means of navigation, subsequently then overtaken by getting into GEAR has not reached back, sufficiently, to prior natural grounding and cultural emergence, and forward to economic effect.

11. Ubuntu to Value Sharing: Transformative Healing Effect – Out of the Divine Will of Africa

Such a true meeting between north and south, enterprise-wise, that is between technology and organization, on the one hand, and nature as well a community, on the other, came through the Cashbuild worker democracy, born and bred in South Africa in the 1980s and 1990s, albeit that business magnate Anton Rupert was also an advocate of co-existence between man and nature. Cashbuild's cooperative architect, Albert Koopman, an Afrikaaner who left school at 14 to set out on his life's cause, following and then parting company from his childhood hero Karl Marx, set out to build upon 'the divine will of Africa' in the course of turning a rurally-based, retailer of building supplies into a fully fledged workplace democracy, dedicated to value sharing. In this culminating 'north–south' chapter we illustrate the nature and scope of such, albeit that ultimately it fell on stoney ground. What was key was the fusion of the natural and communal with the organizational and societal, which takes us into our next 'south–east' case in point, India.

PART IV: CIRCUMNAVIGATING BRICS: INDIA, CHINA, BRAZIL

12. Integral India: South-East – Swadeshi *to* Sarvodaya

The 'south-eastern' BRIC then, to begin with, is India. For a land with such a profound spiritual heritage, it is seemingly now being overtaken by materialism. In this chapter, we shall revisit India, from such a natural-spiritual vantage point, before turning toward technology and economy. In that respect, we start our study on the ground, with the renowned Satish Kumar's latest work on 'Soil, Soul and Society', whereby he grounds India in Gandhi's *Swadeshi,* an economics of place. Thereafter, we turn to the emergent, natural and cultural *Earth Democracy* perspective of the Indian Ecofeminist, Vandana Shiva. For Indian navigation we turn to sociologist Debal Singharoy *'Toward a Knowledge Society'*, and culminate with the case of the renowned *Sarvodaya,* in Sri Lanka, to which Kumar had originally alluded.

13. Integral China: North-East – Chaxugeju *to* Guanxi

In conventional BRICS terms, of course, China is the star player, and yet in our 'north-eastern' integral terms is perhaps the most problematic, because of the social and environmental havoc being unleashed alongside its economic miracle. In this chapter we shall hope to overturn this integral imbalance, by starting out with a grounding of Chinese nature, with the help of Fei Xiaotong charting the foundations of Chinese society, *Chaxugeju,* as he sees it 'From the Soil'.

Thereafter we revisit emergent Chinese culture and society, through the prominent work of the political scientist Lin Chun, focused on the new Chinese government policy of *Xiaokang* (*Moderation*). For navigation we turn to the formidable Chinese management scientist, Zhichang Zhu, for his work on *Confucian Pragmatism*. For ultimate effect we then turn to 'The Dragon's Gift', American development economist Deborah Brautigam's formidable treatise on the Chinese approach to pursuing *mutual benefit* abroad.

14. Integral Brazil: South-West – Eco-Services to Free Trade Re-Imagined

In this final chapter on the 'south-west', that is Brazil, as we begin to close the BRICS chapter, we focus, initially, as per grounding, on the unique natural phenomenon of Amazonia, through its remarkable 'prodigal daughter', Marina Silva, the indigenous Amazonian who recently stood for president, focusing through her on *Eco-Services*. Thereafter we turn, by way of emergence, to Gilberto Freyre, and his 'social theory of the tropics', that is *Tropicology*, which combined his 'western' scientific education with his feel for the tropical 'south'. For navigation, par excellence, we draw on the work of the redoubtable Fernando Cardoso, as sociologist, economist and Brazilian President in the 1990s, 'Charting a New Course' towards *Social Solidarity*. Effectively, and ultimately then, we turn to the remarkable Brazilian polymath, based at Harvard Law School, Roberto Mangabeira Unger, duly, and as we initially intimate in Chapter 2, *'Re-imagining Free Trade'*.

15. Reconstituting the BRICS: Comparative to Integral Advantage

In this final chapter we revisit the original position taken, economically, by the English political economist David Ricardo in the nineteenth century, and subsequently, enterprise-wise, by American business strategist Michael Porter, based at Harvard Business School. We compare and contrast their 'western' approach to our integral own, and conclude with the implication for individual, organization and society of pursuing the latter approach, in each one of the BRICS as well as in the BRICS as a whole. For such we draw on the approach developed by Trans4m of CARE 4 Society, that is; catalysing development; communal activism; innovation-based institutional research; and transformative education.

We now turn from this opening chapter on *Why the Internet is Not the Answer*, which establishes the background to the book, to the second chapter *Emerging Markets to Emerging Societies* which established the foreground so to speak.

Bibliography

1. Olopade, D. (2014) *The Bright Continent: Breaking Rules and Making Change in Modern Africa.* New York. Mariner Books.
2. Lessem, R., Abouliesh, I., Pogacnik, M. and Herman, L. (2014) *Integral Polity: Aligning Nature, Culture, Society and Economy.* Farnham. Gower.
3. O'Neil, J. (2011) *The Growth Map: Economic Opportunity in the BRICS and Beyond.* London, Penguin.
4. Piciga, D., Schieffer, A. and Lessem, R. (2015) *Integral Green Slovenia.* Farnham. Gower.
5. Schieffer, A. and Lessem, R. (2013) *Integral Development: Realising the Transformative Potential of Individuals, Organizations and Societies.* Farnham. Gower.
6. Mangabeira Unger, R. (2004) *False Necessity: Anti-Necessarian Social Theory in the Service of Radical Democracy.* London. Verso.
7. Kropotkin, P. (1985) *Fields, Factories and Workshops Tomorrow.* London. Freedom Press.
8. Evtuhov, C. (2011) *Portrait of a Russian Province: Economy, Society and Civilization in Nineteenth Century Nizhnii Novgorod.* Pittsburg. Yale University Press.
9. Lessem, R. and Schieffer, A. (2010) *Integral Research.* Farnham. Gower.
10. Keen, A. (2015) *The Internet is Not the Answer.* London. Atlantic Books.
11. Berners Lee, T. (1999) *Weaving the Web.* San Francisco. Harper.
12. Mandela, N. (1994) *The Long Walk to Freedom.* New York. Abacus.

Chapter 2

Emerging Markets and Societies: North-Western Conventional Economic Wisdom

Each nation is a compound aggregate of states and inclinations, of wants and resources, of capacities and inventive powers. The territory occupied by each nation is in its turn a most varied texture of soils and climates, of hills and valleys, of slopes leading to a still greater variety of territories and races. Political economy has hitherto insisted chiefly upon division. I proclaim integration – and the ideal towards which society is marching is one of integrated, combined labor.

Peter Kropotkin, Fields, Workshops and Factories Tomorrow

2.1 Introduction

THE THEORY OF COMPARATIVE ADVANTAGE

Comparative Advantage and Economic Development

As we saw in the previous chapter, for Russia's Peter Kropotkin at least, the make up of a nation as a whole, including its nature and culture, as well as its technology and economy, should be taken into account in fostering its development, not only its comparative economic advantage. As we shall soon see, Kropotkin's is by no means a voice in the wilderness, but before we remind ourselves of other related voices, we need to review the conventional economic wisdom on *comparative advantage* that we compare and contrast our own integral approach with. Such a theory of comparative advantage, underlies, in turn, the standardized approach to emerging markets, as per the proverbial BRICS.

For the American development economists Cypher and Dietz (1), on whom we extensively drew in our (2) recent book on *Integral Development*, in an extract from their work on *The Process of Economic Development* (emphasis is mine):

> *If there is one economic theory that the vast majority of economists accept as universally valid, it would be Ricardo's theory of comparative advantage. This theory argues that unrestricted exchange between countries will increase total world output if each country specializes in those goods it can produce at a* relatively *lower cost compared to its potential trading partners. Each country will then trade some of its lower-cost goods for others that can be produced elsewhere more cheaply than at home.* With free trade among nations, all countries will fund that their consumption possibilities have been expanded by such specialization and trade beyond that what would have been possible from their domestic production possibilities alone. *Because of this compelling argument, economists tend to favor free trade, since it is presumed to be 'welfare enhancing' in that the aggregate level of world income is increased.*

Conventional Economic Wisdom – Natural Law to Free Markets

David Ricardo, next to Adam Smith is probably the most famous English political economist in the eighteenth and nineteenth centuries, was himself a commodity broker and financial speculator. Not surprisingly, therefore, he gave pride of place to economic exchange, and thereby to his theory of *comparative advantage*. Two hundred years later, as we shall now see, Jim O'Neil (3), who himself has a PhD in financial economics and was Chairman of Asset Management for the world's most renowned, or indeed notorious, investment bank, Goldman Sachs, wrote his definitive work on *The Growth Map: Economic Opportunity in the BRICS and Beyond*, through which he introduced the BRIC notion for the first time.

The conventional 'western-northern' economic wisdom then, as outlined in this chapter, is grounded in *natural law*, embodying freedom of association, freedom of individual expression, and above all *free trade*; the *emerging markets* as such are deemed to broadly reflect such, and the capitalist system that underlies them; the *Washington Consensus* (IMF, World Bank, WTO), underlies free international trade as a means of overall navigation of such; and ultimately the American style *Business Schools* promote the leadership, the management and the free enterprise underlying economic growth, as an ultimate effect. We now turn specifically to the BRICs in that 'western-northern' context.

Navigation
Technology and Society
International Economic Governance

Effect	Integration	Emergence
Managers, Leaders	*Economic*	Enterprising
Enterprise	*Growth*	Culture
Business Schools		*Emerging Markets*

Grounding
Nature and Community
Natural Law/Free Trade

Figure 2.1 Free trade to free markets

BIRTH OF THE BRICS

Primacy of Economic Growth

For Jim O'Neil, at the time of writing his book on the *Growth Map* in 2011, the aggregate GDP of the BRIC – Brazil, Russia, India and China – countries (South Africa had not been included in his initial list) had close to quadrupled from $3 trillion in 2001, when *O'Neil was the first economist to put such BRICs on the world map*, to $12 trillion in 2011. The world economy had doubled in size since 2001, and a third of that growth had come from the BRICs. Their combined GDP increase was more than twice that of the USA.

In early 2011, moreover, O'Neil decided that the term 'emerging markets' could no longer be applied only to the BRICs and he then referred to such in Indonesia, Korea, Mexico and Turkey in addition and in turn. However, the term BRICS has since stuck, with now a South African addition, and, what goes without saying, is that sole attention is being paid to *economic* growth.

O'Neil as a 'Dirty' Economist

Before O'Neil joined Goldman Sachs in 1995, he had spent most of his years, after his economic studies, as a self confessed 'dirty economist', that is someone who mixed classical economics with the rough and tumble of the trading floor. His speciality was foreign exchange. In 2001, what most interested him about the BRICs was that they all appeared increasingly eager to engage on the global stage.

Whatever had occurred in their past was over and done with. Globalization was happening and they wanted to be part of it. Such globalization, for him then, did not need to be Americanization (Mangabeira Unger below begs to differ), and the BRICs represented 2.8 billion people. Interestingly enough, in conversations about 'emerging' markets that have taken place since, few mention the fact that the original 'dirty economist' who had given birth to the BRICs concept, grew up as a banker and economist, as it were, on the trading floor, and this would invariably influence his outlook.

2.2 The Growth Map

DEMOGRAPHICS AND PRODUCTIVITY

Power of Demographics

It is striking, for O'Neil, how much has changed in just a decade, in the global economy, quantitatively that is, but how little the original BRICs framework, for him at least, has altered. The first reason he gives is demographic, noting that he only takes account of factors that bear upon economic growth. *Because China had dominated the world between the tenth and fifteenth centuries in both size and wealth, and for centuries until then India was the dominant economy, the two combined into 50 per cent of the global economy in those days gone by.* The likelihood then was, and now is, that for these two countries with virtually half the world's population between them, this will happen again.

Productivity Power

The second essential driver of growth, for O'Neil, is productivity. *The more a group of workers can produce with a given set of inputs, from time to materials, the faster their economy will grow.* Moreover, such comparative economic productivity is invariably based, for him, as it was for Ricardo before (Ricardo like O'Neil was a financial trader), on the comparative advantage that each country holds, and the more they hold, altogether, the more advantageous globalization, and free trade, becomes. We now turn to the quantitatively-based Goldman Sachs *Growth Environment Scores.*

GROWTH ENVIRONMENT SCORES

Quantitative, Standardized Indices

As you can see below, Goldman Sachs take into account political as well as economic factors, but all of these are based on quantitative, standardized indices, and no account is taken of the particular nature (other than from a natural *resource* perspective) and culture of each particular country. In other words, demographic, economic and political factors aside, the particularity of a Brazil or a Russia, an India or a China, or indeed a South Africa, in the terms that will underlie our work on *integral* advantage is completely by-passed. Financial economist O'Neil then is no different in that respect from his fellow political economist, and financial trader, Ricardo.

Macro and Micro Variables

Specifically then the Growth Environment Score is based on the following Macro and Micro economic variables (I have put the *technological variables* in italics and underlined the *political ones*, while the normal lettering applies to the purely economic variables):

MACROECONOMIC VARIABLES	MICROECONOMIC VARIABLES
Inflation	*Use of mobile telephones*
Government deficit	*Use of the Internet*
Investment spending	*Use of computers*
External debt	Life expectancy
Degree of openness	Education
	Rule of law
	Corruption
	Stability of government

We now turn very briefly to each BRIC, so called, in turn, starting with the most popular one, for O'Neil in direct investment terms, that is with Brazil, the first such **B**RIC.

BRIC BY BRIC

Brazil: The Most Popular for Foreign Direct Investment

Brazil today is the most popular of the BRICs so far as foreign direct investment is concerned, or at least it was in 2011. The most significant change in Brazil, in recent years for O'Neil, has been the transformation of its political culture. Many people worried that when Lula da Silva, the head of the Worker's

Party, became President in 2003, he might reverse the economic policies of his predecessors, especially that of President Cardoso who had preceded him (see Chapter 14), and who had conquered inflation.

Yet Lula, in O'Neil's terms, succeeded in persuading the lower classes in Brazil – a country renowned for its football and carnivals – that western policies are good for them. In Goldman Sachs' economic terms, it became more western, less Brazilian!

As of 2011 then, Brazil's average wealth was around $10,000 per head, a dramatic rise over the past decade, in that tens of millions of Brazilians have risen out of poverty. From a material perspective that has to be a good thing, while, as we shall see in Chapter 14, from our integral perspective it is a good thing, but only to an economic 'western-northern' point. What about the case of Russia?

Russia: Strong in Technology, Weak in Rule of Law

Russia has one of the best national technology policies in the world, according to O'Neil, with the raw intellectual talent to make it happen. *Russia's history of strong centrally guided education with very high standards of both mathematics and science enable it easily to increase both its use of modern technology and its innovative application in business and government.* At a micro level then Russia is strong in education, communications and computers. Its weaknesses are in life expectancy, the rule of law and corruption. While nothing in this statement is factually incorrect, as we shall see in our Chapters 4–7 on Russia, from an integral perspective the Goldman Sachs interpretation is wholly inadequate, if not outright misleading, with technology and economy dominating over culture and spirituality, in a nation which takes enormous pride in its arts and culture.

India: The Greatest Mystery

India is the greatest mystery, for O'Neil, amongst the BRICs. Its demographics are astonishing, and it has a credible legal system, is English-language speaking and has home grown technology companies which are expanding globally. *At the top of its educational system India produces large numbers of English-speaking technical graduates, who have driven the success of the service industries. They are also highly computer literate.*

However, the vast bulk of the population remains uneducated with very limited access to technology. India's crippling bureaucracy also remains a hindrance to foreign investment. In contrast China, with an equivalent population, strides ahead while India, the world's biggest democracy, often struggles. O'Neil is of course quite right to point out India's great strengths in information technology, but he completely leaves out what the country is most noted for worldwide, in integral terms, its spiritual heritage. In that sense, India is indeed a land of mystery, but it is not that spiritual mystique to which O'Neil is alluding, but rather the fact that the country is a puzzle for him.

The Chinese Economic Miracle – People and Productivity

There is simply no overstating, for O'Neil, China's importance for all of us, not just 1.3 billion Chinese. The entire planet, all 6.5 billion people, is, for him, invested in China's economic success. In 1995 China's economy was worth $500 billion, and it has grown ten-fold in 15 years, averaging 10 per cent growth per annum. By 2010 China had overtaken Japan to become the second largest economy in the world.

The first key, for him of course, to China's extraordinary growth has been its population. Once its government decided to engage with the rest of the world in the early 1980s, this triggered the economic changes that have gathered ever more pace in the 1990s and 2000s. Millions moved into the cities, contributing to and benefiting from China's surge as a global manufacturer. Second, economic growth though, for O'Neil, is about productivity. The number of Chinese people receiving a tertiary education is rising quickly, and the remarkable speed at which Chinese researchers are starting to be among the most successful scientists and engineers in the world is a sign that productivity in key areas is on the rise.

China's Gain is the World's

People, O'Neil goes on to say, feel China's economic gain is their loss and here O'Neil disagrees. A glance at China's growth environment scores well, overall for him, on stable inflation rate, external financial position, government debt, investment levels and openness to foreign trade. It only falls below average on corruption and some areas of technology. In the final analysis for him though, *China pursues its economic interests with remarkable efficiency, not having to worry about voters, elections or rival parties, allowing the government to act with a speed and decisiveness that democracy precludes.* Few would question O'Neil's analysis, of China, from an economic if also a political perspective. However, as we shall demonstrate in Chapter 13, by failing to probe into the nature and culture of the Chinese people, as is the case for Brazil and India, we are left with at best a half-truth, from our own, integral perspective.

O'Neil then turns to the other, new growth markets which are of due concern in pure financial and economic, if not also political, terms.

THE NEW GROWTH MARKETS

N-11: Mexico to Vietnam

There is then a growth addendum to the BRICs. O'Neil has also identified what he terms his N-11 New Growth Markets: Mexico from Latin America, Turkey on the edge of Europe and Asia, Egypt and Iran from the Middle East, Nigeria from Africa, and six countries which span the whole of Asia – Bangladesh, Indonesia, South Korea, Pakistan, the Philippines and Vietnam. Interestingly enough he excludes South Africa, as not being economically significant enough. South Africa's unemployment rate, of 24 per cent in 2011, militated, for him, against the country's inclusion. If a whole continent could be thought of as a country, though, perhaps it would be BRIC-Africa accordingly. Africa as a whole ranks near the bottom of the GES 180-country ranking, though Nigeria has set out to be twentieth in the world ranking by 2020.

Are There No Limits to Growth?

At key moments of human history, for O'Neil, man has found solutions to his most acute problems. An oft-quoted example of this was the great horse-manure crisis which afflicted America's cities in the nineteenth century ... and then came the automobile. O'Neil has great faith then that scientific innovation, wise government policy and free markets can provide solutions which will help us avoid the doomsayer's scenarios. *As nations become richer and individuals prosper, he says, it stimulates business to search for new ideas and creative technologies that will drive the future.* This indeed is the conventional wisdom.

Western critics in that respect may point to China's polluted cities and rivers and call the country's growth unsustainable, but China's leaders see exactly the same problems, O'Neil says, feel them more acutely than those distant critics, and are busy seeking solutions (see the Xioakang policy recently emerging in Chapter 13). *Fossil fuels will be used more efficiently, use of renewables and nuclear energy will expand, and carbon-heavy emissions will be captured before they pollute the environment.* He then turns to consumption.

At the end of 2010 consumption in the BRIC countries came to about $5 trillion, an increase of 250 per cent over 10 years. By 2050 the Chinese could own twice as many cars as Americans, and India nearly three times as many. No industry has moreover benefited more from the rise of the BRICs than luxury goods. In fact there are 200,000 dollar millionaires today in Beijing alone. The art market is also being transformed by the BRICs. In mid 2011, moreover, Kentucky Fried Chicken already had 3,700 restaurants in China. So where is this all headed?

TOWARD A NEW WORLD ORDER

International Economic Governance

If we genuinely wish to pull more people out of poverty, according to O'Neil, into the middle class and facilitate greater trade and wealth creation, then we need to think hard about overcoming the obstacles that still hinder the free flow of commerce.

International economic governance is no longer just a subject to excite economists, he says, it is a vital element of the way the world works today, and one that affects us all. If the G7 then were being formed today it would have to include China. A case could easily be made for Brazil, India or Russia over Canada, and since the introduction of the Euro as a common currency in 1999, there seems little logic to the participation of each individual European member. The days of the western club of democracies, for O'Neil then, is well past its sell-by date. The G20 meanwhile includes the BRICs as well as other Growth Markets in the Next 11, including Korea, Indonesia, Mexico and Turkey. The IMF and World Bank will also need to reform themselves to reflect the new world order.

The Emerging have Emerged

It should be clear by now, moreover, that O'Neil no longer regards the BRICs as, in his terms, *economically* emerging markets. They are a fundamental part of the modern world. They can't be labelled 'emerging' in the same guise as say a Ukraine or a Venezuela. As we shall be pointing out, though, in Chapter 3, there is more to qualitative and integral 'emergence' than meets O'Neil's predominantly quantitative-oriented economic eye.

In London for example, O'Neil is proud to pronounce, the wealth, which has accrued to the BRIC elites, is constantly on display. They buy football teams, the very best residential property and art. The 'season' of social events now has strong Indian and Russian presence. Between 2010 and 2011 the BRICs added 108 billionaires. History, according to O'Neil, suggests that this is not unusual. When countries experience rapid wealth increases, he says, elites benefit most. All that matters for O'Neill is that the trend of the world economy, overall, is growing just over 4 per cent per year, versus 3.7 per cent over the past three decades. Yet a counter argument is provided, as we shall see in the next chapter, by Harvard-based business guru, Michael Porter, who contests the value of the move from an 'innovation' base to a 'wealth' base, in the pursuit of comparative advantage.

International Trade is Good for Everyone

Yet for the over-indebted, burdened nations of the west, selling goods to the rising growth markets, O'Neil maintains, *is* their future. If the BRICs and N-11 achieve their goals it will be good for everyone. In fact, three years from the financial crisis, it seems that the shift in the balance of world growth leadership has been accelerated rather than hindered. So the Brazilians promote investment opportunities in their vast land, the Russians advance their technologies, the Indians pursue their IT-based advantage, the Chinese enhance their status as the low-cost manufacturing hub of the world, the Americans of course have their Silicon Valley, notwithstanding for us the downsides referred to above (see Chapter 1) and the comparative economic advantage of each, he says, pursued in turn and altogether, makes for a better world.

The Winner Does Not Take it All

O'Neil therefore passionately believes, like his illustrious predecessor and fellow financial trader, 200 years ago, David Ricardo, that *one basic trend of international economic theory holds true: overall, international trade is good for everyone.* Tens of millions of US customers, for example, have benefited for years from the success of Walmart bringing in cheap goods from China. As such he finds it irritating to hear and read endless 'distorted stories' of how only a few benefit and increase their wealth from the fruits of globalization, to the detriment of the marginalized masses. *Globalization may widen inequality within certain national borders, but on a global basis it has been, he believes, a huge force for good, narrowing inequality among people on an unprecedented scale.*

Tens of millions of people from the BRICs, as such, and beyond are being taken out of poverty by the growth of their economies. While it is easy to focus on the fact that China has created so many billionaires, it should not be forgotten that in the past 15 years or so, 300 million or more Chinese have been lifted out of poverty. In India the lives of many tens of millions have similarly improved, and perhaps 300 million or more will join them in the next decade or two. *Vast swathes of mankind are having their chance to enjoy some of the fruits of wealth creation. That is* – for O'Neil – *the big story.*

So who is right, Kropotkin and Keen or Ricardo and O'Neil? Well, to help us create a bridge between comparative and integral advantage, we turn to the contemporary Brazilian polymath, and Harvard Law School Professor, Roberto Mangabeira Unger (4), and his *Free Trade Re-Imagined.* Unger, from whom we shall be hearing much more in our penultimate chapter, Chapter 14, on Integral Brazil, is a legal scholar and political scientist, mathematician and economist, sociologist and psychologist, as well as a political activist at one and the same time. If you like, his conventional wisdom is more *south*-western than western-northern in nature and scope, given his combined Brazilian heritage and current US base.

2.3 Free Trade Re-Imagined

NEED FOR TECHNOLOGICAL AND ORGANIZATIONAL INNOVATION

The Limits of Free Trade

The doctrine of free trade, for Mangabeira Unger in fact, as it has been conventionally understood by the likes of Jim O'Neil and indeed interpreted by David Ricardo, is fundamentally defective. In essence, and instead for Unger, a system of free trade will be the more advantageous to those who engage in it *if it allows them the greatest possible experimental freedom to change their practices and institutions of production.*

This, however, may conflict with what free trade has traditionally been understood to be and to require. A single-minded insistence on the maximization of free trade gives too little weight to an imperative that turns out to be vital, indeed of increasing significance: *the need of every country, richer or poorer, to avoid lasting confinement to a particular place in the international division of labour* and to the styles of production, the strategies of development and the sets of institutions that may exert this confining influence. To make these words real, in fact, is to rebel against the institutions in which market economies and the division of labour remain embodied.

The Ricardian approach to comparative advantage, for Mangabeira Unger, as indeed for Michael Porter as we shall see (Chapter 3), deals in the coin of static efficiency. This tells us nothing about the adjacent possible in the history of technological and organizational innovation or of economic growth – the next steps we are able to take, in a given time and place, with the materials at hand.

MORAL SPECIALIZATION WITHIN HUMANITY

A World Divided into Sovereign States

The political divisions within mankind in fact, of which the existence of sovereign states is merely a special case, for Unger, offer expanding opportunities for diversity of experience, vision, organization and action. *The most compelling justification of their separate existence is that they can represent a form of moral specialization within humanity, embodying and developing distinct forms of life and consciousness.* The existence of separate states – or of any other political division of humanity that might take place – is a permanent inducement to diversity of economic arrangements as well as of other non-economic institutions and practices.

It may relate to ways of organizing work, developing and imparting skills, and combining people, ideas and machines. Every one of these features of an economy may take an original turn as a result of the place it occupies within the life of a people. By virtue thus of its separate existence in a separate state, it can more easily develop characteristic experiences and adopt distinctive arrangements. *Astonishingly, however, the all-important relation of diversity to efficiency plays no part in classical conceptions of comparative advantage.*

Indeed China based its development, according to Unger, on the mobilization of its own human, financial and natural resources, rather than foreign capital. It also displayed institutional innovation, seemingly invisible on the *Growth Map*, but as we shall see in Chapter 13, in the way it organized market-oriented activity alongside governmental initiatives. However, its failure to democratize politics or culture has decisively compromised the reach and integrity of such innovations. It has stifled China's collective capacity for self-transformation in the workplace, the school, the state and in society as a whole. For this reason, he says, we should see the Chinese exception less as an omen for the future than as a limited success, brought about at a terrible price, as we shall see.

In fact, and overall as Unger has already said, the distinct, politically organized societies in the world remain the most important sites of difference: difference in institutional arrangements and in forms of consciousness, informing difference in what is produced and how. Difference then is not only part of the problem of organizing a world division of labour helping lift the burdens of poverty, infirmity, and drudgery from mankind; it is also part of the solution to that problem. Without the creation of more difference, the selective machinery of worldwide trade, based on established or constructed comparative advantage, has less material on which to operate and less potential for benefit. The extent to which a particular business bears the imprint of a particular national economy, and of the society and culture of which it forms a part, is nevertheless itself variable. We must understand and use this variation to develop alternatives, he says, to the present organization of market economies and global trade.

A Theory of Self, Organizational and Societal Revision

Free trade will flourish, for him, when the rules of the world trading system are designed to reconcile openness and diversity. The goal is to ensure the maximum of openness to the outside world that is consistent with the maximum capacity for self-revision at home. Without such a capacity, society loses its power to create alternative visions of its own future and to act on them. *The forms of self-revision deserving of special support are those that enable individuals, institutions and whole societies to reinvent their comparative advantages* and to shift labour from repeatable activities, undertaken by machines, to those activities we don't yet know how to repeat.

The basis for the appeal and authority of this specialization is the belief that humanity can develop its powers most fully only *by developing different forms of life, housed in different institutional orders*. The translation of moral difference into institutional divergence would pose a threat to freedom of the individual, moreover, if he were not free to escape the social world into which he happens to have been born and join another one, as for example (see Chapter 14) Brazilian indigenous environmental activist and recent Presidential candidate Marina Silva has done. The people of the world should be in direct communion, their ideas and experiences jumbled by a trading of place (Brazilian Mangabeira Unger now lives and works, at least in part, in the US) as well as of products, that there should be an endless flow of strangers in the midst of every nation, that the walls separating humanity should thus be torn down in the realities of direct encounter among individuals. *All this represents the most radical realization of the idea of an open world economy and the most powerful inducement to collective self-transformation*. Unger now turns to actual, practical proposals.

FREE TRADE REFORMED: THE RECONCILIATION OF ALTERNATIVES

Firstly, Maximize the Possibilities of Co-Existence

Build, step by step, an open world economy in whatever way offers the best promise of reconciling global openness with room for national and regional diversity, deviation heresy and experiment. *The point is not to maximize free trade; it is to maximize the possibility of co-existence among different development strategies, institutional systems, and forms of social life, and then, on that basis, to advance freer trade.*

The formative goal of the trading regime should therefore be the reconciliation of alternative development strategies and alternative versions of economic, political and social pluralism rather than the maximization of free trade. The world should multiply, not restrict, opportunities for countries to opt out of the general trading regime, more like the original GATT (General Agreement on Tariffs and Trade) than the current WTO. It should not be understood as a retreat from the cause of an open world economy. Its effect should be to prevent any fundamental opposition between our stake in diversity and in openness. Countries must find their way by combining elements of falsely universal orthodoxy with innovations responsive to local constraint and opportunity.

Brute Force versus Secondly, a Greater Power and Higher Life

The institutional and ideological adventures of the twentieth century, for Mangabeira Unger, are finished; their conclusion has left contemporary societies in the grip of a small list of living options for the organizing of different areas of social experience. This restrictive institutional canon is the fate of the present societies. To overthrow this fate it is necessary to enlarge that canon. The struggle for such an enlargement, moreover, is bound to take place under *double sponsorship: the brutal rivalry of states, cultures and classes versus the potential appeal of the most powerful belief at work in the world, faith in the rise of ordinary men and women to a greater power and higher life.* This faith requires, if it is to advance, the radicalization of democracy, the economic and educational empowerment of the individual, and the construction of a form of economic growth and permanent innovation that is socially inclusive.

The value of institutional difference, the requirements of institutional innovation, the nature of the way in which we can renovate and enlarge the restricted repertoire of institutional arrangements but which contemporary

Navigation
Technology and Society
Smith and Marx Rediscovered

Effect
Public, Private,
Civic Enterprise
Institutional Experimentation

Emergence
Culture and
Consciousness
Greater Power and Higher Life

Grounding
Nature and Community
Multiple Forms of Co-Existence

Figure 2.2 Re-imagining free trade

societies remain gripped, now that the calamitous ideological adventures of the twentieth century are spent – all these topics turn out to be vital to any effort to rise above the traditional terms of debate between free traders and protectionists.

Thirdly, Rediscovering Smith and Marx

The intellectual alternative, for Mangabeira Unger, is to rediscover and redirect the road along which we have travelled from *Smith to Marx. In that earlier way of thinking, economics had offered and justified a complex of causal ideas and social ideals. It had struggled to relate to the production of things to the structures of society, and the powers of the mind.* Yet our solution today cannot resemble theirs in content. For the established practice of international trade causes Unger to rebel until we reshape both market economies and globalization, not to reject the idea of free exchange and free labour, but to radicalize them as bases for an open national, and world, economy. *We will not shackle humanity to free trade.*

Fourthly, Freedom of Individual Choice turned into Institutional Experimentation

The future lies in using repeatable labour, expressed in formulas that are in turn embodied in machines, to save more of our most important resource, time, for the activities we have not yet learned to repeat.

The goal is to avoid surrendering to the necessary assumptions that tainted Marx's own theory. Our ideas about every national or worldwide regime for market-based exchange, therefore, must operate at two levels. At one level – the one way in which traditional economic analysis has worked – we consider only the freedom to trade goods and services and to combine in their production, people, ideas and things. At another level – the one we must now learn – *we look at the freedom to revise, piece by piece and step by step, the framework of institutional arrangements and assumptions within which we trade and combine.* Our reasoning at the first level should be informed by the second.

All four principles as above, and proposed action, reflecting Mangabeira Unger's *Re-imagining of Free Trade*, are illustrated in the figure above.

2.4 Conclusion

TOWARDS UNITY IN VARIETY

We started out this chapter with an opening quote from Kropotkin that 'each *nation is a compound aggregate of states and inclinations*, of wants and resources, of capacities and inventive powers'. Taking from where he left off, a century ago, Mangabeira Unger has argued that 'the most compelling justification of the separate existence of *sovereign states* is that they can represent a form of moral specialization within humanity, *embodying and developing distinct forms of life and consciousness'*.

Their combined perspectives, compared and contrasted with conventional BRIC wisdom – *the world economy has doubled in size since 2001, and a third of that growth has come from the BRICs* – is closely aligned with our own. That said, Jim O'Neil has performed the world a 'western-northern' service, so to speak, by at least putting the BRICs on the world map, so that, together with Kropotkin and Mangabeira Unger, we can pursue the integral advantage, that is the unity-in-variety, that comes out of the Brazilian, Russian, Indian, Chinese and African combination.

HISTORIC APPROACHES TO UNITY IN VARIETY

Deep Brotherhood and the Group Soul

However, Kropotkin and Mangabeira between them, are certainly not the only ones to share our integral, as opposed to narrowly economic, cause, when it comes to development, evolution or societal renewal. For example, to begin with, for the Indian sage Sri Aurobindo (5), early last century *each society*, he claimed, *develops into a sort of sub-soul or group-soul of our humanity and develops also a type of mind, thereby evolving governing ideas and tendencies that shape its life and institutions*. The group-soul works out its tendencies through a diversity of opinions, wills and diversity of lives. The vitality of its group-life as a national whole depends on such. *A deeper brotherhood between nations, a yet unfound law of love is the only sure foundation possible for a perfect social evolution.*

Senghor's Civilization of the Universal

Secondly, for the African poet-statesman Leopold Senghor (6), who was president of Senegal in the 1970s, beyond the objective of material wellbeing, man aspires to fuller being, to that of his spiritual needs, especially in Black Africa and the developing nations. Africans hunger not so much for American or Russian surpluses, Senghor maintains, as after independence, dignity, science and culture: after *love-in-union.* Such a love-in-union he identified as 'the *civilisation of the universal' representing a symbiosis of different civilisations.*

We now turn from historical to more contemporary approaches, starting with Richard Noorgard's ecological and biological orientation, and ending with Christopher Houghton Budd's economic one.

CO-EVOLUTIONARY REVISIONING OF DEVELOPMENT

Co-Evolutionary versus Mechanistic

For geographer and environmentalist Richard Norgaard, based in California, and writing his work on *Development Betrayed* in the 1980s, a co-evolutionary, as opposed to mechanical, competitive or even cooperative, theory, builds on the idea that species and other system components have a variety of traits that are context specific, and change over time, rather than being universal. For these reasons, co-evolutionary thinking is totally different from cause-and-effect thinking. In fact, *co-evolutionary models of systems can be thought of as endogenously providing change from within, thereby developmental, rather than exogenously from without, as per development.*

A Patchwork Quilt: Individuals to Groups

Through this process, the world can be thought of as having become a patchwork quilt of loosely interconnected, co-evolving social, economic and ecological systems. Within each patch the ecological system evolved developmentally in response to cultural pressures and tended to reflect the values, worldview and social organization of local peoples. In this worldview, what can be known is particular rather than universal. At the same time, in some regions and times, cultural beliefs and social organizations brought aspects of social unity across patches.

Buddhism, for example, spread from India across much of Asia, affecting people's perceptions of nature forever after. Various Chinese dynasties brought parallel, connected social organization to vast areas. These environmental and social constancies led to some nearly universal phenomena across patches. *Generalizations can always be made, but a co-evolutionary perspective helps us comprehend how the loose connectedness between people and their cultures assumed uniqueness between patches.* Houghton-Budd takes the argument, economically, on from here.

STEINER TO HOUGHTON BUDD: TOWARDS A CHOIR OF CULTURES

Choir of Cultures

In the new millennium, in his book in our Gower Transformation and Innovation series, *Finance at the Threshold: Rethinking the Real and Financial Economies* as the concomitant of a single global economy today, for Christopher Houghton Budd (7), a follower of Rudolf Steiner at the Centre for Associative Economics in Britain, will be *a choir of cultures, each able to sound its own note but able also to include the tones of others.* He makes the case that ever since World War 1, this potential has existed and that overlooking, or avoiding, such has been the cardinal feature of humanity's economic affairs ever since.

Global Economy to Commonwealth

What then should be the next 'big idea', Budd then asks, in money and finance in the twenty-first century? Such an idea of a *commonwealth* is that of *a single global economy shared and mutually governed by a choir of the world's peoples.* No one country or people or way of life should impose itself on any other, meaning that Anglo-Saxon dominance would need to give way to promoting economic partnership between peoples, but also that the people around the world would need to identify a future true to their own development, not merely a reaction to past domination.

Human beings everywhere need to give true expression to their deeper destinies and purposes. It could be added that in such a choir of cultures, for Houghton Budd, it will nevertheless be a feature of the English contribution that it will appear in economic form. In particular, it will appear as shifting from possession of the global economy to partnership in economic life.

BACK TO THE BRICS

A Limited Focus on Societal Particularity

Russia's Kropotkin and Brazil's Mangabeira Unger, India's Sri Aurobindo and Senegal's Leopold Senghor, California's Richard Noorgard and English anthroposophical economist Houghton Budd, have all played their respectively historic and contemporary parts in calling for unity-in-variety, culturally and economically. However, where they have fallen short is in identifying the particularity of each of the cultures with which they are concerned. Whereas at Aurobindo, Senghor and Houghton Budd have focused on the particularity of their respective individual cultures, the full variety to which they allude has not been explored. To that extent, ironically enough, Jim O'Neil – in highlighting the BRIC countries Brazil, Russia, India, China, while others have added South Africa – has heralded such variety, even though his 'growth map' has only merely touched economically on such.

Integral Realities and Rhythm

What we want to do in this book, then, is to focus on those particular societies, integrally, in two respects. In the first respect we wish to explore the different worldviews, or realities, that *each of these societies most embodies, naturally and culturally, technologically and economically, contained with what we have termed an all round, integral polity*. Thanks to O'Neil, unconsciously if not consciously, the BRICS enable us to traverse west and west, north and south, thereby constituting, altogether an integral reality. Secondly, and of equal if not greater importance, *we will be reviewing, in each case what we call their integral development rhythm, from* **G***rounding and* **E***mergence to* **N***avigation and* **E***ffect, serving to release the GENE-ius of each.*

Our overall argument is that no society, hitherto, has pursued *integral* advantage, though some may have done so more than others. Indeed we have been so blinded, as Mangabeira Unger has intimated, by the singularly economic logic of comparative advantage, that integral advantage has been severely inhibited. We now turn to the overall, integral rhythm, in Chapter 3.

Bibliography

1. Cypher, J. and Dietz, J. (2009) *The Process of Economic Development. Third Edition.* Abingdon, Routledge.
2. Schieffer, A. and Lessem, R. (2013) *Integral Development: Realizing the Transformative Potential of Individuals, Organizations and Societies.* Farnham, Gower.
3. O'Neil, J. (2011) *The Growth Map: Economic Opportunity in the BRICS and Beyond.* London, Penguin.
4. Mangabeira Unger, R (2007) *Free Trade Re-imagined: The World Division of Labor and the Method of Economics.* Princeton, Princeton University Press.
5. Sri, Aurobindo (1950) *The Human Cycle.* Wisconsin, Twin Lakes.
6. Houghton Budd, C. (2011) *Finance at the Threshold: Rethinking the Real and Financial Economies.* Farnham, Gower.

Chapter 3

Towards Integral Advantage: Integral Realities and Rhythms

The traditional idea of a leader is that of a person who is able to hold a vision, to articulate it clearly and to communicate it with passion and charisma. It is also a person whose actions embody certain values and serve as a standard for others to strive for. The other kind of leadership consists in facilitating the emergence of novelty. This means creating conditions rather than giving directions, and using the power of authority to empower others.

Fritjof Capra (1), Hidden Connections

3.1 Introduction

GENERATIVE EMERGENCE

Quantitative versus Qualitative Emergence

In the previous chapter we introduced the notion of 'emerging' markets, exemplified by the BRICs, while recognizing that *emergence* in such conventional market terms was merely nominal. In other words, all it meant for O'Neil, and other economists like him, was that such economies were growing rapidly, in quantitative terms. There was little qualitative *emergence* explicitly taking place.

Such 'emergence', qualitatively speaking in recent years, has come to the notice, in particular, of biologists and ecologists, as well as complexity and systems theorists, in the social sciences. The most recent of such (2015), has been the American social scientist and complexity theorist Benyamin Lichtenstein (1), for whom *emergence is the creation of order, the formation of new properties and structures in complex systems. When emergence happens, something new and unexpected arises, whose outcomes cannot be predicted.* Emergence then is one of the most ubiquitous processes in the world, and yet one of the least understood. For us, while such outcomes cannot be predicted, thy can at least be anticipated, though invariably the outcomes are somewhat different. What follows, for Lichtenstein, is a description of six properties of emergence.

Properties of Emergence

Such emergent properties, for Lichtenstein, range from relational properties, in general, to collective action in particular:

Relational Properties: when a large number of homogenous agents – for example atoms or molecules or indeed peoples and communities – are put together, the relationships between them lead to emergent properties.

Autocatalysis: much of emergence, in the broadest sense, depends on a cycle of positive feedback within the system, that amplifies certain behaviours and patterns of order, embodying them in the system as a whole.

Symbiogenesis: the 'engine' of order creation here is symbiosis – the association of two or more different species, or for us cultures or societies, that improves the functioning of both.

Collaborative Emergence: at the heart of such social emergence is an ongoing stream of interactions across a large number of individuals or groups. At a micro level this leads to the emergence of patterns between two or several of these; at a macro level these scale up to produce patterns of social interaction that emerge as institutional and societal norms.

Generative Emergence: there are two drivers of generative emergence. The first involves a perception or belief that whatever is produced will be of value to others. The second is enacting, or developing, a method by which knowledge and value gets created, naturally and culturally, technologically and economically, ultimately resulting in integral advantage.

Collective Action: finally is a distinct natural or cultural, social or economic, prototype because it refers to collections of organizations or social entities, which together can exhibit a shared intention or goal.

EMERGENCE AND TRANSFORMATION

Emergence as a Part of Nature

We now turn to our (3) own perspective on emergence, specifically, in the overall context of transformation, generally. As such we introduce our *integral rhythm*. What the new biological, ecological, complexity and systems sciences in fact teach us is that *the very emergence and the maintenance of life is an ongoing transformative, hence emergent, process*. We draw then on nature, literally and metaphorically, for our integral rhythm, thereby underlying an *emerging* market or society as such.

Life then, and, in the context of this book, 'emergent living' economies and societies, are in a state of continual change, not opposing the forces of the environment, but flowing with them. *Life then and the environment are partners in co-creation*. To take another example of this co-creative aspect, aquatic blades of grass reduce stream velocity, thereby forcing the waters to drop their silt load and the decaying plant material they carry along. Both these effects increase channel deposition, which creates more soil and nutrients for plant roots.

Plants grow stronger, denser. This reduces velocity further, creating more deposition. Deposition displaces water. The stream overflows and spreads out, greatly expanding its surface area as it flows over. The water's energy drops drastically. As a result water and silt are spread over a broad channel, nourishing more lush growth. This growth creates greater accumulations of spongy, absorbent, plant material, spreading the slowing water even wider.

Life Creates Conditions for More Life

The interaction between natural energy (physical) and life's energy (human in our case) then is the chief principle of emergence. The interaction is often so subtle, so insignificant that we don't even see it. Each small shift in equilibrium creates another small shift. Each new equilibrium covers the tracks of the previous change. The power lies in the accumulative consistency with which these changes shift equilibrium in life's favour. Life creates conditions for more life. These loops create change, not stability. In fact, stabilizing forces need to follow such change. For us, as we shall soon see, grounding and navigation are stabilizing; emergence and ultimately effecting are transformative. By shaping the development of its environment, life allows itself to be shaped by the environment. Such transformation is equally applicable to individuals, organizations and societies, each one from its own point of original grounding.

While life emerges out of its local environment, or grounding then, it needs to be locally–globally transformed by life as a whole so that it remains life-supportive. This is the essence of the process of transformation in which firstly, the individual unit of survival is simultaneously a unit of transformation, and secondly, the transformation process is the engagement of the individual unit with other units – or individuals, organizations or societies – thereby creating new, intelligent forms without losing the essence of the original. We now turn to our own integral approach to the BRICS, starting with our integral realities, before we turn to our integral rhythm, in which *emergence* plays a key part.

BRICS REALITIES TO RELEASE OF GENE-IUS

Integral BRICS Realities

The purpose of transformation through a co-creative process is to sustain a future in which resources become available to as wide a base as possible, and diverse units of local life work with a common global principle to sustain life as a whole. We begin, as such in the 'south', then move 'east', then to the 'north' and end up in the 'west'. In doing so we traverse the journey of humankind, which by now you will have seen is our overarching transformative reality. In the course of this book on the BRICS, the US and the UK, wherein the very concept of *BRICS* has been derived, represent the 'west-north'; India the 'south-east'; China the 'north-east'; and Brazil the 'south-west'. We ultimately, moreover, and most significantly, position Russia in the Eurasian 'west-east' and South Africa, the 'rainbow nation' as primarily 'north–south'.

Release of GENE-ius

How does this work? To answer that, we immerse ourselves in our transformative realities, and apply our analogous, transformative rhythm. In doing so, we describe *four sub-processes that are crucial for transformation in natural systems*: from the formative Grounding to the reformative Emergence, on to normative Navigation and, ultimately, the transformative Effect, thereby recognizing and releasing GENE-ius. Moreover, and continually, there are feedback loops between one and the other. Notably then, such 'emergence' is specifically *reformative*, qualitatively speaking, something largely ignored by the conventional BRICS wisdom.

Together, these four processes – formative grounding, reformative emergence, normative navigation and transformative effect – provide the basis for an ongoing transformation process (see Figure 3.1 opposite). Clearly, if

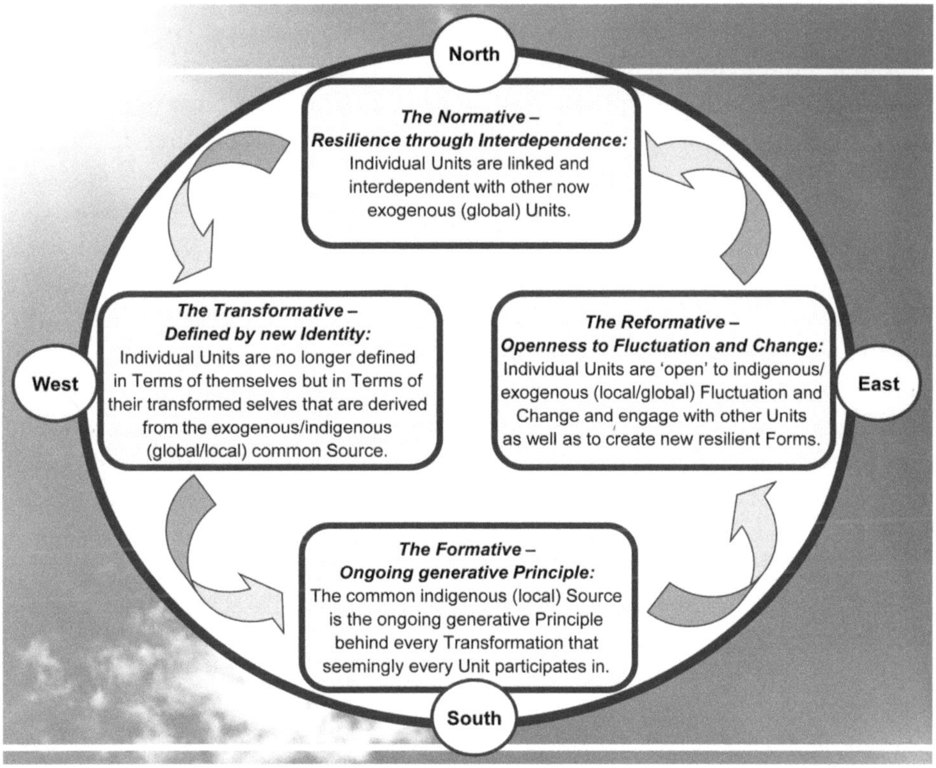

Figure 3.1 Transformation in natural systems

we are looking for a model of transformation, we need look no further than the system of our natural environment that has successfully survived and flourished for millennia. As we saw earlier, nature engages in a continuous transformative process that seeks to sustain life. Interestingly enough the American management guru Peter Senge (4), in his latest book on *The Necessary Revolution*, strongly reinforces this natural orientation:

> *We need to ask, what would a way of thinking, a way of living, and ultimately an economic system look like that worked based on the principles of the larger natural world. And how do we create such a way of living in our organizations and societies, step by step.*

Needless to say, by and large, such a transformative process has not taken place in our societies, explicitly speaking. Quantitative growth of late has taken place, in the BRICS, and in the Pacific Tigers before such, not to mention the 'west' hitherto, but qualitative transformation, has been much less clearly identified.

We now explain how, for us, the natural process works. We need to also bear in mind that our configuration of integral realities – south, east, north and west, – are as much metaphoric as they are literal. Indeed each major society incorporates, potentially if not actually, all of these realities within it.

In the BRICS case, then, each of the five societies has its respectively 'southern' **G**rounding, 'eastern' **E**mergence, 'northern' **N**avigation and 'western' **E**ffect (hence GENE-ius) albeit that, at one and the same time, Brazil has an overall 'south-western' orientation, Russia 'east–west', India 'south-east', China 'north-east' and South Africa 'north–south'.

We start then with nature and life, on the 'ground', to portray our integral rhythm, feeling local, intuiting local–global, thinking global and acting global–local, as it were, before we part from such grounds to enter into society at large.

3.2 Integral Rhythm: Local/Formative to Globally–Locally Transformative

GROUNDING IN THE FORMATIVE 'SOUTH': GENERATIVE LOCAL IDENTITY

Common Source

The rule of the common source, herein drawing on nature, and related in turn to a Russian, Southern African, Indian, Chinese or Brazilian common source in the overall BRICS case, is the same one that enables the transformation of a chrysalis (e.g. Brazilian eco-services) into a butterfly (integral Brazilian economy and society). The caterpillar's organs and tissues dissolve into an amorphous soup-like state only to reconstitute into the structure of a butterfly's body that bears absolutely no resemblance to the caterpillar at all. The chemical complexity of turning into a butterfly is incredible and science still has no explanation for why this metamorphosis has evolved. Some cells know when to die, others digest themselves, some turn into eyes, some into wings.

The whole process of transformation requires a very delicate and precise rhythm between creation and destruction. This rhythm depends on day length, which in turn depends upon the earth's rotation around the earth. *The transformation of a chrysallis into a butterfly is linked to its source in the rhythm of the cosmos*, just as Amazonia, in the example given above, is an intrinsic part of our global whole.

Particular and Universal

How does each cell 'know' how to remain linked to the generative principle of the common source? The answer is simple: the universality of a cell or for that matter, any other unit, is contingent upon it being fully itself. What that means is that in the act of truly being yourself, as per Amazonia-and-Brazil (see Chapter 14), you are at once universal. Therefore, *the role of organizations and societies is to participate in continuously creating and sustaining a common future in which resources and benefits transcend the integral realities, east or west, north or south, of the organization or society and encompass as wide an area as possible.* The only way this can be done is when the society is simultaneously rooted in itself (e.g. *Gram swaraj* as *local awakening* in the *Sarvodaya* 'south-eastern' case – Chapter 12 – as we shall see), while engaging with other societies and the larger environment (e.g. Vishodaya – world awakening) to bifurcate into other forms. We now turn to 'eastern' emergence, still drawing, archetypically so to speak, on the natural world.

REFORMATIVE 'EAST': EMERGING FROM THE WHOLE AS A LOCAL–GLOBAL NON-ENTITY

Resilience through Diversity

Essential to the process of emergence is building resilience through diversity. David Suzuki, the renowned Canadian ecologist writing in *Sacred Balance* (5) refers to the quaking aspen, the white-barked trees as an example of how nature operates as a system. Shoots may grow up from a root more than 50 feet away. So the aspen is really a super organism, a system that is made up of a network of interconnections. But for the system, or society in our case, to remain healthy and thrive and grow, it has to have a diverse landscape. So some parts may grow in moist soil, and through their common underground roots, share the water with other portions, perhaps growing in mineral-rich soil higher up. This was indeed the case, as will be illustrated in Chapter 7, in the 'mixed model' of the nineteenth-century Russian Province, eclipsed by the 'monocultural' form of communism that followed in the twentieth century.

What Suzuki is saying is that if at each level of complexity – cell, organism and eco-system – new kinds of structures and functions emerge, the totality of all life on the planet can be taken as a single entity too. But this totality of life, the convergence of all living and non-living matter into a single system is necessarily dependent on all the divergences that make the system possible. As Nobel laureate Roger Sperry (6) points out, new properties that arise from complexes cannot be predicted from the known properties of their individual parts. These *emergent properties only exist within the whole* (as for example in the Russian Province as a whole, not its component natural and cultural, political and economic parts). No single species is indispensable, but the sum-total of all life, illustrated as we shall see in the Russian case by 'Cosmism' (see Chapter 5) not Communism, maintains the fecundity of the earth.

Genetic Polymorphism – Bridges to the Outside

How does life then achieve its extraordinary resilience? The answer is *genetic polymorphism.* When a species such as the Siberian tiger is reduced to a few survivors, its long-term future is under threat because the range of its genetic variability has been radically diminished and therefore has fewer options to adapt to changes in the environment. Suzuki, like indeed Kroptkin (see Chapter 1) goes on to emphasise how a diverse mixture of gene variants is a fundamental characteristic of a vibrant, healthy species, a reflection of its successful evolutionary history and continued potential to adapt to unpredictable change. Population geneticists believe that *the most successful species are found in places that are connected 'by bridges' to the outside* (as per Chinese *Chaxugeju* or Laws of Association as portrayed in Chapter 13)*). Monoculture then, physically and also for us in terms of humanity, is the enemy of life's evolutionary strategy*. We now turn from grounding and emergence to navigation.

NAVIGATION VIA THE NEWLY NORMATIVE NORTH: RESILIENT GLOBAL ENTITY

Competition and Cooperation

Elisabet Sahtouris (7), contemporary biologist and thinker, writes about the enormous crisis we face because the most central and important aspect of globalization, its economy, is currently being organized in a manner that violates the fundamental principles by which healthy living systems are organized. She writes about natural principles that operate in our bodies and in our families. We intuitively and collectively grasp such principles without any problem. So not many people starve three of their children to overfeed the fourth, or beautify one corner of the garden by destroying the rest of it. But strangely we begin to lose sight of those principles at the level of our local communities, towns or nations.

As international financer, philanthropist and philosopher and George Soros (8) says, 'there is something wrong with making the survival of the fittest a guiding principle of civilized society. This social Darwinism is based on an outmoded theory of evolution'. Once the polymorphic process has taken place, life settles into its new form, assured in its resilience. This brings us into transformative effect.

EFFECT VIA TRANSFORMATIVE WEST: TRANSFORM LOCAL IDENTITY TO GLOBAL INTEGRITY

Inherently Transformative

Each species formed this way becomes part of the transformed ecosystem that thrives because of the simultaneity of individual and universal forces embodied in it. At each level of complexity – cell, organism and ecosystem – new kinds of structures and functions emerge. The totality of life on our planet can be taken to be a single, resilient entity that has remained sustainable for so long because it is inherently transformative. Sad to say this is not so for our economy. Suzuki refers to the single envelope of atmosphere that encircles the earth, while water flows around continents, creating great islands.

That is the reason why the ecosystem is described as an autopoietic (from the Greek, meaning 'self-production') structure, based on the work of the Chilean and French biological duo Maturana and Varela in the 1990s. (9) These two scientists compared autopoietic systems to allopoietic systems. So a car is the latter, as it contains the same molecules from showroom to junkyard. Its identity is given by the manufacturer and nothing changes. By contrast, *autopoietic structures in life change molecules all the time and yet, somehow remain the same.* For us, each of the BRICS needs to be seen as such. So how exactly do they retain their integrity? That is their relationality (see Figure 3.2) with the environment.

A Pattern of Relationships

So, on the one hand, transformation is effectively realized in the individual species and sub-parts, BRIC by BRIC as it were, that thrive through their separate identities. But paradoxically enough, what makes them and the whole ecosystem sustainable is the fact that they are inextricably part of a pattern of relationships: BRICS. The overall process of transformation can be summarized as follows. As mentioned earlier, perhaps the most beautiful illustration of the transformational process in nature is that of the caterpillar

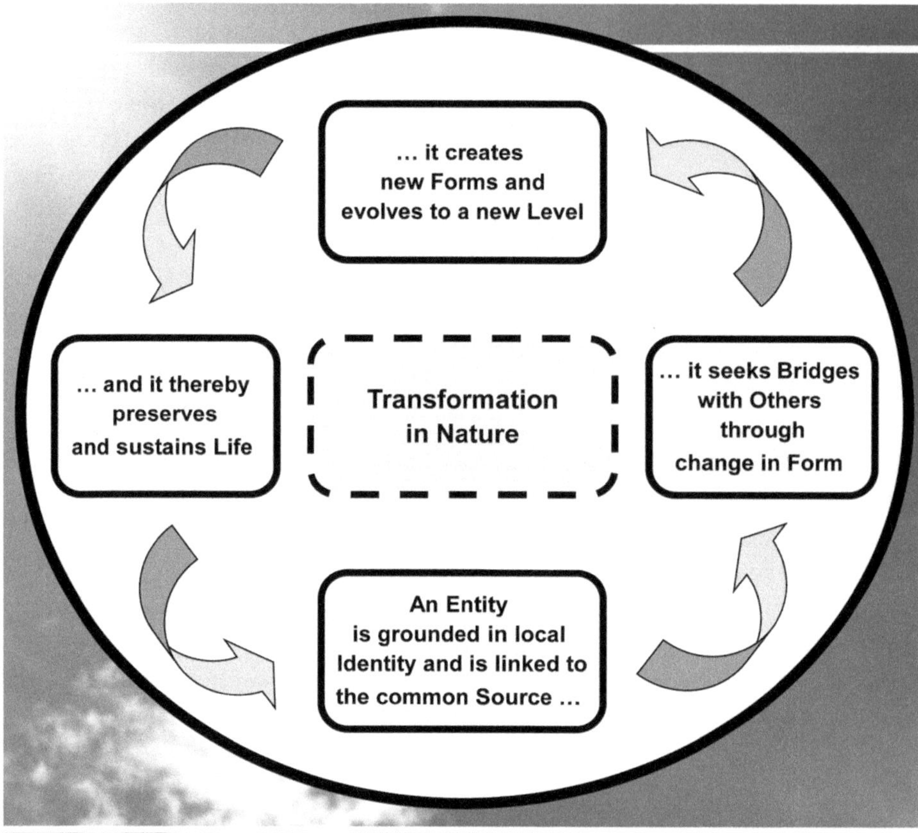

Figure 3.2 Transformation and emergence in nature

turning into a butterfly. The caterpillar's original form (its 'local identity' as again is illustrated by the Russian Province) has to be de-formed and reformed in the chrysallis stage, before, through a course designed or normed by nature, it is ultimately transformed into a butterfly. This was patently not the case when the Bolsheviks took charge and duly ignored what had formatively come before.

We now turn from such a transformational flow, rooted in nature, to our own interpretation of such, embedded in our GENE. To illustrate the proximity of both rhythms, formative to transformative and our GENE, we incorporated the GENE (grounding, emerging, navigating, effecting).

3.3 The GENE: Grounding, Emergence, Navigation, Effect

MANAGING IN FOUR WORLDS

Southern, Eastern, Northern, Western

Through our own ongoing research and development at Trans4m over the past decade, we have evolved a transformational pattern, which we have called the GENE of transformation. This flow embodies the above-mentioned premises and is applied in various forms, always connecting local and individual identity with what we term 'global integrity' as an integrative process. It is in that context that we talk about releasing the transformative GENE-ius of the self, the organization and the society. The GENE is the nucleus of transformational processes based on our (10) original approach to *Managing in Four Worlds* (Lessem and Palsule), drawn out of our integral realities (south, east, north, west), that is southern grounding, eastern emergence, northern navigation and western effecting.

GENE TO GENE-I-U-S

I-U-S

The GENE is set in motion by an inner spark, an initiation of an individual or a community, who either experience an internal impulse for growth, change or transformation which is calling for internal integration, or an outer impulse for such, which is caused by addressing an outer issue. In any case, *it is this initial tension between the I (Individual) and the Other – which we call here the 'U' (You) – that initiates the transformation process*, and which, by working its way through the four stages helps to release the full GENE-*I-U-S* of the living system, whereby the 'S' synthesizes or synergizes the I and the U.

Grounding to Effect

Grounding then, represents the first point of stabilization, in one society or another, as we shall see (Chapter 4–14) for each of the BRICS in turn. For example, in Russia such grounding is in mutual aid, and in India in *swadeshi* (economic of place). As the environment changes something has to give, creating the impetus for transformation and impulse comes from both the inside indigenous) and the outside (exogenous). This is the dynamic, emergent process that follows the stabilizing grounding stage. There is dissolution of the old, for without an opening to change through the influence of an internal or external agency, there is simply no transformational flow. The axis needs to spin out of its original moorings in order for the transformation to emerge as a process, for example as Xioakang (moderation) in the Chinese case (see Chapter 13) while, at the same time, holding onto its ground for dear life!

After the first two G-E stages of grounding and emerging, the process now has to evolve to a stage where it forms itself as a navigating entity. While, for example, in the Indian case this is constituted by a Knowledge Society (see Chapter 12) in the Russian one it is constituted of Anthropoecology (see Chapters 5/6), in both ecological and economic terms. Without this process of explicit articulation the transformation process remains incomplete. Finally, the fourth strand is the one of effecting through an integration of the previous three stages, manifesting itself practically as such, for example as Value Sharing in the South African case (see Chapter 11). Moreover, the four stages are alternatively stabilizing (grounding and navigation) and dynamic (emergence and effecting), one following the other rhythmically, as per, again in South Africa, Earth Jurisprudence (grounding) and Truth and Reconciliation (Navigation) to stabilize the economy and society, and Primal Politics (emergence) culminating in Value Sharing Effect) dynamically. We now follow part of the GENE each in turn.

THE TRANSFORMATIONAL GENE

'Southern' Grounding: Local Identity

The ultimate goal of emergent transformation is to evolve local identity – for your self, organization and society (in this case Brazil, Russia, India, China or South Africa) – towards a form of authentic global integrity. To begin with, you reach into the grounds of your being, and that of your organization or specifically BRICS society, lodged in nature and community. As such:

- *Natural and communal* value provides the *ground* and the purpose (e.g. *swadeshi* in the Indian case – Chapter 12), for everything produced or offered.
- Such value *gives a sense of purpose* to BRIC structures, systems and processes.
- Value *enhances the identity* for those within and without a particular BRIC(S).
- Value *preserves the nature* of a community, organization or society through overall consensus building.

- At their best, *value-based* communities and societies are visionary centred, characterized by a powerful contribution to society, as for example intimated through Nelson Mandela's *Long Walk to Freedom* (see Chapter 10).

'Eastern' Emergence: Towards a Local–Global Non-Entity

Well-grounded, traditional leaders, enterprises, communities and societies, while strongly rooted in particular values, have a static, conserving quality to them. When confronted with modernizing forces, they tend to become either corrupted or subordinated. Rather than drawing upon the GENE they invariably get caught up in, or seek to catch up with, the 'western-northern' mainstream.

As we loosen our socialized grip on our longstanding value grounds, or indigenous source, we need to open up to what is emerging around us, and thereby renew the past, with a view to creating a future out of it. That is, for example, what Kropotkin is calling for (see Chapter 1) in the Fields, Factories and Workshops of 'Tomorrow'. A good model to follow, metaphorically as we have seen, is that of the caterpillar, which, in emerging from an initial egg into a beautiful butterfly, dissolves into a pupa along the way, drawing on its original caterpillar essence. Further, local–global 'emergence', whereby a grounded entity becomes an emergent 'non-entity', can be described as follows:

- Emergence stimulates the transformative journey, in which structures and systems develop and evolve cross-catalytically, as in the Brazilian case of *Tropicology* (see Chapter 14), where 'racial mixing' prevails. It involves processes of destruction and creation, and an intermittent and discontinuous, but *flowing wholeness,* lodged within an interconnected, unbounded field.
- The emergent, *far-from-equilibrium* developments give rise to a new *dynamic balance,* weaving together, past and future, indigenous and exogenous, as per *Future Primal* in the Southern African case (Chapter 9), one world and another; destroying static concepts of structures and systems, leading to a new order, born out of the renewed old one.
- Such emergent processes are therefore *destabilizing*; they creatively 'undo' the rigid structures of the 'west' and orderly systems of the 'north', so that a subsequently *raised consciousness and renewed culture* arises, as reflected, in 'east–west' guise, by Russian *Cosmism* (see Chapter 5).

- What emerges is not merely what happens between structures and systems; on the contrary, processes work around and through structures, making them *porous and permeable,* continually open to new possibilities.
- Without such conscious evolution or indeed 'cosmism', an organization or society remains disconnected and abstract; processes *undo* predetermined notions of order and procedure.
- At their best, process-driven, emergent leaders, organizations and societies, are dynamic, highly *innovative* entities, as in today's China; at their worst totally unpredictable, and lurching from one state to another.

'Northern' Navigation: Building a newly Global Entity

Northern consolidation, combination or conceptualization involves the establishment of new propositions, or institutions, evoked out of what has hitherto emerged:

- Profound theories lead your organization or society to become a *complex system or network,* as reflected in *Confucian Pragmatism* for China (Chapter 13), rather than a simple structure, with interconnected patterns and relationships.
- Systems enhance the notion of order by connecting individual points into linear and *cross-linear relationships,* as per Brazilian Cardoso's *Social Solidarity* (Chapter 14 as we shall see); such systematic linkages serve to enhance predictability, order and control.
- Without such social and economic systems, societal structures, such as those underlying *Truth and Reconciliation* in South Africa (Chapter 10), as we shall see, remain disconnected and lacking in coherence; *systems give direction* to both structure and imagination.
- Such systems and frameworks use *rational analysis* in which the particular follows logically from the general; problems are tackled through attempts at realizing consensus.
- At their best, such rationally and systematically based entities *are ethical,* serving to 'do right', with a collective benefit to all, as was the case in South Africa while Mandela was President; at their worst they are alienating and bureaucratic (as is the case for the ANC in South Africa today).

As we re-emerge (east) out of our value grounds (south) in order to conceptualize ourselves anew (north), different kinds of institutional frameworks are designed. However, they are yet to be internalized. The purposeful navigation of the newborn self, organization or society that we are seeking to establish, represents the *knowing* consolidation of the prior process of becoming. As such the fully-fledged new concept, as an organization or system, product or entity, is established out of the prior fusion of horizons. In fact, the success of the 'north-west' in business, in Europe and America, is born out of just such a 'global' fusion. This has recently been the case for Japan, as a fusion of eastern and western horizons, and, prospectively, as we shall see, may be the case for Russia (east–west) and South Africa (north–south).

We finally turn to a 'west' that duly builds on the rest, not something that we see in the conventional BRICs wisdom, whereby such a 'north-western' worldview stands in isolation form the rest, in terms of our overall integral reality.

Western Effect:Achieving Newly Global–Local Integrity

To realize 'western' efficiency and effectiveness certain culminating steps are necessary, to actualize the local/local–global/global/global–local integral rhythm:

- Structure building requires us to perceive any strategy, for example that of the IMF or WTO, as an *assembly of parts*, like in a machine. It further requires making use of inductive logic, to building up your strategy.
- The structural world is highly differential – categories are created instinctively inside the structure giving a preliminary *sense of order* to the strategic activity.
- Clearly laid-out categories, including a *clear set of aims*, making focus easy, coupled with an easy internalization of knowledge.
- Structures are built on *convergent logic*: for every problem, there is one solution; every cause one effect; there is one way to do a particular thing well, thereby adding value.
- At their best, clearly structured activities lend themselves to effective *problem solving*, with clearly defined sections to each, neatly delegated functions, supervision and monitoring of all required tasks; at their worst the bottom line dominates over all else.

The GENE, in fact, can also be embodied within an enterprise in order to engage the organization in flows of continuous renewal. For that we will turn to Nonaka and Takeuchi's *knowledge creating company*, but before that we need to reinterpret our integral rhythm in what we term 'topographical' guise.

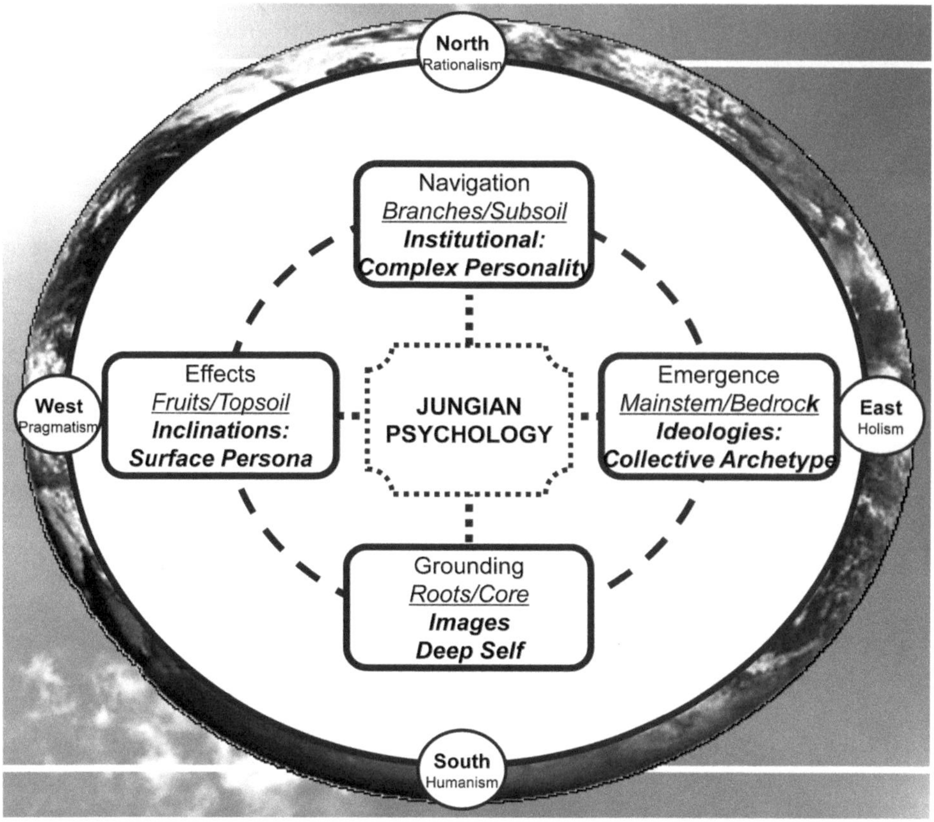

Figure 3.3 Acculturation: Intra-cultural dynamics

3.4 Transformational Topography

INDIVIDUAL PSYCHOLOGY AND CULTURAL STRATIFICATION

The Swiss psychoanalyst, Carl Jung (11), has been a profound influence on our integral approach.

On the one hand, his 'psychological types' – sensing and intuiting, feeling and thinking – have influenced our respectively western and eastern, northern and southern integral realities. On the other hand, his approach to 'layers of personality' have influenced our approach to the integral rhythm of a particular society: specifically grounding *images* or *core* (self); emerging *ideologies* or *bedrock* (archetypes); navigating *institutions* or *subsoil* (personality complex); and *ideologies* or *topsoil* (persona), as portrayed in Figure 3.3 above.

IMAGES, ROOTS OR GROUNDING FRUITS OR EFFECTING

We (12) start by *grounding* ourselves in the historical depths of a particular BRIC, in what we term the *core images or roots*, the deepest layer; we continue *emerging* through *bedrock or ideological mainstem* (second layer), thereafter *navigating* via *subsoil or institutional branches* (third layer), till we reach *topsoil inclinations or fruits* (fourth layer) for ultimate *effect*. Moreover, while this transformation journey from depths to surface represents potential rather than actual, there is a lot of iterative to'ing and fro'ing between levels. In the case of the BRIC societies we shall be reviewing, moreover, topographical elements, as we will see, have invariably been missed along the way.

GROUNDING TO EMERGENCE: ROOTS TO MAINSTEM: IMAGES TO IDEOLOGIES

Core to Bedrock

In between core and bedrock of a particular person, institution or whole community or society, are deeply laden images, rooted in nature, art and religion. In Russia, for example, as we shall see, great writers ranging from Pushkin to Berdyaev, from Dostoevsky to Tolstoy, were profound cases in point. They are potential sources of creativity and innovation. They are the source of transformation, drawn from nature, the humanities or indeed from the depths of religion; that includes language in its original context, informing our imagination.

Similarly, at least for German sociologist Max Weber, P*rotestantism lay at the root of the flowering of capitalism in the modern era. The image of salvation through wealth creation originally infused the hero-archetype in the Anglo-Saxon world*, so clearly embodied in a Richard Branson type of merchant adventurer. Similarly, as we shall see for Russia's Bugakov (Chapter 6), Eastern Orthodoxy and Sophic Wisdom played a similarly imaginative part. We now turn to the topography in between bedrock or mainstem, and subsoil or branches.

EMERGENCE TO NAVIGATION: MAINSTEM TO BRANCHES: IDEOLOGIES TO INSTITUTIONS

Bedrock to Subsoil

In between bedrock and subsoil of a particular society, as it were, are its ideological orientations, primarily represented by its history and philosophies, and its prevailing consciousness. Here we deal with the holistic worldviews that lie well below the everyday surface. Sad to say, as such Russian Cosmism was overtaken by Western Marxism, and Biko's 'Black Consciousness' in South Africa was never applied to economics.

All too often, then, such a cultural bedrock, or mainstem, is globally imported from elsewhere – as was the case for both Russia and China in relation to communism – without being aligned with the local cultural core. This will serve to distort whatever processes of renewal take place, dramatically as we shall see illustrated in the Russian case (see Chapters 4–6 below) unless the potential for disintegration is consciously addressed. Moreover, such an ideological imprint will fall upon stony ground if it is not embedded in the individual as well as organizational consciousness. We now turn from core and bedrock to subsoil, from roots and mainstem to branches and fruits, so to speak.

NAVIGATION TO EFFECT: BRANCHES TO FRUITS: INSTITUTIONS TO INCLINATIONS

Subsoil to Topsoil

At the subsoil of a society are its conceptual and institutional frameworks, duly impacting attitudes and behaviours as outcomes, represented by its prevailing environmental and cultural, social and economic, systems. Built up from our collective intelligence, institutions become the object of concern, including comparative legal systems, political and economic structures, and predominating forms of public, private or civic enterprise. It is here that the 'western-northern' Washington Consensus, aligned with global markets, multinationals and business schools, continue to predominate, across the world stage, at least in the economic arena, and the conventional wisdom on the BRICS is duly aligned with such.

EFFECT BACK TO GROUNDS: FRUITS BACK TO ROOTS: INCLINATIONS BACK TO IMAGES

Inclinations: Attitudes and Behaviours

At the topsoil of a society are its personal inclinations: it is only here that we engage with attitudes and behaviours. Yet, as we might be aware, for example, *the obsessive concern given to leadership and entrepreneurship today reflects such a limited preoccupation with surface phenomena.* They are the ultimate fruits of our endeavours, which ultimately feed back to the roots, but invariably what is lacking is attention to ideologies and institutions in between. In fact these tend to be dominated by 'western' orientations thereby *focused on individual traits and identities, on fruits rather than roots, on effects rather than grounding, emergence, or even means of navigation, in a particular society.*

Overall then, the extent to which each of these cultural layers is well or ill functioning will be dependent upon the degree of differentiation and integration, of both integral realities (east–west, north–south, south-east, north-east, west-north and south-west) and also topographical rhythm (images, ideologies, institutions, inclinations). Moreover, in order to promote such, as we shall see in our concluding Chapter 15, a new kind of activist, catalytic, research and educational institution is altogether required.

DIFFERENTIATION AND INTEGRATION WITHIN A PARTICULAR SOCIETY

Functionality versus Dysfunctionality

In other words, each of the societal layers then, rhythmically speaking, is susceptible to functionality or dysfunctionality, depending upon both the degree of clear-cut differentiation and coherent integration (functionality), as opposed to wildly manifest differences and rampantly cast disintegration (dysfunctionality). In fact, Russia and South Africa stand out today as such rampant cases of disintegration, as we shall see, albeit that these societies could play a seminal integrating part of re-orientation that way.

Horizontal Integrity

In particular, a culture acquires global integrity, with a view to pursuing integral advantage, when each of the layers are both differentiated, analytically, and dynamically integrated, so to speak. Horizontal integrity emerges, when there is purposeful co-creation between diverse worldviews or realities at each horizontal level of the topography, through so-called 'transculturation' as we shall see, in mestizo Brazil (Chapter 14). For example, Japanese Spirit/western technique, as prevailed amongst large scale manufacturing enterprises in Japan in the 1970s and 1980s, was an expression of such an 'east–west' fusion. Similarly, the emergence of 'western' Marxism in the Soviet Union last century was an illustration of the reverse. In the final analysis, both forms of integrity are required in the pursuit of integral advantage.

Vertical Integrity

Secondly, *if there is local resonance between individual inclinations, institutional configurations, ideological orientations and imaginative creations we have what we term vertical integrity.* This has historically, from the eighteenth century onwards, been in evidence in the Anglo-Saxon 'west-north', where individual artistic imagination (e.g. Shakespeare and Byron), political and economically liberal ideologies (e.g. John Locke and Adam Smith), liberal democratic and free market institutions, as well as leadership and entrepreneurial inclinations, have been altogether and mutually aligned.

We now, finally in this chapter, turn to the case of the 'knowledge creating company', or what we also term a 'knowledge and value creating society', to illustrate how such a transformational rhythm may be put into effect.

3.5 The Knowledge and Value Creating Enterprise and Society

KNOWLEDGE CREATION TO CONTINUOUS INNOVATION

Knowledge Creation to Innovation

The two Japanese organizational sociologists Ikijiro Nonaka and Hirotama Takeuchi maintain (14) that the path taken by a knowledge creating enterprise is in essence, to turn knowledge creation into continuous innovation. From the outset, having worked with Nonaka for three years, with a research group under the sponsorship of Germany's Roland Berger Foundation (12), on *Breakthroughs in European Innovation,* I had the sense that his integral approach, aligned with ours, could apply equally as well to society at large.

Nonaka and Takeuchi identified three key 'enabling conditions' for their knowledge creating enterprise (for us also community or society):

- develop intentionally the collective capability to acquire, create, accumulate and exploit knowledge;
- build up autonomous individuals and groups, setting task boundaries themselves to pursue the ultimate intention of organization or community;
- provide a sense of crisis – as well as a lofty ideal – such so-called 'creative chaos' increases tension within the organization.

From our also societal, knowledge *and value* perspective, the following applies:

- develop intentionally *societal* capability to acquire, create, accumulate and exploit knowledge;
- build up autonomous individuals and groups, setting their task boundaries by themselves to pursue the ultimate intention of the *society;*
- provide a sense of crisis – as well as a lofty ideal – such so-called 'creative chaos' increases tension within the *society*.

How then does Nonaka and Takechi's so-called 'hypertext' organization, and for us integral economy and society, serve to promote such?

THE HYPERTEXT ORGANIZATION AND SOCIETY

Start with the Project Layer

Nonaka refers to a 'hypertext' organization, because of its layered nature and scope, which serves to develop, channel and distribute knowledge through duly formed networks. *The top stratum of this kind of enterprise is comprised, not of a CEO or hierarchy of command, but by the 'project team' layer* (see Figure 3.4). Multiple project teams engage in knowledge (and value) creating activities such as new product and systems development. In all such cases the team members are brought together from a number of different units across the business, community or society, and are assigned exclusively to a project team until the project is completed. In fact, in Chapter 7 below, focused on a *Russian Province* in the nineteenth century, we shall illustrate how this communally and societally takes place.

From Project Layer to Bureaucratic System

Alongside this project layer, but occupying a lower order of knowledge (and value) creating significance, is the conventional 'bureaucratic system' with its normal hierarchy of authority. *The project layer, on the one hand, is engaged with developing new knowledge through self-organizing groups. The hierarchical system, on the other, is primarily concerned with categorizing, ordering, distributing and operationalizing such knowledge.* Nonaka and Takeuchi's so called 'knowledge spiral', like *particle* (south-east to west-north) and wave (grounding to effect) as we shall see below, analogous to our own integral reality, and overall rhythm, the project layer is primarily focused upon *'southern' socialization* (grounding) and *'eastern' externalization* (emergence), the hierarchical system is more

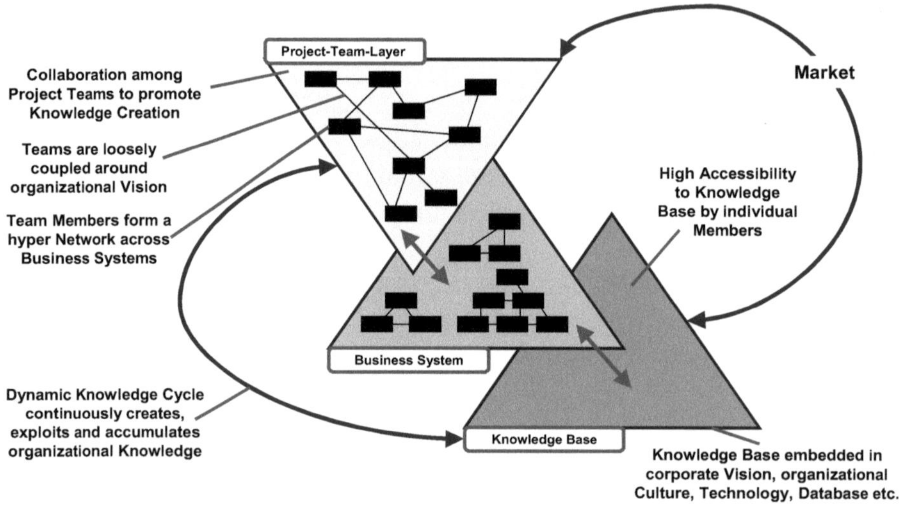

Figure 3.4 The hypertext organization (according to Nonaka et al.)

engaged with *'northern' combination* (navigation) and *'western' internalization* (effect). Underlying both project layer and business, or societal, system, is a 'knowledge (and value) foundation'.

Project Later and Bureaucratic System to Knowledge Foundation

This third layer does not exist as an actual organizational, or societal, entity, but is embedded in vision, culture and technology. Of course, in our context here, societal culture is of even greater significance than the corporate one. Such a corporate or societal vision, for example embodied in Federov's 'Cosmism' (Chapter 5) or Koopman's 'Divine Will of Africa' (Chapter 11) arises from these spiritual, aesthetic and scientific knowledge grounds.

If made explicit, it provides the direction in which the enterprise, community or society should develop its social as well as technological innovations. *Moreover, it clarifies the overall 'field' in which each needs to pursue, for us, integral advantage, for example,* in the South African case *as we shall see, that of* social and economic reconciliation. *Furthermore, while vision and culture provide the experiential and imaginative base formed of tacit (indigenous), aligned with explicit (exogenous) knowledge, technology taps the explicit knowledge generated in the other two layers.*

Designed versus Emergent Structures

This corresponds exactly with the findings of the Austrian physicist and ecologist Fritjof Capra, as intimated at the beginning of this chapter, when he talks in *The Hidden Connections* (16) about the emergence of novelty in human organizations. Designed structures provide the rules and routines that are necessary for the effective functioning of the organization. They enable a business organization to optimize its production processes and to sell its products through effective marketing campaigns. Emergent structures, on the other hand, provide novelty, creativity and flexibility. They are adaptive, capable of changing and evolving.

We now turn to the so-called 'knowledge crew', as opposed to conventional managers and employees, who run such a hypertext organization.

THE KNOWLEDGE CREW

What is seldom recognized is the way in which Nonaka and Takeuchi have dissolved the notion of 'labour', or even 'human resources', and replaced these terms with knowledge creators. *Such a transformation from 'labour' to knowledge is distinctly absent from the 'western' literature on knowledge management, which is much more strongly rooted in technology.* For the Japanese organizational sociologists there are three kinds of knowledge creators: knowledge practitioners, knowledge engineers and knowledge officers.

Knowledge Practitioners or Facilitators

Knowledge practitioners, or for us *facilitators* (see Chapter 15), consist of 'knowledge operators' like technicians who interface with tacit or indigenous knowledge for the most part, and 'knowledge specialists' like computer programmers, who interface primarily with explicit or exogenous knowledge. Such *facilitators develop a strongly personal perspective, a strong degree of openness to discussion and debate, as well as a variety of experience inside and outside the organization, or community, from and through which they are able to learn.* They also acquire a high degree of specific skill-based competence, and functional knowledge, as well as skill in interacting with others.

Knowledge Engineers, Researchers or Catalysts

Knowledge engineers, or for us *researchers or catalysts*, constituting the heart of the knowledge and value creating enterprise or society, are responsible for converting tacit knowledge into explicit and vice versa, thereby facilitating the four modes of knowledge creation. As such they mediate between the 'what should be' mindset of the knowledge officers, or for us stewards, and the 'what is' mindset of the frontline practitioners by creating mid-level business or societal concepts. Such mid-level catalysts synthesise the tacit knowledge of both lower and higher levels, make it explicit, and incorporate it into new products and technologies. They become proficient in *employing metaphors and in developing story lines, to help themselves and others imagine the future. They become adept at communication whereby they encourage dialogue, and grow their competence in developing new strategic concepts.* They are able to develop methodologies for knowledge and value creation, and become equipped with project management capabilities.

Knowledge Officers or Stewards

Knowledge officers, or *stewards* for us finally, are responsible for managing the total knowledge and value creation process at the organizational, or societal, level. They are, therefore, expected to give an enterprise's, or indeed community's or society's, knowledge-creating activities a sense of direction by articulating grand concepts on what each might be, establishing a knowledge vision in the form of a policy statement, and setting the standards for justifying the value of the knowledge that is being created.

In other words, *knowledge officers/stewards are responsible for articulating the company's, or community's, 'conceptual umbrella'*, the grand concepts that in highly universal and abstract terms identify the common features linking disparate business activities into a coherent whole. In short they direct the entire process of knowledge and value creation. They create chaos within the project team, for example, setting challenging goals for would-be leaders, and they have responsibility for selecting the right project leaders or knowledge engineers in key areas.

Finally, they need to be able to interact with team members on a hands-on basis and solicit commitment.

THE KNOWLEDGE AND VALUE SPIRAL

Being, Becoming, Knowing and Doing

Earlier on we alluded to the 'knowledge spiral', which was Nonaka and Takeuchi's equivalent to our societally-based integral realities and rhythm.

Their spiral, as such, is a continuous, self-transcending process through which *an individual, organization or society transcends the boundary of the old self into a new self by acquiring a new context, a new view of the world, an evolved consciousness and knowledge, indeed a new social construction.* In short, it is a journey 'from being to becoming, knowing and doing', in the process, transcending the boundary between self and other, through ongoing interaction. What then is specifically involved?

Local Grounding: Knowledge and Value Socialization

In the first instance an informal community of social interaction provides an immediate forum for nurturing the knowledge and value at each organizational, or communal level. This involves 'southern' grounding, *incorporating altruism, empathy and a sense of reciprocity, Chinese Chaxugeju.* Such is the potential contribution of informal groups to collective knowledge and value creation.

Local–Global Emergence: Knowledge and Value Externalization

Once mutual trust and a common tacit or indigenous perspective have been formed through shared experience, the team needs to articulate the perspective through continuous dialogue. This process activates so called 'externalization', from tacit to explicit, indigenous to exogenous, whereby *participants, acting out of a 'gardening' mentality, engage in the mutual local–global co-development of ideas, as per Shiva's 'Earth Democracy'* (see Chapter 12). This constitutes a holistic 'eastern' orientation. Such dialogue, moreover, should not be single faceted and deterministic, but multi-faceted, providing room for revision or negation.

Newly Global Navigation: Knowledge and Value Combination

The third mode of knowledge and value creation involves the use of social processes to combine different bodies of explicit or exogenous knowledge held by individuals and organizations, as with the South African Truth and Reconciliation Commission, the TRC (see Chapter 9) through such exchange mechanisms as formal meetings, codes of conduct, formalized systems and structures. *The reconfiguring of existing information through sorting, adding, recatagorizing and recontextualizing of such explicit knowledge can, at the same time, lead to new combinations of knowledge and value.* Modern computer-based data processing systems, in fact, provide a graphic example of such.

For Mangabeira Unger (see previous chapter) such knowledge is formulaic. However, importantly for our purposes, such formulae, or now newly global knowledge and value, is born out of prior local, and thereafter local–global knowledge and value, rather than being imposed, or indeed 'caught up with through development', from and through the exogenous outside.

Global–Local Effect: Knowledge and Value Internalization

In the conversion of explicit to tacit, exogenous to indigenous, knowledge and value, finally, that is 'internalization', individual action is important, as has been the case for Albert Koopman in promoting *value sharing* through Cashbuild (see Chapter 11). We are now in the realm of 'western' pragmatism. Individuals internalize knowledge, tacitly, through direct, hands on experience, thereby both reaching out for, and hold onto, what they have procured hitherto. Moreover, for explicit knowledge to become tacit, for exogenous knowledge to become indigenous, it helps if the knowledge is verbalized or diagrammed into manuals, documents, stories, or indeed parables or proverbs, as any good consultant or pastor knows. We now turn to the all-important notion of 'middle-up-down-across' as opposed to top-down or bottom-up.

TOP-DOWN AND BOTTOM-UP TO MIDDLE-UP-DOWN-ACROSS

Beyond Hierarchy and Network

The practical vehicle for activating the knowledge spiral, thereby releasing the knowledge-based vision with the support of the enabling conditions, is for Nonaka 'middle-up-down', and for us 'middle-up-down-across' knowledge and value creation is 'middle-up-down-across'. This he contrasts against top-down or bottom-up approaches, organizationally for him, and also societally for us. In top-down management, set within the context of a vertically-based, autocratic organizational hierarchy much favoured by traditionally based institutions such as conventional bureaucracies, the top executives, or government, create the basic concepts so that lower members, or public, can implement them. Front-line execution thereby becomes largely routine.

We now turn by way of conclusion to this chapter from Nonaka's, as well as our own, knowledge and value creation, to Porter's *competitive advantage of nations.*

3.6 Conclusion

COMPETITIVE TO INTEGRAL ADVANTAGE OF NATIONS

Factor to Innovation Driven Economy

In 1990, the renowned Harvard Business School professor, Michael Porter, noted by us for his specifically 'north-westernized' approach to competitive strategy, came up with his (17) voluminous, and much better balanced in our terms, approach to *The Competitive Advantage of Nations*, now already in its 11th printing. In it he argues, as you can see below, that such competitive advantage is acquired, to the extent that a nation advances:

- from factor driven, largely natural resource based and cost driven;
- to an investment-based orientation, typically attracting foreign investment;
- to an innovation-driven economy, largely technological innovation as such;
- falling away as wealth driven, which in fact caused the recent financial crisis.

We (18) have followed his accumulative logic (in ordinary lettering below), as you can see, but transformed (in italics and underlined) (see Figure 3.5):

- factor, natural resource and cost driven into natural and communal *grounding*;
- economic investment into *emerging*, particular culture and consciousness, our most fundamental differentiator from the conventional economic approach;
- technological innovation into *navigation* via also social science and technology;
- wealth driven into an approach to *affecting* economics and enterprise that builds on what has come altogether before, and finally;
- a form of integral polity that *integrates* nature, culture, society and economy.

Moreover, in our case, one stage builds on the other, iteratively and cyclically, rather than in exclusively linear fashion, and each part is necessary to the ultimate whole. Finally, the Integral Polity (19) to which we allude involved an alignment between environmental, civic, public and private sectors, altogether.

Factor Driven Grounded in Nature and Community	Investment Driven Emerging Culture and Consciousness	Innovation Driven Navigating via Natural and Social Science & Technology	Wealth Driven Effecting through Economy and Enterprise	Integral Polity Alignment Integrating Nature, Culture, Technology, Economy

Figure 3.5 Competitive strategy to integral advantage

PURSUING INTEGRAL ADVANTAGE

We now turn, initially 'east–west' to the first of the bRics we consider in depth, Russia (Chapters 4–7), to illustrate how integral advantage may be pursued, noting that we are revealing potential rather than actual development, in cyclical rather than necessarily linear, guise. After Russia we shall turn 'north–south' to the next of our bricS, that is South Africa (Chapters 8–11). These are our two central cases in point, because, as we have already said, of their overall significance in the world, rather than their economic 'growth rates'.

Thereafter, having already covered the 'west-north', as per the Goldman Sachs view of the BRICs in Chapter 2, we shall turn 'south-east' to brIc India (Chapter 12), 'north-east' to briC China (Chapter 13), and finally 'south-west' (Chapter 14) to Bric Brazil, before we conclude our argument on integral advantage.

Bibliography

1. Capra, F. (2010) *The Hidden Connections: A Science for Sustainable Living.* New York, Flamingo.
2. Lichtenstein, B. (2015) *Generative Emergence: A New Discipline of Organizational, Entrepreneurial and Social Innovation.* Oxford, Oxford University Press.
3. Lessem, R. and Schieffer, A. (2009) *Transformation Management: Toward the Integral Enterprise.* Farnham, Gower.
4. Senge, P. (2010) *The Necessary Revolution: How Individuals and Organizations are Working Together to Create a Sustainable World.* New York, Nicholas Brealey.
5. Suzuki, D. (2009) *Sacred Balance: Rediscovering our Place in Nature.* Vancouver, Greystone Books.
6. Sperry, R. (1982) *Science and Moral Priority.* New York, Columbia University Press.
7. Sahtouris, E. (2000) *Earthdance: Living Systems in Evolution.* Alameda, Metalog Books.

8. Soros, G. (2000) *Open Society.* New York, Little Brown.
9. Maturana, H. and Varela, F. (1991 *Autopoiesis and Cognition: The Realization of the Living.* Boston, Kluwer.
10. Lessem, R. and Palsule, S. (1997) *Managing in Four Worlds.* Chichester, Wiley-Blackwell.
11. Stevens, A. (1991) *On Jung.* London, Penguin.
12. Lessem, R., Schieffer, A., Tong, J. and Rima, S. (2012) *Integral Dynamics: Cultural Dynamics, Political Economy and the Future of the University.* Farnham, Gower.
13. Kaku, R. (July 1997) *The Path of Kyosei.* Cambridge, Harvard Business Review.
14. Nonaka, I. and Takeuchi, H. (1995) *The Knowledge Creating Company.* Oxford, Oxford University Press.
15. Roland Berger Foundation (1996) *The Light and the Shadow: Breakthroughs in European Innovation.* Oxford, Capstone.
16. Capra, F. (2010) *The Hidden Connections: A Science for Sustainable Living.* New York, Flamingo.
17. Porter, M. (1990) *The Competitive Advantage of Nations.* New York, Palgrave.
18. Schieffer, A. and Lessem, R. (2014) *Integral Development: Realising the Potential of Individuals, Organisations and Societies.* Farnham, Gower.
19. Lessem, R., Abouliesh, I., Pogacnik, M. and Herman, L. (2014) *Integral Polity: Aligning Nature, Culture, Society and Economy.* Farnham, Gower.

PART II

An East–West Russian Integral Perspective

Chapter 4

Mutual Aid to Earth Manifesto: Grounding in Russian Nature and Community

> *Perestroika – restructuring – was born out of the realization, in the 1980's, that problems of internal development in the USSR were ripe, even overripe, for a solution. New approaches and types of action were needed to escape the downward spiral of crisis, to normalize life, and to make a breakthrough to qualitatively new frontiers. It can be said that to a certain extent perestroika was a result of a rethinking of the Soviet experience since October, 1917. It was also obvious that the whole world was entering a new stage of development – some call it the postindustrial age, some the information age. But the Soviet Union had not yet passed through the industrial age. It was lagging further and further behind those processes that were making a renewal in the life of the world community possible. Not only was a leap forward in technology needed but fundamental change in the whole social and political process.*
>
> *Mikhail Gorbachev (1),* Gorbachev: On My Country and the World

4.1 Introduction

WHY RUSSIA?

In Pursuit of Integral Advantage

In our pursuit of integral advantage, thereby seeking to qualitatively release the GENE-ius of a *particular* society, rather than merely and quantitatively improve its standardized, economic growth rate, we turn firstly to Russia. Though Russia today has been earmarked, by the likes of Jim O'Neil, as one of the BRIC countries, it is one of the least notable, in purely economic terms, of the four or five. Especially today (April 2015), as it is immersed in the conflict with the Ukraine, beset with economic sanctions as a result, and with oil process steadily falling, it is an unlikely choice. So why focus firstly on Russia?

Russia's Unique Positioning

There are four reasons. Firstly, naturally and culturally, it is uniquely positioned 'east–west-wise' straddling Eurasia. Secondly, and historically as the Soviet Union, it has exerted a major influence on the world over the course of most of the twentieth century. Thirdly, as we shall reveal, it took a huge 'wrong' turn (see Gorbachev's view as above), in pursuing communism early last century, when it could have pursued a fundamentally different direction of its own. Finally, and possible most important for our integral purposes, *Russia has an incredibly rich natural as well as more especially cultural heritage, for its grounding and emergence.* However, overall, we can see some clear fault-lines appearing when it comes to societal navigation, and then ultimate economic effect. In order to transcend such, as we shall now see, we are going to pursue, at least in our mind's eye, integral Russian advantage.

MUTUAL AID TO ZEMSTVA

As such, and to begin with for natural and communal grounding, we shall go back to Kropotkin's *mutual aid,* in the twentieth century, then forward to Gorbachev's 'earth charter', in the twenty-first century (see Figure 4.1). Then we turn to that uniquely Russian emergent idea initiated by Federov, *cosmism,* leading on to *anthropoecology,* before looking into Bugakov's *world as household* as a means of navigation. Finally we incorporate Evtuhov's interpretation of Russian *provintia* for *Zemstva* effect.

Navigation
Technology and Society
World as Household/Anthropoecology

Effect
Public, Private
Civic Enterprise
Provintia/Zemstva

Emergence
Culture and
Consciousness
Russian Cosmism

Grounding
Nature and Community
Mutual Aid to Earth Manifesto

Figure 4.1 Mutual aid to Zemstva

Of course such a nineteenth-century provincial effect is not where Russia is now. We shall seek to explain then, in the four following chapters, why this is so, starting out with the now hidden, perhaps long forgotten, mutual aid Russian heritage.

4.2 Grounding in Mutual Aid

IN PURSUIT OF SOLIDARITY

Mutual Aid to Human Solidarity

Russian twentieth-century geographer, economist, anarchist and evolutionary theorist, Pyotr Kropotkin, to whom we were first introduced in Chapter 1, via his *Fields, Factories and Workshops Tomorrow*, focused (2) on *Mutual Aid* rather than, say, free trade, early in the twentieth century. As such his orientation was towards love, sympathy and sacrifice, in both nature and community, which for him play an immense part in the progressive development of our moral feelings. But it is not love and not even sympathy, he says overall, upon which *society is based*. It is rather based *on the instinct of human solidarity. It is the unconscious recognition of the force that is borrowed by each man from the practice of mutual aid.* For evidence of such Kropotkin reaches back to ancient times.

A wide range of mutual-aid institutions were developed, then, by the creative genius of what Kropotkin calls the 'savage' and half-savage masses, *during the earliest clan-period of humankind* and still more so during the next village-community period. The immense influence that these early institutions have exerted upon the subsequent development of man, down to the present times, induced Kropotkin to extend his research into later historical periods as well. In the process he remarked that 'we have heard so much lately of the harsh, pitiless struggle for life', which was said to be carried out by every civilized man against all his citizens. This led him to oppose such, drawing upon evidence from both animal and also human life in nature and community.

Progressive Refinement and Institutional Regression

While by no means underrating the part played by self-assertion in the evolution of humankind, mutual aid institutions – the tribe, the village community, the guilds, the medieval city – historically, individuals reacted in two ways. *In part they rose up to purify these institutions, to work out a higher form of commonwealth, and in part they endeavoured to break down these protective institutions of mutual support, with no other intention but to increase their own wealth and power.* Unfortunately today, in Russia, there is much more evidence of the latter rather than the former, as the pursuit of integral advantage has gone astray. Why so?

As a backdrop to such, via Kropotkin, we turn, to begin with, naturally and communally, to mutual aid in animals, and thereafter turn to humankind.

MUTUAL AID AMONG ANIMALS

Origin of Species to Descent of Man

Charles Darwin (3,4), in *The Descent of Man,* to a much greater degree than in his *Origin of Species,* pointed out how, in numberless animal societies, the struggle between separate individuals for the means of existence disappears, whereby struggle is replaced by cooperation. The term, which originated from the narrow Malthusian conception of competition between each and all, thus lost its narrowness according to Kropotkin amongst those, like Darwin, who knew Nature. Yet instead of widening such an appreciation, amongst his followers, they narrowed such still more. They came to conceive the animal world as a world of perpetual struggle among half-starved individuals thirsting for one another's blood: witness Russian oligarchs today!

Mutual Support Exceeds Mutual Struggle

The Swiss-French philosopher Rousseau (5), in fact, saw nature, love, peace and harmony as the birthright of the 'noble savage'. He thereby committed the error of excluding the beak-and-claw fight from his thoughts. Yet Thomas Huxley for example, as a follower of Darwin, committed the opposite error. Neither Huxley's pessimism nor Rousseau's optimism represent the whole truth. Indeed, of the scientific followers of Darwin in Russia, one who understood the full purport of mutual aid as a law of nature and factor of evolution, according to Kropotkin (6), was Professor Kessler, Dean of St Petersburg University, in 1880:

> *I obviously do not deny the struggle for existence, but I maintain that the progressive development of the animal kingdom, and especially of humankind, is favored much more by mutual support than by mutual struggle. All organic beings have two essential needs: that for nutrition, and that of propagating the species. The former brings them to a struggle and the latter brings them to support one another. But I am inclined to think that in the evolution of the organic world mutual support plays the greater role.*

The Sociability of Birds and Mammals

Sociability is a common feature, Kropotkin goes on to argue, with birds of prey. The Brazilian kite, one of the most 'impudent' robbers, is nevertheless a most sociable bird. Its hunting associations have been described by Darwin and other naturalists, and it is a fact that when it has seized upon a prey that is far too big, it calls together five or six friends to carry it away. After a busy day, when these kites retire for their night-rest to a tree or to the bushes, they always gather in bands, sometimes coming together from distances of up to ten miles.

Sociability to Compassion

Sociability – that is the need of the animal to associate with its like – the love of society for society's sake, combined with the 'joy of life' only now begins to receive due attention from the zoologists (Kropotkin was writing at the beginning of the last century). We know at the present time that all animals, beginning with the ants, going onto the birds and ending with the highest mammals, are fond of play, teasing each other and so on.

Compassion, moreover, is a necessary outcome of social life. But compassion also means a considerable advance in general intelligence and sensibility. It is the first step towards the development of higher moral sentiments. It is, in its turn, a powerful factor of further evolution, something that Adam Smith (7) had clearly articulated in his first major work on the *Theory of Moral Sentiments*. Therefore, practicing mutual aid is the best guarantee, for Kropotkin, of existence and progress. That is what Nature, for him, teaches us: and that is what all those animals that have attained the highest positions in their classes have done.

That is also what man – starting from the most primitive man – has been doing for millennia; and that is why man has reached the position on which we stand now, as we shall now see.

MUTUAL AID AMONG PRIMITIVE PEOPLES

Nature Tooth and Claw to Strength in Combination

For English seventeenth-century political philosopher, Thomas Hobbes (8), mankind is nothing but a loose aggregation of beings, always ready to fight with each other, and only prevented from doing so by the intervention of some authority. The so-called 'state of nature tooth and claw' was nothing but a permanent fight between individuals. Yet, for Kropotkin, those *species which best know how to combine, and to avoid competition, have the best chances of survival and of a further progressive development.* In the interim, and since Hobbes' time moreover, especially from the nineteenth century onwards, a whole new picture of human institutions has developed, with anthropologists like Lewis Morgan (9) in the US taking the lead.

Social instincts, then, have been in human nature for Kropotkin, even at its lowest stages. The very persistence of the clan organization shows how utterly false it is, according to him, to represent primitive mankind as a disorderly agglomeration of individuals, who only obey their individual passions, and take advantage of their personal force and cunningness against all other representatives of species. *Unbridled individualism is seemingly a modern growth, but is not characteristic,* he says, *of primitive mankind.*

The Social Manners of the Indigenous South

For Kropotkin for example, before the European came to South Africa, in the seventeenth century, the Bushmen of the Kalahari (more of such will follow in Chapters 8 and 9) lived in small tribes, or clans, sometimes federated together. They used to hunt in common and divided the spoils without quarrelling. They never abandoned their wounded and displayed strong affection to their comrades. Yet, they were poisoned by the European settlers, fearing the 'other', like rats, he says, and killed by hunters lying in ambush. The same social manners characterized the African Hottentots, as described by German eighteenth-century explorer Kolben (10):

> *Their word is sacred. They know nothing of the corruptness and faithless arts of Europe. They live in great tranquility and are seldom at war with their neighbors.*
>
> *The integrity of the Hottentots, the strictness of their exercise of justice, are things in which they excel most nations in the world.*

When first meeting with the primitive races, Europeans usually (with the exception of dedicated explorers and would-be anthropologists like Kolben) made a caricature of their life; but when an intelligent man has stayed among them for a longer time, Kropotkin maintains, he generally describes them as the 'kindest' or the 'gentlest' of races on earth. These very same words have been applied to the Eskimos, the Dayaks, the Papuas and other such 'primitives'. We shall see further intimations of such when we come both to South Africa (Chapter 9) and to Brazil (Chapter 14).

MUTUAL AID AT HIGHER STAGES OF CIVILIZATION

Familial to Territorial Union

However, as soon as we come to the so-called higher stage of civilization, we are bewildered by the struggles and conflict it reveals. The old bonds seem entirely to be broken. Tribes are seen to fight against tribes, individuals against individuals, and out of this chaotic contest of hostile forces, mankind is divided into castes, enslaved to despots, separated into states always ready to wage war against each other. At this stage, moreover, the conception of a common territory, appropriated or protected by common efforts, is elaborated, and it takes the place of vanishing common descent. At the same time territorial unions grow up instead of the consanguine unions of old. Consequently, the village community becomes the primary cell of the future organization, with many nations having maintained this character until now. The land, moreover, is the common property of the village community.

A Mir, a Universitas in Itself

Private property in fact, or possession 'for ever' is incompatible, for Kropotkin, with the very principles and religious conception of the traditional village community. *Such a community is not only a union for guaranteeing each one a fair share in the common land, but also is a union for a common culture, for mutual support in all its forms, for protection from violence, for moral conceptions*; and every change in military, judicial, educational or economic matter had to be decided by the village elders.

It was, for Kropotkin as such, a *universitas*, a *mir* – a world in itself.

MUTUAL AID IN THE MEDIEVAL CITY

Common Possession and Self-Jurisdiction

Feudalism, in fact, did not imply a dissolution of the village community. Although the lord had succeeded in imposing servile labour upon the peasants, and had appropriated for himself such rights as were formerly vested in the village community alone (taxes, inheritances), *the peasants had, nevertheless, maintained two fundamental rights in their communities: common possession of the land and self-jurisdiction.*

Surprisingly enough for Kropotkin, no period of history could better illustrate the constructive powers of the popular masses in Europe than the tenth and eleventh centuries. At that time fortified *villages and marketplaces represented so many 'oases amidst the feudal forest', that began to free themselves from the lord's yoke, and slowly elaborated the future city organizations*. In fact this was the intellectual movement that has been described as the Twelfth Century Renaissance and Twelfth Century Rationalism in Europe – the precursor of the Reform – when most cities were still agglomerations of small villages.

The Unique Place of the Guild

However, another element, besides the village-community principle, was required to give these growing centres of liberty and enlightenment unity of thought and action, and powers of initiative. With the growing diversity of occupations, and growing commerce with distant lands, a new form of union was required, and this was supplied by the *guilds*: these were called, for example, *druzhestva* in Russia, *esnaifs* in Serbia and *amakari* in Georgia, duly related, hitherto, to the Roman *Collegia*. All were equals, brothers and sisters, before the guild. Such *guilds were then formed in all forms of work and life: priests, painters, teachers, craftsmen, hunters and peasants. All engaged in self-jurisdiction and mutual support*. In Russia these were traders' *artels*.

In short, the more we get to know the medieval city the more we see that it was not simply a political organization for the protection of certain political liberties. It was an attempt at organizing, on a much grander scale than in a village community, a close union for mutual aid and support, according to Kropotkin, for consumption and production, and for *social life together, giving full liberty to the creative genius of each separate group of art, crafts, science, commerce and political organization*.

Labour Enjoyed Prosperity

The medieval craftsman in fact produced for his guild first, that is for his brotherhood. There was not much room for hired work in the early flourishing periods of the medieval cities, still less for individual hirelings. The work of the weavers, the archers, the smiths, bakers and so on was performed for the craft and the city, and *when craftsmen were hired in the building trades, they worked as temporary corporations, as they still do* (Kropotkin was writing in the opening decade of the twentieth century) *in the artels in Russia, whose work was paid en bloc.*

The results of that new move that mankind made toward cooperation in the medieval city were immense. At the beginning of the eleventh century the towns of Europe were small clusters of miserable huts, adorned with small clumsy churches; arts were in their infancy and learning was found only in a few small monasteries. Three hundred and fifty years later the very face of Europe had changed. The land was dotted with rich cities.

In fact, Kropotkin goes on to say, *at no time has labour before and after in Europe enjoyed such conditions of prosperity*. The fact is that such a medieval guild was not under the control of the state functionaries; it was a union of men connected with a given trade. It had its own self-jurisdiction, its own general assemblies, its own relation with other guilds in other cities: *it had, in a word, a full organic life which, for Kropotkin, could only result from the integrality of its functioning.*

Medieval Rise and Early Modern Fall

The crafts and arts moreover had risen to a state of perfection. Learning had grown and spread. The methods of science had been elaborated; the basis of natural philosophy had been laid down. The way had been paved for all the mechanical inventions of which we later felt so proud. Such were the magic changes, according to Kropotkin, accomplished in Europe in less than 400 years.

In that medieval heyday, in fact, *a cathedral or a communal house* symbolized the grandeur of an organism of which every mason and stone cutter was the builder, and a medieval building appears – *not as a solitary effort to which thousands of slaves would have contributed the share assigned them by one man's imagination, all the city contributed to it.* Each corporation contributed its part of the stone, work and decorative genius to *their* common monument. And each guild bestowed its *love* upon such. And yet when we compare the seventeenth century to the thirteenth and fourteenth, once these free cities were gone, formerly characterizing Scotland, Germany and the plains of Italy, the roads had fallen into an abject state, the cities were depopulated, labour was brought into slavery, art had vanished and commerce was decaying.

MEDIEVAL – MODERN DEMISE

Organic Development Unrealized

The medieval European cities, for Kropotkin then, have undoubtedly rendered an immense service to European civilization. They have prevented it from drifting into theocracies and despotic states of old; *they have endowed it with the variety, self reliance, force of initiative and immense intellectual and material energies it no longer possesses.* Why then were they seized with senile debility by the sixteenth century?

For one thing, mutual aid and support cannot be limited to a small association; they must spread to its surroundings, or else the surroundings will absorb the association. The city, moreover, became divided between the 'burghers' and 'the inhabitants'. The trade, formally communal, became the privilege of the merchant and artisan 'families' and the next step – that of becoming individual – was unavoidable. The same division took place between the city proper and the surrounding villages.

The Creative Genius of the Masses Faded Out

The greatest and most fatal error, for Kropotkin, was for most cities to base their wealth upon commerce and industry, to the neglect of agriculture. This turns Michael Porter's argument (see Chapter 3) on its head. The estrangement of so many cities from the land necessarily drew them into a policy hostile to the land. The division into rich and poor grew deeper. Self reliance and federalism, the sovereignty of the group, the construction of the body politic thereby proceeding from the simple to the composite, had been the leading ideas of the eleventh century.

Then things changed entirely. Students of Roman law and prelates of the Church pronounced from the pulpit, the university chair, and the judge's bench, that salvation must be sought for in a strongly-centralized state. Such a state was placed under a semi-divine authority, whereby one man must be the saviour of society, and that in the name of public salvation he can commit violence: burn men and women at the stake, plunge whole provinces into abject misery. And with this new direction of mind, and belief in one man's power, the old federalism drifted away and the creative genius of the masses faded out.

However, it flows still now, for Kropotkin, and seeks its way to find a new expression which would not be the state, nor the medieval city, nor the village community of the barbarians, nor the savage clan, but would proceed from all of them, and yet be superior to them, in its wider and deeper humane conceptions.

MUTUAL AID AMONGST OURSELVES

Reconstructing Society Based on Mutual Aid

The ethical progress of our race, for him then, viewed in its broad lines, appears as a gradual extension of the mutual-aid principles from the tribe to the always larger and larger agglomeration, so as to finally embrace one day the whole of mankind, without respect to its diverse creeds, languages and races. This is a theme that will be picked up by Sergey Bugakov in his *World as Household* (see Chapter 6), and, prior to such, by Federov and the Russian Cosmists (Chapter 5).

After having passed through the savage tribe, and next through the village community, the Europeans came to work out in medieval times a new form of organization, which had the advantage of providing great latitude for individual initiative, while it largely responded at the same time to man's need for mutual support. *A federation of village communities, covered by a network of guilds and fraternities, was called into existence in the medieval cities. The immense results achieved though were doomed to become prey to the military states, and the surrounding, hostile feudal lords.*

Mutual Aid Put to the Sword

Only wholesale massacres by the thousand, according to Kropotkin, could have put a stop to this widespread popular movement. It was by the sword, fire and rack, for him then, that the young states secured their first and decisive victory over the masses of the people. *For the next three centuries* – from the thirteenth to the sixteenth century – *the States systematically weeded out all European institutions in which the mutual-aid tendency had formerly found expression*. Industry, art and knowledge fell into decay. Political education, science and law were rendered subservient to the idea of state centralization.

The absorption of all social functions by the state necessarily favoured the development of unbridled, narrow-minded individualism. As the obligations towards the state grew in proportion to population size the citizens were evidently relieved of their obligations toward each other. The result, for Kropotkin, is that the theory which maintains men can, and must, seek their own happiness in disregarding other people's wants was triumphant all round – in law, in science, in religion – it conquered over all. *Science loudly proclaimed that the struggle of each against all is the leading principle of nature, and of human societies as well. History took the same line of argument and political scientists traced all progress of science and industry to the same principle.*

Yet Mutual Aid Lives On

However, Europe is, to this day (early twentieth century), still covered with living survivals of the village communities, and is permeated with customs and habits dating back to the medieval period. For example, two thirds of all the forests of Switzerland are communal land (as of the first decade of the last century). The communal forests in the Vaud and Valais, as such, at the same time conform to the rules of modern forestry. Overall, in the Swiss villages, a great number of mutual-aid habits and customs persist.

Switzerland, in fact, is by no means an exception in Europe. The same institutions and habits are found in France, Italy, Germany and Denmark.

Double-Edged British Case: Federation of Trades to Joint Stock Individualism

The repeal of the Combination Laws, in England in 1825, gave a new impetus to the mutual aid movement. Unions and national federations were formed in all trades, and when Robert Owen started his Grand National Consolidated Trades Union, it mustered half a million members in a few months. It was true that this period of relative liberty did not last long. Prosecution began in the 1830s, and the well known ferocious condemnations of 1832–44 followed. Cooperation then, in twentieth-century Britain, was often described as 'joint stock individualism'; and such as it is now, it undoubtedly tended toward a breed of cooperative egotism, not only toward the community at large, but also among the cooperators themselves.

The Proliferation of Russian Artels

Aside from Great Britain, cooperative societies emerged in Holland and Denmark, in Germany especially on the Rhine, in the nineteenth century. It is, for Kropotkin, however, *Russia, which offers the best field for the study of cooperation in an infinite variety of guises*. Informal cooperation through the *artel* from the Middle Ages made for the very substance of peasant life. *The history of the 'making of Russia', and of the colonization of Siberia, is a history of hunting and trading artels or guilds, followed by village communities, and early in the twentieth century there were artels everywhere.*

Among groups of 10 to 50 peasants, who came from the same village to work in a factory, in all the building trades, among fishermen and hunters, among railway porters and convicts on the way to Siberia, among customs house labourers, were some 7 million people. In fact, in the early twentieth century according to Kropotkin, many of the fishing-grounds on the tributaries of the Caspian Sea were held by immense *artels.*

AN INFINITY OF ASSOCIATIONS

Cooperation in Man and Nature

If we take now the teachings which can be borrowed from the analysis of modern society, in connection with the body of evidence relative to the importance of mutual aid in the evolution of the animal world and of mankind, Kropotkin sums up his inquiry as follows:

> *In the animal world we have seen that the vast majority of species live in societies, and that they find in association the best arms for the struggle for life: understood in its widest Darwinian sense – not as a struggle for the sheer means of existence, but as a struggle against all natural conditions unfavorable to the species. Going over to man, we found him living in clans and tribes at the very dawn of the stone age we saw a wide series of social institutions developed already in the lower savage stage, in the clan and tribe; and we found that the earliest tribal customs and habits gave to mankind the embryo of all the situations which made later of the leading aspects of further progress.*

The Ethics of Mutual Aid

However, it is especially in the domain of ethics that the dominating importance of the mutual aid principle appears in full. New religions have always been born at times when mutual-aid principles have been falling into decay, and they invariably found their first supporters amongst the humble, in the lowest downtrodden layers of society, where mutual-aid is the foundation of life. In the earliest Buddhist and Christian communities, in the Moravian brotherhoods and so on, there has been a return to the best characteristics of mutual aid in early tribal life. Therein we find the origin of our ethical conceptions; and Kropotkin affirms that in the ethical progress of man, mutual support – not mutual struggle – has played the leading part. In its wide extension he says, even at the present time, we also see the best guarantee of a still loftier evolution of our race.

What then gets in the way of a country, like Russia, building purposefully on the kind of fertile, mutual grounds to which Kropotkin has continually alluded?

4.3 De-mergence: By-Passing Mutual Aid

TIME OF TROUBLES AND THE CHURCH SCHISM

The Time of Troubles

Of course a lot happened along the historical way. For the great Russian writer, in the twentieth century, Aleksandr Solzhenitsyn (11), in his book on *The Russian Question*, written in the 1990s, points, historically for example, in the seventeenth century to the time of troubles, an anarchic and lawless interregnum when Russia became a battleground for Polish, Swedish and other interests, which lasted from 1605 to 1613.

The Orthodox Church Schism

Thereafter, midway through the seventeenth century, a Church Schism shook the entire country, frail as it already was, to its spiritual and vital foundations. The Patriarch of the time undertook a series of ecclesiastical changes to bring Russian religious practices and texts in line with the Greek Church, and dissenters, since termed Old Believers, met these changes, seen as needless foreign interventions, with fierce opposition. And never again, for Solzhenitsyn, did Orthodoxy in Russia regain the vigorous dynamism which had upheld the spirit of the people for half a millennium.

SERVANT OF EUROPE TO COMMUNIST RULE

Peter I as Servant of European 'Progress'

Thereafter, for Solzhenitsyn moreover, as a 'servant of progress', in the eighteenth century, Peter I failed to grasp that one cannot transfer specific results of western culture and civilization without the psychological atmosphere in which these results had ripened. He also created, for the next 200 years, a ruling class if not always alien to the people ethically, then always alien to them in worldview. Moreover, as a result of Peter's 'modernization' programme Russia lost, between 1719 and 1727 alone, a million of its people, a tenth of the country's population. One would be hard pressed to justify the view of Peter as a reformer, as a reformer is one who takes the past into account and smooths the passage into the future.

All of these historical events got in the way of the pursuit of integral advantage, so to speak, from the ground up, and ultimately became, for Solzhenitsyn, together with the Bolshevik revolution to follow, catastrophe overall.

Stupefying to the Mind and Depraving to the Soul

The history of the 70-year long Communist rule in the USSR, which broke the organic flow of people's lives, is at least today, for Solzhenitsyn, bared to many in all its ugliness and abomination. All the losses suffered by Russia's people for the 100 years since the Time of Troubles pale in comparison to the losses and decline in the 70 years of communism. The USSR lost no fewer than 45–50 million people during that period. It mowed down those who stood out by protest, resistance, critical thinking, talent or authority in their circle. The most morally or intellectually valuable people, for him, were extirpated. The 'Victory' of 1945, at the end of the Second World War, materialized in the fortification of Stalin's dictatorship and the total depopulation of villages.

All those who escaped extermination were for decades bombarded by a propaganda stupefying to the mind and depraving to the soul, and all were expected to show continuously renewed signs of obedience. *The 'industrial success' of the USSR was in fact embodied in a lifeless economy: the deformed poor quality production of goods that were not in demand, the environmental deformation of enormous expanses and the plundering of natural resources*. All of such moreover, instigated under the guise of Marxism, was influenced by the very same 'west' that Peter had followed, a 'north-west' in our terms, contrasted with the 'west-north' (see Chapter 2) albeit a distorted version of such. However, the Bolshevik Revolution was ultimately stopped in its course.

How so?

4.4 Perestroika to Earth Manifesto

WAS SOCIALISM BUILT IN THE SOVIET UNION?

The October Revolution

It was only then in the latter part of the twentieth century, that a Russian emerged who was to build, and further evolve, partly consciously and partly unconsciously, on the kind of grounds or foundations that Kropotkin had identified in his country's soils. That was Mikhail Gorbachev. What was the backdrop to such? The October 1917 revolution, for Gorbachev (12), was termed a socialist revolution, and the Soviet Union was proclaimed a socialist state and even held up as a model. Later it was argued that it was 'Developed Socialism'. Was it really a *socialist* revolution that took place? Gorbachev quotes a statement by Lenin: 'Our revolution up until the autumn of 1918 was, to a significant degree, a bourgeois revolution'.

For the revolution was obliged objectively, before all else, to carry out the tasks of such: reorganizing the structure and character of the government, making a fundamental transformation in the system of land ownership, and resolving the nationalities question were all problems that had not been solved. In October 1917 the victors in the revolutionary struggle confronted a society shaken to its foundations by the unprecedented slaughter and destruction of the world war. The material basis for socialism had not yet been created by capitalism.

The October revolution did destroy the autocratic machinery of state, for Gorbachev, and put an end to the legacy of feudalism in the countryside. In addition, basic principles for industrial development were sketched out. After Lenin's death in 1924, and up to the end of the 1920s, a struggle went on in Russia between differing conceptions of how to move forward in the future. By the beginning of the 1930s Stalinism had triumphed in the Soviet Union.

Dictatorship of a Small Ruling Group

Gorbachev's view then is that a harsh and even cruel totalitarian system triumphed at this point. How was it possible for this to occur? Because of their backwardness he says, notwithstanding prior traditions of mutual aid, people were not prepared to accept genuinely democratic ideals. *Stereotyped ideas about 'our good father, the tsar' had taken deep root in the mass consciousness. This was the psychological soil in which Stalinism was able to grow. Also, such stereotypes have not been overcome, even today.* It also cannot be forgotten that the Bolsheviks inherited a country in the depths of chaos.

What Gorbachev sees in Lenin's last texts is a different person from what had come before – a person who, after leading the country into and through the revolution, understood that mistakes had been made. These ideas of Lenin, though, and his New Economic Policy, were completely set aside by Stalin. What then was it that was defective in the Bolshevik model of socialism? Firstly, for Gorbachev, it was a crudely schematic model based on ideological principles that could not withstand close examination. Stalin's interpretation of these deepened their harsh and dogmatic character. His version became a quasi-religious doctrine based on intolerance and ruthless suppression of all who in any way did not fit on this bed of Procrustes. Secondly, the most generalized principle of the Bolshevik 'model' was the *'dictatorship of the proletariat'. In effect it turned out to be a dictatorship by a small ruling group at the top of the hierarchical apparatus that served it.* How did Gorbachev fit in with such?

HOW GORBACHEV BECAME GREEN

Grounded in Deprivation

Gorbachev was born in the Stavropol region of the North Caucasus, one that had witnessed countless invasions and been a crossing point of many and varied cultures and civilizations. As a child he lived in poverty in a traditional cabin with an earth floor. His family slept on top of the Russian stove, and in winter a calf and in spring hens and ducks were kept under the same roof. In 1933, while still a child, Stavropol suffered a famine, which was described in neighbouring Ukraine as 'planned starvation', artificially brought about by the government. But more than anything else, *collectivization had ruined agricultural production by destroying traditional peasant life, and banishing the best farmers, the kulaks, to Siberia.* In that terrible year nearly half the population of his village, Privolnoye, starved to death, including three of his own family. The farmers, moreover, had to hand over almost the whole of the harvest to the army and the armament production workers. There were no supplies for even the most basic daily needs.

Face of War to a New Form of Serfdom

Villagers sowed hemp and sheared sheep; grandmothers fetched their old spinning wheels and looms down from the attic; they even made their own footwear from cowhide, soaking the soles in Masut. Salt came from the salt lake 50 kilometres away; they learnt to use soda to make soap; they struck sparks with flint or manufactured matches from explosives scraped out of unexploded shells. Despite all this the following episode more than anything else shaped Gorbachev's abhorrence of war.

In March, 1943, just as the snow was beginning to melt, he set off with a few other lads to hunt for 'trophies' in the nearby undergrowth. They happened on the remains of a group of soldiers who had fallen in battle: decomposing bodies in shreds of uniform, half devoured by wild animals, skulls in rusty helmets, bleached bones of arms and hands still clutching rifles, empty eye-sockets staring up at them. This face of war, this image, remained in Gorbachev's memory forever. Whenever he heard of some new conflict or yet another act of terrorism, he thought of those soldiers as he listened to matter of fact reports on casualty numbers.

No Care was Given to the Earth

During those post-war years in fact he also became aware of the power of nature: the enchanting world of the steppe with its endless distances where corn-crakes sing in the ripening wheat at sunset, where soft breezes murmured and a myriad of stars shine in the sky at night. *At difficult times in his life nature had always offered him refuge. For him it was not 'environment' or a 'place of leisure and relaxation' but a temple in which he experienced feelings that were almost religious.* Meanwhile the natural disasters visited on the Soviet Union in the post-war years showed Gorbachev how dependent we are on nature. In 1946 almost the whole harvest in his region, and indeed in nearly all grain-growing areas, was ruined by drought.

The higher Gorbachev rose on his career ladder, meanwhile, the more he saw before him the picture of the economic, social and ecological crisis for which the Soviet Union was heading. Not until he became General Secretary, though, did he become fully aware of the details. No care was being given to the earth, the fount of our existence; it was exhausted and laid waste. The state gave precedence to heavy industry, which worked mainly for all aspects of armaments manufacture, and to the mining of mineral wealth, the sale of which financed the arms race.

Millions of hectares had been expropriated for military purposes. The construction of gigantic dams and the resulting artificial lakes needed for hydroelectric power stations had not only ruined the stocks of fish (in a country that had once been famous for fish delicacies), but also caused 14 million hectares of the most fertile land to be flooded. The careless application of pesticides had polluted fields, rovers and lakes, and irreparably damaged flora and fauna. Especially affected was the far North where, for Gorbachev, barbaric methods of oil and gas extraction had devastated parts of the tundra, the natural habitat of indigenous tribes.

GLASNOST, PERESTROIKA AND ACCELERATION

Starting with Glasnost

In 1985 he was elected Chairman of the Communist Party, which meant he became head of state of the USSR. By that time he had already developed a number of ideas for reforming the country.

Gorbachev presented society with three aims: glasnost, perestroika, and acceleration. An essential prerequisite for the reforms that he gave the name perestroika was glasnost or transparency, which gave people the possibility but also the right to speak the truth. How could these reforms be put in train if one did not tell the truth about the actual situation? Moreover the country had to very quickly come to grips with the new technologies if it did not want to be pushed to the edge of the civilized world as electronics and computer technology forged ahead with their contribution to the process of globalization.

Taking up the Ecological Cause

And the first topic taken up by the newly awakened citizenship was that of ecology and the living conditions of the many millions of the Soviet population. In 90 towns of the Soviet Union, in fact in every large industrial centre, people were living in an environment of polluted air, water and oil. Women and children suffered the greatest ill health. For ecological reasons then Gorbachev decided to close 1,300 factories either forever or until they could be modernized. Under pressure from public opinion and the awakening of civil society he also put a top to the absurd 'pharaoh project' that planned to reverse the flow of Siberia's mighty rivers. It could have led to natural disasters in the whole Eurasian region.

Aftermath of the Chernobyl Catastrophe

The Chernobyl catastrophe, which taught not only Gorbachev but hopefully the whole of humanity a lesson, befell the USSR in April, 1986, a year after he had been brought to power. According to the experts there was one chance in a million that the crew of the Chernobyl power station would make all seven mistakes that were needed for the catastrophe to happen at once. But happen they did. Chernobyl turned Gorbachev into a different person. What lessons then did he learn from the greatest technological catastrophe in human history?

Firstly, Chernobyl became a decisive test for the new policy of glasnost. Whatever may have been written about the matter, the following, he says, is the truth about what really happened. His government colleagues and he decided on the very first day to publish all the details about the catastrophe as soon as it reached them. Second, his belief in the absolute reliability of technology was shattered. All technological processes, which might have a negative effect on the health and life of the population required supervision by society. Third, his time-scales changed drastically: the half life of the radioactive isotope most damaging to health that escaped from the cauldron of Chernobyl is 30 years, thereby affecting the health of populations for a long time to come. What right have we to burden our descendants with such a problem? And fourthly, Chernobyl stiffened *Gorbachev's resolve to establish new international contacts and establish emphatically that we are a single humanity sharing a single planet.*

Gorbachev Foundation – East Meets West or Otherwise

In 1990 Gorbachev endeavoured to create a new system of international relations on the basis of peace, the recognition of human rights and without any ideological pressure, were marked by the award of the Nobel Peace Prize. Since, by then, he had been ousted from his post as President, simultaneously with the disappearance of the Soviet Union, he decided to devote his future to his country and humanity. He set up the Gorbachev Foundation in order to develop further the idea of the new thinking and the ideas of a new humanitarian civilization for the twenty-first century, and for a new 'earth charter' for our planet.

The Earth Charter

In fact, in 1997 biologists and economists calculated the cost of nature's gifts to us – clean air, clean water, fertile land – to amount to 33,000 billion dollars per year. Not that nature is waiting to be paid, but it is not so that our descendants will have to raise at least half that sum in order to put right the polluted environment we are leaving them. In the preamble to the Earth Charter then, of which Gorbachev (13) was a co-author at the beginning the new millennium, it was said:

> *We stand at a critical moment in Earth's history, a time when humanity must choose its future. As the world becomes increasingly interdependent and fragile, the future at once holds great peril and great promise. To move forward we must recognize that in he midst of magnificent diversity of cultures and life forms we are one human family and one Earth community with a common destiny. We must join together to bring forth a sustainable global society founded on respect for nature, universal human rights, economic justice, and a culture of peace. Toward this end, it is imperative*

> *that we, the peoples of the Earth, declare our responsibility to one another, to the greater community of life, and to future generations.*

4.5 Conclusion

LOCAL MUTUAL AID TO GLOBAL EARTH MANIFESTO

We have seemingly come a long way, via the *Earth Manifesto,* and indeed the *Gorbachev Foundation* that gave rise to it, from Kropotkin's *Mutual Aid.*

And yet it is not such a long way. For Gorbachev (14):

> *We must join together to bring forth a sustainable global society founded on respect for nature, universal human rights, economic justice, and a culture of peace. Toward this end, it is imperative that we, the peoples of the Earth, declare our responsibility to one another, to the greater community of life, and to future generations.*

Such is arguably 'mutual aid' writ large, moving from a local to a global scale.

The interesting question is why Gorbachev had to be ousted from his position as President of the Soviet Union, in the process, in order to then form the Gorbachev Foundation, whose overall concern has been with our planet in general, rather than with Russia now specifically?

WHAT INHIBITS LOCAL GROUNDING EMERGING LOCALLY/GLOBALLY?

Towards Interdependent Local–Global Emergence

Why then did Russia bypass its own communal grounds, as prolifically lodged in the craft-based *artel,* as we have seen, and the *obschchina* (rural commune) as we shall see? Why does a society not build up automatically from its own foundations, so that it can emerge from within, albeit in the process drawing from without? Why did the Soviet Union, at the turn of the last century, lurch toward 'western' communism, rather than draw, as we shall soon see, on its own form of *cosmism?*

For Alexander Solzhenitsyn (15), writing in 1990, the year his citizenship was restored, looking ahead to *Rebuilding Russia:*

> *For a given people, with its specific geography, history, traditions and psychological make-up, the task is to set in place a structure that will lead to a flourishing of this people rather than to its decline and degeneration. Such a structure must necessarily take national conditions into account: 'Stand in the crossroads and look, ask for the ancient paths: which is the good way? Take it and you will find rest for yourself' (Jeremiah 6:16)*

This is the issue to which we shall turn in the next chapter, with a view to co-evolving a local–global 'eastern–western' *emergent* Russian culture and consciousness, as opposed to one where the 'west' – in both capitalist (west-north) and Marxist (north-west) guise – dominates over the rest. For, in pursuing integral advantage, building upon prior local nature and community, this form of *interdependent eastern-western emergence is the next port of call.*

Bibliography

1. Gorbachev, M. (2000) *Gorbachev: On My Country and the World.* New York, Columbia University Press.
2. Kropotkin, P. (1914) *Mutual Aid: A Factor of Evolution.* New York, Dover Publications.
3. Darwin, C. (2004) *The Descent of Man.* London, Penguin Classics.
4. Darwin, C. (2008) *The Origin of Species.* Oxford, Oxford University Paperbacks.
5. Rousseau, J.J. (1998) *The Social Contract.* Ware, Herts, Wordsworth Editions.
6. Kropotkin, P. (1914) *Mutual Aid: A Factor of Evolution.* New York, Dover Publications.
7. Smith, A. (2009) *The Theory of Moral Sentiments.* Paris, Book Jungle.
8. Hobbes, T. (2008) *Leviathan.* Oxford. Oxford University Paperbacks.
9. Morgan L (1985) *Ancient Society.* Phoenix, University of Arizona Press.
10. Kropotkin, P. (1914) *Mutual Aid: A Factor of Evolution.* New York, Dover Publications.
11. Solzhenitsyn, A. (1994) *The Russian Question: At the End of the 20th Century.* London, Harvill Press.
12. Gorbachev, M. (2000) *Gorbachev: On My Country and the World.* New York, Columbia University Press.
13. Gorbachev, M. (2005) *Manifesto for the Earth: Action Now for Peace, Global Justice and a Sustainable Future.* Forest Row, Clairview Books.
14. Gorbachev, M. (2005) *Manifesto for the Earth: Action Now for Peace, Global Justice and a Sustainable Future.* Forest Row, Clairview Books.
15. Solzhenitsyn, A. (1990) *Rebuilding Russia.* London, Harvill Publications.

Chapter 5

Cosmism to Anthropoecology: Grounding to Russian Emergence through Culture and Spirituality

The development of Russian national consciousness, in a full fledged way, dates back to the 18th century. In opposition to the European outer directed social and cultural reforms of Peter the Great, oriented 'westwards', Russian peculiarities were then defended by historians and writers. this inward spiritual freedom was extolled especially by the so called 'slavophils'.

Thomas Marasyk (1,2), The Spirit of Russia

5.1 Introduction

GROUNDING TO EMERGENCE

Local–Global East–West

Natural and communal, local *Grounding*, as we saw in the last chapter, provides a sense of place, of identity. This then was abundantly and historically the case for the Russian *artel*, or the village commune, the *obshchina* as we shall see, which thereby stabilizes a society.

It is *emergent* culture and consciousness which then provides a cultural, spiritual or philosophical, local–global positive dynamic, set against the negative forces of warfare, despotism or totalitarianism, as we have seen in the Soviet case. In our integral terms, as such, and harking back to Porter's *Comparative Advantages of Nations* (Chapter 3) this is the spiritual equivalent of economic investment. Where grounding is local, emergence is local–global, involving a fusion of cultures, or Eurasian in Russia's case. However, such emergence may be confused, rather than creative, as such, crisis-ridden rather than richly complex.

THE RUSSIAN QUESTION AND ITS NEGATION

Time of Troubles, Bolshevik Revolution and Oligarchs

For Solzhenitsyn (3) in fact, toward the end of the last century, *today a cruel, beastly and criminal society is being created, and the current crisis is much more than an economic one*. What is lacking, for Solzhenitsyn, is a focus on building upon the integrity of the nation (our integral advantage). When he alludes to nationality he does not mean *blood*, but always a *spirit*, a *consciousness*. The Russian spirit and culture has existed for centuries, and all those who feel themselves to be a part of such are *Russians*. How then did the once powerful Russia fall so low? For him there were three such 'diseases', as he saw it, first *the times of troubles* in the seventeenth century, second the 1917 *Bolshevik Revolution*, and third *the rise of the Russian oligarchs today*. These three, altogether, could not have been mere accidents.

Some fundamental flaws of state and spirit, he says, are to blame. If, for four centuries Russia squandered the people's strength on superfluous externalities, and in 1917 could so blindly succumb to the cheap calls to theft and desertion, must not the time have come to pay? And of course even more recently (March 2015) we see the Russian people marching on the Moscow streets in the wake of the assassination of opposition leader, Boris Nemtsov. The character of the Russian people, so well known to its forebears, so abundantly depicted by its writers and observed by thoughtful foreigners – this character was continuously oppressed, darkened and mangled, he says, during the entire Soviet period.

Shall Our People Be or Not Be

The 'Russian Question' at the end of the twentieth century stands then unequivocal. *Shall our people be or not be?* Today, Solzhenitsyn claims, we hear talk only of the economy, and it is true that Russia's exhausted economy strangles it. But, he says, *we must salvage our character, our national traditions and culture, our historical path*. For him, *we must build a moral Russia or none at all*. In fact the Russian illustrious physics Professor Timashev once accurately remarked, according to Solzhenitsyn (4):

> *In every condition of society there are, as a rule, several possibilities, which, becoming attainable, emerge as tendencies of societal development. Which of these tendencies are realized and which are not, cannot be forecast with absolute confidence. This depends on how they come into contact with others.*

USES OF THE OTHER

The East is Europe's Other

In fact this matter has recently been addressed by Iver Neumann (5), as Head of the Russian Research Centre at the Norwegian Institute of International Affairs. In his book on *Uses of the Other*, the idea of Russia entering European civilization, historically so to speak, had always had its flip side in the idea that it was emerging from an Asiatic one. Parallels, politically and otherwise, were often drawn between Russia and the Ottoman Empire. *The Russian then is forced to play the role of barbarian. The 'east' is indeed Europe's other, and it is being continually recycled in order to represent various 'non-European' identities.*

These metaphors of Russians as nomadic barbarians, always on the move, pegging their tents on the outskirts of Europe, looming like an incubus, belong to a fixed imagery, for Neumann that may also crop up occasionally in, say, a French representation of the British. The crucial difference is that in the case of Russia, this is a regularly invoked feature of discourse throughout the nineteenth century and beyond. *The idea of the barbarian at the gates, then, lent a particular flavour to European strategic discourse on Russia. Russia was depicted as an ambiguous presence on Europe's border*, a presence that could be associated with Europe, but also with China.

Cold War to 'Common European Home'

During the so called 'Cold War', at the time of the Soviet Union and the 'west', the representation of Russia as an actual military and to some extent also a political threat (today with Putin, Crimea and the Ukraine the same recurs) was so pervasive that it was ubiquitously used in the delineation of a period of European history. *The 'other' inscribed itself in the temporal dimension of the European self identity by giving a name to a period of its history; the Cold War.*

Indeed, it was the Soviet initiative to end the Cold War by means of an application by Gorbachev to join Europe: via his slogan of the 'Common European Home'. European reactions to these applications ranged from bafflement that such an application should be necessary, to assertions that the Soviet Union was mostly in Europe, but not of Europe, to wariness that the intention was to decouple western Europe from the United States.

These reactions mirrored the two pervasive representations of the Soviet Union of the Cold War period. The dominant version was of an Asiatic/barbarian power that had availed itself of the opportunity offered by the Second World War to intrude into Europe by military means. In 1945 Churchill is said to have maintained that the 'barbarians' – the Soviet Union – stood in the heart of Europe, and Konrad Adenauer, the German Chancellor at the time, wrote that 'Asia stands on the Elbe'. Interestingly enough there was no explicit reference to the power of emergence, in the Russian case, through east–west fusion.

Europe's Liminar

Russia rather then stood out in its 500-year history of always just having been tamed, civil, civilized; just having begun to participate in European politics; just having become part of Europe. We will see variations on this theme recurring, in fact, as we make our way through the other BRICS. Since the Enlightenment Russia has, furthermore, if not also Africa and Brazil, India and China at large, been seen by the 'west' as a pupil and a learner, whether a successful one (the dominant version of the enlightenment), a misguided one (the alternative version of the Enlightenment), a laggard who should learn but refuses to do so (the dominant version of the ninetenth century), a truant (the twentieth-century version), or a gifted but somewhat pigheaded (the resent version) one. Russia, like the European colonies hitherto, in whatever territorial shape, by whatever name, as whatever representation, has a history as Europe's liminar. Why then is this 'Russia' so often depicted as the 'other'?

5.2 Berdyaev's Russian Idea

TWO STREAMS JOSTLE WITH EACH OTHER

A Nation of Contradictions

For the twentieth-century Russian historian and philosopher, Nicholas Berdyaev (6) – in seeking to express, toward the middle of last century, the idea of Russia rather than adopt a purely empirical, political and economic perspective on its makeup – *the Russian people are a conglomeration of contradictions. In respect of such polarization and inconsistency they can be paralleled only by the Jews;* it is not a matter of chance that precisely in these two people there exists a messianic consciousness. The inconsistency and complexity of the Russian soul, moreover, may be due to the fact that *in Russia, two streams of history – east and west – jostle and influence each other.*

Elemental Strength Combined with Weak Sense of Form

There is then, in the Russian soul, something that corresponds to the immensity, the vagueness, the infinitude of its land, its spiritual geography thereby corresponding with the physical, great plain of Russia. *There has been, specifically, a vast elemental strength in the Russian people aligned with a comparatively weak sense of form.* For this reason its people have found difficulty in achieving mastery over the country's vast expanses and reducing them to orderly shape. In our terms, Russians experience difficulty in moving from the emergent cultural and spiritual whole to navigating the political or economic part, thus fusing, holistic 'eastern' art and philosophy and rational 'north' systems and technology. An exception, as we shall see in the next chapter was cosmist scientist Tsiolkovsky.

They have not been a people of moderation and have rather gone to extremes, from communism to capitalism, for example, neither of which is intrinsically their own. *Two principles lay at the foundation of the structure of the Russian soul, a natural, Dionysian, elemental paganism and an ascetic, monastic Orthodoxy, that is anarchism and despotism,* a heightened individualism and impersonal collectivism, revolt and slavery. *Moreover, a fundamental category in Russia is motherhood, identified with the Trinity,* for Berdyaev, *that is Mother Earth being more vividly expressed than the Heavenly King, Jesus Christ.* As we shall see later it is also reflected in the Slavophile notion of *integrality.*

Leaving Indigenous East Behind;Veering Exogenously to the West

The exogenous reforms of Peter the Great, for Berdyaev, were imposed from above by force, rather than generated middle-up-down-across. Russia had to emerge from a position of isolation and seclusion as a result of the Tartar Yolk and Muscovite Tsardom. There were traits in Peter 1, in fact, which may be compared with the Bolsheviks. He brought Russia in touch with western absolutism of the enlightened kind. The power of the nobility, top-down, increased, in alienation from the people, bottom-up. Serfdom ensued. *The western culture of the Petrine eighteenth century then was a superficially aristocratic borrowing and imitation, a rehash of Voltaire. Independent thought had not yet awakened. It was only in the nineteenth century that the Russians learned to think.*

We now turn specifically to the Russian notion of destiny.

5.3 Russia has a Destiny

WESTERNIZERS VERSUS SLAVOPHILES

The Russian Philosophy of History

It had long been a feeling that was native to Russians (Berdyaev stresses 'feeling' rather then 'knowing') that Russia had its own particular destiny, that the Russian people are a particular people. Pyotr Chaadaev in the first half of the nineteenth century maintained that Russian self-consciousness had to pass through the bitter rejection of self, as a dialectical movement in the development of the Russian idea. In Russia there is a pre-eminent example of virgin soil. Its very backwardness provides the possibility of choice. Hidden potential forces will be able to discover themselves in the future.

The Russian philosophy of history, moreover, was obliged before all else to solve the problem of the meaning and significance of Peter's reforms, which had, so to speak, sliced Russian history in two. Is the historical path of Russia, on the one hand, the same as that of exogenous western Europe, that is to say, the path of common human progress, or common human civilization, and is the peculiarity of Russia to be found only in its backwardness? Or has Russia, on the other hand, a special indigenous 'eastern' path of its own with its civilization belonging to a different type? *The westernizers accepted Peter's reforms entirely, and in their view the future of Russia lay in taking the western path. The Slavophiles believed in a special type of eastern culture springing out of the spiritual soil of Orthodoxy.*

Rationalism Built on Integrality

The Slavophiles, for Bedyaev in fact, confused their ideal of Russia, their ideal utopia of the perfect order of society, with the historic past. But the westernizers fell into an error of a different kind; they confused their ideal of what was best for Russia with that of western Europe. The resolution, for us as for him, lay as an emergent local–global 'non-entity' in between, thereafter creating a newly global entity, born out of prior identity:

> *The Slavophiles were bent on the organic and on integrality, and fought against Western rationalism. Russian thinking was much more integral on the one hand, and indeed prone towards the totalitarian on the other, than the thinking of the West. For Westernizers, conscience is replaced by law, regulations become a substitute for the inward impulse, even*

charity is turned into mechanical business; anxiety is for political reforms. For us, then, the 'western' rational self needed to build on the 'eastern' integral other, to fore a new Russian entity.

Communalism versus Communism

For Berdyaev, moreover, a sense of community does actually belong to the Russian people in a greater degree than to the peoples of the west, but in a particular respect. They have less of the western individualism, but their communalism has spiritual connotations, constituting a metaphysical property of the Russian people. As such it is not tied in any form to economic or social life, though Kropotkin, at least historically, may have argued otherwise. In that spiritual guise then, it may neither be strongly communally grounded, nor ultimately economically effective. Ultimately then *we can see an incongruity emerging between a spiritually oriented communalism and materially oriented communism, bereft of original, natural and communal grounding in mutual aid.*

THE CLASH BETWEEN PERSONALITY AND WORLD HARMONY

Man through Communism Falls into a New Idolatry

The theme then of the clash between individual personality and world harmony is very Russian. This is the same problem as the conflict between the individual person and the universal whole. It was a conflict, as we saw in the previous chapter, that Gorbachev attempted to resolve, through a newly conceived Soviet Confederation. While he was on the side of world harmony, Yeltsin embodied the strong Russian personality, and never the twain did meet. Tolstoy (7), moreover, shared in the idea that Russia was called to express the brotherhood of man.

Socialists with a Russian Spirit

If the world of 'socialism', then, is not taken in its doctrinaire and exogenous Marxist sense, one might say that socialism is indigenously rooted in Russian nature and culture. *The Slavophiles,* for example, repudiated the western bourgeois interpretation of private property. *One and all they hoped that Russia would escape the wrongness and evil of capitalism, that it would be able to pass over to a better social order while avoiding the capitalist stage of economic development.* And they considered Russia's backwardness as conferring on her an advantage. Of all the peoples of the world, they maintained, it was Russians who had a community spirit.

Concrete People Rather than Abstract Nation

In fact *narodnichestro* – folk populism – is a phenomenon that is peculiar to Russia aligned with Russian nihilism and anarchism. It had many different manifestations, but overall it was *a root belief in the people as the guardians of truth and right. A distinction was drawn between the people and the nation, set in opposition to each other.* The people, as such, are a concrete, for us 'grounded' community of living persons, whereas a nation is an abstract, for a 'navigational' idea. The latter is regarded as a vampire that sucked the blood of the people, a parasite on the people.

The Russian sociologist, Mikhailovsky (8), known for his approach to *subjective socialism,* affirmed the conflict between the individual as a concrete human subject, and abstract, objective society as such. When a society is victorious as an organism, then the individual is turned into an organ of society, into a function. *One must strive for the sort of organism of society in which the individual is not an organ or function but the highest end. Such a society, for him, was a socialist one.* Capitalist society in fact also turned the individual into an organ and a function of the maximum degree.

ANARCHISM, NIHILISM AND DISCONNECTION FROM THE RUSSIAN STATE

The Poisoned Liberation of Labour

Berdyaev now turns to another field, the field of literature in which Russian genius flourished. There were people who had a strong sense of sin, who were no strangers to the Russian social theme and who displayed the creativity of genius. In the front rank of such were the writers Tolstoy, Dostoevsky and Soloviev. These great Russian writers were representatives of the religious *Narodnichestvo.* They believed in the righteousness of simple working people. *The Russian genius, in contrast with the western European one, when it has reached a summit wants to mingle with the earth and the people.* The west knows no such repudiation of one's own aristocracy, wealth and fame, as for example exhibited by Tolstoy, who revolted, with unprecedented radicalism, against injustice.

Populist Russian Nihilism versus Universalist European Culture

The people of western Europe, for Berdyaev in fact, rarely had any doubts about the justification of their culture. They considered themselves to be the heirs of Mediterranean Greco-Roman culture and they were believers in the sanctity of its traditions. At the same time the culture presented itself to them as universal while all the rest of the world was barbarian. This point of view was particularly clear-cut among the French. Nihilism, in contrast, is a typically Russian phenomenon and it grew out of the spiritual soil of Orthodoxy.

Hatred for the conventional lie of civilization, as such, led to the search for the truth in the life of the people. This is displayed most clearly in Tolstoy. In 'nature' there is greater truth and right, there is more of the divine than in 'culture'. Everywhere and always Tolstoy depicts the truth of life which is near to nature, the truth of labour, the profundity of birth and death, in comparison with the falsity of the so-called 'historical' life in civilization.

In this view, truth is to be found in the natural and unconscious, as opposed to the civilized and conscious. Tolstoy's (9) desire was to fuse his life with that of the labouring people; in the suffering he endured he was very Russian. He had a reverence for Confucius, Buddha, Solomon, Socrates and Jesus Christ; but for him these sages were not propagators of culture but teachers of life. He connected with simplicity, whereas culture is complex. Tolstoy, as such, was close to the ground, to the concrete lives of his people, and as such, nihilistically, disconnected from the centralized state.

The Russians do not like the State

Anarchism, like nihilism for Russians then, is a creation of the Russians. Interestingly enough, such theories were created pre-eminently by the highest stratum of Russian gentry. Of such, the chief and most extreme were Bakunin and Prince Kropotkin, as well as Count Tolstoy.

For Berdyaev, ironically then, the Russians do not like the state, and are not inclined to regard it as their own; they either revolt against it or meekly submit to it. They feel the evil and sin of all authority more strongly than do the people of the west. The growth of the power of the state, which sucks all the power out of the people, had, as its reverse side, the Russian desire to resist, a withdrawal from the state physically or in spirit. Such a Russian schism, in this case between the people (our grounds) and the state (our navigation) Berdyaev goes on to say, is a fundamental thing in Russian history.

Anarchy and Slavophilism

There is, specifically moreover, a powerful anarchist element in the ideology of the Slavophils. The Slavophils have had no love for the state and authority; they saw evil in all authority. Their idea that the cult of power and glory, which is attained by the might of the State, *is foreign to the make-up of the soul of the Russian people,* was a very Russian idea. For the Russian philosopher Leontyev, Russian statecraft is the creation of Byzantine principles combined with Tartar and Germanic elements. The anarchist *Bakunin* (10) *thought that the Slavs themselves would never create a state, for they lived in brotherhood and communities.* Like all Russian anarchists he was an opponent of democracy, reacting negatively to the prospect of universal suffrage, such representation of the people for him giving rise to governmental despotism.

He made the grim prediction, moreover, that if any people attempted to realize Marxism in Russia, it would result in the most terrible tyranny the world has seen. *In opposition to Marxism he asserted his belief in the elemental nature of the Russian people. A free and brotherly society, as such, of producing associations,* would arise of its own accord. Kropotkin, as we have seen in Chapters 1 and 2, believed in a natural disposition to cooperation.

Anarchism as an Ideal of Freedom

Anarchism is opposed then not to order, but to authority, force and the kingdom of Caesar. *It is an ideal of freedom, of harmony and order which arises from within,* that is to say, it is the victory of the Kingdom of God over the kingdom of Caesar. A very original feature in Dostoyevsky (11) is that freedom is to him not a right of man but an obligation, a duty. Freedom is not ease, it is a burden. Berdyaev has formulated such an idea in this way, that it is not man who demands freedom from God, but God who demands it from man. To the Roman idea, which is founded upon compulsion, he opposes the Russian idea, which is founded upon the freedom of spirit. This brings us onto Russian philosophy, and its most famous exponent, Soloviev.

5.4 Russian Integral Worlds

RELIGIOUS RUSSIAN PHILOSOPHY FUSED WITH GERMAN IDEALISM

Questions of Philosophy and Psychology

There were no philosophers in Russia of such a stature as that of its writers, like Dostoevsky and Tolstoy. Russian academic philosophy, for Berdyaev, was not distinguished by any particular originality. A philosophical environment only began to take shape, academically so to speak, in the 1880s, when the journal *Questions of Philosophy and Psychology* began to be published.

The Union ofTheoretical and Practical Reason

Perhaps the greatest Russian philosopher was Vladmir Soloviev. Russian religious philosophy in fact awoke from a long intellectual sleep as the result of a jolt it received from German philosophy and chiefly from Schelling and Hegel, with which it ultimately became fused. Religious philosophy, as opposed to theology, presupposes the union of theoretical and practical reason and the attainment of integrality in apprehension. The programme of independent Russian philosophy was first sketched out by Kireevsky and Khomyakov (12), as they passed through the School of German Idealism, but exerted themselves to adopt a critical attitude to what was the high-water mark of European philosophy in their day, Hegel and Schelling. Kireevsky wrote:

> *How necessary philosophy is; every development of our intelligence requires it; our poetry lives and breathes by it alone; it alone gives a soul and integrality to our infant science, our every life itself borrows from it the beauty of its order. Now from whence in Russia does it come? German philosophy can never take root in us. Our philosophy must develop from our life. It must be created out of our current problems. It needs to be the dominating interest of our corporate and individual existence.*

Unfortunately, neither Khomyakov nor Kireevsky wrote a single philosophical book, but limited themselves to philosophical essays. But they both had remarkable intuition, striving toward integral knowledge. As seen by the Slavophils, moreover, Catholicism gave birth to Protestantism, which gave birth to Hegelianism, which passed onto dialectical materialism. *The fundamental idea of Russian philosophy is the idea of the concrete existent, of the underlying real existence that preceded rational thought.*

Development of an Integral Spirit

Russian religious philosophy in particular insists upon apprehension by the integral spirit, in which reason is combined with will and feeling. Mikhailovsky, Kireevsky and Khomyakov, in addition to Soloviev (13), are all bent on such an integral view. It was characteristic of Russian thought then in the nineteenth century that the non-religious tendencies of the Russians, that socialism, anarchism, nihilism and narodnichestvo had a religious theme. Dostoevsky understood this absolutely. It was Soloviev, though, who had a unique philosophical perspective on the Russian nation as a whole.

Integral Creativity, Knowledge, Society and Life

All the spheres and levels of the societal organism must be found here, in a completely free synthesis. Each of them, for Soloviev, is equally necessary for the integrated fullness of the organism. For example, in the first case, mysticism in an internal connection with the fine arts and with applied art forms a single organic whole. The goal here is mystical – the interaction with the higher world by means of inner creative activity. If we call this first substantial unity of creativity, 'theurgy', let us call it *integral creativity.*

To continue, for Soloviev, the second member of the religious whole – theology – is a harmonious union with philosophy and science forming *integral knowledge.* For theology, the enormous significance of independent philosophy, having elaborated its own forms of cognition, an independent science, furnished with complex instruments of observation and experimentation enriched by vast amounts of empirical and historical material, is readily apparent. Only the kind of theology, which is grounded in independent philosophy and science, may, along with them, be transformed into integral knowledge.

Russia's Integral Role in the World

Finally, normal relations in the social sphere are determined by the fact that the higher level of this sphere – spiritual or sacred society – forms a free internal union with the political and the economic, constituting an *integral society.* Altogether these constitute an *integral life,* and the bearers of such, first and foremost, to humankind, are, for Soloviev, the Russian people. But, since integral life in its essence is free of any exclusivity, it will necessarily spread to the rest of humankind. As such the formation of a uni-total, universal human organization in the form of integral creativity, integral knowledge and integral society is to be Russia's role in the world.

Interestingly enough, one of the arch proponents of such integrality since, has been the polymath Rudolf Steiner, on whose work we (14) prolifically draw, from his own Slav perspective (Steiner was born in Croatia).

INSTEAD OF COMMUNISM, COSMISM

Cultural Emergence

This brings us, finally, onto Russian so-called *cosmism*, which seemingly has fused together the Slavophile 'east' and the 'west'– ernizer, the indigenous and the exogenous, the spiritual and the material, within the Russian soul. This facilitates its cultural emergence, so to speak, and to some extent its scientific and technological navigation, but much less so politically and economically. That is where arguably, as we continue to see today, society's fault-line is to be seen, with a view to its overall pursuit of integral advantage. While the 'west' has its historically prominent political and economic thinkers, such as John Locke and Adam Smith, in Russia the likes of Federov and Bugakof remain in the shadows, while Marx hitherto, and arguably now Adam Smith, stand in the light.

5.5 The Russian Cosmist Project

GENERAL CHARACTERISTICS OF COSMISM

Expansive Appeal in Russia Today

Serving today, if only in the margins, as a living example of Berdyaev's definition of the 'Russian Idea', is *Cosmism,* according to Russian historian George Young (15), as Fellow of the Centre for Global Humanities at New England University in America. It is at least discussed, as such, and *debated in large crowded halls at frequent academic conferences round the country, and is the subject of a multiplying number of academic articles, dissertations, and scholarly books,* presented in both print and electronic media.

Yet, most of the leading figures, outside Russia, are largely unknown. The major Russian Cosmists, in fact, are the religious thinker Nikolai Federov, the poet and philosopher Vladmir Soloviev, the religious philosophers Bulgakov, Berdyaev and Florensky, and the scientists Vernadsky and Tsiolkovsky.

Definitions of Cosmism

To many of today's Russian students of Cosmism, its approach to world problems – *seeking unity, wholeness and universality by facing and attempting to overcome a multitude of apparent contradictions* – represents Berdyaev's characterization of the Russian soul, at its best, in action.

AMATEUR PHILOSOPHY AS A PASSION

Philosophy as Extra-Curricula

Unlike Russian literature, Russian music or even art, Russian philosophy is little known outside its homeland. This is not because, for Young, Russians have neglected philosophical questions, but because they have gone about it in their own way, usually avoiding paths favoured by followers of, for example, Descartes, Kant and Mill. Since for most of the nineteenth century, moreover, the study of philosophy in Russian universities was either prohibited or, when permitted, allowed to range only from Plato to Aristotle, philosophical discussion remained an extra-curricula activity. *Because then philosophy could not be a profession, it had to be a passion. The major contributors to Russian thought then have not been trained academicians, but gifted amateurs.*

As such not only in the nineteenth century, but throughout the history of Russian thought, even to the present century, the line between literature and philosophy has never been as sharply drawn as in other traditions. From Pushkin, Gogol, Dostoevsky and Tolstoy, onto Pasternak and Solzhenitsyn, writers whose talents are primarily literary have made significant contributions to Russian thought. The leading cosmists, as we shall see, can be viewed in a similar light.

Thought as a Call for Action

Federov and the Cosmists eventually offered a symbiosis of westernizer and Slavophile positions, welcoming western scientific and technological rationality, but turning them toward Slavophile goals of communal wholeness, unifying activity and spiritual consensus – all contained in the well-known Slavophile concept of *sobernost*. Federov, and later the *Cosmists, believe that their projects, combining science and spirituality, represent precisely that inner integrative path that Russia should follow in order to be true to her historic mission.* Federov, Solovyov and Bulgakov, for example, all propose models of an all-embracing communal life more radical than the socialist communes proposed by the Marxists in the 1960s.

We now turn to the person, who, more than any other, originated the Russian notion of Cosmism, Nikolai Federov.

THE MOSCOW SOCRATES' COMMON TASK

Concerned with War, Hunger and Kinship

A phrase often used to characterize Federov (1829–1903) is the 'Moscow Socrates', who also happened to be the second cousin of Prince Kropotkin. In many ways Federov did lead a Socratic life indifferent to status and comfort, preferring oral to written transmission of ideas, relying on friends and disciples to propagate his teachings, using his place of work, the Moscow library, as a teaching space, as Socrates used the Athenian agora. *His abiding concerns, in life, were to address the problems of war, hunger and the absence of kinship.* In fact Dostoevsky and Tolstoy were attracted to Federov's ideas even before they got to know him, having been alerted to his ideas by one of Federov's disciples.

A Man on a Mission: Loved by his Students

Although he did not attend university he received a good school education, and after the lyceum began his years of wandering through southern and central Russia, serving as a teacher of history and geography. Loved by his pupils he was regarded by his superiors as a nuisance and crank. Overall he maintained that *by pursuing knowledge for its own sake rather than applying it, the learned merely aided those who would wage war.* After his initial years as an itinerant teacher then, Federov, via a disciple, secured a post at Moscow's leading public library. He would work there for the next 25 years. As Young puts it:

> *During his long life in Moscow, Federov lived alone, frequently changing addresses but usually renting a small, closet-sized room. He slept on a humpback trunk. The only coat he wore was more rag than coat. At home he would have a light meal and then talk with friends who dropped by. He would sleep for two or three hours till midnight and then read till dawn, then set out for the library for a new day.*

He was a man on a mission to pursue the 'common task', in five respects: holistic, relational, projective, business-like with a difference, transformative.

THE COMMON TASK MEANS BUSINESS

Restoring Wholeness

For Federov the 'common task' was to reverse the natural flow of life toward death as disintegration and death as fusion, and to restore everywhere a wholeness that insures both the integrity of the unit and the unity of the whole. The model – or icon – for the universe 'as it should be' is the mystical quality of the Holy Trinity, neither fused nor disaggregated, both three and one, for us, altogether then, becoming four!

Rosdstvo – Joining the One to the Many

Rosdstvo, usually translated as 'kinship' or 'relatedness' is a concept central to Federov's thought. The Russian rod is commonly used in everyday life for 'to give birth', 'to be born', as well as 'relative', 'homeland', and 'national-people-folk'. It is what joins one to home, to parents, to enduring relationships. It also joins the one to the many, the personal to the universal, each one of us to everything in the entire cosmos.

Subjective and Objective to Projective

Federov's view, moreover, is that true knowledge is neither subjective nor objective, but projective – *projektivnoe*. Properly understood, the universe, consisting not only of human interactions but of physical and chemical interactions as well, is not an 'object' whose existence is dependent on or independent of our existence as 'subjects'. Rather it is a 'project', which we shall either direct or fail to direct, yet for which we must bear ultimate responsibility. *'Projectivism' is Federov's bridge between, and alternative to, idealism and materialism.*

Delo – Common Task – Means 'Business'

In fact such projectivism, the bridge between the 'world as it is', and 'the world as it ought to be', the difference on a universal scale between chaos and cosmos, is *delo*, a word that can mean 'business', 'affairs', 'matter', or 'activity'. For Federov, it is *delo* – the common task – applied to fields of knowledge that will transform everyday current *-ology* into *-urgy*. *Orthodox Christianity, for him as such, assumes the radically active cosmic project of resurrecting the common task (delo), as a Christian alternative to Marxism or to a secular culture dominated by the erotic instinct, or bestial passion.* Federov seeks thereby to combine 'Active Christianity' with 'Active Science'.

Transform Humanity and Cosmos

The goal of Federov's 'common task', in the final analysis, is the transformation of both humanity and the cosmos, of both the inner and the outer, spiritual and physical, microcosmic and macrocosmic. We now turn specifically to the work and thought of Cosmist Sergey Bugakov, to whom we shall devote a whole chapter, on would-be Navigation. For Young he is the 'religious cosmist', and for us, as for Evtuhov, the economic one.

COSMIST ECONOMICS AS TAKING GOOD CARE OF THE UNIVERSE

The Philosophy of the Economy

Following in the footsteps of the common task was Sergey Bugakov's (1871–1944) first major work (15), and the one that best illustrated his Cosmist views: *The Philosophy of the Economy*, as such. The Russian word for 'economy' suggests with its root the word 'husbandry', 'landlordship', 'proprietorship', 'management' and ultimately 'house-holding', resonating well with Federov's 'common task'. *Bulgakov extends the meaning of economy, then, to taking good care of the universe.* Far from a 'dismal science', economics becomes a sacred, priestly care of all that God has entrusted to us.

We now turn from cosmist economist, Bulgakov, from whom we shall hear much more in the next chapter, to firstly, its most prominent astrophysicist, Konstantin Tsiolkovsky, and secondly, the Russian natural scientist, and well-known cosmist, Vladmir Vernadsky.

LAYING THE FOUNDATION FOR SPUTNIK

Withdrawing Deep Within

In the 1870s, while working in the library, Fedorov went out of his way to serve a special group of ragged young scholars whom he liked to call his 'stipendiates'. One of these was Konstantin Tsiolkovsky (1857–1935), then a 16-year-old raw youth who had arrived in Moscow from a provincial village with no friends, no money and minimal education. Nearly deaf from a childhood bout of scarlet fever, solitary and a daydreamer, as he himself put it: '*... as an outcast from society I used to withdraw deep within myself, to pursue great goals as to deserve the approval of others ...*'. Isolated in his rural village, this gifted child had to come to Moscow to learn, and there he found his ideal teacher, Federov.

Released from the Chains of Gravitation

Duly inspired by the work of the French fantasy writer Jules Vernes, Tsiolkovsky acquired the feeling for an eternal striving toward the sun, to a release from the chains of gravitation. While studying in the Moscow Library, because he was deaf, Federov walked up to Tsiolkovsky, and wrote on a piece of paper:

> *I'm going to do mathematics with you, and you'll help mankind build rockets so that we will finally be able to know more than the earth. People need a distant view, because only those who are thinking about the future are real and present.*

After his Moscow apprenticeship with Federov, he returned to his native village, and ultimately qualified as a science teacher, while dreaming of interplanetary travel. In that year of his first teaching experience he began to make notebook sketches of rocket-powered spaceships. But what distinguished Tsiolkovsky's imagination from that of any of his contemporaries is that after writing fantasy narratives and drawing pencil sketches, he developed the mathematical formula that could make the realization of these fantasies possible, laying the foundation for the 1957 launching of Sputnik. As a Soviet historian of science wrote:

> *Tsiolkovsky was the first to do most of the things necessary to make, launch and sustain life inside rockets as we now know them ... he developed aerodynamic test methods for rigid air frames; he solved the problem of rocket flight in a uniform field of gravitation; he calculated the amount of fuel required to overcome the earth's gravitational pull.*

Releasing Genius

Like Federov and many esoteric writers before him, Tsiolkovsky considered the macrocosm and microcosm to be structured upon the same organic principles, and the perfection of the inner man and the outer world to be mutually interdependent. All the planets in our solar system, for him, and, indeed, all material bodies and gaseous clouds in the cosmos, contain life in one form or another. For him *a genius is one who comprehends and channels messages from higher beings into earthly projects, the poet who hears the muses, the inspired inventor who turns a dreamed universal symbol into a useful object.*

BIOSPHERE TO NOOSPHERE

The Good of the Planet

Both Tsolkovsky himself and Vernadsky were indeed such geniuses. Of the major Cosmists, Vladmir Vernadsky (1863–1945).was the most thoroughly academic, in the best sense of the term. Human beings for him were first and foremost inhabitants of the planet, one component in a cycle of physical and chemical interactions and transmutations, and as such they possessed an obligation to think and act for the good of the planet as well as for their own personal comfort and wellbeing. *We are then, in a very deep sense, related to all on our planet as we are to animals, vegetables and minerals, as well as to other human beings, and as the rational component of the biosphere, we have a responsibility, literally to all.*

Philosophy and Spirituality Aligned

Vernadsky was not religious in any conventional sense, but he was a deeply spiritual thinker, well read in the literature of the world's religions, and in eastern and western philosophy. He recognized that a unified view of nature, the idea of the interconnectedness of all, had for millennia been at the heart of much religious and philosophical speculation, and so at the deepest level he found no conflict between philosophical and spiritual views of the world.

Foremost Allegiance to the Biosphere

Free science then, more than any other intellectual activity for Vernadsky, could bring genuine benefits to human beings. As inhabitants first and foremost of the cosmos and the planet, *human beings owe allegiance to the biosphere more than to any nation, ethic entity, economic class or system.* For him *the biosphere represents the planet's sheath of 'living matter', and the noosphere represents the biosphere's emerging sheath of 'thinking matter'*. Among the new concepts and terms that Vernadsky introduced to science are the 'ubiquity of life', the 'pressure of life', the 'thickening of life', and the 'speed of life'. For Vernadsky then:

> *In the intensity, complexity, and depth of modern life, man forgets in a practical sense that he himself and all humanity, form that which he may not be separate from, and is inescapably linked with the biosphere. In reality, no one living organism finds itself in a free circumstance on Earth. All these organisms are constantly and inextricably linked – first of all in their food and breathing – with the material/energy environment around them. Outside of it they cannot exists in natural conditions.*

Honoured then in his own day as a brilliant experimental scientist, Young maintains, whilst many of his manuscripts were kept in the drawer during Soviet times, Vernadsky nevertheless gained iconic status as a scientific thinker. He was at the same time a pioneer environmentalist, exhibiting a mode of integrity, dignity and rectitude in a time and place where such qualities in prominent individuals were in short supply. He is then a figure revered in Cosmist studies in Russia today, and Young hopes in time he might be equally honoured elsewhere. What about, finally, Cosmist offshoots in our current day and age? What is ultimately the institutional embodiment of such?

ISCRA: INSTITUTE FOR SCIENTIFIC RESEARCH INTO COSMIC ANTHROPOECOLOGY

Peaceful Development

The central institution for the study and propagation of Russian Cosmism today is the N.F. Federov Museum-Library housed in the Central Children's Library in Moscow. The idea for a special museum devoted to Federov and his intellectual heirs developed through a seminar in the 1980s directed by the literary scholar Svetana Semenova, who has been writing about Federov's ideas since the 1970s. The Museum-Library itself was officially chartered in 1993, and has since been directed with unflagging devotion and energy by Semenova's daughter Anastasia Gacheva.

By now, hundreds of papers have been published in the 'Federovian Readings' series, analyzing Federovian and other Cosmist ideas both in themselves and in relation to other Russian and international philosophical tendencies. *A few titles from related conferences indicate the themes involved: 'Toward a Peaceful Development of the Cosmos'; 'A Noosperic Assessment of Global Problems'; and 'From Egotism to a Systemic Worldview'.*

Cosmic Anthropoecology

These and the similar papers published after conferences are merely the tip of the iceberg. Panels, round tables, commemorations, video presentations and displays supplement the individual papers given. Participants include academics in the humanities, natural and social sciences, from Russian and international universities and institutes, independent scholars, writers, artists, journalists and government officials. The best-known Cosmist institute, as such, is ISRICA in Siberia.

Since the early 1990s, in Novosibirsk, Siberia, under the aegis of the Russian Academy of Sciences, the Institute for Scientific Research in *Cosmic Anthropoecology has been investigating telepathic communications between human subjects on earth and unidentified forces in the cosmos.* Basing their experiments in part on Vernadsky's theory of the noosphere, they have mainly based their research on the controversial astrophysicist Nikolai Kozyrev. *Time,* according to Kozyrev, is *a spiralling movement of energy,* of 'torsion waves', pervasive throughout the cosmos. His theory reinstates the ether as a fluid medium of energy underlying everything in the universe – western scientific equivalent of *chi, prana, akasha.* We are now ready to conclude.

5.6 Conclusion: Communism to Cosmism

A SAVING ALTERNATIVE TO THE WEST?

Cosmism specifically, for Young then, is often seen as *a positive, spiritually advanced alternative to the previous all embracing ideology of Communism,* a more comprehensive thousand-year plan to replace five-year plans that did not work in the Soviet era. Cosmists who have written about the history of Russian philosophy find that their approach offers a grand synthesis of all Russian thought: *Slavophiles and westernizers, progressive and conservative, religious and scientific, mystical and realistic, national and universal.*

The more we can all know about the traditional cultural and intellectual tendencies of a country, in this case Russia, the better. The Cosmists, for Young then, present as *clear and deep a look as any into the past, present and potential future tendencies of what has been called the 'Russian soul'*. Fedorov, Berdyaev, Bulgakov and Florensky all proposed their ideas in part as *a saving alternative to what they considered to be a broken, ailing western tradition.*

RUSSIAN GROUNDING AND EMERGENCE BEREFT OF NAVIGATION AND EFFECT

Interestingly enough George Young is located at a Centre for Global Humanities, in New England, and as such completely disconnected, say, from a Harvard School of Government, Law School or Business School, and all the more so from the Chicago School of Economics, which altogether make our 'western' economic, if not also political establishment, world go around. More specifically, in our Russian context, Cosmism, as an offshoot of mutual aid if not also the earth charter, in some not unreasonable respect, is a million miles away from the Kremlin and the Russian oligarchs, today so to speak.

From the vantage point of pursuing integral advantage, hitherto in Russia if not also the Soviet Union as a whole, an exogenous form of 'western' Marxism, as a 'force of mind', has been imposed on the indigenous 'Russian Soul'. This has seemingly happened for two reasons. First, since the time of Peter the Great, Russia has looked to the global 'west' to 'modernize' its local, traditional institutions. Secondly, its own local–global emergence, through the likes of Federov, Berdyaev, Dostoevsky, Soloviev, and more recently Solzhenitsyn, has not yet resulted in a viable enough system of navigation, so to speak, serving to turn its nature and culture into sustainable systems and technologies.

We get somewhat close to such navigation, via Bulgakov's (17) *philosophy of economy* as an offshoot of emerging cosmism, to which we now turn. At the same time we need to recognize, as will also be the case for South Africa that follows next, that there is no agency within society to facilitate the pursuit of integral advantage, be it Russian, South African or otherwise. It is to that crucial issue that we shall turn in our final chapter. But next, in Chapter 6, we look at *the world as household*, taking on from where anthropoecology leaves off.

Bibliography

1. Masaryk, T.G. (1919) *The Spirit of Russia – Volume 1.* London, Allen and Unwin.
2. Masaryk, T.G. (1919) *The Spirit of Russia – Volume 2.* London, Allen and Unwin.
3. Solzhenitsyn, A. (1990) *Rebuilding Russia.* London, Harvill Publications.
4. Solzhenitsyn, A. (1990) *Rebuilding Russia.* London, Harvill Publications.
5. Neumann, I. (1999) *Uses of the Other: The 'East' in European Identity Formation.* Minneapolis, University of Minnesota Press.
6. Berdyaev, N. (1948) *The Russian Idea.* New York, Macmillan.
7. Bartlett, R. (2013) *Tolstoy: A Russian Life.* London, Profile Books.
8. Mathura, E. (2004) *Foundations of Sociological Subjectivism: The Social Thought of Mikhailovsky.* London, Athena Press.
9. Bartlett, R. (2013) *Tolstoy: A Russian Life.* London, Profile Books.
10. Masaryk, T.G. (1919) *The Spirit of Russia – Volume 2.* London, Allen and Unwin.
11. Berdyaev, N. (2009) *Dostoyevsky: An Interpretation.* San Rafael, CA, Semantron Press.

12. Jakim, B. and Bird, R. (1998) *On Spiritual Unity: A Slavophile Reader.* Hudson, New York, Lindisfarne Books.
13. Soloviev, V. (2008) *The Philosophical Principles of Integral Knowledge.* Cambridge, William Eerdmans.
14. Lessem, R. with Schieffer, A. (2015) *Integral Renewal: A Relational and Renewal Perspective.* Farnham, Gower.
15. Young, G. (2011) *The Russian Cosmists: The Esoteric Futurism of Nikolai Federov and his Followers.* Oxford, Oxford University Press.
16. Bulgakov, S. (2000) *Philosophy of Economy: The World as Household.* New Haven, Yale University Press.
17. Bulgakov, S. (1993) *Sophia: The Wisdom of God.* Hudson, New York, Lindisfarne Books.

Chapter 6

Anthropoecology to the World as Household – Russian Navigation: Philosophy of Economy as Social Science

> *Active cultivation of the natural world firstly is an economic activity; its primary elementary form is the family. The second basic form of society, which is inextricably linked with the first, determines the relationship of people not to nature but immediately to each other, and has its direct object not people's labor, but people themselves in interaction as members of a collective whole. Such a political society is engaged with lawfulness or a system of rights. The third form of society is determined by the religious character of the person, not his material existence (economic) or lawful existence (political) but now his absolute existence in sacred society.*
>
> *Vladmir Soloviev,* The Philosophical Principles of Integral Knowledge

6.1 Introduction

NATURAL AND COMMUNAL GROUNDING TO SOCIAL AND ECONOMIC NAVIGATION

Inhibited Knowledge and Value Creation

Over the course of the last two chapters, 4 and 5, we have traced a Russian path of prospective, integral advantage, from local grounding in mutual aid, through local–global emergence through cosmism. At the same time, we need to recognize that such grounding in nature and community reaches back to the Middle Ages, communally, if not through many millennia, naturally, so that much has faded in the Russia's memory. We have pointed out, moreover, that there is no agency in such a society to facilitate such grounded recall, and indeed to promote the interconnection between east and west, if not also north and south.

Even more speculative than such natural and communal grounding is the emergent culture and consciousness, in Russian society at large, to further build, locally–globally, on such fertile grounds. While Russia, stretching uniquely across Eurasia, has the distinctive potential of bridging east and west, more often, in its history, one has been opposed to the other, both internally and externally. As such, whereas the somewhat invisible cosmism is a unique blend of Slavophile (eastern) and westernizers, the much more visible 'western' import, communism, decimated the country over six oppressive decades. Instead of a local–global fusion, the global Marxism triumphed over the local brand of socialism, with anarchism lodged somewhat awkwardly in between.

What is altogether remarkable is the strength and vibrancy of what Berdyaev has called the 'Russian Idea', from a cultural and spiritual perspective, and yet how invisible it remains to most, without, if not also within the country, in today's Russia. As we have pointed out, one of the limiting factors, indigenously, is the ability to further evolve, from grounding and emergence to now navigation, or in Nonaka and Takeuchi's knowledge-creating terms (see Chapter 3) from local socialization and local–global externalization to global knowledge combination. Sergey Bulgakov, as we shall now see, has at least gone some of the way towards such, taking on from where cosmic anthropoecology has left off.

Philosophy and Economy

Sergey Bulgakov, as we have seen, was indeed one of the major figures of the so called Russian Silver Age. As economist, philosopher, publicist, politician and founder of a Christian Socialist party, during his 'second life', when exiled from the Soviet Union in 1922, he became arguably the twentieth-century's foremost Orthodox theologian. Thus his unique amalgam (1) of philosophy and economics – *Philosophy of Economy* – was an attempt to formulate an alternative philosophy that preserved what he considered Marxism's main insights yet eliminated its disregard for individual dignity.

BULGAKOV BIOGRAPHY: FALL AND RESURRECTION

From Orthodoxy to Marxism

Sergey Bulgakov was *born into a family of provincial priests,* stretching back six generations. An intensely religious and church-oriented childhood was followed by a loss of faith at the age of 14, partly under the influence of German philosophy. *During his years at Moscow University in the 1890s, in his 20s, Bulgakov established his reputation as one of Russia's leading Marxist intellectuals.* He believed, as such, that capitalism was a necessary stage of development for all nations and therefore denied the possibility of a 'special path' for Russia.

Disenchanted with Communism

On the crest of his success, Bulgakov traveled to Berlin to pursue his doctoral studies in capitalism and agriculture, but by 1900 he found it difficult to conclude his dissertation, which he had originally conceived in Marxist vein. *By the time he returned to Russia* that year he was in a state of spiritual crisis. The crisis was to establish the new parameters of his intellectual life for the ensuing two decades; *from this moment began an intensive search for a worldview to replace Marxism that had proved inadequate.* Bulgakov, the once prominent Marxist, now became an equally prominent participant in the renewal of art, literature and philosophy in Russia known as the Silver Age. He experienced and gave voice to the period's 'discovery' of idealism and eventually of a re-visioning of Orthodox Christianity.

Founding Christian Socialism

Dissatisfied then with western style political parties, he tried to found an alternative Christian Socialist party, but with limited success. He did, however, become a major figure in a widespread movement for the religious 'reformation' of society among the intelligentsia, both in Russia and in the rest of Europe. What more specifically then was its nature and scope?

6.2 Philosophy of Economy

THE REVOLT AGAINST POSITIVISM

A Re-evaluation of Darwin and Marx

Bulgakov's search for a new social philosophy was part of a broader European movement that historians have described as 'the revolt against positivism'. *At the turn of the twentieth century, thinkers throughout Europe questioned the foundations of nineteenth-century attitudes towards science, literature and society.* In social thought the questioning of dominant nineteenth-century beliefs frequently involved a re-evaluation of Marxism and a dissatisfaction with the application of Darwinian theories to social life. The revolt against positivism took a variety of forms: German neo-Kantism, Sigmund Freud's 'discovery' of the unconscious, Husserl's phenomenology, and French post-modernist Saussure's approach to language as structure are leading examples.

Questioning Progress

What did Bulgakov mean by 'positivism', and why did he consider it an inadequate basis for a vision of society? To a large extent, he equated positivism with 'a theory of progress'. *He spoke for an entire generation of Russian intellectuals, including Berdyaev, when he claimed that positivism, as a code of social morality, sacrificed the good of present generations for the future.* Belief in science, as such, had attained the level of religion. Positivism then in general, and Marxism in particular, subjugated the needs of individual human beings here and now for the sake of collective humanity in the future. His own response was that of a 'philosophy of economy'. In this book, as we shall see, *Bulgakov replaced Marx's vision of society as a class struggle based on material interests, in which the mode of production determined social forms and ideologies, and at the crux of that view stood the relation between man and man.*

Towards a Sophic Economy

He took as his point of departure, in that guise, an imagined original state in which man and nature lived in perfect harmony. To this initial state, analogous to the State of Nature postulated by John Locke or Jean-Jacques Rousseau, Bulgakov (2) gave the name 'Edenic economy' – the world before original sin. Yet the world in which we currently live is fatally separated from that harmonious state. Prisoners to our material needs, this is the world that Marx took to be our only one, basing his doctrine of economic materialism on the 'fallen' state of humanity. In this imperfect world Bulgakov then turned to a biblical notion – Sophia – as a way out of mere labour that characterizes the fallen world. Sophia is joy, play and wisdom. The economy, even if Eden has been lost, could once again become 'sophic'.

People's relations to each other would now be defined not by contract but by virtue of their common inspiration and participation in the shared task of nature's resurrection. The idea of Divine Wisdom (Sophia) was particularly close to Bulgakov because of its important role in the Orthodox (Greek and Russian) liturgy. Sophia moreover was much broader than Christianity; it had its roots in Gnosticism and Judaism and had parallels in Platonism (the World Soul); indeed this illusive and beautiful divinity would not be alien to a Muslim or Buddhist.

Fall and Resurrection

Bulgakov then substitutes a 'resurrective' model – the Christian cycle of Fall and Resurrection – of history for the linear 'theory of progress' associated with positivism, and indeed with both capitalism and communism. A 'sophic economy' as such was *not a paradise to be achieved on earth but a constantly present vision inspiring us to work for the restoration of the harmony of nature and culture that humanity lost in the Fall.*

This Christian philosophy of history anticipates the use of this same resurrective model by the existentialist philosophers, particularly Germany's Heidegger, whose notion of 'throwness' corresponds with Bulgakov's description of history as a result of the Fall. Such a sophic economy was also an ethic – one that prescribed joyful labour 'in Sophia' as an antidote to the grim eking out of existence that was so prevalent in life and accepted as necessary by Marxism and other economic doctrines.

Anthropoecology: Uncovering Inner Spirit as Opposed to Outer Form

The central feature of Bulgakov's sophic economy then, and one that complements the rejection of a linear conception of history and emphasis on process rather than ends, is its *replacement of social theory – Marx's – that, like most social theories of the eighteenth and nineteenth centuries, described society in terms of external forms (institutions, classes, forms of government), by a vision that instead stressed the internal content or 'spirit' of society.* What went on in the mind of the individual and social economic actor – the *khoziain* or proprietor – was as essential a part of the economic process as its ultimate goals or economic structure. The same, for us, applies to a society as a whole. Bulgakov, moreover, was part and parcel of an overall Slavophile philosophical movement in Russia in his time, also linked, as we saw in the last chapter to the Russian cosmists, generally, and to anthropoecology (inner man and inner nature), specifically.

BULGAKOV AND THE NINETEENTH-CENTURY RUSSIAN PHILOSOPHICAL TRADITION

Khoziaistvo means both Economy and Household

As early as 1874, fellow Slavophile, Vladmir Soloviev, as we saw in the previous chapter, perceived a 'crisis in Western philosophy', and specifically a crisis of positivism vis à vis his integrality, 20 years before it erupted on the European scene. Following their German Romantic predecessors, Soloviev and his fellow Slavophile philosophers argued against the 'rationalism' of western philosophy. Bulgakov's *Philosophy of Economy* then was premised on an interaction of two major disciplines. He believed that *philosophy and political economy existed in artificial isolation and that insights from each discipline could be productively brought to bear on the other,* as also illustrated by anthropoecology. In fact *khoziaistvo* in Russian, as the title and sub-title of Bulgakov's book intimates, means both economy and household.

Addressing the Real Concerns of our Life

Bulgakov then, like many of his predecessors, was concerned above all with constructing a worldview that addressed the real concerns, as per household, of our life in the world, that treated human beings as active creatures, thereby economic, interacting with the world around them. What he termed an interaction of the disciplines of philosophy and economy was a restatement of Russian philosophy's preoccupation with life. *Bringing the concerns of political economy to philosophy was a means of introducing the realities of labour, wealth and poverty into an otherwise meaningless abstract intellectual exercise.*

Specifically, in placing the problem of man and nature (anthropoecology) at the centre of his view of society, Bulgakov gave voice to a major but sometimes implicit concern of *Russian philosophy, which had firstly absorbed a preoccupation with man's relation to the world around him from German Romanticism.* Secondly, then *his focus on the inner spirit followed a Russian tradition of concern with organicism and wholeness.* Thirdly and finally, in seeking to make labour, or activity, into an epistemological principle, Bulgakov, like fellow cosmist

Federov, continued Russian philosophy's disdain for 'armchair philosophers' passively ensconced in the safety of their study: *philosophy must engage with life and is of interest only insofar as it helps us understand and eventually transform the world.*

Labour and Sobernost

Meanwhile the linking of the individual with the collective in the notion of *sobernost*, and thereby the sense that *individual personality could find full expression only in interaction with the larger community*, marks Bulgakov's Slavophile philosophy. By proposing labour as a philosophical principle, moreover, Bulgakov meant that he, as a *philosopher, must look at the process of man's life in the world as the starting point of philosophy, and as such, man as an active, working creature.*

Bugakov Lost and Found

The history of *Philosophy of Economy* as a text reflects then the larger story of Russian religious philosophy. The book was widely read and discussed, according to Russian historian Catherine Evtuhov, among educated Russians in the first years after its publication in 1912. However, it was erased from public consciousness as the aesthetic and social utopias of the Bolshevik Revolution crowded out non-Marxist and anti-Marxist philosophies. It was then to be reborn in a wave of popularity that greeted Silver Age philosophy and literature, in the 1980s, as the Soviet Union collapsed. *Bulgakov's work has then received a new immediacy in recent years, as Russia redefines its identity.*

6.3 The Problematic Philosophy of Economism

NEED TO OVERCOME THE PHILOSOPHY FROM WITHIN

Limited Horizons of Economic Thought

One of the most outstanding traits of contemporary humanity's outlook, for Bulgakov, is what he termed the 'economism' of his epoch (he was writing in the first decade of the twentieth century). Such must not be denied, he says, but *overcome from within*, explained in its limitations as a philosophical 'abstract principle' in which one side of the truth is sold as the whole truth.

The limitation of the horizons of economic thought, thus revealed, find expression not so much in the prevalence of the philosophy of economism, but in its naïve dogmatism. *It is as though the dogma of economism were the only possible, and moreover the self-evident, philosophy of economy generally.* No specialized investigation is conducted from scratch, so to speak; rather it begins, like life as it were, in the middle, for it always depends on an entire series of contingent or certain axiomatic principles, that is, it is always, according to Bulgakov, dogmatically conditioned. *Only scientific inquiry that can be acknowledged as 'critical' can be conscious of such dogmatic contingency.*

The discipline of economics currently finds itself (Bulgakov was initially writing a hundred years ago) in a severe philosophical crisis. The advent of economic materialism has left economics completely devoid of any philosophical basis and turned it into an abstract manipulation of empirical facts and observations, so that it can barely be taken seriously as a science. As a result, the philosophical examination of the basic principles of economic thought and action has become imperative; such, for Bulgakov, is the task of the philosophy of economy.

Philosophy as General Meaning; Science as Specific Explanation

We might say, then, that philosophy seeks the collective explanation of the living meaning of phenomena studied by science in their individuality. This is why adjacent fields of inquiry are outside the reach of science: its tacit assumptions are precisely the proper task of philosophy. Thus *political economy and the philosophy of economy, for example, both study the economic process, but one, political economy, engages in detailed analysis, whereas the other, philosophy of economy, looks for general meaning.* Economic activity in this sense is but part of life as a whole. *Nature is thus the natural basis of culture; it is the material for the economic activity; outside of nature, economic activity is as inconceivable and impossible as concrete experience is impossible outside life.*

We now turn to Bulgakov's interpretation of the basic economic functions, in terms of the world as household.

6.4 The Basic Economic Functions of the World as Household

FROM CONSUMER DEMAND TO CONSUMPTION AS INHALATION

Exhalation and Inhalation

Economic life, in the world conceived as household, can ultimately be reduced, according to Bulgakov, to a metabolic process, to something like circulation or an alternation of inhaling and exhaling. *In the language of political economy, production corresponds to exhalation, consumption to inhalation.* The economic cycle consists of these two acts. For this reason he asks the general question *how is economy possible?* Reduced to two particular questions, of the world household, he asks: how is production possible, and how is consumption possible? We start with consumption.

Consumption as Nourishment

By *nourishment* in the broadest sense, he means *the most generic metabolic exchange between the living organism and its environment*, including not just food but respiration and the effects of the atmosphere, light, electricity, chemistry and other forces on our organism, insofar as they support life, in the context of the world household. The world enters us through all the windows and doors of our senses and, having entered, is apprehended and assimilated by us. *In its totality this consumption of the world, this ontological communication with it, this communism of being, lies at the foundation of all our life processes, and of our world household.*

The boundary between living and nonliving, for example, is actually removed in food. *Food is natural communion – partaking of the flesh of the world.* Every particle of the food we eat or indeed consume (and every atom of the air we breathe) is in principle the flesh of the world. Food in this sense uncovers our essential metaphysical unity with the world, as a household.

For Bulgakov then, if food is a means of communion with the flesh of the world, regardless of its shape and quantity, then partaking of Christ's flesh and blood in the form of bread and wine is communion with the flesh of the Son of God. This then is the divinized flesh of the world, which can also be conceived only dynamically. And as food maintains mortal life, so the Eucharistic meal means to partake of immortal life. Once again then, communion supplants communism.

Metaphysical Communion of the Universe

Thus the possibility of consumption is, in principle based on the metaphysical communion of the universe, on the primordial identity of all that exists, thanks to which metabolic exchange and circulation are possible. It is premised, above all else, on the unity of living and non-living, on the universality of life, and the integration of the world household. The appearance of life, its nourishment and expansion, are possible only because the entire universe is a living body. We now turn from consumption as inhalation to production as exhalation.

FROM FACTOR OF PRODUCTION TO PRODUCTION AS EXHALATION

Production as a Work of Art

Secondly, we face the question how is production, in the world household, possible? Production is the exertion of the subject on the object, or man on nature, such that the subject of the economic process imprints or realizes his or her idea, objectivizes his or her goals, through the object of his or her economic action. The object item, the non-I, gets saturated therefore in human teleology, and realizes a model or idea projected in advance in the subject. In this aspect the product of any finished productive act is like a work of art, which is characterized by the mutual penetration of matter and form through the idea.

As the German Romantic philosopher Schelling so beautifully has said, according to Bulgakov (3): '*the world becomes objective for us only through action*'. The relation between the I and the non-I, then, is a relation between two worlds or two energies in constant interaction. Thus man's economic relation to the world, theoretical-practical, subjective-active, ideal-real, is of primary significance both for epistemology and for general philosophy. *The changing relationship between the subject and object, the unfolding of the I in nature, is life, that is growth, movement, is dynamic.* It is this living, active, economic 'I' that ought to be, for Bulgakov, the point of departure for philosophy and economy in the world household. Only this can be the basis for the possibility of production.

Labour Connects Subject with Object

The blind, elemental or instinctual labour of nature, as such, now becomes the conscious labour of man. Thus the living connection between subject and object, the bridge leading the I into the world of realities and irrevocably connecting him to the world, is labour – human reality, objectivized anew and thus objectivizing the world around us.

Labour then, which occupies so much space in theories of political economy, thus acquires primary importance in epistemology as well, in the context for Bulgakov of the world as household. Political economy, in contrast, has as a result of its lack of philosophical sophistication and the limitations of its spiritual horizons, failed to use this principle properly, to find an appropriate place for it.

Labour is More than Productivity

First of all political economy – in theory in the work of Adam Smith (4), in practice in the case of most of his followers – narrowed the concept of labour to 'productive' labour, expressed in material goods. Consequently, *attention was focused on this single aspect of labour, the objective one, which is actually its periphery, while its significance as a bridge between subject and object, by means of which the subject comes into the object and realizes its ideas, projects and models, was entirely neglected.* Scientific technology too evades this question, in its complete concentration on working out detailed practical problems.

But if political economy with its 'economic materialism' knows labour only in its products or objects, and misses it in the subject, than an analogous error repeats itself in the opposite pole – in Kantian subjective idealism. The Kantian subject is idle, for Bulgakov (5), devoid of any working energy.

Labour is Full of Human Possibilities

All of knowledge, then, is the economic projection of future answers through questions posed. Here the object of exertion through labour is the external world, and object of cognition full of possibilities as infinite as those offered by the external world as an object of economic action. In this sense, knowledge is economic action, the subject, or I, coming to the non-I, and the primordial unity of the I and the non-I, the subject and object, is realized in each cognitive act. What existed in a dreamy, potential state as the unconscious, or as the possibility of knowledge, becomes actualized in consciousness. We might say then that the economy is a cognitive process turned sensual or externalized, whereas cognition is the same process, but in an ideal, non-sensual form. Every conscious, intentional overcoming of the opposition of subject and object, as such, in the ideal or sensual sphere, is an act of labour.

The significance of labour therefore, so underestimated by epistemology, has found a certain appreciation in political economy. Labour, however, is usually placed among the factors of production, along with land and capital, in the theory of the production of material goods. Yet, although this classification may have some specialized relevance, it is entirely devoid of general philosophical meaning. In this respect the so-called 'labour theory of value' is more interesting. Here labour has a unique value as the basis of the value of goods. Yet it is understood, by Marx (6), in an extremely narrow sense, merely as applied to explaining the mechanism of process and the theory of exchange value.

We now turn to economy and history, and to knowledge in the context of such.

6.5 On the Transcendental Subject of Economy

MAN AND HUMANITY

Integral Historical Development

Although empirically it is true, for Bulgakov, that economic activity takes the form of a myriad of separate acts, if we look at it dynamically, over time, we see that it is actually a unified and connected activity whose subject is not the individual but the whole world as household. The human economy then develops both extensively and intensively, so that at each historical stage at least some part of the preceding process becomes integrated into the present; the present grows out of the past, assimilating it organically, similar to the way in which foetal development recapitulates biogenesis. But at the same time the new species, this integral of the preceding historical series, contains within itself some new element, and this is what constitutes historical development in nature and in human history – what we call emergence. This creativity, this constant introduction of new elements is what renders historical processes – among them the economy as household – possible.

Knowledge and Economy

Knowledge and economy, moreover, cannot exist independently: knowledge creates models and plans essential to economic organization and itself exists only as part of the economic system. *Man cannot progress in knowledge without simultaneously realizing the progress in practical life. Economy is knowledge in action; knowledge is economy in theory.*

The economic process is actually a synthetic effort, both extensive and intensive, to possess a single object through labour and economic activity (this is known as the development of 'productive forces' (7) in the language of Marxist political economy). The single subject of economy, the world soul for Bulgakov, acts in history through an indefinite quantity of separate, independent centres – individual human minds and wills. Its unity becomes realized only in multiplicity. He then turns to his notion of a 'sophic economy'.

THE SOPHIC ECONOMY

Starting with Self Determination

Through economic activity, man is capable of transforming nature according to his will; he constantly creates a cultural reality – new goods, new knowledge, new feelings, new beauty – alongside the 'natural' world that is given to him. We live then in the consciousness of the constantly growing power of economic activity, which in turn opens up limitless opportunities of the creation of culture. *All creativity, moreover, requires labour, effort, will – all symptoms of self determination.*

Since man is obviously not all-powerful, he cannot create from nothing but must draw on the existing world in re-creating his new, artificial world, the world of culture. He can imprint his ideas on the created world, experiment with it, and find in it the answers to his questions; in economic activity, the new world of culture takes shape. But where does he find the images, the model ideas on which he bases his creativity?

Sophia and Humanity

The empirical world is immersed in a 'process', in time and space, in history, and as such is imperfect and disharmonious; yet, like humanity itself, it is never wholly separate from a higher metaphysical reality, from the divine *Sophia that soars above the world, illuminating it through reason, through beauty, through economy and culture. Sophia and humanity maintain a living interaction, like a plant's nourishment through its roots.*

This life comes about not through labour or economic activity but through birth, that is through the realization of a primordial life force, likened to Federov's *rosdstvo* (see previous chapter). We can broaden the sphere of life, perhaps even resurrect life, but we cannot create it. Divine Providence, as such, manifests itself in the universal connectedness of the world, in the gradual generation of life in all aspects before man, in man's first steps in history. And this logos of things also makes the economic process possible.

Fall and Resurrection

The initial immediacy, the intuitiveness of contemplation, the identity of knowledge and consciousness, the subject-objectness of being in Sophia (8) have all been lost in recent times, and knowledge has become abstract and distant. Fragmentation has replaced solidarity, and the struggle for survival becomes the law of life in the human as well as the animal world. The purpose of economic activity, in the aftermath of such, is to defend and to spread the seeds of life, to resurrect nature. *Economic activity then overcomes the divisions in nature, and its ultimate goal – outside of economy proper – is to return the world to the life of Sophia.*

He then turns from economics, specifically, to science, generally.

6.6 The Nature of Social Science

THE ECONOMIC NATURE OF SCIENCE

Labour Expanded on Science and Production

Science then firstly is a social process involving labour and directed toward the production of ideal values, that is, of knowledge, which is necessary and useful to man for various reasons. As a process involving labour, it is a branch of man's economic activity generally, which is directed toward supporting, defending and expanding life and which is at the same time an organic part of life.

The labour that is expended on science, as such, pursues two fundamental aims: to broaden experience or accumulate knowledge (which can be compared with the inherited creation of material wealth passed from generation to generation serving to build roads, cities, farms factories); and to organize such, to generalize such scientifically into concepts and laws (which can be compared with the accumulation of capital, the capitalization of the products of labour or the purposes of production).

As the miner carves new ores from the cliffs, so the scientific worker calls the new into being – which he does not create but exposes and liberates – to life, forth from the darkness. This labour is conducted according to a definite plan.

Science and Production Rooted in Life

Science's economic nature manifests itself in the manner in which it is, secondly, rooted in life. As in the production of economic goods, in the narrow sense of the world, labour is expended for the production of commodity values having utility, so in science the production of the ideal goods, the labour of research, is directed toward the satisfaction of needs dictated by life. *Life impulses and practical needs have called different branches of knowledge into being at different periods.*

SCIENCE AND LIFE

Life is an Unceasing Economic Process

Science, overall then, is a function of life; it is born in the process of labour, and *the nature of all labour is economic, that is, has the aim of defending or expanding life.* Life never rests; it is in a state of ceaseless tension, actuality, struggle. Life is in this sense an unceasing economic process. An economic orientation to the world, moreover, includes a theoretical orientation to the world, that is science a necessary tool.

Economically Oriented Scientific Worldview

Our time (early in the twentieth century) is characterized by a terrible intensity of economic energy, expressed equally in the development of science and in the economic conquering of the cosmos. This intensity is expressed in the extreme immersion of the subject in the object and is accompanied by a certain displacement of the centre of consciousness.

But although science transforms the world into a lifeless mechanism, it is itself a product of life, and a form of the subject's self-definition in the object, and thereby, as we see below, expressed through the phenomenology of economy. In that sense Bulgakov is drawing philosophically on his central European colleague Edmund Husserl (9). Of course this is different from the conventional capitalist or socialist view of economics.

6.7 The Phenomenology of Economy

THE TASK OF POLITICAL ECONOMY

Riveted to the Economic Particular

The sense of economy as an interaction of collective humanity and nature, sophic or indeed anthropoelogical in its foundations and endowed with cosmic meaning, is not of course present in the minds of particular economic actors as they go about their practical lives. Their attention, riveted to the particular, remains ignorant of the whole, world as household as it were.

Labour then, as the sweat of our face, bears the stamp of slavery in its elements, of banishment from paradise, of the inability to live in harmony with creation. *Poverty and want pose the questions, and human labour and utility shape the answers.* The essence of the economic process as a whole then, and its transcendent principles for Bulgakov, are almost completely overshadowed by the general race for wealth – a competition that fragments a single, unified economic process into disparate, fractional particles.

Transcending Economic Man

'Economic man', as such, is a sermon for commercialism, naively exposing political economy's central nerve and revealing the focus of its orientation. The first obstacle we encounter, in relation to it moreover, is *the vagueness of its most basic concept, wealth,* which is as amorphous and unclear as most 'real life' notions. *The mercantilists defined wealth as money, the physiocrats as agricultural products, the free traders as industrial products, the socialists as material goods, and Ruskin as human life;* each is right from their own relative point of view.

Man though is spirit incarnate and spiritualized flesh – a spiritual and material being. This is why there is no distinct boundary between the material and the spiritual and why everything has two sides; from this standpoint everything should be included in the science of economy, in the world as household. This is not the way of a conventional 'western' approach to economics.

POLITICAL ECONOMY'S SCIENTIFIC STYLE

A Typically Stylized Collective Type

'Deductive' political economy, in fact, is constructed completely on a particular representation of a typical, or average form of behaviour, any departure from which is seen as irregular or accidental. The infamous 'economic man' – that crucially instrumental concept of political economy that we can either deny with Ruskin or Carlyle, as a slander of reality, or judiciously apply so long as we find it of practical use, ever conscious of its contingent ad practical nature – is precisely such a stylized collective type.

Political economy's basic principle is that the phenomena of economic life are typical or repetitive forms of the general methodological premise of economic regularity. Yet this statement obviously excludes not only the individual but anything that is historical. *It is assumed that the entire inventory of economic reality and causality has already been accounted for and that beyond that nothing can happen.* Marx's (10) prognosis, for example, concerning the evolution of capitalism to socialism is typical in that respect; it is premised entirely on *ceteris paribus* (other things being equal) and constitutes a mental extrapolation of just one tendency, generalized from isolated aspects of contemporary reality.

Born Under the Star of Commercialism

Political economy in the final analysis has long concerned itself with theories of economic value, but has not included in its purview a problem that is really important, namely the theory of value of economic theories in themselves. Political economy was born under the star of commercialism, that is, of completely practical motives, of the need to figure out the complexities of the economic mechanism. It *is the child of capitalism and is in turn the science of capitalism.*

6.8 Economic Materialism as a Philosophy of Economy

ECONOMIC MATERIALISM AS PHILOSOPHY AND AS SCIENCE

Economic Materialism: Economic Based and Cultural Superstructure

It is of course simple to dismiss economic materialism, as is true for every theory that poses a significant life problem, by turning away in impotence or from lack of interest; *the problem must ultimately be overcome only by positive means, having acknowledged its truth and understood its motive but declined its limitations and perversions.* Fundamentally then, economic materialism represents a metaphysical or at least meta-empirical philosophy of history, something like a *historical ontology.* The history of philosophy, for Bulgakof, is full of examples of such unconscious metaphysics. *Economic materialism's central Marxian (11) theory of the 'base and superstructure'*, as such, addresses the ontological problem. According to this theory *all of mankind's historical life in its external and internal, political and social, cultural and spiritual manifestations is but a superstructure above the economic base.*

Vulgarized in Benthamism

Marx's economic materialism, according to Bulgakof moreover, is vulgarized in Benthamism (the English utilitarian economic philosopher in the nineteenth century called for 'the greatest happiness of the greatest number'). It degenerates into an effort to explain everything by greed and perceives only an economic explanation for the greatest historical developments. The history of the Reformation turns into the history of pig farming and landholding in the sixteenth century, the history of early Christianity into the history of slavery and the proletariat in the Roman Empire. *History, which appeared to Bentham (12) as a struggle among individual interests, became for Marx a struggle among class interests, and the idea of class struggle as an explanation of the historical process took shape.*

THE CONTRADICTIONS OF ECONOMIC MATERIALISM

Labour, Nature and Culture

The basic idea of economic materialism is that economy has the defining role in history and in life, or that all of culture is of an economic nature and bears the imprint of economy. It approaches the world as an economic household. *For Bulgakof, as for Federov rather, man* does not create anything anew that did not already exist in nature in hidden or potential form, but he *brings life forces to the fore, realizing its possibilities through labour.* Labour, directed both toward the external world and toward man himself, expended in the production both of material goods and spiritual values, *creates something that, in counter-position to nature, primordially given, bears the name of culture.*

The Political Economist Paralyzes the Philosopher

The blunder of economic materialism then, is that instead of placing the problem of economy with all its premises at the centre of attention, and providing an independent philosophical analysis, economic materialism takes the concept of economy ready-made from a specialized science, namely, political economy. Marx, the political economist, here paralyzes Marx the philosopher, something that applies even more to his followers. *If philosophy is interested in the interconnections between phenomena as a whole, specialized science, which bears the mark of scientific pragmatism, intentionally focuses on one side of things.*

Political economy therefore is satisfied with a definition of labour that, for example, for Adam Smith, and for David Ricardo, to whom we referred in Chapter 2 and who has inspired the title of our book, or Karl Marx, was directed only toward the production of material goods or exchange values. Political economy, like Ricardo's theory of comparative advantage, then remains distant from political anthropology and even further removed from natural philosophy. Economic materialism, in that sense, is nothing other than a philosophical delusion of grandeur on the part of political economy elevating itself to the rank of historical ontology. And here *Hegel has really been stood on his head: for him it was logic that had such ontological significance, not as a specialized science as we know it today, but as a theory of general forms of consciousness and being;* for Marx political economy was merely a specialized science, and acquired its significance as such.

Turning Social Science into a Natural Science

Economic materialism wants to be a philosophy of history, whereas, for Bulgakov, by its logical structure it is a sociological rather than historical doctrine. It *strives, for Marx (13), to turn a social science, including history, into a natural science, that is to establish immutable, uniform laws of social life.* Having come across 'laws of development' of society, we can scientifically predict its future.

Hence a developed nation shows the way of future development to a 'backward' nation. By 'natural science' is meant a perception of events from the standpoint of their similarity or typicality, and not from the standpoint of their individuality and uniqueness, as per historicism. That is why, over time, economic materialism has generated so many confusions, constantly changing its logic or colouration depending on circumstances. In fact, truly scientific elements are dissolved in utopian ones, but the utopian are hidden behind a mask of scientism.

Economic Materialism Does Express a Particular Life Truth

Beyond this philosophical value, though, economic materialism does express a particular life truth – practical and oral rather than theoretical. The economic tragedy of human life has found expression in this sorrowful theory, and its pessimism contains profound sincerity and truthfulness: the economic slavery of man to man, the eternal struggle among people because of wealth, for Bulgakov expressed in God's judgement on sinful man and all creation.

In this imperfect world, as we saw above, Bulgakov then turned to a biblical notion – Sophia – as a way out of mere labour that characterizes the fallen world. Sophia is joy, play and wisdom. The economy, even if Eden has been lost, could again become 'sophic'.

6.9 Conclusion: East Meets West

ENTERING A EUROPEAN ERA WHERE RUSSIA MUST LEAD

Leading the 'West' Out of its Cul de Sac

Creative culture, for Berdyaev as for Bulgakov, is impossible without tradition, without one's distinctive character. Only by its indigenous culture does each people serve exogenous world culture, in national flesh and blood. We must, for Berdyaev, love western culture, but we must also repay our debt to western thought, to which we are obligated for much. We are now entering an epoch, he says, when Russian philosophy can and must lead western philosophy out of its dead end.

Immature Westernizing to Mature Vision

We need to bear in mind, for Berdyaev moreover, that Russia's westernizing tendency was that of an immature youth. The Russian westernizing consciousness is atheistic and materialistic. Yet the consciousness of western nations is by no means such. They also contain religious truths. It is not only on the graves of Karl Marx, but also of those of Hegel and Schelling that Russia stands. Russia, the east and west – that is the universal theme that our generations and the next are destined to develop.

Russia stands then, for Berdaev as for Bulgakov, at the centre of two currents of world history: eastern and western. Only Russia, he says, can resolve the question of the east for European culture. If Russia has a world mission, this mission is the unification of the east and the west in one Christian humanity. That is a far cry from the Russia of Marxism or of today's oligarchy.

EMERGENCE INHIBITS NAVIGATION

Russia Forever in Transition

For Iver Neumann (15), in his *Uses of the Other* then, as we saw in the previous chapter, if in our ongoing representation of Russia we do not allow for more reflection of how the deeply entrenched patterns reviewed here in 'the Russian idea' remain a more-or-less unacknowledged factor, we will add our voices to the chorus that confirms the dominant version of Russia as a learner, at least in a political and economic respect, forever about to make the transition into Europe, if not into Asia as well.

In fact Russia's political and economic backwardness Neumann says – that is, its low degree of functional differentiation of power between politics and economic, between state and society – meant that *the country continuously had to face up to the challenge posed by the more highly differentiated and therefore more efficient economic order in Europe.* This was particularly the case for the 'northern' and 'western' European countries, of course, in the twentieth century, and even more so, for the United States of America. Of course, though, the possibility always existed that some new idea may emerge and spawn a specifically Russian model for political and economic organization, but none is explicitly apparent as yet.

Standardized Western Fare

The problem then, as matters currently stand, is that such a new model, in systematical, navigational guise, is yet to emerge, and Russia is by no means alone in that regard. Pass through the corridors of academic powers, in the Soviet Union or indeed in China hitherto, in the schools of economics and of management (now business schools) and you would in the past (from 1920–80) have been taught standard Marxist theory, imported from Great Britain where Marx and Engels spent most of their productive lives. Turn the clock forward, to Russia in the new millennium, and it is now the US and the UK who rule the economic and business roost, with *standard 'western' theories of economics and business administration pervading these new business and economic academic corridors.* Such 'western' conventional wisdom is then passed on, knowingly or otherwise, to practitioners.

We may be dismissive of such economic and business tomes, most especially those Americans long winded ones, but they reflect the very systematic nature and scope that is absent in Russia, or other such emerging nations today. Instead, then, of building on Bulgakov, rendering his *Philosophy of Economy* more systematic, we have economics 101, and the neo-liberal policy makers, and practitioners, to follow.

Shock Therapy – In the Absence of Knowledge Creation

In the absence of such, then, we have 'shock therapy' as per the US neo-liberal macro-economist Jeffrey Sachs (16), on the one hand, or the Russian oligarchs on a micro enterprise level, on the other. For if you fail to draw naturally and communally on your own roots, or grounds, and what is emerging beneath your own feet, culturally and spiritually, you will inevitably suffer 'shock' as you come out into the 'western' or 'northern' open, from your 'eastern' or – as we shall see later (Chapters 8–11) 'southern' grounds. Moreover, *as you come out of shock, you will resort, as Russia has done, to a lowest common denominator, politically and economically, rather than drawing on the richness of your own nature and culture, to ultimately navigate your way.*

In other words, in *knowledge creating* guise, as per Nonaka and Takeuchi (see Chapter 3) instead of creating your own knowledge and value, integrally, you, on the one hand, loosely draw from others' global ('western') 'combinations', rather than from your own economic philosophy like that of Bulgakov's local–global 'externalization'. On the other hand, and subsequently the political and economic knowledge you 'internalize' is necessarily extremely shallow, because you do not draw on your own natural and cultural depths. This is particularly ironic in the Russian case as the very notion of 'integral knowledge' emerged, via Soloviev, on home cultural grounds, but has never been developed for political and economic purposes. Russia has shown, historically though, that it could be different in effect. So we turn from here, for such, onto a Russian Province: *Niznhii Novgarod.*

Bibliography

1. Bulgakov, S. (2000) *Philosophy of Economy: The World as Household.* New Haven, Yale University Press.
2. Bugakov, S. (1993) *Sophia: The Wisdom of God.* Hudson, NY, Lindisfarne.
3. Bulgakov, S. (2000) *Philosophy of Economy: The World as Household.* New Haven, Yale University Press.

4. Smith, A. (2003) *The Wealth of Nations.* New York, Bantam Classics.
5. Bulgakov, S. (2000) *Philosophy of Economy: The World as Household.* New Haven, Yale University Press.
6. Marx, K. (1992) *Capital.* New York, Penguin Classics.
7. Marx, K. (1992) *Capital.* New York, Penguin Classics.
8. Bugakov, S. (1993) *Sophia: The Wisdom of God.* Hudson, NY, Lindisfarne Books.
9. Husserl, E. (1970) *The Crises of the European Sciences.* Evanston, IL, Northwestern University Press.
10. Marx, K. (1992) *Capital.* New York, Penguin Classics.
11. Marx, K. (1992) *Capital.* New York, Penguin Classics.
12. Smith, M. and Burston, W. (1983) *The Collected Works of Jeremy Bentham.* Oxford, Clarendon Press.
13. Marx, K. (1992) *Capital.* New York, Penguin Classics.
14. Jakim, B. and Bird, R. (1998) *On Spiritual Unity: A Slavophile Reader.* Hodson, NY, Lindisfarne Books.
15. Neumann, I. (1999) *Uses of the Other: The 'East' in European Identity Formation.* Minneapolis, MN, University of Minnesota Press.
16. Schwartz, A. (2006) *The Politics of Greed: How Privatization Structured Politics in Central and Easter Europe.* New York, Rowan and Littlefield.

Chapter 7

Portrait of a Russian Province: Nizhnii Novgorod Zemstvo Effect

> *When we imagine ancient Russian society, we do not see castles, noble knights or kings. You see instead a countless multitude of small communes scattered over the face of the land, each representing its own small world. These small communities merge into larger ones.*
>
> *Jakim B. and Bird R. (1),* On Spiritual Unity: A Slavophile Reader

7.1 Introduction: Integrity of a Russian Province

MUTUAL AID TO ZEMSTVO

Thwarted at a National Level

In this final chapter on Russia pursuing its integral advantage, we ironically have to turn the clock back to the nineteenth century, to locate such, albeit at a provincial level. For neither Russia specifically, nor indeed the Soviet Union generally, have succeeded in pursuing such integral advantage, as a whole. Both were too busy trying to catch up with the 'west', as per Peter the Great in the eighteenth century or Lenin and then Stalin in the twentieth, all too often oppressing their own people in the process, rather than, as per Nikolai Federov (see previous chapter), Russia as a whole 'projecting itself'. Mikhail Gorbachev, as we saw in Chapter 4, was the one to probably get closest to pursuing such integral advantage (see Figure 7.1), but he was, on the one hand, stopped prematurely in his tracks, and, on the other hand, was never able to formulate his own integral approach to economics.

Integral Advantage Pursued at a Provincial Level

That said, over the course of the last three chapters, culminating now in an effective portrayal of a Russian *Provintsia*, we have illustrated, via Kropotkin

Navigation
Science and Society
World as Household
Bulgakov

Effect
Public, Private
Civic Enterprise
Zemstvo
Evtuhov

Emergence
Culture and
Consciousness
Cosmism
Federov

Grounding
Nature and Community
Mutual Aid to Earth Manifesto
Kropotkin

Figure 7.1 Mutual aid to zemstvo

(grounding in mutual aid), Federov (emerging through cosmism towards anthropoecology), and Bulgakov (navigating through the world as household), integral advantage may be pursued in Russia. The effective means toward that end has been a typical Russian province in the nineteenth century, mediated by what we have termed an integral polity (2), the local zemstvo.

We now turn to such an integral provincial portrayal as a whole.

THE HEART OF THE COUNTRY

Niznhii Novgorod

Specifically as such Professor Catherine Evtuhov (3), a Russian historian based at Georgetown University in Washington DC, set out *to uncover the nature and scope of a typical Russian province in the late nineteenth century,* in the reform period after the emancipation of the serfs. She chose Nizhnii Novgorod province, in the heart of Russia. Her intention was to uncover not only what is unique to a Russian province, the size of Belgium or Greece, but also what is generalizable to the nation as a whole. Moreover she wanted to *illustrate the nature and scope of such a local, or regional, Russian consciousness, lodged in a typical 'province'.* In the process, as we shall see, she overturns the conventional wisdom on Russia's primarily agrarian heritage, and thereby intimates that there is something more integral here, in our terms, than meets the conventional historical, political or economic eye.

The Zemstro and the Age of Congresses

In fact the last third of the nineteenth century, for her, was the 'Age of the Congresses'. Every action of the Nizhnii Novgorod's zemstvo (local government) had become inscribed in larger, national Russian efforts. Whilst the oldest and best-known civic institutions remained the Free Economic Society and the Russian Technical Society, a plethora of ad hoc associations or regular meetings appeared 'middle-up-down-across' in every profession and organization. *A network of 'invisible threads' linked the provinces to each other and to the nation as a whole.* How was this achieved?

PURVEYORS OF THE PROVINCE

Researchers and Catalysts

Pivotal to all of such, for Evtuhov, were what she calls the 'purveyors' of the province. These were not specifically *provincial activists*, but more especially particular persons *whose goal was to depict, describe, conceptualize, present and promote the province.* In an organizational context, Ikijiro Nonaka, as we have seen (see Chapter 3) would call such 'knowledge engineers', and we call them researchers and catalysts. Evtuhov introduces, then, four such nineteenth-century catalysts, so to speak, who ultimately fulfill our effective Russian purposes.

Annal of Pavel Mel'nikov

The son of a minor landowner and graduate of Kazan University, Pavel made his mark as editor of the recently established *Gubernskie vedemosti* which he transformed from a terse compendium of governmental directives into a vibrant annal of local life and history. He also made his mark as an ethnographer. At the same time, these researches bore fruit in Mel'nikov's extraordinarily rich and basically sympathetic two-volume fictional account *In the Forests* and *On the Hills.*

Alexsandr Gatsiskii – Defending the Provincial Idea

The purveyor par excellence was Gatsikii. Author of some 400 articles on local history, popular religion, archaeology, ethnography and statistics, he entered the national limelight in the 1970s as *defender of the 'provincial idea', the notion that Russia's provinces had a crucial role to play in national development.*

Andrei Karelin – Taking Provincial Culture to an International Audience

Karelin was first of all an artist. He took his camera inside the bourgeois household, capturing on film images of families, ladies distributing charity, girls in conversation, loving couples and other domestic scenes. As such he was a purveyor of the provincial bourgeoisie. His prize-winning expositions *brought the most intimate details of provincial culture to an international audience.*

Vaslii Dokuchaev – Founder and Purveyor of Soil Science

Founder of the discipline of soil science, Dokuchaev was the son of a provincial priest. A graduate of the Slomensk seminary he came to Petersburg to study at the Theological Academy at the height of the reform era, in 1967. He abandoned his theological studies then in favour of natural history at university. By 1870 his successes in geology and mineralogy had earned him an appointment as *Curator of the Geological Collection at St. Petersburg University.* His fate became linked to Nizhnii Novgorod as he worked on the book that established his professional reputation, *the Russian Chernozem (1883),* arising out of a three-year intensive study of the local soils.

Creating Knowledge and Culture

Mel'nikov, Gatsiskii, Karelin and Dokuchaev, like innumerable others, helped create nineteenth-century knowledge and culture in Nizhnii Novgorod. If, in our usual conception, nineteenth-century Russia appears as a vast, uniform, centralized state, socially and economically polarized, primarily agrarian and resistant to change, the picture that emerges for Evtuhov is very different. *Instead of only peasants and landlords, we see a countryside peopled by wooden-spoonmakers, fishnet weavers, itinerant icon sellers, and the middlemen and creditors who maintained this subsistence economy.*

Some forms of artisan activity – notably sheepskin processing, steel products and wooden implements – were successful enough to compete with factory production. Even within the province of Nizhnii Novgorod, we see an exchange economy in which the rich south-eastern black-soil provinces supplied the infertile northern forest areas with grain, while the latter kept the south provided with timber and wood products. *Instead of a centrally administered state, we see the predominance of local initiative in the crafting of the cadaster (public register), on an extremely high scientific level, in order to orchestrate the fair and equitable distribution of local taxes – an important function of the zemstvo.* Indeed, the flourishing of local statistics and the collection of documents of local history, and the promotion of local culture, brought the province into synchrony with analogous developments in other European regions.

Finding Out What Was There

Evtuhov's goal has been quite simply to ask what was there, rather than what was not or what went wrong. Without denying that Russia remained more dependent on its agrarian economy than its European counterparts, she proposes that agrarian reform – as well as industrial revolution – can result in intensive social change. It can result specifically in the emergence of groups of people who then work to further agricultural-industrial economic development, together. The Russian province presents one variant, one combination of factors, in a general and diverse European pattern. As such, the provincial economy builds from the ground up, with nature and community.

7.2 Ecology and Economy: Soil, Forest, River

FASHIONING THE SOIL

Local Climate to Relief

We can think of the parameters of the interaction, in the Nizhnii Novgorod region, in terms of the trinity of soil, forest and river. Thomas Kuhn has accustomed us to think of scientific revolutions in terms of a paradigm shift. Dokuchaev's revolution in soil science fits Kuhn's pattern, according to Evtuhov, nicely. *He saw soil as a natural historical body*, resulting from the collective influence of six underlying factors: the subsoil's climate, flora and fauna, geological age and the relief of the locality.

Grounded in Multiplicity and Variability

Each of the above is a *soil-fashioner, representing an endless series of degrees, variations, peculiarities, altogether related to each other.* The soil, in other words, lay at the intersection of a variety of apparently external factors; studying it seriously required bringing into play insights from minerology, geology, chemistry, physics, meteorology, biology and geography. If it is possible to speak of a specific result of this many-layered, complex approach, it would be multiplicity and variability. We now turn from soil to forest.

PRIMORDIAL, AGRICULTURAL AND INDUSTRIAL FOREST

Between Forest and Steppe

Romantic poets like to talk of primordial forests. In Eurasia natural scientists and geographers have classified five distinct natural 'belts' related to such, moving from north to south: tundra, forest, forest-steppe, steppe and desert, Nizhnii Novgorod itself falling between forest and steppe. Forests, however, are susceptible to the effects of human activity, and are amongst the earliest targets of exploitation through human society.

Diverse Forest Industries

Virtually all forms of industry in the northern districts of Nizhnii Novgorod were directly related to the forest itself. The major rivers were deep enough to be used for floating timber, which was cut down for local use and export. The rivers were also used to float tar and leather. Local kustar (peasant) craftsmen made carriages, wheels, barrels, troughs, spoons, dishes and shovels; they manufactured wood coal and turpentine. The most systematically damaging form of activity for the forest, however, was the deforestation that gave way to agriculture. We now turn from soil and forest to water.

RIVER, RAVINES AND RIVER ECONOMY

Multiple River Beds

In the local context, the Volga looked rather less like the mighty current of the song and legend, pushing forward all the way to the Caspian, and more like an enlarged version of the uncertain, meandering streams and rivers on which it depended for its sustenance.

The Volga's multiple river beds yielded a whole vocabulary of physical concepts, moreover, describing its volatility and changeability. A *zaton* was a quiet spot abandoned by the current; a *porva* was formed when the current disrupted to its old riverbed; a *volozhoc* ('little Volga') was a dead-end arm of the main river; and a *log* was a mini-lake. An *iar* was an unexpectedly steep part of the lower bank created by erosion; a *rynok* was a peninsular projection into the river. Overall then, the theme of constant flux characterizes the river environment even more than it does the soil.

Link between Europe and Asia

It was the river economy, in fact, that transcended the narrow boundaries of the province itself and transformed Niznhii Novgorod into a link between Europe and Asia. Locally, rivers were the backbone of a rich and productive fishing industry, the smaller rivers provided a local outlet for the kustar (art and craft) industry, while the appalling institution of human-powered barge hauling was a source of income for a local workforce.

Altogether the interaction between nature and economy, science and technology, was ever present.

MULTIPLICITY, CHANGEABILITY AND INFINITY IN THE NATURAL ENVIRONMENT

Man and Nature – Oikonomia, Khoziaistvo

Yet while the relatively low profile of soil and atmospheric science, in the emerging scientific revolution in Europe, had meant that Dokuchaev had not yet made it into the international canon of 'great names', as did, for example, his contemporaries Mendeleev and Pavlov, his work was part of a conceptual revolution in geographically related sciences. Such seminal work might be described as *the explosion of rigid categories and the discovery of multiplicity, changeability and infinity in the natural environment.*

In that sense his work, for Evtuhov, was both pre-modern and post-modern. Most significant, firstly as such, is the incipient picture of human interaction with the natural environment, and between economy and environment – economic life as per Russian *khoziaistvo* – that emerges. Secondly, what is fascinating for her is the harmonious balance between the very different types of grounded economic activity that defined the region. Examined in such a local context, the classic statement about Russia as above all an agrarian country, for her, loses any precision or meaning. While agriculture did predominate in the south-east corner of Nizhnii Novgorod, trade and industry – especially handicrafts – evolved naturally in the north and south-west; in fact the heavily forested northern districts had to import grain while exporting manufactured goods.

Agriculture and Industry Intertwined

Neither kustar (artisanal production) nor 'real' industry – such as the famous Sormovo shipyards, which housed some of the first workers' communities in Russia in the 1840s – can possibly be considered as 'auxiliary' to a mythically primary activity of agriculture. For many people, the high level of skill and technique required for all kinds of leather, wood and metal manufactures were the source of professional pride as well as a dominant source of income. The same of course goes for trade, whereby the Nizhnii Norvorod mercantile infrastructure was extremely sophisticated. Everything in Nizhnii was about trade, from lavish balls to Old Believer (the original Orthodoxy) icon sellers. We now turn from nature and economy, agriculture and industry, to Evtuhov's so called local economic rhythms.

7.3 Emerging out of Town and Country, Culture and Nature

MULTIPLICITY AND DIVERSITY OF ECONOMIC STRUCTURES

Intersecting Forms

The separation between city and countryside in Russia, for her, remained partial even up to the early nineteenth century. Life in Niznhii Novogrod pulsed to the rhythms of the surrounding countryside, as well as to the rhythms of commercial enterprise and those created by the religious calendar. Two points, for Evtuhov, are critical here: the multiplicity and diversity of emerging economic structures and activities on the territory of this single province, and the constant, active interchange and motion within such.

Economic historians take more or less for granted the basic distinctions between *agriculture, industry, trade and commerce. In the Russian experience,* particularly in the world of the nineteenth-century province, these manifestly different forms of activity *intersected, forming, if not a coherent unity, at least an infinitely connected continuity*. This is consistent with the nature and scope of emergence, both culturally and, in this provincial case, economically.

Types of Economic Space

Nizhnii Novgorod province straddled three types of economic space, roughly coinciding with the ecological regions outlined above. Firstly, from the south-west it bordered on the central *industrial region* that surrounded Moscow.

The thick forests beyond the Volga created a second space, where *timber and fishing* industries predominated. The south-east, thirdly, was mainly *agricultural*, a final extension of the rich black-soil belt stretching up from southern Russia.

Evtuhov now turns specifically to the issue of land, closely interconnected with the liberation of the Russian serfs in 1861.

CULTURE, AGRICULTURE AND ECONOMY

Land at the Forefront

One of the thorniest issues in the transition from a serf economy to a 'free' one is the question of land – its distribution and possible redistribution. A key distinguishing feature of the Russian reform, in the 1860s, was the decision to liberate the serfs with land; *the architects of the Russian peasant emancipation chose to place the land question at the forefront*, constructing the elaborate mechanism by means of which peasants were able to purchase the land they farmed over the course of the last half century.

Economic or Cultural

The Polish-American neo-liberal economic historian Arcadius Kahan, a follower of the Chicago School's Milton Friedman, perceived the 'essence' of the economic process over the entire 1860–1913 period in Russia as 'the growth of the market economy', through the development of an industrial sector, and a more efficient use of physical and human resources. Thus the local guidebooks in Nizhnii Novgorod reported forest products as the province's number one industry, followed by metalwork and felt manufacturing. However, as 'proto-industry' so to speak, the *factories were scattered over an extended territory and worked in small workshops rather than being clustered in a single factory.* Such 'industry', as per Kropotkin's *Fields, Factories and Workshops*, moreover, was as much an expression of local culture as of enterprise.

CULTURE AND ECONOMY IN PAVLOVO AND SORMOVA

From Dispersed Proto-Industry to Mutual Aid

The steelworks of Pavlovo and Vorsma had their own origin myth, as such, which doubles as historical mythology and as a metaphor for the structure of a dispersed 'proto-industrial' enterprise. The traditional Pavlovo structure proved remarkably resistant to change, assimilating mechanization and various efforts at factory organization while maintaining a stability of traditional forms. From 1858 to 1895, as such, 75 per cent of workers performed their tasks at home. The Pavlovo region, moreover, had an unusually well-developed network of credit institutions, and it proved a fertile field for experimentation in mutual aid, cooperative organizations, education and artisanal museums.

Sormovo, meanwhile, was a major landmark and world unto itself. The combination of mechanical, iron-smelting, shipbuilding and railroad-engineering and manufacturing employing 8,500 workers made it one of Russia's largest.

A church, a sanatorium, schools for women and men, a canteen, a Sunday school and library, and a hospital were among the services provided, funded in part by a voluntary contribution from the workers' wages. As such Nizhnii Novgorod industry found resonance in literature: Gorky's *Mother* was for Sormovo what *Sons and Lovers* became for D.H. Lawrence's home town Nottingham. We now turn to the great fair, Europe's largest at the time.

BRINGING TOGETHER EAST AND WEST

The Great Fair at Nizhnii Novgorod

The largest fair in nineteenth-century Europe, based in the province, brought together east and west: merchants from Bukhara in Uzbekistan and China rubbed shoulders with Armenian traders and central Russian textile manufacturers. Yet the fair simultaneously represented the culmination of a multitude of local and regional trade networks, and a great festival that transformed the city on the Volga and Oka for two months in the year. Markets for other products dotted the province, moreover, with each market having its particular specialization, depending on local manufacturers.

Economic and Religious Rhythms Overlapped

A merging of economy and spirituality, moreover, is inevitably the case when the church calendar is the most reliable tool for calculating the passage of time. The two major trade congresses then were timed to coincide with Epiphany and the feast of St John the Baptist, respectively. Artisans' work seasons often began and ended on religious holidays; wheel makers, for example, ended their labours on the feast of the Protection of the Mother of God, when they returned to the land.

In the provincial context, the greatest obstacle to expansion of industrial enterprise, moreover, was the absence of organized and accessible loan-granting institutions, whether banks, credit associations or mutual funds. *The Old Believer brotherhood, still basing itself on Greek orthodox traditions, oftentimes persecuted as such, rested solidly on mutual aid. This is why there were no paupers or poor peasants among them.* The religious connection functioned as financial insurance, extending not just to natural disaster but to indigence and business mishaps. We now turn to Evtuhov's artisanal case study.

7.4 Institutional Navigation: An Artisanal Case Study

THE PROVINCIAL WORLD AS HOUSEHOLD

Russian East–West Economic Variation

In a world where the spectacular successes of industry in the west provided a model for growth, Russian economic thinkers turned their attention to aspects of their own economy that might set Russia completely apart, and create a different model or fundamental 'east–west' variation on the general 'western' economic theme. The organization of the various forms of production, as such, divided into three basic categories. *Practitioners might operate entirely independently, as individuals; they may work as a household, with a division of labour among family members; and finally a few businesses were organized along industrial lines,* with, in this final instance, full-blown factories and hired workers with no stake of their own in the enterprise. All three moreover, as per Bugakov (see previous chapter), may be envisioned as variations on the theme of provincial household.

PROTO-INDUSTRIAL ECONOMIC MODELS

Mutual Aid and Mutual Interaction

Alongside all of such, was the issue of credit, which ultimately led to the formation of mutual assistance societies, much heralded by Kropotkin (see Chapters 1 and 2) of paramount importance for small-scale enterprises of Nizhnii Novgorod artisans. Such credit institutions, interestingly enough, included those formed by the Bureau for Social Welfare; a private bank formed with funds donated by a guild-merchant and a female honorary citizen. In addition, the Department of State Property sponsored 20 loan and 16 savings institutions, while the Department of Private Property Development set up rural banks in each of its seven branches; some peasant societies and already established their own financial institutions for grants, deposits, loans, aid to orphans, insurance and tax payments.

The easy and regular movement between work on the land and 'proto-industrial' manufacture, overall then, might lead us to question some of the difficulties of transition that have so attracted the interest of historians of the 'hyphenated peasants' who, toward the close of the nineteenth century, left their villages for the lure of the cities. *Might there not have been a more natural and organic link between city and countryside, one that continued the customary or traditional interaction between agricultural production and manufacture?*

To what extent then, overall, have our conventional means of categorizing rural versus urban, bourgeoisie versus peasantry, got in the way of development? Moreover, where are the economic and development models, both macro and micro that fuse the two together? We now turn from natural grounding, and then natural, cultural and economic emergence, altogether, onto institutional navigation, as we have just seen to ultimate effect: in numbers, images and biographies.

7.5 Integral Effect: Numbers, Images and Biographies

BEYOND STATISTICS

Qualitative and Quantitative Effect

The temptation is great, for Evtuhov, when speaking of 'society' or the 'social', to turn immediately to established sociological categories of class, status, profession, organization or party, peasant society, working class or bourgeoisie, and cite comparative statistics accordingly. Yet in our daily practice, we experience the 'social' by means of a more fluid and less structured apprehension, a definition of life in the world, duly aligned with Bugakov's world as household.

Knowledge from Within as well as Without

In the Nizhnii Novgorod provincial world as such, the gathering of statistical data was characterized by a number of features that, while not by any means unique in the nineteenth century, placed a distinctive mark on the materials collected. Among these Evtuhov singles out a tendency to *conflate numbers with verbal description, with the result that statistical study merged with local ethnography.* Moreover, the fact that such information was collected by a cross-section of local intelligentsia, *resulted in a 'deep-within' knowledge of things local.* Finally, what was notable was the shared passion for uncovering local conditions and history.

Vibrant Community of Exchange and Artisanal Production

Nizhnii Novgorod in fact is distinctive, in nineteenth-century Russia then, in the intensity of its commercial and enterprise. But this vibrant community of exchange and artisanal production is much more characteristic of Russia at the time than we tend to think. Certainly there can be no more dreadfully inaccurate portrayal of the country, according to Evtuhov, than as characterized exclusively by agricultural production.

Yet Marxist-Leninist historiography, with its insistence on a persistent 'feudal system', until 1861 portrayed it as such. To the extent, therefore, that the Soviet Union succumbed to Marxism in the twentieth century, so it refuted its own communal grounds, emergent culture, and resultant economy and society. Russians rather, from the medieval period onwards, were a people of trade and small-scale production. Everything, in other words, is not what it seems: *this dynamic, fluid and infinitely colourful world is the diametric opposite of the ossified and therefore ultimately conflict-ridden social universe of earlier historiographical tradition.*

BETWEEN ART AND ETHNOGRAPHY

The Art of Painting with Numbers

Provincial statistics as an end result, then, might be seen as the art of painting with numbers: from the vast production of apparently dry data emerges a vivid social and economic portrait of the province's inhabitants. If the portrait was a conscious creation of the data gatherers, Evtuhov's historical reading a century later brings out features and aspects that may or may not coincide with the concerns of the original counters.

Here is one such example.

Peasant, Scribe, Businessmen and Philosopher: Petr Bankal'skii (1832–91)

Bankal'skii was a member of the urban lower middle estate in Nizhnii Novgorod. At Prince Gruzinskii's school he finished two grades, and shone in arithmetic, before being taken out by his parents to live, as he described it, 'among the peasants' until he was seventeen. In 1849, he then struck out on his own, going off to the city to seek gainful employment. He worked at the fair and as a grocery clerk until finding his first vocation as a scribe for a local association for artisanal production, himself becoming a member, thereby leaving his peasant background behind.

Partly in response to the inexorable pressures of Russian life, and in part through his own irrepressible enthusiasm, he found himself to be a man of several trades and spheres of activity: public service, commercial enterprise and philosophy. By the late 1870s, he was to become a much-respected citizen, elected speaker of the city duma for several four-year terms. *Banka'skii was noted particularly for his defence of the poorer members of the city population and his extensive efforts to make city institutions a part of local life.*

While he was such an active citizen through his social standing by profession he was a businessman. He ultimately opened a tavern and then moved onto cafeterias on board the many ships that plied the Volga and Oka Rivers. During these busy years, Bankal'skii complained, however, that he had no time to read anything 'edifying', as he put it, to reflect on scientific matters, or to mix with educated people. In fact, by the late 1860s, success in business gave him the leisure time to do what he really wanted. He began then his third career: the pursuit of philosophical knowledge. As he himself told the story:

> *The first learned book that I came upon destroyed many of my previous opinions and I fell into doubt. Before taking leave of my previous conceptions, I turned to the Bible and particularly to the book of Genesis. In this book I saw, at first, much that was unclear and mystical, yet there was also in me the conviction that Moses, as a prophet, could not have known what science has now discovered, for even if he had been writing merely as a learned person, even then he would have had to have a definite point of view, and more so since he was writing according to inspiration from above. For this reason I sought to understand what seemed incomprehensible to me. On the other hand, each learned book showed me something I had not known, and I tried as much as I could to make sense of this too.*

Reconciling Science and Religion

His doubts and reflections ultimately led him to a reconciliation of the claims of science and religion – a position he elaborated, with a wealth of detail, in two books: *The Powers of Nature in Accordance with the Biblical Account of the Six-Day Creation* published in Moscow in 1874, and *The History of the Origins of the Heavens, the Earth and the Three Kingdom of Nature: Mineral, Plant and Animal: According to the Revelation of Holy Scripture and According to Scientific Investigations* which came out in 1889 in Nizhnii Novgorod. His cosmological system was more or less a recounting of the biblical story of Creation, weaving in, as he went, bits and pieces he picked up from Darwin, Kant, Humboldt and contemporary Russian science as well. He was particularly fascinated by key moments of transition: from the 'world ether' to its coagulation in planet earth – the creation of matter and the creation of life. When he died in 1891 his friends declared on his 'epitaph':

> *His life was one of constant labor*
> *Labor of the mind, but not a search for glory*
> *He fought and struggled for good with his mind*
> *And his labor was not empty amusement.*

For our purposes, his life story serves to illustrate that nature, culture, science and enterprise, altogether embodies in his own integral polity, so to speak, Bankal'skii was capable of straddling them all. For Gatskii, his biography as such, and that of the province, if not ultimately that of the nation at large, were potentially, if not actually, one and the same. Turning individual part into societal whole was what the pursuit of integral advantage was all about. We now turn to provincial consciousness, more generally.

PROVINTSIA: PROVINCIAL CONSCIOUSNESS IN EFFECT

Diversity, Variability and Mutability

How might we draw up the balance of this excursion into the social world of the nineteenth-century province? The picture that emerges from evocations through numbers, images and biographies confirms Evtuhov's general theme of diversity, variability and mutability through time and space. Yet, at the same time, we can note a remarkable convergence of all three methods – statistical, photographic and biographical – representing a particular social stratum that figures prominently in provincial consciousness.

Middle-Up-Down Across

Indeed, it coincides remarkably with the stratum that Gatsiskii identified as provintsia – those individuals who were neither aristocrats nor peasants but somewhere in between and who made up the backbone of local society. Through the statisticians' number we see the significance of the artisans both in the towns and the countryside; the tendency to small and middling landholding on the one hand, and an industrial and commercial middle on the other; the difficulty of drawing a direct link between industrial activity and urban centres; and an ethnic diversity, in one of the central Russian provinces, that belies the apparent simplicity of statistical categories.

We now turn to local administration, generally, and to the 'zemtsvo' specifically, for us a form of 'integral polity' at a provincial level, serving thereby to align nature and culture, society and economy.

7.6 Managing the Province: Integration through Zemstvo

ZEMLIA: ORIGINATING LOCALLY FROM THE LAND

A Unique Territorial Assembly

A half century after the French social philosopher de Tocqueville's travels in the United States of America, whereafter he popularized the notions of civil society and civic association, the Spanish writer Dona Emilia Pardo Baza (4), famous for her introduction of the Russian novel into the Spanish-speaking world, waxed eloquent on the subject of Russian provincial government

> *Among modern institutions, particularly worthy of attention is the 'zemstvo' or territorial assembly. Analogous to our Provincial Councils, but of a more liberal nature and a healthily decentralizing spirit. All classes have a seat in the assembly. What effect would it produce in one of our provincial councils to see, alongside the frock coats and topcoats, the jacket with engraved silver buttons of an honest peasant? In Russia the emancipated serf debates together with his ex-lord. The format of this sort of local parliament is democratic in the extreme: the cities, the laboring class and the and the landowners elect the representatives, and the assembly devotes itself to the modest but most interesting practical questions of hygiene, health, security, and public education.*

National Enlightenment

Pardo Bazan had never set foot in Russia, deriving her knowledge from knowledgeable colleagues and from Russian literature. Still she put her finger on those features of the Russian 'zemstvo' that made it a unique institution in nineteenth-century Europe. More specifically, she noted, *an entire network of zemstvo-run schools was created under the jurisdiction of the Ministry of National Enlightenment, whose function was to teach basic literacy to the children of the newly free peasants.* The zemstvos also established what was virtually a socialized health care system, with the character of the rural physician becoming a major new figure in the post-emancipation countryside – and in Russian literature as well.

Zemlia – Originating from the Land

The new political institution, moreover, by no means began its existence in a vacuum, becoming immediately inscribed in a web of cultural references and inheritances. The very term, *zemstvo,* had a deep resonance for contemporaries. The term comes from *zemlia* – the land. More importantly the word had an archaic sound and evoked images of a sixteenth and seventeenth-century Muscovite political structure, in which representatives from the land had gathered periodically in a *zemskii sobor* (council of the land) that advised the tsar. The zemstvo's inheritance from the past, in fact, had another dimension: its meetings took place in the quarters of the old Gentry Assembly, thus underscoring the replacement of estate based institutions by a more broadly rounded, multistate body.

In fact, at a time when European countries were just beginning to develop welfare legislation, in the latter part of the nineteenth century, the Niznhii Novgorod zemstvo presents a unique example of local management of social needs. We now turn from provincial administration to culture.

Concept of a Cultural 'Nest'

For Russian nineteenth-century linguist Vladmir Dal, a regional culture, or 'cultural nest' may be comprised of a well-tended high school or seminary with gifted teachers, a wealthy public library, a public lecture series in a local university, energetic self-educational circles, the activity of a local scientific society, or indeed their mutual interrelations. Thus the 'nests' that he urged his students to investigate included *education, the press, theatre, art, as well as socio-economic phenomena.*

Creating a Local Intelligentsia

In fact one of the key moments in Nizhnii's cultural and intellectual life took place outside the city and even the province, with the founding of Kazan University in 1810, providing a regional centripetal focus and helping to create a local intelligentsia. The Niznhii Novogrod gymnasium moreover, founded, at a secondary level, included instruction in religious instruction, Russian literature, history, geography, maths, physics, natural science, law and languages. It ultimately offered courses, also, in business and accounting. Such educational institutions were often closely associated with prominent publications.

A Local Voice should Play its Part in the World of Ideas

The Petersburg publicist Mordovstev (1830–1905) thereby sympathized with their goals, that provinces, like capitals and major cities, whereby they should *speak their own independent language, make their voices heard in the general forum of the human world, and that this voice should play a significant part in the world of ideas*. At the same time he lamented the fact that the centres tended to eclipse these peripheries.

Gatsikii moreover, as we have seen, made the case for decentralization, whereby the provincial life and energy should proliferate alongside that of the capital cities. *True progress consisted in the infinitely broad dispersal and dissemination of knowledge and intellect, not just concentrated in the 'one', but spread among the 'many'.* The intelligentsia in the capitals, he said moreover, hung up on reaching and communicating with the peasants, whereas they should be focusing on the provinces, the 'middling' population of Russia's regional centres and zemstvos that were becoming the backbone of Russian society. To the extent that they failed to do so, they inhibited the middle-up-down-across knowledge and value-creating process to which we have alluded (see Chapter 3). We now turn to literature and music.

A Cultural Milieu for the Development and Reception of Scientific Ideas

The harvest, sowing, productivity, prices, as well as, speaking more broadly, health and prosperity, are ultimately contingent on meteorological conditions. On the local level, in Niznhii Novgorod, the weather-forecasting infrastructure was provided by the Astronomy Circle and the Zemstvo Agricultural Museum. Observation of the heavens was another, related provincial passion. The Circle of Amateurs of Physics and Astronomy was founded in 1888 and flourished until the First World War. Like the Lunar Society (1765–1813) in Birmingham a century earlier, the above Circle provided a cultural milieu for the development and reception of scientific ideas.

Provincial Culture – Creation of a Local Consciousness

Commemoration and historical consciousness became transformed into a collective task with the creation of the provincial archival commissions, established by decree from the central government in 1883. The commission's primary aims were preservation and research. In keeping with prevailing trends, local ethnography and archaeology were a dominant concern. Local history, moreover, figured prominently in the commission's activities, the more recent such history, the greater the interest in individual personalities, as a continuation of Gatsiskii's biographical principle.

If one were to speak of a 'provincial culture' distinct from that of the capitals, one of the key loci for its emergence was the museum. *For residents of provincial Russia, the notion of museum evoked not so much an art collection as an assemblage of historical, ethnographic and natural-scientific artifacts.* One of the first natural-historical museums was founded in Niznhii Novgorod in 1888 by soil scientist Dokuchaev, to whom we referred to above; its aim was not only to display soil types, meteorological tables and examples of handicrafts but also the education of visitors. Eventually *a network of such museums became a means for the dissemination of information and the creation of a local consciousness throughout Russia.* Eventually the museum would unify different branches of scientific investigation, including the social sciences – economy, ethnography, history. This brings us back full circle to the 'philosophy of the common task'.

Philosophy of the Common Task

For Federov, who worked as a teacher of history and geography in a string of provincial towns for 14 years before becoming a librarian of the Rumiantsev Museum in Moscow in 1874, through his 'philosophy of the common task':

> *Knowledge must be proved not only through small scale experiments, conducted by a special estate of scientists in physical offices and laboratories, city-style, but knowledge must also be proved country-style, through experiments on natural scale, through the transformation of the earth form a self-propelling elemental force into an earth mover propelled by the entire human race as navigator.*

Provincial scientific societies and their communications with each other become sanctified, thereby, as liturgy, as an impassioned quest to transform nature from a temporary enemy into a permanent friend. Fedorov's larger project, entailing the ultimate resurrection of past generations as a substitute for procreation, drew profoundly on his deep knowledge of provincial life and culture.

And so we turn, ultimately via the provincial zemstvo, from nature and culture, science and society, to politics and economics.

LOCAL VISION – GLOBAL STRUCTURE

Province as Intermediary

For nearly half a century, Evtuhov concludes, historians, sociologists and political scientists have sought to work out the relationship of state versus society, of policy implemented 'from above', as opposed to grass-roots initiative 'from below'. She has suggested, in that respect, that, in Russian provinces (and in Niznhii Novgorod in particular), in the nineteenth century, *the process of governance was characterized at every level by a more or less productive interaction of central initiative and local response* – or, more precisely, of centrally designed structures and the articulation, within the framework established by these structures, of local visions.

Khoziaistvo:The Rise and fall of the Provincial Economic Household

The primary such illustration of such, overall, was in the management of the local economy, or *khoziaistvo.* The provincial 'household' (individual and communal) became invested with symbolic value, as an expression of a political or quasi-political vision. However, such a local-central (periphery-core) consensus tended to collapse by the 1890s because the zemstvo's visionary capacity had far outreached the functioning of the state.

The Local and National Political Rhythm

Politics meanwhile functioned at four levels, local, local-national, national and national-local:

- *local institutions* proper, of which the statistical committees of the town dumas, and the provincial and district zemstvos were prime examples;

- *mediators*, the agents for special commissions, who at critical junctures could play a defining local–global role;
- immediate representation of imperial power in the institution of *governorship;*
- and finally, *corporate and civic* organizations.

On all levels, we can note an interactive, cooperative exchange between the state and the institutions and the individuals on which it of necessity depended to make its policies work. The interchange might take the form of 'zealous service' by individuals or the consensual creation of common spaces where local institutions might implement policy.

The mechanism of government can be schematized in terms of central (largely contentless) initiative prompting avid local responses and the local elaboration of the actual mechanisms to bring the initiative to fruition. A process of give and take then follows, in which local visions frequently transgress the boundaries acceptable to the central state; more initiatives follow to curb such, and so on. If the enthusiasm of the local actors outgrows the central framework, a social movement might be born. We now turn finally to *The Idea of Province* including the locally self-governing zemstvo contained within it.

7.7 Conclusion: The Idea of Province

PROVINCE AS BIOGRAPHY: GATSISKII

Province as Total Biography

The central, and most self-conscious figure in this process of self-definition, of 'the idea of the province' embodied in Niznhii Novgorod was *Alexsandr Gatsiskii: organizing statistical investigations of artisanal production, publishing guidebooks and local histories, promoting the provincial press, and proposing the principle of a 'province as a total biography'.* Moments of inspiration and glimpses of the transformative potential of this daily labour formed an integral part of provincial consciousness.

Gatsiskii's future was in fact determined by the timing of his return to Nizhnii Nogorod: the fateful year of 1861, when, as he put it, 'the era of liberation moved certain people to the forefront. *At a time of spiritual uplift, of general energy, strength, and hope, everyone who feels God's spark in him abandons his reluctantly inhabited hole and gives himself, so far as his strengths and talents allow, to the common enthusiasm'*. Gatsiskii immediately decided to devote the whole of his energies to the new challenges facing the Russian provinces.

Passion for Enlivenment

His true passion lay in enlivening the local newspaper. He socialized with well-known writers, drafted projects for a charitable and legal society, headed the district school council, was elected to the Imperial Geographical Society, travelled to the ethnographic exhibition in Moscow (1867), as well as defending the needy in court cases, becoming an honourable member of the Nizhnii Novgorod All Estate Club (participated under its auspices in organizing a cooperative society), participating in the first Russian Archaeological Congress, being invited to join the Nizhnii Novgorod Club for the encouragement of commerce and attending the Eighth International Statistical Congress in St Petersburg (1872). When it became clear that the government apparatus was no longer a comfortable home, someone like Gatsiskii could now take refuge in the zemstvo – being elected as a delegate in 1877 and become head in 1878–80.

Love, Unity and Agreement

Gatsiskii then, while a patriot of Niznhii Novgorod, was an even greater proponent of a more general idea of 'province'; *provintsiia* had a good deal to contribute to, and to counterpose, that centralized culture that laid monopolistic claims to represent culture as a whole. The 'provincial idea' of the 1880s was a secularization of Shchapov's – the Russian historian and activist – regional coexistence and interaction in 'love, unity and agreement'.

PROVINCE AS LOCAL ECONOMY

Multiplicity and Variety

One of Gatsiskii's main points, then, had been that *provintsia* really exists. Evtuhov thereby cites, as general characteristics of Russian development in the second half of the nineteenth century, the growth and expansion of cities, the development of a commercial culture based on retail trade and exchange of services, the emergence of a variety of clubs and organizations, the richness of provincial theatre and the multiplicity of local journals and newspapers, or the appearance of national journals that catered for 'middling' tastes in the city and countryside.

In Niznhii Novgorod local specifics included the influence of wealthy and respected merchants and, in a province with a particular intensity of religious life, a greater than usual social activism on the part of local clergy.

Economy as Household

For Evtuhov moreover, a more useful philosophical notion for conceptualizing the dynamic commercial and cultural world of the Russian provinces belongs to the philosopher Bulgakov (see previous chapter) who, in his 1912 book, *Philosophy of Economy,* proposed that we see the world as household or as economy. Bulgakov spoke of *khoziaistvo* as 'the struggle of humanity with the elemental forces of nature with the aim of protecting and widening life, transforming it into a potential human organism'.

Economy *(oikonomia)* was conceived as the working, interactive relation of man and nature. For Bulkagov as we have seen, the essential economic functions were production and consumption: if, on the one hand, humanity, as the transcendental collective subject of economy, consumes nature – the object – by eating it, then it also, through labour, on the other hand, humanizes and revives an inert natural landscape. *The economic process itself – inspired by Sophia, the Divine Wisdom – becomes the creative essence of human existence. Science has a particular role in this process, as the contemplative moment to guide action.* Using this notion, Evtuhov proposes we can look at the province as a household or local economy. At roughly the same time as Bismarck's famous (or infamous) state-implemented social insurance scheme, the Russian zemstvos were, in rather more improvised fashion, beginning to provide medical services, working to control cholera and syphilis epidemics, constructing elaborate plans for fire insurance, establishing pension plans, trying to conserve forests, and coping with emergencies of various sorts.

Khoziaistvo: Locally Anchored Economy

Bulkakov's concept helps to formulate an essential principle of provincial life, namely *the intrinsic power of economic life, at a local level, as politics.* The provincial mode of existence in the second half of the nineteenth century (that is after emancipation) involved the formulation of concrete visions – of *credit institutions, a national income tax, plans for railways, organizations of museums,* and so forth – and their articulation and discussion at zemstvo meetings. And indeed, congresses, meetings and umbrella organizations mushroomed in the final third of the nineteenth century. Physicians, lawyers, statisticians, and agronomists sought larger forums for mutual consultation. The Free

Economic Society, the Russian technical Society, the Geographical Society, the World Fir, all played their role.

What is useful about the *khoziaistvo* concept is that it helps us see how deeply anchored these organizations and congresses were in the intimate details of local problems and issues, also explicitly incorporating science.

Shifting Boundaries – Local to Global

The provincial idea, meanwhile, was about local personalities like Gatsiskii, about life stories that began and ended at a local level, and that do not fit comfortably with standard notions of a privileged elite, on the one hand, and an impoverished peasantry, on the other. *The 'provincial idea' was about a common task and a common self-consciousness, about an enthusiastic effort to manage the local economy, to provide social insurance, medicine, sanitation, education and culture that previously had been the domain of landlords.* The landlord was replaced by the club, the zemstvo, the scientific society and so forth. *Provinstia* as such had shifting boundaries, sometimes coinciding with a local administrative unit, sometimes covering a geographical region, like Nizhnii Nogorod, and sometimes referring even to a larger spiritual entity that united people from all over Russia.

Challenging Marxist-Leninist Assumptions

Yet 'province', for Evtuhov, has even another value. The peculiarities of a location, or lived space, are always of interest to its inhabitants. It is possible to become fascinated by intrinsic details of topographical layout, domestic architecture, the ebb and flow of streams, a neighbour's family dramas and issues of school reform. 'Local colour' is a constant in human existence. In the twentieth century, then, *the universalizing model of Marxism-Leninism eclipsed or even obliterated local and regional factors. A provincial vantage point, then, fundamentally challenges such economic, political and cultural assumptions.*

Twenty years ago Russia would have been described, in the nineteenth century, as predominantly agrarian, with the countryside dominate by landlords and peasants. What we have seen here, in Niznhii Novogrod is quite different. How then was Russia governed? Again, not so long ago, the answer would have been presented with great clarity: the Russian Empire was highly centralized, verging on the despotic, with a total absence of democratic institutions. What Evtuhov has presented is much more varied, sometimes quite the opposite, in many cases combining local initiative with 'high science'.

Her hope is that once we study Russia in this way, we might put the constituent parts back together in a new way. They will ultimately result in a picture of Russia far different from the one we are accustomed to seeing through a centralized, horizontally oriented historiography. In this sense her work is a beginning rather than an end. May such an end then be a very different one from the one we are seeing in Russia March, 2015) today, not least because of the way it has been consistently misrepresented, in the twentieth and twenty-first centuries, both within and without.

We now turn, in the next four chapters, to South Africa, thereby turning from 'east–west' to 'north–south'.

Bibliography

1. Jakim, B. and Bird, R. (1998) *On Spiritual Unity: A Slavophile Reader.* Hodson, NY, Lindisfarne Books.
2. Lessem, R., Abouliesh, I., Pogacnik, M. and Herman, L. (2014) *Integral Polity: Aligning Nature, Culture, Society and Economy.* Farnham, Gower.
3. Evtuhov, C. (2011) *Portrait of a Russian Province: Economy, Society and Civilization in Nineteenth Century Nizhnii Novgorod.* Pittsburg, Pittsburg University Press.
4. Valliere, P. (2001) *Modern Russian Theology: Bukharev, Soloviev, Bulgakov.* Grand Rapids, MI, William Eerdmans Publishing.

PART III

North–South African Integral Perspective

Chapter 8

Wild Law to Earth Jurisprudence: Grounding Southern Africa in Local Nature and Community

> *Magqubu Ntombela was always involved in the natural world. He had really known no other and so had become part of it and in constant harmony with the ebb and flow of the days and the seasons. When the hyena called beyond the fire Magqubu would answer, as it was for the lion, the zebra, the rhino and the wildebeest. It was the same with the trees: each one was different and alive, and for him an extension of ourselves. He talked with the waving themeda grass or the bateleur eagle, the vulture, or the Natal robin singing form a quiet kloof (valley). There was a constant dialogue with the wild world.*
>
> *Ian Player (1),* Zululand Wilderness, Shadow and Soul

8.1 Introduction

DARK EYE, ECOLOGICAL INTELLIGENCE, WILD LAW

South African 'North–South' Icon

In our journey 'east–west', across Russian Eurasia, we traversed the spiritual and the material, from Russian Orthodoxy to secular Marxism, from Slavophile to 'Westernizer', from Bulgakov if you like, as an 'eastern' philosophy of economy, to Marxist-Leninism, if not also economic liberalism. Counteracting rather then reinforcing that east–west perspective then, communism and capitalism sit on the same side of the 'western' fence, albeit the one (liberalism) being arguably western-northern and the other (socialism) northern-western.

Navigation
Science and Society
Ubuntu : Truth and Reconciliation

Effect
Public, Private
Civic Enterprise
Value Sharing

Emergence
Culture and
Consciousness
Future Primal

Grounding
Nature and Community
Wild Law/Earth Jurisprudence

Figure 8.1 Wild law to value sharing

It is very different when we journey fully 'north–south', as we shall now see. For one thing there are no such explicit political and economic systems on which to draw. *While the 'north's' strength is rationalist philosophy and the 'south's', albeit much less commonly recognized until of late, is a more humanistic orientation, the latter is all too often disguised* by the repressive political regimes that we have associated with much of Africa and South America.

Wild Law to Value Sharing

However, our focus at this second, pivotal point, is not on the 'south' per se, but on 'north–south' for which we turn to South Africa. In fact, like Russia, which has exerted great influence on the world for good and for ill, in modern times, the same applies respectively to 'apartheid' and 'post-independent' South Africa. In fact, *probably the most iconic figure of the second half of the twentieth century, Nelson Mandela, came from South Africa.*

In this chapter then, on South Africa's *Grounding*, we start out by engaging naturally and communally with Ian Player's *Zululand Wilderness, Shadow and Soul* (see Figure 8.1 and quotation above), Afrikaaner Laurens van der Post's *Dark Eye of Africa*, historically, Ian McCallum's *Ecological Intelligence* as well as ultimately Cormac Cullinan's *Wild Law-and-Earth Jurisprudence* currently. All modern day 'bushmen' as it were, before emerging, culturally and spiritually, with South African-Hawaian political scientist, Louis Herman's *Future Primal.* Our next, and most prominent port of call, by way of socio-political *navigation* is Mandela's and Tutu's *Truth and Reconciliation.* Finally, enterprise-wise, we turn to Anton Rupert's approach to *Co-existence* (Rupert was a soul mate of Ian Player's through their conservation activities) and more specifically to Koopman's Cashbuild, to the *value sharing* that he brought to prominence in the 1990s.

LEFT IN THE NIGHT OF THE HUMAN SPIRIT

Indigenous World

Laurens van der Post was an Afrikaans explorer, adventurer, writer and philosopher, in the latter half of the twentieth century, who seemed to have a particular affinity for the indigenous people of his land. For him, in fact, the White man ('northern') had discredited the Black man's ('southern') way of living, and of dealing with the forces of nature about and within. Then he had obliged him increasingly to live in a way that forced him to reject the institutions, customs, initiation rites and rituals whereby for centuries he had struck a balance between those overwhelming aspects of nature that were incomprehensible to reason. Having discredited this ancient or indigenous way of living the White man had not yet put an honourable alternative in its place. For Van der Post (2) then:

> *No human being or society, however self-sufficient or rational it may appear to be, can live without these institutions which deal with those aspects of life which cannot be explained rationally. No group of human beings can be left indefinitely outside in the night of the human spirit, in the beast infected jungle which lies beyond the conscious fortifications which civilized culture raises for us in life'.*

Identified with the Bushman

Laurens was born in South Africa in 1906, to an Africaans family living out in the bush veld. Most of his adult life had been spent with one foot in southern Africa and the other in Europe and Asia. His independent expedition to the Kalahari Desert in search of the Bushman was the subject of a famous documentary film:

> *My own story began with the Bushman stories. I had a nurse, Klara, who was a Bushman woman, a Stone Age person. Hers was the first human face I can remember. I looked into her eyes and it was always as if I looked at the first dawn of the first day. It was one of the dearest faces. Even as I talk about it I am filled with the most incredible emotion. (Van der Post)*

8.2 The Story of Our Time

DECODING STORIES

We now turn to 'the story of our time' courtesy of Van der Post. People, he complained, always laughed at Bushman stories and said they had no meaning. They had no meaning, he argued, because we onlookers had lost the key and the code. We had lost the meaning of their indigenous stories. So he started in 1952 to decode them. This was after he had returned to Africa, war shattered, at a time when he was beginning his life again:

> *My story was moving into a new phase, and I had to begin it again. And it almost seems to me as if in this there's a parable for all of us. All of us who are discouraged, who sit back and say what's the point of trying, well this is heresy to me, because the story is timeless. Life is timeless. If we play our role in it we redeem it from time.*

EVERYTHING IN LIFE IS A STORY

The Significance of Myth

For Van der Post, then, *everything in life is a story. The story of mankind, then, is history, and without history we have no meaning.* Both, moreover, are part of the same indivisible process for which Laurens had such a passion. Stories provide us with our sense of wonder. They provide us with the sense of living mystery in life. They help us to heighten our sensitivities, our perceptions, our awareness.

The story presents the options and possibilities of life that might have been and still can be lived. Van der Post's great mentor, the Swiss psychoanalyst Carl Jung (3), whom we introduced in Chapter 3, said that in every disturbance of personality one could discern the elements of a personal story. And the person could only be healed by our getting hold of the story. That *story is the personality's most precious possession, the secret key to unlock the door which barred reality in all its dimensions both within and without from entering the personality and transforming it.*

Departure and Return

There are moments, moreover, of individual and national crisis where the past is not an inevitability, but presents life with the opportunity of a creative course of new action. For example, for Van der Post, with a story you go on a journey in space and time, in life and creation, always travelling. *The deepest of all the patterns in the human spirit, in fact, is that of departure and return, and the journey implicit in between*. The life of man is the journey, a voyage such as that of Odysseus, the wanderings of the Israelites from bondage in Egypt in search of the promised land, the strange walkabouts of the aborigines in the never-never of Australia, and of the stone-age people in the vast wasteland of southern Africa. The same pattern leads to the Tao of China, and the one and only way of Confucius, and the New Testament parable of the Prodigal Son.

> *Man's supreme task in achieving wholeness was twofold: to resolve the imbalance in the spirit of man not only between the superior and suppressed functions but also across the great divide of the introvert and extravert. This represents an exhortation to all men and women to realize how important it is to work towards raising what was dark and inferior within oneself to the same honourable state as what was light and superior without any sacrifice to the illuminated values.*

The most difficult points of dialogue to establish bridges across are those which separate our four worlds, most particularly those straddling north–south. This brings us to Van der Post's *Dark Eye of Africa.*

8.3 *The Dark Eye of Africa*

EUROPE AND AFRICA

Excessive European Rationalism

For Van der Post, nothing describes the origin of things more authoritatively and movingly than the description of genesis in the Bible. First there is the spirit moving ceaselessly over the great and formless waters of time in search of flesh and blood to give it life and reality. Then comes the word:

> *I feel that before a new spirit can come to painful birth in this painful terrible conflict in Africa and find true and just expression in a new form of society and human reality, there has first to be a new form of society and human reality, there has first to be communication, the word, to give it form and expression.*

The human spirit, then, is being served by words, ideas, and world-concepts that have become totally inadequate for the meaning which it is trying to express and the being which it is trying to create. It is the *excessive 'northern' rationalism and the fanatic adherence of 'western' man to outer physical reality,* Van der Post argues, *together with his over-valuation of the demonstrable objective world around him which is the cause of much of his undoing.*

We Deny Africa its own Unique Creativeness

There are all manner of invisible and imponderable values which the European has neglected in his own life and therefore ignores in the lives of those in his power, or those with whom he is thrown into contact, and those factors sooner or later combine in rebellion against him. The explosions which are blowing European man out of so many parts of the world and which are making so many so-called inferior, less cultured and less civilized nations increasingly mistrustful of him, are caused largely by neglect of these great imponderables in himself, and therefore inevitably in others. *We force the African continually to take from us and prevent him from giving to us in his own rich way. We deny Africa its own unique creativeness* (the same could indeed be said for Russia) *and then the whole world faces the consequences.* That leads to ongoing African, and Russian-Ukrainian, unrest.

THE BLUEPRINT OF MISUNDERSTOOD TIME

Cosmic Reality

As Van der Post sees it, then, there are four dimensions, four levels of reality, wherein African unrest is germinated. *First* of all there is the *cosmic,* universal dimension, also identified by the Russian *Cosmists,* albeit for them Africa is a distant land. For most of us Time is only a 'when', a linear current measured by ticking of clocks over which it flows like water over a wheel, a measure completely at our disposal over which we make dates and keep our business appointments. We are so caught up in this linear movement that we never stop to consider that Time may also have a content and a nature, a specific meaning of its own which makes it not merely a 'when' but also a 'what' and perhaps, more importantly still, also a 'how' and a 'way' to eternity.

> *I suggest therefore that incorporated somewhere in the inner patterns of misunderstood time there exists a blueprint from the master architect of life itself, a chart of the ultimate design of being which ceaselessly communicates to us our own unique share in Time's fashioning. Or, if you like a more modern comparison, I believe there exists a kind of radar which, if we are properly tuned in, can bring us to our appropriate*

> *landing ground through the thickest fogs and darknesses of existence. The moment we neglect to fly by this radar, then increasingly panicky unrest invades our aboriginal hearts and minds and infests our behavior, institutions and societies like a new black plague.*

Van der Post is therefore convinced that in the first place the unrest in Africa is part of an infinitely wide disquiet about the current trend of our life in this earth. On that level the unrest in Africa is universal unrest.

Global Reality

The second level is global as opposed to cosmic. Van der Post views this global conflict as a struggle between the haves and the have-nots, between under-dog and top-dog, between under-culture and top-culture, which we would call a 'western' reality, as per the overall impact of 'globalization'. In that dimension the unrest in Africa is part of a world unrest.

European Reality

The third dimension is on a European level. Two complementary partners vie with each other, the one wanting to conserve and contain, the other wanting to break out and change, a classic and a romantic urge. It is significant in the main that the Conservative tends to side automatically with the white man in Africa, while the Socialist tends to identify with the black man. The fourth dimension is peculiarly African.

The Fourth 'Primeval' Dimension

In Africa specifically, and the 'south' generally, there are still primeval territories, scenes of unexploited mountain and lake, river, plain and forest, and patterns of vivid animal life that you can see nowhere else in the world. The bushman makes gods of all the animals that surround him; the Hottentots kneel to an insect, the praying mantis; the Bantu listens to the spirits of his ancestors in the roar of the lion and in the noise of his cattle stirring. Then suddenly European man burst upon he scene, from the 'north'. A long period of pure reason which began with the Reformation and had been stimulated by the French Revolution was deeply at work in the European spirit, setting him at variance with his intuitions and instincts.

European man walked into Africa by and large totally incapable of understanding Africa, let alone of appreciating the raw material of mind and spirit with which this granary of fate, this ancient treasure house of the lost original way of life, was so richly filled. He had, it is true, an insatiable appetite for the riches in the rocks, diamonds and gold, but not for the precious metal ringing true in the deep toned laughter of the indigenous people around him.

SOCIETAL REBIRTH AND AWAKENING

No group of human beings, for Van der Post, can be left indefinitely outside in the night of the human spirit, in the beast-infected jungle which lies beyond the conscious fortifications which civilized culture raises for us in life. If a community cannot get within the protection of these fortifications by fair means it will do it by foul. If civilized reason and conscious strength will not aid it, then animal cunning and brute force will. If it cannot learn the discipline of proportion freely from within, he maintains, it has to learn it from disaster without.

Now in a deep sense every man has two profound sides to his being, a child of darkness who is equal and complementary to the more obvious child of light. Whether we know it or not we all have within us a natural and instinctive man, a dark brother, to whom we are irrevocably joined as to our shadow. Now the white man of Africa sees reflected in the natural dark man around him that dark aspect of himself that he has rejected. The black man is therefore condemned to play that part which the increasingly exacting projection of the white man expects of him. He is therefore prevented from being himself and from living out his own unique being.

The whole problem of modern culture, as seen from a north–south perspective, expresses the need for some transcendent factor or purpose wherein neither white nor black, neither natural – nor 'wild' as we shall see – nor thinking man, will have to be sacrificed to one another. Instead both will be joined and made complete in one transcending purpose. After all, the two opposites of electricity need no longer be expressed through the bright and dangerous medium of lightning but can now be transformed and resolved together into a source of creative energy.

AFRICAN MICROCOSM – GLOBAL MACROCOSM

Van der Post in fact maintains that the unrest in Africa in all its facets – European, cosmic, global and African – is plainly an extension of our own individual interest. *Modern man with his grievous and crippling realization of having lost the sense of his own beginnings, with this agonizing feeling of great and growing estrangement from nature, and from the wild, finds that life holds up Africa like a magic mirror* miraculously preserved before his darkening eyes. In this great glass of time the innermost reflections of this ancient, timeless spirit stare out at him, and he can, could he but realize it, rediscover therein his despised and rejected natural self.

I believe the greatest of all mirrors of our age is Africa. We all, east and west, north and south and bewildered twentieth (and twenty-first) century man, stare into it as if hypnotized, but we do not see and recognize in it the reflection of our own hidden selves. Nevertheless the interest of the world is compelled by events in Africa because, unconsciously, the world apprehends that Africa may know the secret of its own lost and hidden being. Without this miraculously preserved Africa, without this land and its allegiance to the original meaning and charter of life, this timely reflection may not be possible.

We need a sense of wonder for it is part of our wholeness and keeps us humble. One of the more harmful by-products of the excessively one-sided scientific concentration of the past centuries, Van der Post maintains, has been the tendency to eliminate the sense of the mystery of life in men and to depreciate any feelings which lie outside the range of our conscious awareness. The process too was made easier as European civilization became more and more a metropolitan culture and man's conquests in the physical world increased the distance between man and nature. So man's natural contacts with the great mysteries became more remote. Africans so far have not lost contact with that great mystery, and its influence on their make-up is immense. For the African in his archaic way can experience their full blast of the ancient spirit of man to the full. Indeed each nation, for him, travels, consciously or otherwise, on a mythological journey.

THE MYTHOLOGICAL JOURNEY

Tell me then, Van der Post goes on to say, what is the myth within history that is seeking to express itself through the life of a nation and I'll tell you what that nation is and may become. To this day, for him, Africa is largely an Old Testament land, which still needs temples and prophets and a David (Mandela for example) for Goliath far more than it needs parliaments, politicians and trade unions (though for us it needs those too!). The particular myth of Van der Post's Afrikaaner countrymen presupposed a great trek through a great unknown wilderness, alias 'wild law' as we shall see, to a land of promise. It was a necessary and inevitable phase in the development of their myth.

No living myth can be pinned down to one particular phase of its inherent development or to one consciously selected and favoured aspect of itself. It too is a moving finger that writes and has written moves on. If we deny it its onward movement it will go back and re-write the lesson on the rough blackboard of life with some extra lines on disaster thrown in after school hours. It works in this way because it contains the rounded vision of life without bias, fear or favour for any of its parts.

One time-honoured myth is that in which man is chosen and called upon to perform a perilous journey. The journey itself is not a mere changing of place, an exchange of geographical locations but a change of being, a becoming. The task involves travelling from the familiar being man receives from his parents to the distant being he has neither known nor seen in this other invisible dimension of the spirit. The golden fleece, the promised land on the other side of the great desert, are both symbols of the brave new being with which the journeyman who has travelled the whole way with his myth is rewarded. Writing in the mid 1950s Van der Post called upon his countrymen to move out of the physical plane of their journey and to carry it onto the mind and the spirit.

Seemingly F.W. De Klerk, almost 40 years after Van der Post wrote his book, responded to the call. The Africaaners were called upon by their visionary countryman:

> *to free themselves from the Egypt of their worldly senses, from captivity in the Babylon of their outer histories, and to carry the myth forward into a realm where race and physical being have no automatic privileged meaning, but where kinship is determined by the deeper and abiding considerations of life, for all those who, whatever their color of race, have answered the ancient challenge and have committed themselves to the journey of becoming.*

This is exactly what the New Testament did to the Old. It freed the Hebraic myth from racial bondage as the Israelites were released from Egypt, destroyed its limited meaning and carried it forward into a wider non-racial validity. It opened thereby a whole new continent to the spirit of man and discovered a far greater new world than ever did Columbus or any of the sailors of the seven seas.

MAKING YOUR BEING OF YOUR TIME

It seems that it is not enough, Van der Post maintains, that a man should be born in his time. His mature, Odyssian task is to make his being of his time. Most of us are of our time only in a technical sense; we use it rather than express it. The time of day and inner time are often eras apart. Twentieth-century man in one profound sense has not yet been born. We have seen in our age a worldwide revolt against the vested economic interests and privileges derived from the discarded past. What still we have not realized is that there are vested interests of the mind and spirit, tyrannies and despotic tracts of knowledge and history that hem us in and stand between us and our twentieth-century experience and meaning.

We are like a profoundly preoccupied person limping painfully along the highway of being, not noticing that he has his bread-and-butter foot on the A.D. pavement while his other, mythological foot, still drags in some B.C. gutter. Few individuals and few nations are capable of being their time on both dimensions. Very few of us can accept the demands and necessities of our age as a problem of the unrealized being within ourselves. There is in most of us a dark gap between what we are and what we are challenged to be and only the myth, like a bloodhound on our trail, to drive us into bridging the distance.(4)

We now turn from Africa's 'dark eye' to ecological intelligence, so called, before ending this chapter with 'wild law' and 'earth jurisprudence', constitution or ultimate grounding, in this 'north–south' case.

8.4 Ecological Intelligence

REDISCOVERING OURSELVES IN NATURE

Remember Where We Have Come From

Ian McCallum (5), South African sportsman, psychiatrist, therapist and wildlife guide, believes, as does Van der Post (though McCallum was writing 50 years later), that *our identity is ultimately associated with a deep historical sense of continuity with wild places and the animals that live there – that we have an ancient, genetic memory of where we have come from*. These are the places that permit us to say 'it is as if this place is in my blood, it is as if I have come home'. The cure for home sickness, then, is to remember where we have come from. It is to rediscover that original church within oneself and to remember that the wild areas of the world are the landscapes of the soul and that the creatures who belong there are soul-makers.

We readily speak of the spirit of adventure and the spirit of science, of soul mates, soul places and the dark night of the soul. The words are at the tip of our tongues. They are intrinsic to our descriptions of kinship, belonging, connection and continuity. And we know what they mean, even if we cannot fully explain them. They may well be linked to neuro-circuits, neuro-transmitters and circulating hormones, but how they are linked we will probably never know. It would seem they cannot be measured. Does that make them any less real? McCallum thinks not.

ZIZIPHUS MUCRONATA. THE TREE OF LIFE

The Natural Folklore of the Nguni People

There is not a culture in the world, for him as for Van der Post, that does not have myths, legends or fairy-tales of the origins of the world, of heroes and villains, of how we ought to behave or otherwise. Central to the folklore of the Nguni people of South Africa, for example, is the *Ziziphus mucronata.* They call it the tree of life. At any time of the year you will find on this tree a combination of green, yellow and brown leaves – the phases of youth, adulthood and old age.

A striking feature of the ziziphus is its thorns. Appearing as a double row, they are placed along the length of every branch in pairs, each thorn directly opposite the other. One of the pair points robustly outward and forwards holding the other curves back and inward in the opposite direction. The Nguni legend says the thorns tell us something about ourselves – that we must look ahead to the future but must never forget where we came from.

In the image of the backward-looking thorn of the ziziphus is the explanation of the human-nature split: we have forgotten our animal past. It is therefore the direction of our healing. Follow your dreams, but never forget your roots. Together the thorns say yes and no. They are poetic. One row points toward the future and to what they might become, and the other toward the Earth and our origins. They represent the push of the human spirit on the one hand, and the pull of the soul on the other, the wings of psychology in one direction and the roots of our biology in another.

Nguni Legends and Greek Myths

Remember where you have come from, say the Nguni legends. Know thyself says Apollo. The thorns are paired, keep the balance, say the Nguni. Nothing to excess, say Apollo. Honour the ancestors, say the Nguni. Honour the Gods, says Apollo. The first admonition, to know thyself, is the big one. It is to remember where we have come from. It is to deepen our awareness of our human origins, of species dependence and the transient nature of things. To know thyself is to understand our wild nature. The psychological instincts of the predator are in our blood. It is to discover that our identity is not restricted to a personal ego, but includes a sense of self that is both ancient and evolutionary.

SPIRIT AND SOUL: LIGHT AND DARKNESS

Animals Are in Us

Animals in fact, for McCallum, are in us and with us. We share their genes and their juices. Made up of countless molecules, cells and complex organs, each one of us is the carrier not only of the pattern of the embryonic gill slits and tales, but the entire history of life also. Every hydrogen atom in our bodies originates from the time of the Big Bang; every atom of iron in our red blood cells is a leftover of supernova explosions; every atom of oxygen and carbon is a gift from our sun. They are the foundations of a new way of thinking about who and what we are in relationship to the Earth and the Nature.

The Great Myth of Pan

When the great myth of Pan is reviewed, it should become clear that the pagan God of the wild did not die at all. Instead he went underground. His hiding place, for the past two thousand years, has been in the shadowy depths of the human psyche. Psychologically, the death of Pan can be interpreted, in similar guise to Van der Post's *Dark Eye* as the repression of the instinctive, spontaneous, raw or wild parts of the psyche that occurred with the rise of monotheistic consciousness. Great Pan did not really die, however, for nothing in the psyche dies. Like molecular particles, which can be changed but not destroyed, ideas can be repressed, yes, but extinguished, no.

What has ensued is an ongoing battle between Light and Darkness, with wild nature, including the wild parts of ourselves, cast in the role of Darkness, a phenomenon to be conquered, civilized and subdued. The history of colonialism bears testimony to this claim, an example of which was the 1492 'discovery' of

America by Columbus, the same year that the Jews, by royal edict, were evicted from Spain. It tells us that the enemy is 'out there'. It has played right into our genetically driven need for territory, rank, status, security, esteem, attachment and belonging – us versus them. But it has done more. It has defined the 'other' as different, be this Russian or African, to be subdued and thus lesser than us.

OUR ANIMAL NATURE AND OUR SENSE OF PLACE

Kinship of Science and Soul

It is time to shed our prejudices, McCallum goes on to say, against things that are wild, untamed or unconverted – more especially our animal nature. *Historically almost every animal has in some way struck a cord in the human psyche – the phoenix and the centaur, the birds and domestic animals.* They are on family crests and they are in our dreams. More than 40 constellations in the southern sky are named after them and every second sports team has an animal totem. We have toy animals and listen to animal stories. They are in our blood and our imagination. And now, with the unravelling of the human genome, we have proof of a kinship of science and soul. *Life without animals would be unthinkable. It is what the poets and shamans have been trying to tell us for years. Let us remember our wild side.*

Sense of Place and our Sense of Self is Linked

Our sense of place and our sense of self, in the final analysis, is linked – our identity is somehow associated with a deep historical sense of kinship with wild places and animals and we are dependent on both of them, in McCallum's view, for our psychological health. In almost all traditional cultures, animals have been and remain the guiding spirits of the shamans, those rare individuals whose role, more than anything else, has been that of defending the psychic integrity of their communities. Chief Seattle (6) wrote in 1855 in a letter to the president in Washington:

> *We know the sap which comes through the trees as we know the blood that courses our veins. Every part of the Earth is sacred to my people, every shining pine needle, every sandy shore, every mist in the dark woods, every shadow, every humming instinct. The rivers are our brothers. They quench our thirst. They carry our canoes and feed our children. So you must give to the river the kindness you would give to your brother. We are part of the Earth and it is part of us.*

We now turn from philosopher Van der Post and naturalist McCallum to environmental lawyer Cormac Cullinan, all of them South African.

8.5 Walking on the Wild Side

NATURE AND CIVILIZATION

A False Dichotomy

It is precisely, for South African environmental lawyer Cormac Cullinan, thereby aligned with both Van der Post and also McCallum, *the false dichotomy between the 'wild' and the 'law', between 'nature' and 'civilization', that we need to overcome.* Like the Chinese symbol for Yin and Yang, both are part of the whole, and it is dynamic balance that is key, not the triumph of one over the other.

Wildness as Life Force

Governing then in a manner that stamps out wildness and promotes the dull conformity of monoculture is not desirable. Much of what is best in us is contained within our wild hearts. *Wildness is associated with creativity and passion, with that part of us which is most connected with nature.* It can also be understood as a metaphor for the life force that flows through us all and drives the evolutionary process. In this sense it has an eternal, scared quality that both defines us and connects us most intimately with this planet. Wildness is a quality that can only be experienced by straying off the orthodox path of civilization as we know it. In many cultures, moreover, wildness is associated with wisdom. We now turn to 'wild law', and to 'earth jurisprudence'.

WILD LAW

Earth Jurisprudence

Wild law in fact for Cullinan, expresses Earth jurisprudence. It recognizes and embodies the qualities of the Earth system within which it exists. As an approach it *seeks both to foster passionate and intimate connections between people and nature, and to deepen our connection with the wild aspect of our natures.* It tends to focus more on relationships and on the processes by which they can be strengthened, than on end points and 'things' such as property. It protects wilderness and the freedom of communities of life to self regulate. It aims to encourage creative diversity rather than impose uniformity.

Community Health

Customary based, indigenous law systems, which place a high value on the health of communities, view crimes and social conflict as symptoms of deterioration in the social bonds that create a community, which may include the dead, animals and deities. Probably all human communities once regulated themselves with the purpose of ensuring that their members lived in accordance with the requirements of the wider ecological community. This was seen as necessary for the health of the human society. Unfortunately, the customary laws and practices of those indigenous peoples who still prioritize maintaining a mutually enhancing relationship with their habitat, have had virtually no influence at all on the governance systems of the dominant cultures.

Inspiration from Indigenous Peoples

For Cullinan then, the dominant cultures of the twenty-first century could learn important principles and techniques from the systems of governance of those indigenous people that would be useful in developing more Earth-centred structures for our times.

Three good reasons for taking a closer look at indigenous cultures are: firstly, certain cultures did manage to evolve laws and other means of regulating human conduct that enabled them to live successfully over long periods of time as part of a wider community of living and non-living beings. Second, there is a dearth of plausible new ideas about how to govern ourselves in a manner that will improve our relationship with the rest of the Earth Community. The fundamental issue we are dealing with here, our relationship with the Earth, is as old as humanity itself. We would be foolish indeed not to consult the fantastic library of different techniques of human governance that have succeeded over thousands of years. Third, after being in the stifling, virtual monoculture of governance thinking for so long, it is inspiring to be exposed to worldviews outside of it.

A Question of Natural Rights

Imagine we are talking of rivers rather than people, on the question of rights. We would conclude that a fundamental river right, that is the riverine equivalent of a human right, would be the right to flow. If a water body could not flow it would not be a river, and so the capacity to flow is essential to the existence of a river. Therefore, from the perspective of a river, building lots of dams across it, and extracting so much water from it, that it ceased to flow into the sea, would be an abuse of Earth rights. Cullinan now turns to governance per se.

ELEMENTS OF EARTH GOVERNANCE

Natural and Social Bonds

The intimate cooperative relationship between many generations of farmers and their local environment produces seeds that encapsulate the needs of both; nutritious enough to justify the farmer's efforts, resilient enough to cope with the variability of the micro-climate, and specifically adapted to the availability of soil nutrients, evolutionary experience, water and light in the place where it evolved.

The seed does not, however, contain the whole story. Essential to its continued propagation by humans is a context of traditional knowledge and practice about how to plant, cultivate, harvest, store and cook the seed. Associated with these are specific skills and technologies and cultural practices such as rituals to celebrate and honour the process.

The Integrity of Life Forms Count for Nothing

There is all the difference in the world between developing seed varieties in a manner that will benefit the human community by producing more food within the constraints of the particular social and ecological system, and genetically engineering seeds that can be mass-produced and owned for the purpose of increasing profits and the price of shares on the stock exchange. In Cullinan's view, genetically engineered seeds have been manipulated by humans, not to fit in with and contribute to a particular environment, but rather to co-exist with a patented herbicide developed for the same purpose. These are products not of long term intimate relationships, the timeless communion between members of an Earth community, but of hurried, forced unions in the sterility of a corporate lab. *In this world the accumulated wisdom of evolutionary experience and the integrity of life forms count for nothing, and the share options of the CEO for everything.*

Strengthening the Web of Life

If the human cultures that currently dominate the planet were to change their worldview so that we once more understood that the role of humans is primarily to fit in with, and contribute to, the larger Earth system and process, the purpose of governance would change. It would no longer be important to try to make national and world Gross National Product grow year after year, or to increase international trade for the sake of it. Our governance efforts would focus rather on re-constituting our society's image, of itself, and in reconstituting the sophistication of our regulatory systems to ensure that the net impact on humans strengthened the web of life.

Balance, Reciprocity and Justice

Earth jurisprudence, for Cullinan ultimately, must take account of the central importance of balance in the natural world. Not the stasis of equal weights on each on of the scales of justice, but the ever changing flux, the creative disequilibrium of the universe, always moving always changing, but never moving on one direction for long before swirling back to seek equilibrium or re-establish the past pattern again. Linked to the question of balance is the principle of reciprocity – for every taking there must be a giving. As every good farmer knows, if we take from the soil we must relinquish and nourish it, or else it will become barren. Our vast taking from the Earth in the past will require huge giving in the future. He then turns to the law of the land.

THE LAW OF THE LAND

Sacred Land

Many indigenous cultures and philosophies, for Cullinan, believe that the life force or vital energy that animates us also flows through, and is concentrated in, the rocks, plants and soils. This means that we share a subjective presence, soul or consciousness with Earth. In other words, it is more accurate to conceive of land as being part of the physical body of a living being than as an animate object. Indigenous people throughout the world believe that people belong to and are shaped by the land, rather than vice versa.

Land as Property

Yet the dominant cultures understand land as property. Land in the eyes of the law is therefore a thing, an object that may be bought and sold, and by definition devoid of any personality or sacred qualities.

> *Each of us is attached to the soil of this beautiful country. Each time one of us touches the soil, we feel a sense of personal renewal (Nelson Mandela, Inaugural Speech, 1994)*

Once it has been cut up and pegged down, land is sold in the market. By defining land as a commodity the dominant legal philosophies legitimize our exploitative relationship with the land.

THE TERRAIN AHEAD

Indivisible Continuum

Cullinan hopes that we will remember once more that, like the forests, we live on Earth's flanks, that we will understand again the necessity, and beyond that the great purpose, of adapting ourselves to the mountains (like the Table Mountain opposite which he lives in Cape Town), rooting ourselves deeply in its soil until no one can say where one ends and the other begins. *Nature, human nature and culture will then be recognized once more as an indivisible continuum.*

He pleads for a recognition of the fact that governance needs 'soul', not in the sense of an immortal soul, but in the sense of a quality of depth, connection, closely associated with the wild creativity that runs through the heart of humans back into wild spaces and times that are our heritage and to which we belong. *We are made of the same soil and breathe the same air as the Earth Community. Yet many of us have wandered far from it, so that we no longer recognize with whom we have co-evolved.*

8.6 Conclusion

TRADITION AND MODERNITY

The Living Reality of Place

The need for recognition of the living reality of place, of earth and of myth exists deeply in Africa. What is needed there is not destruction of its Old Testament myths but rather the prevention of their regression and archaic proliferation so as to bring them up into the light of day and to give them all of their contemporary meaning. In that meaning Van der Post asserts that there is room in community and spirit for all races and colours in South Africa.

The great danger, as he sees it, emanates from the fact that we are not aware enough of our meaning, vocation and purpose there. No matter what solution we arrive at must be preceded by an enormous extension of the awareness of modern man in Africa, an expansion that will allow all the instinctive values which play such a great role in the life of the black man around us also to play a legitimate role in our lives. These need inevitably to express themselves in a liberalization of our institutions and a broadening of the relationship between its constituent members.

THE ABORIGINAL LANGUAGE OF THE SPIRIT

Natural and Synthetic

The 'southern' black man and the 'northern' white man in Africa, primitive natural and civilized synthetic man, personify two ancient aspects of man that are continually at war in the heart of the individual. The onlooker of this vast drama in Africa, is apt to mistake the conflict without for the conflict that rages within himself and to imagine that by taking sides in Africa he is really helping to resolve the problem. There is a whole natural language of the spirit that Van der Post claims we have lost and can no longer receive or read. It is what he calls the 'aboriginal language of spirit' (7):

> *If we could only gain access to it again and learn to read its hieroglyphic script anew, in the silence of our hearts, the barbarisms of mind which have produced such terrible wars in our societies would be revealed to us and brought back to lawful proportions. I believe that one way to rediscover that language is for us to honor the primitive man in our societies. We have acquired great power in the physical world, but before we can go further, without disaster, we must match it with greater understanding of ourselves and our natures.*

We now turn from local nature and community, from the wild law and earth jurisprudence that underlies such identity from the 'north–south' perspective portrayed here, to local–global culture and consciousness, in South Africa.

Bibliography

1. Player, I. (1997) *Zululand Wilderness, Shadow and Soul.* Cape Town, David Philip.
2. Van der Post, L. (1955) *The Dark Eye of Africa.* Cape Town, Lowery Publishers.
3. Stevens, A. (1991) *On Jung.* London, Penguin.
4. Sections of this chapter have been reproduced from Lessem, R. and Schieffer, A. (2015) *Integral Renewal: A Relational and Renewal Perspective.* Farnham, Gower.
5. McCallum, I. (2005) *Ecological Intelligence – Rediscovering Ourselves in Nature.* Cape Town, Africa Geographic.
6. Cullinan, C. (2004) *Wild Law: A Manifesto for Earth Justice.* Totnes, Green Books.
7. Van der Post, L. (1955) *The Dark Eye of Africa.* Cape Town, Lowery Publishers.

Chapter 9

Future Primal and the Truth Quest: Emerging through Local–Global Culture and Consciousness

By studying the interconnected relationship between growth and order in the universe, the ancients were also exploring what lies at the very core of life – the elements that makes it sacred.

HRH Prince Charles, Tony Juniper and Ian Skelly (1), Harmony

9.1 Introduction

INSIDER-OUTSIDER: LOCAL–GLOBAL

Ever Present Origin

Van der Post's fascination with the bushman, and the sense and sensitivity of McCallum and Cormack for the wild, as we shall now see, was shared by his fellow countryman Louis Herman, from whom we shall extensively quote in this chapter. All past cultures and civilizations, for Hawaii-based South African born political philosopher, Herman (2), have had some intuitive sense that humans lived within a larger process – a story whose ultimate origin was the most profound and sacred mystery. For the central European integral thinker, and macro-historian, Jean Gebser (3), noted for his seminal work on our *Ever Present Origin*, we invariably need to turn back to our origins, to find a sustainable way forward. Each society, for Herman then, had a cosmology, a story of origins that formed the foundation of its way of life and guided its economics and politics.

South Africa to Hawaii and Back Again

Herman is currently a political philosopher in the University of Hawaii's West Oahu's Department of Political Science. He was born into an orthodox Jewish family in South Africa, the only Jewish family in a rural Afrikaaner community. He then emigrated with his family when he was 12 to England, proceeded to study medicine there at Cambridge University, then went to live on a kibbutz in Israel, thereafter studying political science at the Hebrew University. He finally ended up as an academic in Hawaii, while making ongoing visits to South Africa to renew himself. He is therefore a perfect case of a local–global insider-outsider in Africa.

Today, however, for most, as Van der Post, McCallum and Cormack, have already intimated (see previous chapter), *the primordial experience of the mystery of our earthy origins has ceased to be a moral force in our lives.* All our dominant institutions, from the global marketplace to the factory model of industrial production, were constructed on the basis of a radically constricted understanding of the place of the human in the cosmos generally, and of our particular society specifically. This has applied, as we have seen, hugely, to modern day Russia, as well as to South Africa.

We urgently need a new vision of politics and economics that is attuned to our local and global reality.

THE PERSONAL AND THE PLANETARY – A PRIMAL RESONANCE

Early societies then, immersed in an unpolluted wilderness on which they depended absolutely, recognized the primal resonance between the natural world and human consciousness and explored it through their shamanic systems of religion and healing. When we approach politics from such a perspective, for Herman, magnificent possibilities emerge: of ways of life profoundly better, truer and more beautiful. This involves an ongoing process of creative searching.

9.2 Bringing Soul Back into Politics – Truth Quest

TO SEEK AND TO LIVE THE BEST POSSIBLE LIFE

Debased to Ennobling Politics

Our modern use of the word *politics* in fact has become as thoroughly debased and misunderstood as the practice it is commonly used to describe – seeking and wielding power over others for personal gain. On the scale of public opinion, politicians rank, according to Herman, somewhere between prostitutes and used-car salesmen. The whole business of politics is considered as far from its Socratic roots, for Herman, in philosophy and 'cultivating virtue' as one can get.

To move out of this dead end, for him, we need to retrace our steps to find a way forward. If we go back two and a half thousand years to Ancient Greece, we can find the origin of the word *politics* in the Greek *polis* – the self governing, autonomous, democratic city state – where 'politics' simply referred to the affairs of the polis, and as the concern of all, it was regarded as the most ennobling and meaningful of all human activities.

Search for the Good Life

Herman then uses the word *politics* in the original, inclusive sense, to mean the *universal human struggle, individually and collectively, to seek and to live the best possible life.* Political philosophy can then be reconnected to its original Socratic intention as the search for 'the good life'. This has two primary aspects. *On the one hand, there is what Socrates called 'the improvement of one's soul'*, or what we loosely understand as personal growth, since the Greek word for soul is *psyche*, from which we get our psychology. *On the other hand, there is the improvement of one's society*. Traditionally, this sort of Socratic knowledge was called wisdom. By contrast, in today's universities, 'political philosophy' refers to an obscure sub-speciality within the discipline of political science.

WE HAVE ABANDONED THE TRUTH QUEST

Unashamed Self Interest

So here, for Herman, is our central failing. We have created a political culture that has eliminated *in principle* the need for the individual to consider and take responsibility for the good of the whole. We have abandoned the truth quest in public life. Our system is set up so that political and economic decisions that are made according to the conviction that if individuals, organizations and nations follow self-interest, the 'invisible hand of the market' will automatically convert selfishness into the best possible outcome for the largest number.

This has in fact led to a global economic system that rewards a few individuals with grotesque quantities of wealth, rivalling the GDP of small nations, while a billion people go hungry. *Never before has so much power over so many been concentrated in the hands of so few in the service of unashamed self interest.* All the while the collective frantic energy of globalized humanity continues to pollute and plunder the planet. How did this globally, so to speak, come to be?

'BIG HISTORY' TOWARDS THE FOURTH REVOLUTION

First the Primal Revolution – Egalitarian Community

Looking back over the past 200,000 years of human existence, Herman identifies three sudden leaps in human self understanding – three revolutionary discontinuities in our way of being. *The initial 'primal revolution' was associated with fire making and the appearance of language and symbolic culture.* With this leap into the realm of imagination and self-awareness came an expanded arena of real freedom, creativity and choice; with choice came the reality of good and bad choices.

Humanity was confronted for the first time with 'morality' or 'the best way to live'. In compact bands of nomadic hunter-gatherers this question was constantly addressed in the everyday flow of discussion and storytelling. *All participated in the life of the self-sufficient, more or less egalitarian community, where political economy was based on simple reciprocity, cooperation, caring, sharing.* All had some direct experience of the social and cosmological whole.

Second the Agricultural Revolution – Hierarchies of Wealth and Power

Around 10,000 years ago, for Herman, agricultural civilization started walling out the 'wild'. Ground was held, ploughed, seeded, irrigated, harvested and defended. The initial domestication of wild plants and cereals was most probably the achievement of the woman-as-gatherer and her plant wisdom. The first Neolithic civilizations on old Europe were, as far as we know, correspondingly peaceful and egalitarian in nature and goddess worshipping societies.

Over time agricultural civilization made possible growth in population, which was accompanied by an increasing division of labour, specialization in knowledge, and more sharply defined hierarchies of wealth and power. Hunters became soldiers, shamans became priests, and captives became slaves who built the fortifications and monumental architecture that defined cities. Warrior societies became more patriarchal, and the power and influence of women declined. Religious and political wisdom passed into the hands of scribes, bureaucrats and professionals.

Third the Industrial Revolution – Rational Self Interest

The most recent leap in human awareness has been accomplished through industrial capitalism, inspired and guided by the political philosophy of Liberalism, which advocated *freeing the rational self-interested individual from the constraints of religion, tradition and arbitrary government. Liberalism helped liberate the individual from a calcified and corrupt feudalism.* It produced the astonishing understandings of modern science and its near miraculous technology.

But this revolution, for Herman, has deformed crucial dimensions of what it means to be human – in particular, the organic connection to other humans and to the larger world of nature from which our humanity emerged. We face a situation, Herman says, where humanity has become almost godlike in its technological prowess but demonic on how it directs that power.

The Fourth-coming Consciousness Revolution

Arguably then, today, according to Herman, we are on the cusp of a 'fourth revolution' in human self consciousness. Thanks to science and critical scholarship we have a depth of understanding of all three revolutions that no previous generation could have hoped for.

We are in a position to recognize the enduring, but partial truths of each and to integrate their wisdom in a higher, more inclusive synthesis. Such an understanding would join together what has been fragmented; *it would integrate the earth-based wisdom of primal societies, which sustained humanity for nine-tenths of the time we have been human, with the achievements of classical civilizations and the past 400 years of science and industrial capitalism.* It would bring us into a fuller and more creative partnership with the evolving earth community. What, for Herman then socio-politically, could this mean?

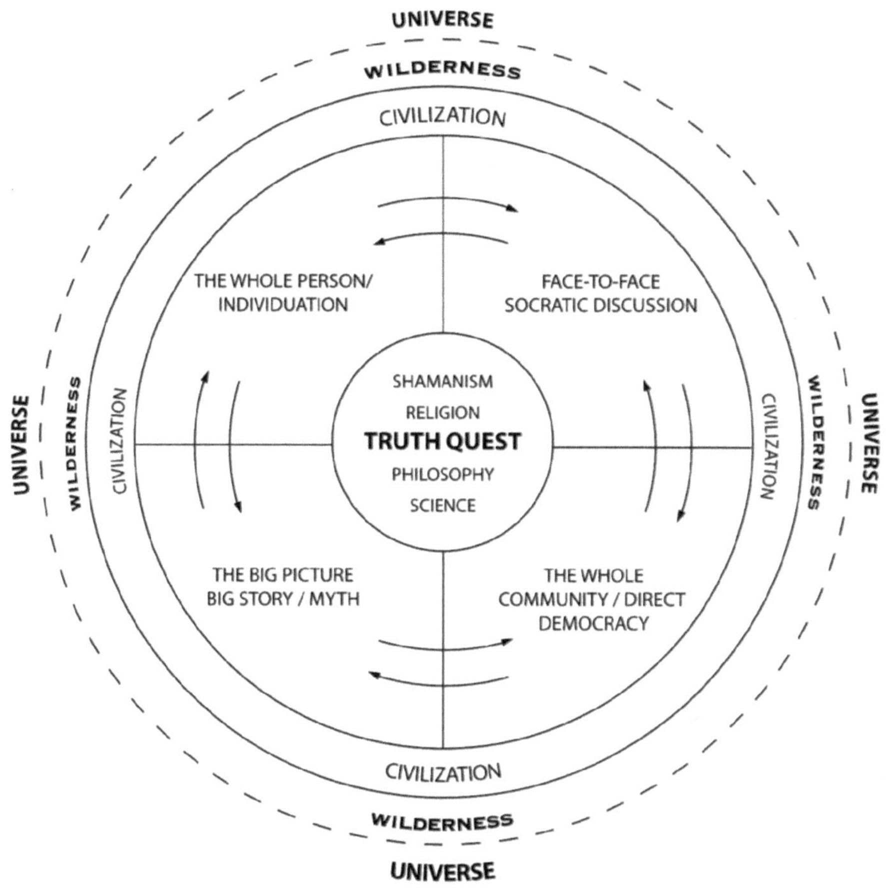

Figure 9.1 The mandala of primal politics

A FOUR-PART 'TAO OF POLITICS'

Future Primal

Future Primal, as Herman terms it then, presents a model of what he calls the 'truth quest' as an archetypal dynamic of the human search for order. The model itself indentified four interconnected elements, these being, duly connected with our release of GENE-ius:

- the self understanding of the searching, growing *individual*
- honest face-to-face *discussion*
- participation in a *democratic community*
- the construction of a *big picture* of our shared reality.

Universal Symbol of Order

Together, for Herman, these constitute a four-part structure (see Figure 9.1 above) that can be represented graphically as a mandala, with four quadrants. *The mandala also is, appropriately enough, the oldest and most universal symbol of order, representing the relationship of the searching individual to the cosmos.* Since the model seems to express an archetypal structure of the search for order that is rooted in the primal human condition – the autonomous creative individual, in face-to-face community, embedded in nature – we find it reappearing at those creative moments of transition in history where one order is collapsing, a new one is emerging, and the big questions resurface. This is the situation, for Herman, in which we find ourselves today.

This means the vision of *Future Primal* differs from past paradigms of politics in recognizing that the ongoing search itself – the primal truth quest – needs to be at the centre. It is also resonant, as we can see, with our own model for the release of GENE-IUS (see Chapter 3).

9.3 Out of the Wilderness

THE JOURNEY OUT AND IN

Hard and Soft

In fact Herman's four-part model, building on those fellow South Africans Van der Post, McCallum and Cormack that came before, is resonant also with our own integral approach. This altogether involves rethinking our politics, as per our *Integral Polity* (4) in light of the scientific story of our evolutionary origins, thereby *requiring us to connect the hard evidence of archaeology and palaeontology to the 'soft evidence' of our inner experience of what is good, true and beautiful*, the 'holy trinity' so to speak. The journey out and in recognizes that the outer wilderness world of primates is related to the inner wilderness of our psyche, that there remains an ancient consciousness that still breathes and pulses inside every one of us.

JUNG IN AFRICA, AFRICA IN JUNG

This World Had Been Mine for Millennia

C.G. Jung (5), to whom we have alluded several times already, describes his own experience of dropping down into the early times of our African ancestry while travelling in Africa. He woke up early one morning on a train from Mombasa to Nairobi and looked out the window at the first rays of sunlight as the trained curved around a steep cliff. There on a jagged rock above the track he saw a slim brownish-black figure standing motionless on a long spear looking down on the train. For Jung:

> *It was as if I were this moment returning to the land of my youth, and as if I knew that dark-skinned man who had been waiting for me for five thousand years ... I could not guess what string within myself was plucked at the sight of that solitary dark hunter. I only knew this world had been mine for countless millennia.*

Evolutionary Dynamic

His own experiences amongst the Swiss peasantry, and subsequent meetings with African 'witch doctors' and Native American shamans, opened him to the in-between and the full range of the para-psychological occult, present throughout history. He discovered a striking repetition of symbols, narratives and themes across cultures and times. *He called them patterns of archetypes of a collective unconscious, part of an evolutionary dynamic that changes over time.* Jung's work, then, allows us to understand mythology as the inner history of the archetypes, mediated through the creative imagination of individuals and cultures and canonized in religion, art and cosmology. In this understanding, past, present and future become separate facts of a single reality – what Jean Gebser (6) called the 'ever present origin'.

This brings us back once more to Van der Post.

THE LOST WORLD OF THE KALAHARI

The Divided Self

When Herman opened Van der Post's famous book on *The Lost World of the Kalahari*, he recognized, with some shame, how cold and hard our proud scientific detachment was compared to the Bushman's passionate full-blooded knowing. For Van der Post (7) then, reflecting on his own divided self:

Today we tend to know statistically and in the abstract. We classify, catalogue and subdivide the flame-like variety of animal and plant according to species, sub-species, physical property and use. But in the Bushman's knowing, no matter how practical, there was a dimension that I miss in the life of my own time. He knew these things in the full context and commitment of his life. He participates so deeply in one another's being that the experience could almost be called mystical.

However limited his anthropology, Van der Post seemed to have grasped a profound political insight: that the war between his own opposite forces represented the sickness of our civilization in microcosm, the split between Afrikaner and African, 'civilized' and 'wild', modern and primordial. The San Bushman, even today – constrained, compromised and impoverished as they are in the Southern African Kalahari – should not be seen as lost, exotic or pathetic but rather should be honoured as custodians of a global cultural treasure – inheritors of a culture consistently fashioned by an unbroken connection to the original human homeland. Herman then applies his 'mandala of primal politics', retrospectively of course, to the bushman.

PRIMAL POLITICS

An Economy of Caring and Sharing

In a competitive market economy, for Herman then, relationships often become a means to enhance one's own material wealth. *!Hxaro* – a Bushman process of giving, receiving and sharing gifts – inverts this by understanding wealth as a resource to develop the symmetrical bonds of friendship. Their 'Zen affluence', in American anthropologist Marshall Sahlins (8) terms, minimizes material demands and creates a wealth of time and energy to serve a life rich in relationships and mutual care. There is a tantalizing sign, for Herman moreover, that such *!Hxaro* relationships are emerging in the west (as we saw in Chapter 4 they emerged long before also in the east), ranging from formal cooperatives, as per mutual aid, to complementary currencies.

Direct Democracy – Everyone a Chief

In the west, for Herman then, we have an individualism of competition leading to division of labour, specialization and hierarchies of wealth and power. Bushmen have an individualism of cooperation, according to him, leading to an egalitarian democracy that promotes universal access to the full range of humanizing experience – cultivation of the whole person. The Bushman formula is rooted in the economy of hunting and foraging, which provides the most unshakable foundations of any society for individual self-sufficiency. *Since the division of labour is minimal, virtually all individuals have the basic knowledge, ability and resources to live directly off the land, gather food, make clothing and build shelter.*

Cultivating a Whole Human Life

Here then is the paradox: precisely because of the material simplicity of Bushman society, each individual can develop a greater inner wealth, cultivating a whole human life. For the most part, *each member of the band participates in all the definitive humanizing activities: producer, provider, teacher, learner, follower, artist, musician, dancer and healer.* Everyone has a direct voice in the ongoing discussions and helps create the consensus that constitutes governance. The archetypal events of a human cycle – birth, growth, maturity and death – are ubiquitous and public. The full range of human emotions – love and hate, anger and tenderness, meanness and generosity – are similarly on public display in the full context of the lives of the protagonists.

Face to Face Discussion

Below the foaming surface of conversation, anthropologists have identified a range of conversational styles and strategies for investigating problems, understanding opposing points of view, coming to consensus and acting collectively. Decisions are seldom the outcome of a single, formal debate. Men, women, young and old participate, talking together, for days if necessary, until every point of view has been considered.

The San, for Herman, exemplify what Socrates proposed: that the power of discussion is not simply a mechanism to resolve conflicting ideas; it's a mode of inquiry that in itself helps individuals recognize a deeper shared unity of need and purpose. Like the nomadic San, and not unlike Federov (who did at least write a little) Socrates wrote nothing and repeatedly drew attention to the superiority of discussion over text and lecture. He pointed out that discussion, unlike text, connects ideas and abstractions to their authors as whole embodied human beings. Each faces the other, sharing the same space and time, fully exposed as an instrument and embodiment of political truth.

Unlike the prepared lecture, with its one-way flow of information, discussion requires all participants to think on their feet. Voice tone, facial expression and body language can reveal unscripted meaning: degrees of warmth and hostility, respect, trust and finally intention. For Socrates, as in shamanic systems of knowing, intention helps determine outcome. Most importantly, the simple fact of sharing language, space, time and self consciousness reinforces the need to care for a shared humanity. We need one another to be most fully ourselves.

The Big Picture – Everyone a John Locke

In summary then for Herman, the three dimensions of experience most characteristic of the traditional Bushman are also the three most removed from our own 'western-northern' way of political life, whereby politics and the quest:

- take place in public, through *open-ended face-to-face discussion* and storytelling in an egalitarian and democratic situation;
- *embedded in a living wilderness ecology* where animal and human communities regularly cross the boundary separating them;
- *embedded in the inner invisible dimension of the psyche*, represented by the innermost circle, the truth quest.

Bushman's Ultra-Polis

From the point of view of the classical Greek polis we can regard the Bushman band as the ultra-polis; smaller than the polis, more personal, more egalitarian, totally self-sufficient, and with universal participation in discussion as the primary medium of both the truth quest and governance. This is the political-economic foundation of deep democracy, a discussion-based epistemology that feeds and is fed by the *arête* of the whole person. In a real sense, *each Bushman,* for Herman then, *is the author and creative agent of his or her own political cosmology in a far more robust fashion than the citizen of the bureaucratic nation-state. Everyone is Socrates, everyone John Locke.*

Herman then turns to the primal future born out of such a primal past.

9.4 Our Primal Future

PRIMAL RESURGENCE

Building up a Primal Dynamic

Obviously, he says, we can no longer follow the truth quest by hunting and gathering in the wilderness. Even if we wanted to, we have lost the vast expanse of unspoiled, game-filled country needed to keep more than a handful of humans alive. But we can recognize the complex of primal politics, according to Herman, as ubiquitous within us all. *Our wilderness origins fashioned our creative self-consciousness, which is both expanded and balanced by following the primal dynamic: face-to-face communication within a caring community of individuals, passionate for living and learning in a mutually enhancing resonance with the natural world.* This is the truth quest, he says, and it is our primal inheritance. We can ignore it and repress it, or we can cultivate it in all our endeavours and bring it into a creative engagement with the reality we find ourselves caught up in: a civilization rushing to self destruction while displaying tantalizing possibilities of a more beautiful, joyful way of life.

The Failure of the Current Model of Farming

Today, for Herman, hunting and gathering has been replaced by agriculture as our most fundamental and intimate relationship to the natural world. Agriculture is the area in which humanity touches the earth most directly; agriculture shapes and is shaped by the most fundamental values of society. One of the hard realities the big picture of the quest confronts us with – and perhaps the one that is most likely to cause our collapse – is the failure of the current model of farming. *We are enmeshed in an oil-intensive, corporate dominated, mechanized, wasteful, polluting industry that is eroding the soil, destroying wilderness and accelerating climate change.* Forty per cent of the terrestrial surface of the earth has been transformed by farming, which, Herman maintains, now uses 70 per cent of all fresh water consumed.

Since we cannot expand agricultural land without dramatically adding to climate change and destroying biodiversity, we have two immense practical challenges: to control our global population, and to farm more intensively and sustainably. To do this we need to come to a compelling shared understanding of our reality, and for this we need to make the truth quest the centre of our politics.

We are a Product of the Evolving Earth

This, according to Herman, both empowers and constrains us. As we have seen, primal societies, still close to experience, generally organized their politics in the ways described by the mandala structure, with the shamanic quest at the centre. Today immense cultural and economic forces seem to undermine all efforts to live according to the primal dynamic.

Locked into the self interest and materialism of industrial capitalism, facing environmental devastation and social collapse, we find it too easy to despair and indulge in escapism or fatalism, as if it were too late to do anything but go shopping and wait for the arrival of the apocalypse. But such a response is based on a distorted perception of the larger reality. The bigger, deeper picture reveals that our capacity to respond creatively to our predicament is amplified by the breadth and depth of our vision, and that as we grasp the bigger picture the way forward is illuminated and we become empowered and transformed.

THE PERIAGOGE – A REVOLUTION IN THE SOUL

A Soulful Wake-Up Call

The primal perspective makes us aware, for Herman then, that one of the primary political 'institutions' is the individual. Ultimately any political change begins, ends and is carried forward in the life of each person. For this reason a *periagoge – the waking up of the soul and its reorientation to the truth quest* – is at the centre of Herman's primal politics.

Concern for the wellbeing of others, which extends to the entire non-human community of being, is inherent in our nature and expresses an intrinsic connectedness and a need to be of service to others. Primal societies exemplify and reinforce this attitude. Altruism, generosity and heroic sacrifice in the protection of the community seem to be as much part of the human condition as our more oft celebrated selfishness and greed. The imperative of the *periagoge* (wake up of the soul) means we serve our higher selves by serving others.

NELSON MANDELA'S PERIAGOGE

Personal and Societal Transformation

One of the most striking and inspiring stories in recent times of an individual opening to truth, becoming transformed, and then catalyzing a comparable process in the entire nation, according to Herman, is that of Nelson Mandela (9) – the first black President of post-apartheid South Africa (we shall hear much more from him in the next navigational chapter), whose leadership helped avert a race war. His story is well known, but its connection to primal politics, in Herman's terms, is not. In fact, separated from his wife and family, and condemned to a life of hard labour, Mandela might have been consumed with hatred for Afrikaaners. Instead the opposite happened; he discovered the humanity of the oppressor and in the process he expanded his own humanity. *This personal transformation made it possible for him to catalyze a similar transformation in the psychology of the nation, culminating in the 'miracle' of the negotiated revolution* to which we shall refer in our next chapter.

Ubuntu – I Am Because You Are

Mandela for Herman, as we shall see, had the good fortune to be 'raised by a village', enjoying the benefits of an extended family and a warm caring community surrounded by the beautiful rolling hills of the Transkei in the Eastern Cape. *This early grounding in the human and national community later made it easier for him to recognize a common humanity with an Afrikaaner enemy.* Mandela, subsequently then, while in prison, carefully studied the psychology of his oppressor. He read widely in Afrikaans' history, poetry and literature and took every opportunity to engage his white wardens in prison, always politely, always in Afrikaans. He was surprised to find that many were poor country boys with little education, who must have reminded him of his own simple beginnings. *Mandela saw clearly that their fear was real; they felt that everything they loved – their language, history and culture, their entire way of life – meant nothing to the blacks and would be quickly swept aside once a black majority was in power.* Apartheid was first a strategy for survival, which then became a strategy for exploitation.

In 1994, when Mandela was inaugurated as president of South Africa, Herman tells us, he invited three of his former prison wardens to be guests of honour. In emphasizing the commonality between the two peoples, African and Afrikaaner, Mandela underlined his faith in the universal value of what Africans call *ubuntu* – the notion that under the deformations of ideology, creed and dogma, one find a deeper common humanity. Mandela's strategy followed the boundary crossing wisdom of the Native Americans, which was also the *thuru* of the Bushman shaman and the dialectic of Socrates: one gains a bigger picture and grows by engaging with opposites. As we saw in primal societies, such a discipline requires a degree of psychological wholeness – the inner security that comes from the process of individuation.

For Nelson Mandela and South Africa, the miracle of the negotiated revolution was a moment of transcendence within a wider culture of materialism and power politics. The result was a multiracial ANC government based on constitutional democracy, though in some respects it has since and inevitably become dysfunctional and corrupt. What does this more generally mean, for Herman, and his new-old paradigm, so to speak, of primal politics?

9.5 The Mandala Structure of the Primal Quest

FOUR PRIMARY VALUES

Four World Archetype

Reflecting on the questing human individual as he or she emerges within the primal community, according to Herman as we saw at the beginning of this chapter, we can identify four primary values and processes that constitute the necessary, minimal coordinates of the quest. This structure, for him, functions like a Jungian archetype, a deeply rooted way of thinking and behaving. The four quadrants of the mandala, like our own integral realities, represent the distinctiveness of each element (see Figure 9.1 above). The surrounding circle represents their interconnected-ness in continual dynamic interaction, converging in the unity of the single centre-point – the quest itself.

We now deal with each of the four elements in turn.

THE WHOLE PERSON, OR INDIVIDUATION

All is Contained within our Story

Firstly then, since all our knowing is inevitably refracted through our unique trajectory through life, all we have to teach is contained within our story. *As we struggle to grasp a shared reality, we are forced to reflect on our uniqueness and to recognize that of others, and so we find ourselves returning to the wisdom of the Delphic Oracle: 'Know Thyself'.* Certain social structures enhance this process, others repress it.

The small size and self-sufficiency of the primal hunting group impelled every adult to participate in all the definitively human activities: hunter, gatherer, artist, healer, musician, learner and teacher. Conversely, the social hierarchy and division of labour of classical and industrial societies restrict the degree to which the individual can play multiple parts in the life of the community. The Greek ideal of *arête* or excellence, was the cultivation of the whole person, the consummate amateur who would participate creatively in all aspects of life, and thus grasp the fullest range of what it meant to be human.

The Native American Medicine Wheel

An even fuller expression of the whole person is found, for Herman, in the more differentiated, but still egalitarian, shamanic traditions of the Plains Indians of North America. In the Cheyenne teachings, for example, the mandala of the medicine wheel could also represent an individual's entire journey through life, from birth to infancy through youth, maturity, old age and death. The medicine wheel could also represent the full range of possibilities for human temperament, rather like Jung's psychological types. As Hyemeyohsts Storm (10) puts it:

> *But any person who perceives from only one of these Four Great Directions will remain only a partial man. For example a man who possesses only the gift of the North will be a wise man, but he will be cold. And the man who lives only in the East will have the clear sighted vision of the eagle, but he will never be close to things. After each of us has learned of our Beginning Gift, our first place in the wheel, we must grow by seeking understanding in each of the other four great ways. Only in this way can we become full.*

Attraction of Opposites – White and Black

There is, for Herman moreover, an attraction between the opposites that serves wholeness. As a white in South Africa he was attracted to black culture; as an Israeli, he found Palestinian culture fascinating. By following this impulse, we can balance our dominant way of looking at the world, *when we seek out and integrate opposites, we get a bigger, truer picture of the human condition. As we participate in the life of larger humanity, we can grow psychologically, spiritually and intellectually.* Jung (11) called this path of healing through wholeness individuation.

In fact, for Herman, the more punishing and rigid the society, the more the ego refuses to recognize its connection to its opposite. This deforms our ability to grasp and accept that we live in-between the great opposites of reality. Nelson Mandela, who struggled against the racist apartheid regime, embodies the individuated, morally mature statesman. His capacity to discover and affirm within his own soul the Afrikaaner oppressor transformed both himself and his jailers. His example made it possible for a majority of South Africans, poised on the edge of a racial war, to envision a multiracial polity and a non-violent reconciliation after apartheid. The good life requires this paradoxical individuality, one grounded in a loving relationship to the entire community of beings.

FACE-TO-FACE SOCRATIC DISCUSSION

Confronting our In-Between Situation

Face-to-face discussion, secondly, confronts our personal truths with that of others. We face as such diverse individuals, each on his or her own trajectory through life. Face-to-face communication offers a direct way for grasping the dialectical logic of truth through contradiction, since *it confronts us in the most inescapable way possible with our in-between situation.*

Bushman Politics

As we saw, such politics swam, as it were, in an ocean of discussion and storytelling. In such a situation the individual was stimulated and challenged to keep thinking and move around the medicine wheel of life – to keep growing as an individual.

THE WHOLE COMMUNITY AND DIRECT DEMOCRACY

Direct Democracy in Mqhekezweni

Direct democracy, thirdly for Herman, expresses the value of communication free from the distortions of concentrated wealth and power. It also expresses a society's commitment to providing the education and resources necessary to maximize the individual's participation in face-to-face decision making. Nelson Mandela (12) gives us a vivid description of direct democracy from his youth, when he lived with the Regent at Mqhekezweni, the seat of the tribal chiefdom of his Thembu people. For Mandela then:

> *Everyone who wanted to speak did so. It was democracy in its purest form. There may have been a hierarchy of importance amongst the speakers, but everyone was heard, chief and subject, warrior and medicine man, shopkeeper and farmer.*

Each One of Us is a Chief Over Himself

We also see something approximating direct democracy in the early days of the Israeli kibbutz, with which Herman had become personally familiar during the time he spent in Israel, when all adult members of the community gathered in the general assembly to make collective decisions for the community through face-to-face discussion. The San Bushmen, meanwhile, had no powerful chiefs: *'Each one of us is a chief over himself'*.

THE BIG PICTURE, THE BIG STORY – MYTHOS

Epic Narratives

Big pictures, fourthly and finally according to Herman, are symbolic representations of the whole. They are vision paradigms, worldviews and epic narratives that serve to connect the lives and passions of the individual to larger, more encompassing realities – family, tribe, nation, civilization, species and ultimately the living earth and the evolving cosmos. *Without such nested pictures of wholes within wholes, or stories within stories, we drift, unprepared, easily surprised and distracted. Energies become dissipated, and we lapse into selfishness or cynicism.*

In Between Worlds

These big pictures only become politically significant and morally compelling to the degree that they are processes through the mill of other mandala components – self-reflecting individuals, similarly motivated, in free discussion within the community. Today, according to Herman, we are in crisis because we are in between cosmologies. Liberalism was a radically truncated cosmology that undermined big picture thinking and attempted to turn material self-interest into a transcendent principle of order. The bankruptcy of its eighteenth-century assumptions, for him, about nature and human nature, are becoming obvious, and new cosmology is gradually emerging. This represents an extraordinary synthesis of the wealth of accumulated civilizational wisdom woven together within the great arc of the evolutionary story.

The outlines of this new cosmology are clearly visible, but institutions have a life of their own. We created our institutions out of a constricted and distorted, all too often 'western-northern' global worldview. We can now re-create them in the light of our larger, truer local–global understanding, and in doing so we shall start healing ourselves, our society and our planet.

9.6 Conclusion: The Mandala of Primal Politics as an Ideal

ORIGINATION TO TRANSFORMATION

In conclusion then for Herman, the mandala dynamic emerged in small-scale, self-sufficient, self-organizing, local communities still living close to nature – the original human condition. However, we can see it reappear in history in times of social upheaval and transformation. We see it, for him, in the creative ferment of the Renaissance, with an explosion of interest in the natural world and the celebration of the whole person as 'Renaissance Man'. We see it emerging again out of the chaos of the English Civil War in the seventeenth century before the institutions of Liberalism had hardened, when peasants, driven off manorial estates, seized public land and organized themselves into a variety of democratic and spiritually-based communities like the Levellers and Diggers.

We find elements of the primal now reappearing during our contemporary crisis. We have seen it in the early Israeli kibbutz, and more recently in a steadily growing eco-village movement that builds from the kibbutz model ideal. Integrating the localized principles of self-sufficiency and sustainability with a spiritual relationship to the larger 'global' community of being. We can see primal principles emerging in the small Buddhist nation of Bhutan, and we see them exemplified by spiritually attuned leaders of liberation movements, such as Mahatma Gandhi, Martin Luther King and Nelson Mandela.

MOVING BETWEEN OPPOSITES

The lesson of the primal polis, according to Herman finally, is that all moves to decentralize power, locally, need to proceed in parallel with strategies for universalizing commitment to the truth quest, globally. *Democratizing wisdom requires cultivating the ability to move between opposites: local and global, the individual and the collective, humanity and wilderness.* Decentralization backfires if it focuses exclusively on electoral mechanics, which can simply privilege the lowest common denominator of prejudice – for example racists voting to expel foreigners. Every step toward devolving power requires a corresponding effort to augment the truth quest – to grasp the bigger picture and see the connections between part and whole, self and other, enemy and friend.

Since the mandala of primal politics is rooted in the deep structure of what it means to be human, it can function effectively as an ideal and offer criteria for development, without having to be fully embodied in small-scale communities.

Its values can guide us, according to Herman, whatever institutional or historic setting we find ourselves in. *The more completely we understand the big story telling us into being, the better able we are to respond creatively to the challenges of our moment by applying the discipline of the mandala.*

We now turn to the full story of Mandela's *Long Walk to Freedom*, which, aligned with truth and reconciliation, becomes the centrepiece of our navigation in this north–south context, altogether set within the framework of exchange and reconciliation infused with a combination of 'southern' *ubuntu* and 'northern' *Christian* values.

Bibliography

1. HRH Prince Charles, Tony Juniper and Ian Skelly (2010) *Harmony: A New Way of Looking at Our World.* London, Harper Collins, Blue Books.
2. Herman, L. (2013) *Future Primal: How Our Wilderness Origins Show Us the Way Forward.* Novato, CA, New World Library.
3. Gebser, J. (1955) *The Ever Present Origin.* Ohio, Ohio University Press.
4. Lessem, R., Aboluei sh, I., Pogacnik, M. and Herman, L. (2014) *Integral Polity: Aligning Nature, Culture, Society and Economy.* Farnham, Gower.
5. Burleson, B. (2005) *Jung in Africa.* London, Continuum.
6. Gebser, J. (1955) *The Ever Present Origin.* Ohio, Ohio University Press.
7. Van der Post, L. (2002) *The Lost World of the Kalahari.* New York, Vintage.
8. Sahlins, M. (1972) *Stone Age Economics.* New Brunswick, NJ, Transaction Publishers.
9. Mandela, N. (1995) *The Long Walk to Freedom.* New York, Abacus.
10. Storm, H. (1988) *The Seven Arrows.* New York, Random House.
11. Jung, C. (1992) *Psychological Types.* London, Routledge.
12. Mandela, N. (1995) *The Long Walk to Freedom.* New York, Abacus.

Chapter 10

Truth and Reconciliation: Navigating Towards Freedom

> *At the opposite end from healing is the illness of not being able to accept or even tolerate those who are different from us. Worse, this inability encourages suspicion, fear, and resentment. This it is an illness of the collective psyche when different cultures don't understand one another. The history of humankind is plagued by this psychic disease that has caused much pain and disappointment in the world. Methods of healing, then, must take into account the energetic or spiritual condition that is in turmoil.*
>
> *Malidoma Patrice Some (1),* The Healing Wisdom of Africa

10.1 Introduction

INTRODUCING THE TRC

Grounding and Emergence Prior to Navigation

In pursuit of integral advantage, from a north–south natural-societal perspective, we first grounded ourselves in primeval nature, ecological intelligence, and earth jurisprudence. Secondly, and thereafter as well as alongside, we drew from an emergent primal polity, incorporating a central truth quest, and surrounding 'four worlds': direct democracy, a big picture, Socratic discussion and personal individuation.

The 'truth quest' moreover, in a South African context, constituting its emergent centre-piece, has indeed been embodied in Nelson Mandela as a person and, for us, in the Truth and Reconciliation Commission (TRC) as an institution. The TRC proved to be *a unique amalgam of northern Christian principles of love and forgiveness, on the one hand, and the southern spirit of 'ubuntu', on the other*. While harrowing in its overall nature, it was at the same time an inspiration to the South African nation, and to the world at large, insofar as it embodied the spirit of reconciliation upon which Mandela's new South Africa had been built. It also had the potential as we shall see, but sadly not yet realized, to offer a new kind of economic as well as social and political ethos for the country.

EXCHANGE AS RECONCILIATION

Exchange in Newly Integral Guise

South African academic and theologian John de Gruchy (2), in his book on *Reconciliation – Restoring Justice,* wrote that the Greek words translated in the New Testament by *'reconciliation' or 'reconcile' are compounds of the Greek 'to exchange', and this in turn is derived from the Greek word meaning 'the other'.* The words thus carry with them the sense of exchanging places with 'the other' and therefore being in solidarity with rather than against, such 'an other'.

Interestingly enough, economics generally, and business specifically, is also built on exchange, albeit in a somewhat different context. However, the potential does exist for developing a new approach to economics and enterprise, in such a 'north–south' context, that builds upon reciprocity and exchange. Reconciliation in fact has to do with, putting it colloquially as De Gruchy does, God making us friends. Thus reconciliation in Pauline theology refers to the way in which the love of God in Jesus Christ turns enemies into friends thereby creating peace. Not only humanity, but the whole created cosmos is included in God's act of reconciliation in Christ, thereby linking redemption and creation.

Integral Advantage in Reconciliation

Reconciliation then is God's overcoming estrangement and establishing a new relationship not just with individuals coming to faith, but also with the world in all its complex relationships. More importantly, for Paul the language of justification derives from a special understanding of justice, namely justice as restorative rather than punitive. God's justice, in Paul as elsewhere in the scripture, has far less to do with the law-court and much more to do with healing relationships and social justice with a particular bias towards the poor and the oppressed. At the heart of De Gruchy's argument is the conviction that *reconciliation is about the restoration of justice, whether it has to do with our justification of God, the renewal of interpersonal relations, or the transformation of society. Therein integral advantage lies.*

BUILDING A HOME FOR BLACK, WHITE AND BROWN

The Formation of the ANC

Following the Anglo-Boer War in fact, early on in the last century, every effort was made by the British colonial authorities to reconcile the two settler communities in a united white nation. But blacks were excluded by the constitution of the Union of South Africa in 1910, and subsequently systematically deprived of their land and rights. This led, in response, to the formation of the of the African National Congress in 1912, a movement that sought to unite all blacks, irrespective of ethnic background in the struggle against their exclusion and deprivation.

After centuries of gestation scarred by violent conflict, 'two nations' were thus born. Ever since the fundamental 'national question' facing South Africa has been around the relationship between them, the 'white nation' seeking to be exclusively European, and the 'black nation' seeking to build an inclusive African identity. Apartheid was the logical outcome of the first; the struggle for liberation and a non-racial democracy was the inevitable project of the second.

Let My People Go

The first South African Nobel Peace Prize winner, Chief Albert Luthuli (3), who received the award in 1961, wrote in his *Let My People Go!*

From the beginning our history has been one of ascending unities, the breaking of tribal, racial and creedal barriers. The past cannot hope to have a life sustained by itself, wrenched from the whole. There remains before us the building of a new land, a home for men who are black, white, brown, from the ruins of old narrow groups, a synthesis of the rich cultural strains we have inherited.

THE WHOLE TRUTH AND NOTHING BUT THE TRUTH

National Reconstruction

More than 20 years later, a newly independent South Africa, in establishing its Truth and Reconciliation Commission (TRC) under Archbishop Tutu's guidance (4), *expressed the following conviction with a passion commensurate with his own ministry of reconciliation:*

There is a movement, not easily discernible, at the heart of things to reverse the awful centrifugal force of alienation, brokenness, division, hostility and disharmony. God has set in motion a centripetal process, a moving towards the Centre, towards unity, harmony, goodness, peace and justice; one that removed barriers. Jesus says, 'and when I am lifted from the earth I shall draw everyone to myself' as he hangs from the cross with out-flung arms, thrown out to clasp all, everyone, everything belongs. None is an outsider, all are insiders, all belong. There are no aliens, all belong in one family, God's family, the human family.

Ubuntu: I Am Because You Are

The sociality of humanity means, as such, that we only exist in relation to others, something expressed in the term *ubuntu*, which is repeatedly used in South Africa, included in the founding documents of the TRC, to describe the process of reconciliation. This means that *we come into being as persons through encountering and embracing the 'other'*, whether neighbour or enemy. For only within such a relationship is there genuine reciprocity of wills. The alternatives are the limitation that comes with atomistic individualism or absorption into an undifferentiated mass. So what, more generally, was the implication of *truth* and reconciliation in South Africa?

METANOIA AND THE FOUR TRUTHS

Restorative to Personal Truth

Like our 'four worlds' then, and indeed Nonaka and Takeuchi's knowledge spiral (Chapter 3) there are, for De Gruchy, four forms of truths, which can also be aligned with Herman's primal politics:

- the truth of *healing* or *restoration* contained within 'southern' *community*;
- as well as the *dialogic* truth emerging through an 'eastern' *big picture.*
- *objective* scientific truth sought in our 'northern' *Socratic discussion;*
- the *personal* truth constituted through our 'western-style' *individuation.*

Metanoia at the Centre

In effect these 'truths' may be likened not only to the 'four worlds', and to Louis Herman's primal politics (see Figure 10.1). Truth, moreover, serves the

	North *OBJECTIVE* Socratic Discussion	
West *PERSONAL* Individua tion	*Centre* *METANOIA*	*East* *DIALOGIC* Big Picture
	South *RESTORATIVE* Communal Democracy	

Figure 10.1 Worldview, knowledge and truth

cause for reconciliation and justice only when it leads to a genuine *metanoia,* that is a turning around, a breaking with an unjust past, and a moving towards a new future. This would be embodied in Mandela's *Long Walk to Freedom.*

COVENANTING TOGETHER TO RESTORE JUSTICE

Towards A Rainbow Nation

Nelson Mandela (5), as cited in his *Long Walk to Freedom,* in his inaugural speech in May 1994, declared: 'We enter a covenant that we shall build a society in which all south Africans, both black and white, will be able to walk, without any fear in their hearts, assured of their inalienable right to human dignity – a rainbow nation at peace with itself and the world'. *Reconciling is about building bridges, about allowing conflicting stories to interact in ways that evoke respect, build relationships and help restructure power relations.* This means that we have to go beyond an agreement to co-exist across those rivers that divide and find ways to engender common endeavour.

A Covenantal Relationship

Forging such relations means respecting difference without allowing difference to foster sectarianism and division. It means recognizing the way in which power has been abused in serving self-interest and developing structures of inequality and injustice, and seeking ways to achieve equity rather than protection of vested interests. *A covenantal relationship,* in other words, *goes further than a social contract because it is concerned about reconciliation rather than mere co-existence.* Indeed it is in the process of forming such covenants between black and white, man and nature, business and society, management and worker, that South Africa's integral advantage is constituted, naturally and culturally, socially and economically.

10.2 Freedom and Transformation

RELEASING GENIUS

In fact, in our (6) previous work on *Transformation Management,* initially cited here in Chapter 3 we recast Nelson Mandela's long walk to freedom in terms of the release of GENE-ius, as per Grounding and Emergence, now Navigation with a view to Effect. Here are selective excerpts from such transformation – if not strictly speaking 'Transformation Management' – of Mandela as an individual, the ANC as an organization, and South Africa as a society, heralding, prospectively at least, the integral advantage on which this current book is based. Pride of place here, in the context of such a long walk, and the place of navigation therein, is given to the so-called Robben Island University.

GROUNDING: LOCAL IDENTITY: NATURE AND COMMUNITY

The young Mandela was no more than five when he became a herd boy looking after sheep and calves in the fields. He discovered the almost mystical attachment that the Xhosa have for cattle, not only as a source of food and wealth, but as a blessing from God and a source of happiness. From then he dated his love of open spaces, simple beauties of nature, and clean line of the horizon. Nature then was his playground. Whereas his father once told stories of historic battles and heroic Xhosa warriors, his mother would enchant the young people with Xhosa legends and fables that came down from numberless generations. These tales stimulated their childish imagination and usually contained some moral lesson.

EMERGENCE: NATIONAL NON/ENTITY: CULTURE AND CONSCIOUSNESS

In 1937, when Mandela was 19, he went on to Wesleyan College in Fort Beaufort, about 175 miles southwest of Umtata. Fort Beaufort was one of a number of British outposts during the so-called Frontier Wars, in which a steady encroachment of white settlers systematically dispossessed the various

Xhosa tribes of their land. Over a century of conflict warriors like Makhanda and Maqoma, who were imprisoned – and indeed died in Robben Island – by British authorities, achieved Xhosa fame. In his final year at the Wesleyan College we were informed that the great Xhosa poet, Krune Mqhayi, was to visit the school.

Mqhayi (7) was actually an *imbongi*, a praise singer, a kind of oral historian who marks contemporary events and history with poetry that is of special meaning to his people. At one point his voice rose and said '*The assegai stands for what is glorious and true in African history; it is a symbol of the African as warrior and the African as artist* ... we cannot allow these foreigners who do not care for our culture to take over our nation. I predict that one day the forces of African society will achieve a momentous victory over the interloper. For too long we have succumbed to the false gods of the white man. But we shall emerge and cast off the foreign nation'. It was that experience in young adulthood that spearheaded Mandela's struggle, as a lawyer and as an activist, over the course of the next 27 years, for freedom for his people, and, once sentenced to life imprisonment, another 27 years of incarceration would follow, during the course of which 'Robben Island University' was established.

NAVIGATION: TOWARDS AN AFRICAN NATIONAL ENTITY: POLITY TO UNIVERSITY

In the period of internment, Robben Island was known as 'the university'. This was not only because of what Mandela and his fellow inmates learned from books, or because prisoners studied English, Afrikaans, art, geography and mathematics, or because so many of the comrades earned multiple degrees. Robben Island was known as the university because of what they learned from each other. *They became their own faculty, with their own professors, their own curriculum, their own courses. They made a distinction between academic studies, which were official, and political studies, which were not.*

For a number of years Mandela taught a course in political economy. In it he attempted to trace the evolution of economic man from the earliest times to the present, sketching out the path from ancient communal societies to feudalism to capitalism and socialism. He was by no means a scholar and not much of a teacher, and he would generally prefer to ask questions than to lecture. *His approach was not ideological, but it was biased in favour of socialism, which he saw as the most advanced stage of economic life then evolved by man.*

TRANSFORMATIVE EFFECT: TOWARDS GLOBAL INTEGRITY: POLITY TO ECONOMY

Mandela's actual release, after a protracted period of negotiations with De Klerk's Nationalist government was on 11 February 1990. At the age of 71 his life was beginning anew (8):

> Friends, comrades and fellow South Africans. I greet you all in the name of peace, democracy and freedom for all. I stand here before you not as a prophet but as a humble servant of you, the people. Your tireless and heroic sacrifices made it possible for me to be here today. I place my remaining years in your hands.

Although few today will remember 3 June 1993, it was a landmark in South African history. The multi-party forum voted to set a date for the country's first national, multi-party, non-racial one-person-one-vote election: 27 April, 1994. A month later the multi-party forum agreed on a first draft of an interim constitution. It provided for a bi-cameral parliament with a 400-member national assembly elected by proportional representation from national and regional party lists, and a senate elected indirectly by regional legislatures.

The first stage of our election effort involved what were known as People's Forums. ANC candidates would travel all over the country and hold meetings in towns and villages to listen to the hopes and fears, the ideas and complaints, of our people. The forums were parliaments of the people, not unlike the meetings of the chiefs of the Great Place that Mandela witnessed in his rural home as a boy. He revelled in the People's Forums. No one ever before had come to solicit their opinion and what should be done in their own country. The ANC, meanwhile, drafted their Reconstruction and Development Program (RDP), which outlined our plan to create jobs through public works, to build a million new houses with electricity and flush toilets, to extend primary healthcare and provide ten years of free education to all South Africans, to redistribute land through a land claims court, and to end the value-added tax on food. The document was translated into a simpler manifesto called 'A Better Life for all', which became the ANC's campaign manifesto.

If we fast forward then 20 years, we will find that the RDP process has in fact not been realized. Political liberation there may have been, but not economic liberation, and this is where Ramphele Mamphele, the ex-partner of Steve Biko, medical doctor, university vice chancellor, and ultimately political activist picks up the story. In constituting her Agang Party in 2013 (ultimately she was the only one of her party to win a seat in the 2014 elections), Mamphele sought to restore and renew Mandela's long walk to freedom.

10.3 Learning to Walk Together

TOWARDS SOCIO-ECONOMIC RECONCILIATION

A Journey of Healing

For Ramphele (9), as she originally argued in 2008, in her *Laying Ghosts to Rest: Dilemmas of Transformation in South Africa,* and thereafter put into political Agang (a Sotho-Tswana word for 'Let us Build') effect, through the launch of her new political party, in 2013, South Africa had lost its way. Its people, as a whole she said, needed to learn anew how to 'walk together'. As such it is embarking on a journey of healing the wounds of the past that perpetuate the disempowering social relations that characterize South African society today. The rhetoric of *ubuntu,* as we shall also see in the next chapter then, without evidence of the affiliative strategies of mutuality, reciprocity and capacity for empathy and emotional bonding with those at the bottom of the social ladder, only serves, for Rhampele, to confirm with poor people that there is something wrong with them. Many internalize the myth that their poverty is of their own making and reflects their worthlessness to society.

The truth and reconciliation process in South Africa in the mid-1990s, she goes on to say, was a resounding success in dealing with gross violations of human rights when people dug deeply within themselves to confront and ritualize the beginnings of a healing journey for both South Africans and the country. It is unfortunate, though, that the TRC process was deliberately designed to exclude all but gross violations of human rights. The political logic was understandable: compromise that involved letting go of retribution for socio-economic injustices was essential for a political settlement to be reached with the apartheid government of the day. But the importance of establishing the broken chain of human connectedness in the post-apartheid period was seriously underestimated. South Africa missed the opportunity to ritualize acknowledgement of its ruptured society as a foundation for starting a deeper healing process. *Failure to address the impact of violations of socio-economic rights in the transition to democracy has effectively then privatized the healing of social pain in South Africa.*

Ubuntu: Isolated Subjects to Co-Citizens

Ramphele (10) then proposes, in her next work on *Conversations with My Sons and Daughters* that the current generation pays more attention to how the country's legacy and the social pain its causes are impacting upon South Africa's social relationships. We need to ask how much social pain may have affected the country's ability as a society to live out the *ubuntu* ideals that as South Africans people are rightly proud of. Has the exclusion of, and discrimination against, the majority population made the country more determined to live out *ubuntu* or not? How much social pain are we inadvertently continuing to inflict on those who remain excluded from opportunities while we repeatedly affirm our adherence to *ubuntu.*

The process of democratization requires commitment by citizens and leaders alike to embark on a journey to unlearn the authoritarian culture of the past, which still permeates South African homes, schools and workplaces and some civil society structures such as trade unions and churches. It is Ramphele's view that *the transformation of South African identities from those of subjects to citizens requires a commitment to a journey of healing.*

What kind of leadership is required for such?

LEADERSHIP FOR COMPLETING THE TRANSITION

The People Have to be the Liberators

South Africa is, in the second decade of the new millennium, again at a crossroads as a country, Ramphele maintains. It managed the first transition to democracy by working together as civil society groups internally and later linked with the exiles in the liberation movement to achieve a glorious victory against apartheid. The country is now challenged, to complete the transition and make freedom a reality in the daily lives of ordinary citizens.

During the first few years of transition South Africa was blessed with able leadership that steered it towards a mass-based approach in the march to freedom. *The journey started in earnest with the 1950s ANC-led defiance campaigns, the 1960s PAC anti-pass law campaigns, the 1970s Black Consciousness Movement student-led protests that gave way to labour and civic association mass mobilizations.* The relentless bid for freedom ultimately overwhelmed what has been seen until then as an impenetrable fortress of white domination. The leadership for this mass-based movement was provided by ordinary people: in street committees, churches, factory floors and in every situation in which people found themselves. They became, to paraphrase Mahatma Gandhi, the change they wanted to see in their own country.

Nelson Mandela, South Africa's founding father as first president, was the first to recognize the power of ordinary people, and to leverage it to initiate settlement talks with his captors in jail. The liberation movement formations outside and inside the country also realized that the real liberators had to be the people themselves. The ANC in exile was forced by developments post-1976 into accepting the importance of complementing the internal mass-based to the system of apartheid instead of undermining them.

This internal mass-based movement became increasingly led by faith-based leaders such as Anglican Archbishop Desmond Tutu, Muslim scholar Farid Esack and the Reverend Allan Boesack of the United Reformed Church. The focus was initially on mass mobilization against governance without representation of the majority, whereas the ANC outside mounted a successful propaganda campaign that discredited the apartheid government. International pressure mounted and ultimately divestment and disinvestment in the apartheid economy undermined the foundations of white privilege. The stage was set for the successful negotiated settlement that ushered in the freedom South Africans enjoy today.

The Time has Come to Heal the Wounds

Meanwhile Mandela resisted the hero-worship that was showered upon him. He insisted on affirming the role of others in the struggle for freedom, such as Walter Sisulu, Govan Mbeki and Ahmed Kathrada (11), rather than placing himself above his fellow citizens. His famous words at his inauguration were:

> *The time has come to heal the wounds. The moment to bridge the chasms that divide us has come. The time to build is upon us … We have triumphed in the effort to implant hope in the breasts of millions of people. We enter into a covenant that we shall build the society in which all South Africans, both black and white, will be able to walk tall, without fear in their hearts, assured of their inalienable right to human dignity – a rainbow nation at peace with itself and the world.*

This leads us back to *ubuntu*.

UBUNTU, RAINBOW NATION AND THE PROCESS OF HEALING

The 'I am because you are' – *ubuntu* – in the above 'rainbow nation' light, should be the touchstone, for Ramphele, of South Africans' social relationships. People should therefore distance themselves from those who use *ubuntu* as a slogan to market themselves in both the private and public sector without any intention of living its values. We need, moreover, to learn from other cultures as well about the importance of *ubuntu*, especially in framing how we lead. For Burma's Aung San Suu Kyi, whom Ramphele (12), now explicitly exhibiting *A Passion for Freedom* cites as such:

> *The quintessential revolution is that of the spirit ... To live the full life one must have the courage to bear responsibility for the needs of others ... one must want to bear that responsibility.*

To what extent has South Africa made the 'revolution of the spirit' its focus to guide its post-apartheid social relationships? Is it true that instead of becoming the nation at peace that Mandela spoke of at his inauguration, people have come much further apart? *The process of healing*, for Ramphele, *has yet to begin and for that the country needs the humility of spirit to acknowledge the need for it and commit to work with others in their homes, community, at work and in the wider society to achieve it.* The second step allied to mind-set change is the need for a new language to reflect the vision South Africa is committed to. The journey from subject to citizen has to include discarding the expressions that promote the very passivity we seek to root out in psycho-social relationships. Citizens are not passive recipients of whatever largesse comes from those in government or some other form of authority. The notion of 'service delivery' may have arisen from a desire by the country's first government to be seen to be 'delivering' on the promises of freedom. But no government in the world can have the capacity and resources to 'deliver services' on the scale needed to eradicate poverty and inequality to a very passive citizenry.

The language of 'delivery' reinforces the very subject identity that Ramphele's 'walk together' approach is seeking to shift into a citizen identity characterized by the exercise of rights and responsibilities. Sustainable development is only possible through active engagement of citizens in all phases of the process.

South Africa needs its people, firstly, to be the geniuses that shed the mantle of fear in exchange for that of courage to lead its citizens out of the morass of fear and false loyalties that undermine good governance and the building of bridges across the widening chasms in society. Secondly, people need to live their, and their country's, dreams. The third step of the journey involves strengthening and deepening leadership among citizens. Heroic politics is limited in its ability to sustainably drive change precisely because of the narrow reach of leaders in a pyramidal system of power. One of the reasons for the resilience of the student-led Black Consciousness Movement (BCM) in the 1970s and the Mass Democratic Movement (MDM) in the 1980s, was the practice of holding leadership development seminars and workshops that created safe spaces for activists to hone their leadership skills. *Not everyone can be a leader in the traditional sense, but each of us has leadership capabilities in niche areas that need to be identified and developed.*

The core, overall task for Ramphele, in South Africa, is a process of healing, that of 'laying ghosts to rest', which is the key, for her, to transformation.

HEALING AND TRANSFORMATION

Towards Transcendence

The process of transformation to normalize South Africa has at its core then, for Ramphele again, (13) as first intimated above, the laying to rest of lingering ghosts lest they continue to haunt our future. The most stubborn ghosts are those whose names we are often too afraid to mention: racism, ethnic chauvinism, sexism and authoritarianism. Yet effective transformation is predicated on acknowledgement of each ghost by calling it by name, engaging with it to transact unfinished business and bidding it to make peace with bygones.

South Africa has been fortunate enough to have in its midst transformative leaders with special qualities who have laid some ghosts to rest already. But the task is not complete, and much work remains to be done.

The Path to Healing is Long

Transformation of a society entails a complete change in both form and substance, a metamorphosis, as happens in the life cycles of insects as butterflies. The transition from an invisible egg, to a larva, then a pupa, and finally an insect with all its beautiful colours takes the butterfly through significant changes in form and substance. The scale and scope of the transformation South Africa embarked on after apartheid is without precedence. The country has had to wrestle simultaneously with political, economic and social transformation at all levels. The term 'transformation' is used here to denote fundamental changes in the structures, institutional arrangements, policies, modes of operation and relationships within society.

South Africa, according to Ramphele, had no model to guide its transformation from the apartheid past to its envisaged future. It had to find its own way. A central challenge in the transformation process is the quality of the human capital base it has inherited from apartheid. The past has its beauty, she says, but it also has its ugly parts. The country had little choice but to embrace the reality of the past as a whole. As such, South Africans have had to struggle to find closure on many issues related to that past. This is in part because the wounds are still raw. It is also because people have had difficulty acknowledging the depth of the trauma. *Wounds fester partly because as a result of people's denial of their extent and their impact on attempts to transform society. Past wounds have a long history, so that the road to healing is long.*

The Scarring of the Black Psyche

Frantz Fanon (14), the Martiniquan-born Algerian based psychiatrist-revolutionary in the 1950s and 1960s, showed, in his *Black Skin-White Masks* how the colonial situation had debilitating consequences for oppressed people's personalities and identities. The structures of colonial society condition them to see the world, including themselves, through the eyes of the oppressor. Such societies are always hierarchical, with their oppressor and valued as 'good', and the oppressed and their culture as 'bad'. *The oppressed, adopting this view themselves, become alienated from themselves and their cultures. Fanon called this 'the scarring of the black psyche'.* Some of the symptoms of this condition include a socially induced inferiority complex, self-hatred, low self-esteem, jealousy of those seen to be progressing (both black and white) and sometimes a defensive romanticization of the black culture.

Hence the central message of Steve Biko, as founder of the Black Consciousness Movement in the 1970s, was that psychological and cultural liberation of the mind of black people was a precondition of a successful struggle for political freedom. As Biko (15) put it:

> *... hence thinking along the lines of Black Consciousness makes the black man see himself as a being, entire in himself, and not as an extension of broom or additional leverage to some machine.*

Laying the ghosts to rest, then, entails transcendence beyond normal human experience. Transcendence is usually associated with the spiritual realm. In a sense, South Africa's transformation has at its best moments delved deep into the collective consciousness and touched the spirit of the nation. It was at these moments that people rose above the ordinary and achieved extraordinary things. Transcendence requires openness to a radically different frame of reference; it takes one beyond the known into the unknown, demanding courage and a willingness to take risks. *Most analyses of the South African condition tend to focus on material issues in the socioeconomic and political domains. Yet human beings as the main actors in history are framed in significant ways by spiritual and psychological impulses that go beyond material needs.*

We are inclined to underestimate, as such, the importance of deep matters of the soul that distinguish humans from other members of the animal kingdom. *We are at our best as human,* as Ramphele puts it, *when our souls and minds are in harmony with what we do and how we relate to others.*

LIBERATION THEOLOGY TO BLACK THEOLOGY

In Pursuit of Spiritual Freedom

Material freedom disengaged from inner spiritual freedom, then, puts us at risk of losing the focus on the larger purpose of freedom – freedom to be fully what we can be in a democracy. From the 1960s therefore, liberation theology added a spiritual dimension to the discourse and practice of resistance politics. The Black Consciousness Movement embraced it and popularized it as Black Theology. Trevor Huddleston's stance against apartheid embodied in his 1950s work as an English Anglican priest amongst the people of Sophiatown, Johannesburg, inspired the likes of Desmond Tutu and others to stand on the side of the oppressed people in their ministry. The 'conversion' of such people as Beyers Naude, the South African cleric and theologian, a member of the Afrikaaner establishment Broederbond who became an anti-apartheid activist, reflects the impact of the spiritual on the freedom struggle. Those who lived in exile before this infusion of spiritual discourse missed out, as such, on an important dimension.

Jonathan Sachs (16), Chief Rabbi of the United Hebrew Congregation of Great Britain and the Commonwealth, cited here by Ramphele, presents an interesting perspective from Judaism.

> *In Judaism, faith is not acceptance but protest, against a world that is, in the name of the world that is not yet but ought to be ... It is impossible to be moved by the prophets and not have a social conscience ... the world will not get better of its own accord. Nor will we make a more humane place by leaving it to others.*

We now turn back, by way of conclusion, to Mandela himself.

10.4 Conclusion

NEED FOR INSTITUTIONAL EMBODIMENT OF THE LONG WALK TO FREEDOM

Individual Icon to Iconic Country

All too often, for our South African, north–south purposes, what we find is that what is valued is the individual man or woman, Mandela in this case as a local and indeed global icon, rather than what he embodied, institutionally and societally, and thereby the integral advantage, so to speak, that he pursued in the course of releasing South African GENE-ius.

It is not difficult to see how Mandela was grounded in, and indeed continually revisited the nature and community of his childhood years, in Qunu. It is also clearly apparent that both he and the ANC of which he was part, emerged, through their long walk to freedom, as if on the kind of mythological journey to which Van der Post has alluded. Moreover, it is not difficult to see the direct democracy in his communal heritage, the big picture of which he was a leading part, that is the *long walk to freedom*, the Socratic discussions in which he and his comrades engaged at Robben Island University, and the process of individuation which Mandela profoundly underwent, from freedom fighter to national reconciler. Above all, his means of navigation was *truth and reconciliation.*

NEED FOR SOCIAL AND ECONOMIC TRANSFORMATION

Economic Liberation Missing

However, there was one big, missing element, which revealed itself ever more, in the period during Mandela's own premiership, and thereafter that of Mbeki and Zuma to follow. In the worlds of Archbishop Tutu (17), as instigator of the Truth and Reconciliation Commission at the outset:

> *In South Africa today, the resources of the state have to be deployed imaginatively, wisely, efficiently and equitably, to facilitate the reconstruction process in a manner which best brings relief and hope to the widest sections of the community; this reparation is as balm being poured over the wounds to assist healing.*

However, and most significantly, he went on to say:

> *In South Africa, at the same time, the whole process of reconciliation has been placed in jeopardy by the enormous disparities between rich and poor, between the mainly rich whites and the mainly poor blacks … unless blacks gain access to clean water, electricity, decent health care, decent education, good jobs and a decent environment – we can just kiss reconciliation goodbye.*

VALUE SHARING – INTERDEPENDENCE AND TRANSFORMATION IN SOUTH AFRICA (ITISA)

CODESA Enterprise

In fact within the business community, in the post-independence period, indeed starting in the 1980s before, there has been one lone voice, taking seriously what Tutu and Mandela had been calling for: social and economic reconciliation. While Black Economic Empowerment (BEE) has played a part in such, it has served overwhelmingly to establish an African capitalist elite, a far cry from Mandela's and Marx's 'to everyone according to his means to everyone according to their needs'. In effect, the RDP was abandoned in the latter part of the 1990s in favour of getting into GEAR (Growth, Employment and Redistribution) following the conventional economic wisdom.

The one lone 'north–south' voice has been that of Albert Koopman, through the worker democracy, the CODESA *value sharing* enterprise he established at South Africa's Cashbuild, and the movement for Interdependence and Transformation in South Africa (ITISA) he and his colleagues created in the 1990s.

Unfortunately, by the new millennium it had been dissolved, as a worker democracy, and had returned to being a conventional business. We take up this story in the next chapter, focused on transformative effect in a north–south context.

Bibliography

1. Some, M.P. (1997) *The Healing Wisdom of Africa.* New York, Tarcher.
2. De Gruchy, J. (2000) *Reconciliation – Restoring Justice.* Cape Town, SCM Press.
3. Luthuli, A. (1963) *Let My People Go.* London, Fontana Books.

4. Tutu, D. (2000) *No Future Without Forgiveness.* Cambridge, Perfect Paperback.
5. Mandela, N. (1994) *The Long Walk to Freedom.* London, Abacus.
6. Lessem, R. and Schieffer, A. (2009) *Transformation Management: Towards the Integral Enterprise.* Farnham, Gower.
7. Mandela, N. (1994) *The Long Walk to Freedom.* London, Abacus.
8. Mandela, N. (1994) *The Long Walk to Freedom.* London, Abacus.
9. Ramphele, M. (2008) *Laying Ghosts to Rest: Dilemmas of Transformation in South Africa.* Cape Town, Tafelburg.
10. Ramphele, M. (2012) *Conversations with My Sons and Daughters.* Rosebank, Johannesburg, Penguin Books.
11. Ramphele M (2012) *Conversations with My Sons and Daughters.* Rosebank, Johannesburg, Penguin Books.
12. Ramphele, M. (2013) *A Passion for Freedom.* Cape Town, Taffelburg.
13. Ramphele, M. (2008) *Laying Ghosts to Rest: Dilemmas of Transformation in South Africa.* Cape Town, Tafelburg.
14. Fanon, F. (2008) *Black Skin, White Masks.* London, Pluto Press.
15. Mngxitama, A., Alexander, A. and Gibson, N. eds (2008) *Biko Lives: Contesting the Legacies of Steve Biko.* New York, Palgrave Macmillan.
16. Sachs, J. (2004) *Dignity of Difference: How to Avoid the Clash of Civilizations.* London, Continuum.
17. Tutu, D. (2000) *No Future Without Forgiveness.* Cambridge, Perfect Paperback.

Chapter 11

Ubuntu to Value Sharing: Transformative Healing Effect – Out of the Divine Will of Africa

> *We have to admit that there are moats and gulfs that divide us, we have to recognize them; but our aim ands our task should be to build bridges across them, not to deepen and extend them, least of all to block up or demolish such fords and causeways as our conventional way of life leaves open for our use. Partnership provides the key to reconciliation and co-existence.*
>
> *Anton Rupert (1),* Priorities for Co-existence

11.1 Introduction

RECONCILIATION – ONLY TO A POINT

Mandela, Tutu, Ramphele

As intimated in the previous three chapters, original grounding in *Earth Jurisprudence*, with a view to South Africa's emerging *Primal Future*, has been implicitly navigated through Mandela's 'Long Walk to Freedom', in pursuit of *Truth and Reconciliation*, but only to a point. For in terms articulated in the last chapter by Archbishop Tutu (2):

> *unless houses replace the hovels and shacks in which most blacks live, unless blacks gain access to clean water, electricity, decent health care, decent education, good jobs and a decent environment – we can just kiss reconciliation goodbye.*

The ultimate transformative effect of *value sharing*, with the one Cashbuild exception to be articulated below, has been supplanted by Black Economic

Empowerment (BEE), with its 'western-northern' as opposed to 'north–south' connotations, hitherto brought to the surface by the late Steve Biko's *Black Consciousness.*

BLACK CONSCIOUSNESS

Steve Biko (3) was in many ways the architect of the Black Consciousness Movement during the apartheid years, ultimately paying for such with his life, also taking on from where Van der Post (*Dark Eye of Africa*) and Herman (primal politics) had left off:

> *A people without a positive history is like a vehicle without an engine. They always live in the shadow of a more successful society. yet one can extract from our indigenous cultures a lot of positive virtues that can teach the westerner a lesson or two. The oneness of community, for instance, is at the heart of African culture. The easiness with which Africans communicate with each other is not forced by authority but inherent within them.*

Black Consciousness, for him then, is an attitude of mind and a way of life. By seeking to run away from themselves and emulate the white man blacks are insulting the intelligence of whomever created them black. *Freedom therefore is the ability to define oneself with one's possibilities held back not by the power of other people but only by one's relationship to God and to nature.* If one is free at heart, no man-made chains can bind one to servitude. As people existing in a continuous struggle for truth, we have to examine and question old concepts, values and systems, set within the kind of primal political context that Herman has advocated.

UBUNTU: I AM BECAUSE YOU ARE

Giving the World a Human Face

The attitude of seeing people not as themselves but as agents for some particular function either to one's advantage or disadvantage is, for Biko, foreign to the African. We are not, he says, a suspicious race. We believe in the inherent goodness of man. We enjoy man for himself. We regard our living together not as an unfortunate mishap warranting endless competition amongst us but as a deliberate act of God to make us a community of brothers and sisters jointly involved in the quest for a composite answer to the varied problems of life.

Whereas then a Westerner is geared towards using a problem-solving approach following very trenchant analysis, the African approach is that of situation-experiencing. The Westerner has an aggressive mentality. When he sees a problem he will not rest until he has formulated some solution to it. He cannot live with contradictory ideas in his mind; he must settle for one or the other, or else evolve a third idea in his mind, which harmonizes or reconciles the other two. And he is vigorously scientific in rejecting solutions for which there is no basis in logic. He draws a sharp line between the natural and the supernatural, the rational and non-rational, and more often than not, he dismisses the supernatural and non-rational as superstition.

Africans being a pre-scientific people, for Biko then, do not recognize any conceptual cleavage between the natural and the supernatural. They experience a situation rather than face a problem. By this is meant that they allow both the rational and the non-rational elements to make an impact upon them, and any action they may take could be described more as a response of the total personality to the situation than the result of some mental exercise. As such Africans would obviously find it artificial to create special occasions for worship. Neither did they see it as logical to have a particular building in which all worship would be conducted.

Africans believed that God was always in communication with them and therefore merited attention everywhere and anywhere. In rejecting western values, therefore, they are rejecting those things that are not only foreign to us but that seek to destroy the most cherished of our beliefs – that the corner/stone of society is man himself – not just his welfare, not his material being, but just man himself with all his ramifications. Africans reject the power-based society of the westerner that seems to be ever concerned with perfecting their technological know-how while losing out on their spiritual dimension. For Biko then:

> *We believe that in the long-run the special contribution from Africa will be in the field of human relationships. The great powers of the world may have done wonders in giving the world an industrial and military look, but the great gift still has to come from Africa – giving the world a human face.*

So, the question inevitably is, why do we seemingly see so little of such '*ubuntu*' in Africa generally, if not also in South Africa specifically. Now we turn to Biko's ex-partner, in the struggle years, Ramphele Mamphele, who, in the last 2014 elections, felt the ANC had been failing to take the *Long Walk to Freedom* on, and therefore established her own political party – *Agang* – of which she is now a lone parliamentary representative.

AGANG: TO BUILD

Towards a Process of Healing

Agang, the Sotho term 'to build', is the political party of that name recently formed in 2013 by Ramphele, a South African medical practitioner, business-woman, university vice chancellor and social activist, to align freedom, transformation and conversation in uniquely South African guise. The guiding image for her (4), appropriately so for a medical doctor, is *the process of healing.* Most of her life (5) as she writes in her book *A Passion for Freedom,* has been dedicated to the struggle for justice and freedom in her country, taking on from where Mandela left off.

For Ramphele (6), overall, South Africa has fallen prey to two fatal flaws. It has:

- fallen into the trap of heroic politics with the ANC governing as a liberation movement that had not transformed itself into a modern political party
- failed to tackle the challenges of systematic restructuring of the economy to lay the foundation for the realization of socio-economic rights and inclusive prosperity.

It is the second of these statements with which we are most concerned at this culminating point, in South Africa's prospective pursuit of integral advantage.

Towards Socio-Economic Reconciliation

Learning anew to 'walk together' entails embarking on a journey of healing the wounds of the past that perpetuate the disempowering social relations that characterize South African society today. The rhetoric of *ubuntu* without evidence of the affiliative strategies of mutuality, reciprocity and capacity for empathy and emotional bonding with those at the bottom of the social ladder, only serves, for Rhampele, to confirm with poor people that there is something wrong with them. Many internalize the myth that their poverty is of their own making and reflects their worthlessness to society.

The truth and reconciliation process in South Africa in the mid-1990s was a resounding success in dealing with gross violations of human rights when people dug deeply within themselves to confront and ritualize the beginnings of a healing journey for both South Africans and the country. It is unfortunate, though, that the TRC process was deliberately designed to exclude all but gross violations of human rights. The political logic was understandable: compromise that involved letting go of retribution for socio-economic injustices was essential for a political settlement to be reached with the apartheid government of the day. But the importance of establishing the broken chain of human connectedness in the post-apartheid period was seriously underestimated. South Africa missed the opportunity to ritualize acknowledgement of its ruptured society as a foundation for starting a deeper healing process. As for Tutu, so for Ramphele: *Failure to address the impact of violations of socio-economic rights in the transition to democracy has effectively then privatized the healing of social pain in South Africa.*

Subjects to Co-Citizens – A Journey of Healing

Ramphele then proposes that the current generation pays more attention to how the country's legacy and the social pain it has caused are impacting upon South Africa's social and economic relationships. We need to ask how much social pain may have affected the country's ability as a society to live out the *ubuntu* ideals that as South Africans people are rightly proud of?

Has the exclusion of, and discrimination against, the majority population made the country more determined to live out *ubuntu* or not? How much social pain are we inadvertently continuing to inflict on those who remain excluded from opportunities while we repeatedly affirm our adherence to such? The process of democratization in fact requires commitment by citizens and leaders alike to embark on a journey to unlearn the authoritarian culture of the past, which still permeates South African homes, schools and workplaces and some civil society structures such as trade unions and churches. It is Ramphele's view that *the transformation of South African identities from those of subjects to citizens requires a commitment to a journey of healing.* One such citizen, and a business citizen at that, as we shall see, was Albert Koopman.

The Legacy of Socio-Economic Neglect

The legacy of systemic socio-economic neglect, Ramphele goes on to say, as did Archbishop Tutu before her, is at the core of the unfinished agenda of acknowledging the impact of colonialism and apartheid. Unfortunately, history has no precedents of such socio-economic reparations in a situation where there are neither victors nor vanquished. South Africans have to find their own model to make peace with this aspect of the past, by both understanding and transcending the stubborn ghosts that haunt it. How might this be accomplished?

THE GENETIC PROCESSES OF HEALING

Personal to Integral

Such a journey of healing, Ramphele's (7) overall life mission, to transcend the stubborn ghosts that haunt us, individually and collectively, starts with personal stories. These personal histories then become a 'river of life', just like Mandela's *long walk to freedom*, thereby going into rewriting the national history – personal rivers of life flowing into the nation's river of life. Textbooks, for her, have to be rewritten to enable people to process the pain, see their history through different eyes and move beyond it. The personal and national are intertwined and it is difficult to build a democracy when a country's personal history still hurts. Community activist Martha Cabrera, a mentor of Ramphela's in Nicaragua, cites four GENEtic processes:

- *grounding in the personal sphere*: recognizing crises, wounds and healing;
- *the emergent historical/cultural sphere*: how our personal life is marked by a country's history and the national culture, how many dysfunctional strategies our culture has, and how they are expressed and ultimately transcended;
- *navigating through the organizational sphere*: what organizational form we establish, as per the ANC or the TRC in the South African case;
- *effecting transformation via the integral sphere*: actualizing the developmental model that acknowledges and promotes healing of social and economic pain.

We now turn to Koopman, Cashbuild and ITISA (Interdependence and Transformation in South Africa), as an illustration of all of such, in the social and economic arena. As was the case for Nelson Mandela, we shall let Albert Koopman (8) tell the Cashbuild story in his own words, thereby reinforcing the point that Van der Post makes (Chapter 8), that Africa, or for us the 'north–south', is a biblically laden land of heroes, including for example Biko and Luthuli (*Cry for Freedom*), Mandela and De Klerk (*Long Walk to Freedom*), and now Albert Koopman (*Building on the Divine Will of Africa*).

11.2 The Cashbuild Story: Healing Divides – Becoming a Worker Democracy

I ENTERED LIFE AS A MORAL FIGHTER

Entering Life as a Clean, Moral Fighter

I was raised as a street fighter. My mother died when I was 13 and my father lived in Mozambique, 1,240 miles from me. Set free at a very early age I had to learn to survive. That meant dealing with people, including people who had hang-ups, and people who wanted to do me in for what I believed. *The one thing that I learnt as a result was that I was going to enter my life as a clean, moral fighter, someone who sterilized his bicycle chains before he entered the fight of interpersonal relationships.* Unlike the animals with claws and teeth, God gave me his supreme gifts; choice and intellect. Making use of these two gifts I was able to observe my fellow-man going about his daily activities and make his life more meaningful. From this I acquired my moral purpose.

Combining the Rationality of the North with the Humanity of the South

The story you are about to hear, then, is one of my personal experiences in an African context, through my involvement as the Chief Executive of a Cash and Carry Building Material Merchant in South Africa. It is a story of success and many failures, a story of victories and sadnesses in my attempt to create an excellent company, to put it mildly, in a somewhat turbulent society. *It is the story of how a white (northern) man in Africa became a white African (southern). It is the story of how I combined the rationality of the First World with the humanity of the Third.*

NORTH AND SOUTH INITIALLY FAILED TO MEET

I Did Not Know Enough About the South to Know Where to Start Looking

Cashbuild was started as a wholesaler in 1978 and became a very successful business in a short space of time. Situated predominantly in the rural areas of South Africa and focusing on the black housing market, our staff complement consisted of 84 per cent black, 13 per cent white and 3 per cent Indian. However, by mid 1982, with 12 outlets, profits started sliding. *Everything 'northern' was in place – systems, procedures, technology, combined with a booming market – but something was going wrong and I did not know enough about the south, at that point, to recognize where to start looking.*

We embraced our cardinal principles of giving value to our customers, being innovative, adaptable and totally committed to the business as well as having efficient organizational structures, but obviously something was changing and we did not know what it was. Our hierarchy was well displayed on the walls of all our outlets, everyone was placed in neat little boxes with prescribed job descriptions and functions, and no one was achieving our objectives as had been laid out! I came to the conclusion that we had a lot of trained men but no actual committed soldiers.

I Started by Saying I Am Sorry

It was clear that our organizational structure was autocratic, as was my own personal management style. We had to change, but how? What if people started seeing me as soft, when I became more participative and democratic? What about the chaos that might occur during the period of transition? Well there was no other way to do it at the time but by MBFA – Managing by Fumbling Around. *There was no alternative but to plunge in at the deep end and to risk my neck and possibly be forced to say 'I'm sorry' for my original way of doing things.* I immediately commissioned an attitude survey and found that pro-company feelings, to the tune of 89 per cent in 1980, had slipped to 74 per cent in 1982.

I Was a Pompous, Egocentric and Distant Northerner

Typical remarks of the predominantly white, first world (northern) management team about the majority of our third world (southern) workforce were 'there's no way one can train them; they're too badly educated'; 'they simply won't open up as people and talk about their aspirations, needs and fears because of cultural barriers'; 'none of then understands our business and they simply don't care'. Remarks about myself were even more demeaning. 'You're pompous, egocentric, and very distant from what's happening at the coal-face'.

UNCOVERING THE DIVINE WILL OF AFRICA

Management 'North' Pulling One Way, Workers' 'South' the Other

Key questions went through my mind. Why do the workers actually work? What is their social or Divine Will? What went wrong in Cashbuild with respect to capital and labour? What were we actually trying to achieve as a business organism? *How do we bring together the rights of people, their spiritually-based humanity and the economic process as represented in the workplace?* Subsequently, I conducted a succession of brainstorming sessions to uncover the purpose of Cashbuild's existence. It soon became clear to us that one purpose existed in management's head and another in the workers'. Management 'up north' was pulling one way and the people 'down south' another. There was no transcendent purpose linking one with the other.

Listening to and Interacting with the Other

Meanwhile, in the course of launching, and participating in, company workshops over a period of six months, *it became clear to me that active listening and intensive interaction between people made each aware of the other's spirit*. Day in day out I was confronted with people's vitality, their reasons for being, and their creativity. I became aware that there was a spirit or soul that lay deep within each person, which needed awakening. However, our current Cashbuild organization was patently incapable of releasing it. North was north and south was south and never the twain did meet!

Beginning to See the Light

Typically a Chief Executive, after fighting like hell to get to the top, goes into hybernation once he gets there and forgets his leadership role. In order to enrich his own existence he all too often forgets his responsibility to benefit his followers. Until this point I had become just such a self-centred person. Perhaps now, though, I had begun to see the light.

ESTABLISHING OUR CARDINAL PRINCIPLES

Northern Management Principles Needed to Embrace our Southern Workers' Spirit

Arising out of 3,000 issues that came to our attention through the brainstorming sessions, we drew up a set of cardinal principles emerging out of the interdependent relationships that existed between customer, employee, company, competitor and motivation. We realized, at the same time, that the 'northern' principles would have to embrace the 'southern' spirit of every employee, so they were spelled out as follows:

- we recognize that the marketing process of getting goods from supplier to customer is the concern of every employee and that we have to liberate him/her to achieve this;

- we want to strive for quality service through people and keep our system as balanced as possible through on-the-job training, motivation through better supervision, self measurement and statistical control rather than boss control, giving people a say over their workplace;
- we recognize that quality service and total productivity will only come if we rediscover the spirit of (wo)man within the workplace, providing job enrichment by changing the work people do;
- people need to belong to and identify with the company's cause; customers must be satisfied through committed people.

Southern Spirit; Northern Organization

At every workshop session, which subsequently followed, we probed all the obstacles which stood in the way of our following our cardinal principles. No stone was left unturned and over a period of one year we listened to why people worked, with whom they preferred to work, and what they saw would be the design of the perfect workplace. After spending extended periods of time living amongst our black employees, experiencing life within their communities, and consulting with them directly, *I found I had to review my whole understanding of the people I employed, as well as how they saw their relationship with our business and with its philosophy.* The degree to which aspects of indigenous 'southern' culture were to become 'spiritualized' in the workplace was to depend on the type of 'northern' organization imposed upon the individual, including the degree to which the organization would allow expression of these elements.

TURNING OUR THINKING ABOUT PEOPLE UPSIDE DOWN

I Realized Capitalist Exploitation Could No Longer Exist

I was therefore forced to seek a way in which we could spell out and determine our objective common interest in the production of commodities – customer service (southern) – to replace capital's pure interest in increasing profits (western). Lots of meetings, small group activities, discussion groups and open two-way communications had to form as much of the way we ran our business as did the work itself.

Everything had to be focused upon the common interest of creating wealth and fostering an understanding amongst workers that the correct management of capital benefits the organization as a whole. This correct management, in turn, could only occur if the worker was democratically involved in contributing towards the overall success of the organization. I visualized that in this manner so called capitalist exploitation (of the 'southern' community) would no longer be able to exist.

Creating the Freedom to be Enterprising

We had to turn our thinking about people upside down and look at our business totally differently. The perception of capitalist exploitation at Cashbuild had to be changed. This change needed to be achieved not merely through some superficial 'western' programme of empowerment, but through an active 'northern' restructuring of the hierarchy, to liberate the work ethic. *We had to design an organization that was truly free so that the cooperation between all individuals in fact became its own sustainable social form.* We needed a social form that could accommodate the freedom to be enterprising, as well as harnessing the spiritual consciousness of all our employees. Enter our CARE philosophy – Cashbuild's Aspirations with Regard to Excellence.

CASHBUILD'S CARE PHILOSOPHY

Establish 'Northern' Code of Conduct and Release 'Southern' Consciousness

In essence our so-called CARE philosophy sought to bring about a balancing of power within the organization. At that stage, in 1982, authority was vested with management (but no power) and power with the unions (but no authority). *Firstly, we built in mechanisms for the protection of individual rights vis à vis the organization, through a 'northern' code of conduct. Secondly, CARE groups were formed to give expression to the 'southern' spiritual consciousness of individuals, serving as a vehicle for discussion of issues affecting their working life.* Groups were formed at five levels – general labourers, semi-skilled personnel, junior, middle and senior managers – each with their own majority elected President. Thirdly, these groups were to engage with the economic process, sharing information about efficiency and productivity, and learning about as well as influencing the company's wealth creating process.

CARE by the People for the People

A CARE philosophy designed by the people for the people spelled out how our workplace should be regulated, and set out the rules of the business game. Some of the salient points were:

- a commitment to *joint decision making* at all levels, with everyone playing their part in finding solutions to problems;
- an *open and free culture* with everyone in the organization having access to any line manager;
- *a team consisting of different races*, sexes and cultural creeds, none of which were to be discriminated against;
- *a belief in the 'Extra Mile'* concept, with the customer centre stage as such, both for the organization and for the individual.

After the philosophy was translated into seven languages and a little booklet given to each and every employee to read, we felt we could start moving into the future. Our view towards people changed dramatically as we recognized that:

- each employee had his own rights, will to work, and wanted some control over his/her destiny;
- we needed to understand the cross-cultural complexities of our workplace through continuous interaction;
- the company would place no limits on human growth.

Yet the resistance to change continued.

RESISTANCE TO CHANGE

They Told it Like it Was

Whilst our CARE horizon extended over five years I found, after only 18 months, that resistance to change had become an inordinate obstacle. Indeed we started experiencing that people actually cared for the company, and began to find such meaning and purpose in their work that productivity was considerably enhanced. But the euphoria was short lived. After many consultative workshops we decided to have a major get together to assess our performance so far. As the management team, our ears fell off – they told it like it was!

> *'Mr Koopman, I would like to resign as President because my fellow men see me as siding with management; they're no longer carrying out my instructions'.*

> *'I have no power. Although my people voted me in I cannot get my manager to act on their requests. He simply is not interested'.*

'The company has cheated us for so long. Why is it suddenly changing. We don't believe in it'.

'My manager told me the other day that he sees me as a threat and will not cooperate with me'.

'We don't trust our manager. He is prejudiced against blacks'.

'What happens to my family if I die'.

In other words, the process of healing, as Ramphele (9) has indicated, takes a long time, to overcome the ghosts of the past, and the new Cashbuild was only half way through, with the journey of the hero, in this case Koopman, in mid-stream. And he had his own hosts to slay, along the way, before he was to be transformed, in truly north–south guise.

THE ADVENT OF VENTURECOM

Southern Social Selves Disconnected from North-Western Economic Processes

We were sure that our belief in raising spiritual consciousness was valid, but we could now see our employees expressing their 'southern' social selves as apart from the 'north-western' economic process. While they perceived their labour power as intimately associated with themselves as human beings, they still saw the company as viewing their labour content as part of the production – distribution – consumption process. They were being treated as commodities, just as previously implied by Nonaka and Takeuchi, from their 'eastern' perspectives (see Chapter 3).

Crying Out For Participatory Democracy

Cashbuild's CARE structures, as nominally democratic, were still substantively separating management and worker. What they were crying out for was for participatory democracy, thereby integrating their economic and social selves, so as to relieve labour power of its commodity character:

- no one can demand productivity from anyone, but I can create a climate within which social man is willingly productive;
- I cannot manage people, only things, but I can create a climate within which people take responsibility and manage themselves;

- one cannot demand quality from people, but I can create conditions at work through which quality work is a product of pride in workmanship.

Create a Human Face

So these new conditions we thought would help to create the human face (to which Steve Biko has referred), and which I had been looking for earlier. *Exploitative capitalism demands quotas, productivity and quality, all as part of a commodity outlook on life. People remain part of the production-distribution-consumption process, without their spiritual work or social ethos being recognized.* The protagonists of class consciousness, meanwhile, became a rallying point in the name of social justice, without actually giving expression to the human face.

Soft Variables: Enterprise and Labour – Hard Variables: Capital and Land

We promptly decided at Cashbuild to pursue our own course, dividing control of the business into soft variables (enterprise and labour) and hard ones (capital and land). A convention of some 200 workers was held and the ground rules were established:

- respect human dignity and individual *freedom of speech;*
- allow everyone to have *access to company results* and performance standards;
- give everyone *a role in developing company policy;*
- improve the quality of life of all employees outside the work sphere through *active community involvement.*

Frightening the Hell out of the Capitalist Fraternity

Views and feelings just poured out of the hearts of the workers for the first time. The basis for removing barriers ('isms') between capital and labour was still the CARE groups, but this time around we were talking team – total team, only us. This was our company. It was proposed that a governing body of five people be constituted to each outlet – the VENTURECOM – with each person being democratically elected to hold a portfolio, save for the manager who was appointed to the Operations Portfolio, based on his or her expertise.

This portfolio was concerned with the 'hard' variables whereas the Safety, Labour, Merchandise and Quality of Work-Life portfolios were the 'soft' ones. Moreover, each of these managers was continually assessed by lower levels in the hierarchy. *The subsequent newspaper headlines – 'Cashbuild – the company where workers have the right to dismiss their managers' – frightened the hell out of the capitalist fraternity.*

Distributive Justice and Workplace Security

Yet precisely because that right existed within the workforce we never needed to use it. In fact this Cashbuild VENTURECOM system was socialistic in that it reinstated distributive justice and offered security against destitution. It was likewise capitalistic to the extent that individual expression was given its due reward, and group development its due recognition. Our system thus gave expression to the work ethic and also to the enterprising spirit of people.

REVIEWING MY LEARNING CURVE

Protracted Soul Searching: North and South Need Each Other

So where were we now (Koopman was writing in the 1990s)? As newly appointed Managing Director, back in 1982, I had first begun to realize that the internal workings of the organization were simply not matching up with external demands. Profits were going down. To me, power had been a thing, a toy. My 'north-western' nature was individualist and competitive. I was the only person existing in the world. I saw coercion as the way to get things done. So when I confronted the results of our attitude survey I was inevitably confused.

At the end of a protracted period of soul searching I began to realize that I had been using power and the 'ism' through which it had to be executed in pursuit of the protection of my class. In a sense I was still a product of the industrial society, and my 'north-western' self had thereby forgotten that there was actually no such thing as the means of production. There were only people who actually work machines in order to produce. Without the 'southern' people, the machines and the factories would stand still. Without the effort of 'north-western' enterprise, there would be no progress in humanity. Here was my key to change. I could now see that if I recognized and restored the dignity and pride of the workforce I could achieve a new human spirit that would drive the enterprise for the betterment of all. I would therefore be able to change, not by losing my individual competitive value system but by finding 'southern' solidarity as Managing Director with all the people in the organization, thereby:

- taking employees on a journey to *strength their relationships* with management;
- *turning all employees into stakeholders* of the organization;
- aggressively *addressing the distributive aspect* of the business, through profit sharing, in the ultimate interest of the business, its workers and their families;
- *promoting excellence* of quality and productivity, within the organization, and *fostering a communal climate for its achievement.*

Establishing a Superordinate Goal and a Philosophy of Social Justice

At the structural level I had to restore meaning into people's lives, by constructing a code of ethics around which people could be rallied for the common purpose. This involved:

- a superordinate goal for the enterprise through the people themselves;
- a philosophy of social justice and equality, pride and dignity amongst all.

I found later that this last point was in fact the spark for all endeavours, and took precedence over any of the other technical systems, rewards or structures we introduced. It reflected, in fact, the Divine Will of Cashbuild, which in its turn manifested the parallel Will of the communities which the company represented. It reflected the difference between competitive, north-western 'having', and cooperative 'south-eastern' being. What did this all mean?

THE AFRICAN WORK GROUP

Establishing a Place of Discourse: A Traditional Indaba

In my ten years of experience at Cashbuild, then, I had observed that the African work group (see Table 11.1 below) regarded their fellows primarily in terms of 'southern' morals and emotions rather than in terms of their 'northern' roles and functions. Traditionally, blacks have emerged through the spoken word. Wisdoms were carried forward as metaphors and stories as opposed to the written word, which preserved information for western cultures. So 'southerners' (as Biko and Herman have both intimated above) will tend to think aurally and emotionally, which is why they would think aloud and use continuous discussion as the main part of their reasoning process. The traditional indaba (place of discourse) had, at its base, the removal of all dissent before the group could proceed.

Table 11.1 The north–south divide

Competitive versus Communal	
North: Individual Competitive ⟷	**South: Group Communal**
Profit for me is derived from self-interest.	Profit to me is a vote of confidence my society gives me for service rendered to that society.
I am actually exclusive from my fellow man.	I am mutually inclusive.
I prefer to be a self-actualized person.	I prefer to be a social man.
The more I have, the more I am.	I am, therefore I share and give.
I demand productivity from People.	I prefer to create a climate in which people will be willingly more productive.
I am actually an aggressive kind of Person.	I am actually a receptive kind of a person.
I look you in the eye and challenge you.	I bow my head and show my respect.
My concern is for production.	My concern is for people.

So I needed to tap more purposefully into what I called 'the divine will of Africa'.

Tapping into the Divine Will of Africa

The African work group therefore has to clear dissent by engaging interactively with the morality of an issue. Thus performance is valued less for its own sake than for the sake of the group. Such a 'divine will' then, reflected in the 'southern' work groups that I came across at Cashbuild, is hidden between the lines of the following passages:

- Africa shows a strong *reverence for ancestors* and other departed relatives who are believed to be able to affect the living.
- Africa sees that the principle of *age is an important source of wisdom.*
- Africa places a *high value on ceremony and ritual* in many aspects of social life.
- Africa attaches *great importance to group life and to social harmony,* thereby placing a high premium on consensus in group endeavours.
- Africa is extremely social through its *spontaneity of self expression* and ease of communication; correctness of speech as a prerequisite for social standing.
- Africa can forgive and forget very readily because of its *great capacity for reconciliation.*

Having effectively, after a long and painful, but ultimately very rewarding period of reconciliation, within and between 'north' and 'south' and indeed transformation, in a business and economic context, I left Cashbuild in seemingly safe hands, to attempt to spread the 'value sharing' world more widely in South Africa'.

11.3 ITISA: Worker Democracy to Value Sharing

DEMOCRATIC ENTERPRISE TO VALUE SHARING CONSULTANCY

The Legacy of the Great Indaba

By 1994, Cashbuild had 72 outlets of which 56 were in South Africa and 16 in surrounding African countries. Company turnover had reached the equivalent of some one hundred million US dollars, a significantly profitable undertaking. The CARE groups and VENTURECOMMS were still well in place and every year all the management together with employee representatives would gather together for three days, for a 'Great Indaba'. The issues discussed would range from wage and salary increases to housing loan schemes, combined with major strategic issues, the agenda for it being compiled from one year prior to the great meeting.

The objective is that by the time the Great Indaba comes, everybody in the company has had a say and all the Venturecomm representatives who will be attending have a record of how each branch member feels about the issues raised in the Indaba document. All proposals are voted after extensive debate and decisions are taken as positive if there is a 75 per cent majority. What then about the daily life of a Cashbuild branch?

A DAY IN THE LIFE OF THE BRANCH

The lifeblood of Cashbuild, in the 1980s as well as in the 1990s, is the branch operation. This is described by South African management consultant and researcher Elton Bondi, as of a Wednesday morning in 1995, at the Thaban'Chu branch nearby an African township. Employees could best be described as highly aggressive towards the competitor, and many showed a profound knowledge of Cashbuild's bulk buying power.

I was truly amazed by the level of business understanding and high degree of loyalty demonstrated by employees wearing overalls who packed corrugated iron most of the day.

The second overall impression was that of relaxed humour. One feels, in fact, like an outsider to a tight family unit, who share their own customs and values. The communal 'southern' spirit of Cashbuild obviously lived on in the 1990s, together with the practice of value sharing that takes place through the CARE groups, the Venturecomms and the Great Indaba.

VALUE SHARING

Spreading African Humanism in Business

Albert Koopman left Cashbuild in 1987 to help form ITISA – Interdependence and Transformation in Southern Africa – a participatively oriented management consultancy. His successor as chief executive was Gerard Haumant, Albert's longstanding associate in Cashbuild, a Frenchman with a chemical engineering background on the one hand, and a radical orientation on other. Not surprisingly Haumant, while honouring the southern foundations of the organization, gradually reinforced the systematic, 'northern' influence (10). Together with his colleagues at ITISA (Interdependence and Transformation in Southern Africa) then, Koopman has been attempting to spread his brand of African humanism across business enterprises. The underlying approach involved sharing value to add value.

Politics Cannot be Separated from Economics

Most notably moreover, within ITISA's 'southern' context politics cannot be separated from economics. Therein lies the primal southern force of unity.

'The three interrelated facets of society, namely authority, economy and community, form an interdependent whole. If they are in open interaction with one another it is called a democracy', says Koopman. Whereas the AUTHORITY pole stands for the rationality of the 'north', and the COMMUNITY pole for the humanism of the south, the ECONOMY represents a force of pragmatic

Economy

Authority Community

Figure 11.1 Primal unity

integration. In business, Koopman maintains, the equivalent of the economy is creating and keeping customers through adequate performance. *If, for whatever reasons, the relationship between 'northern' authority (management and shareholders) and the 'southern' community (employees and trade unions) breaks down, then the organization's 'western' economy (performance to create and keep customers) will suffer.*

AUTHORITY, COMMUNITY AND ECONOMICS

Profiting Society through Wealth Creation

The combination of these three, then, form not only the politics of society and the sociology of organizations but also the dynamics of business. Each of these elements, moreover, is built into the fabric of the enterprise politically and authoritatively through the institutionalization of justice and dignity; socially and communally through communication, and economically and commercially through wealth creation. For Koopman then:

> *We understand that communication is the sharing of meaning of our stated objectives. Each employee has the right to remain informed on matters affecting his life. As teamwork is the seed of human accomplishment, and participation the sap of human growth, so justice and freedom are the combined and moral fruits of human endeavour. We share a mutual respect, in common purpose and respect for our diversities of interest, applied through a principle of non-violation of each other's rights, individual against individual, individual against company, labour against capital, white against black, man against woman, management against worker, or the reciprocal of any of these. We invest money to buy plant, put up buildings, purchase materials, and pay running expenses. The wealth created, however, is not driven by self interest, but rather serves as a reward and vote of confidence in us by society, for the services we render to that society. We understand that our wealth creation process will only remain paramount if individuals are able to retain a wealth creating consciousness. Freedom to create wealth through a freeing of spirit will be our ultimate drive. For we realise that it is only through wealth creation that we remain free.*

11.4 Conclusion

WHAT INHIBITS LOCAL GROUNDING OF INTEGRAL ADVANTAGE IN NATURE AND COMMUNITY?

Never a Prophet in Your Own Land

Today Albert Koopman is based in Vancouver, and could not be further removed from Cashbuild, physically if not spiritually. All too often the adage, 'never a prophet in your own land', applies, at least over the long term. All too often Cashbuild was dismissed as the product of one unique man, whose achievements could not be replicated across the South African stage. As such, the link between Mandela's and Tutu's *truth and reconciliation*, De Gruchy's four truths – *restorative, dialogic, objective and subjective* – and Cashbuild's *value sharing* was never made. In fact, when I approached Cashbuild, recently in 2014, to ask about the legacy of the Koopman years, the company having by now returned to conventional private enterprise status, I was told I should talk to their advertising agency! What then is going on in a South African 'north–south' context?

Footloose Grounding

To begin with, that is with grounding in nature and community, the likes of Van der Post (*Dark Eye of Africa*), McCallum (*Ecological Intelligence*) and Cormack (*Wild Law/Earth Jurisprudence*) are not exactly drops in a South African ocean, but they are somewhat rare breeds. There is an identifiable *wilderness movement* in South Africa, and its leading light, Ian Player, as a world-renowned environmental activist so to speak, died only last year. At the same time, its leading spokesman Laurens Van der Post somehow lost his way, in the new South African because he sided with the Zulu-based Inkatha party, rather than with the ANC.

In one respect then, this 'grounding movement' has fallen out of favour with the current political establishment, and in another respect it is 'too white'. The black South African, at least for now, tends to *be* at one with nature rather than writing about it.

A Voice in the Wilderness

Despite the fact then that Mandela himself has clearly articulated his closeness to nature and community, for his own grounding, such gets left totally out of account by the political (ANC) and economic (westernized) establishment. It is left in no-man's land. In fact the closest we do get to such a Southern

African perspective on nature and community that is recognized by those able to access his somewhat esoteric work is that of the South African Zulu sage, Credo Mutwa (11). Indeed his close associate, through their shared interest in the African white lions, Linda Tucker (12), has quoted Mutwa as saying:

> *Western man has come to believe that he is the master of all living things, and that nature is there to be tamed at best; despised, broken and destroyed at worst, this has led to a very dangerous situation: the belief that human beings can build a shining technological future without animals, trees and other life-forms. Until this attitude is combated, he says, and erased from the human mind, Westernized human beings will be a danger to all earthly life, including themselves.*

However, it is difficult for the political and economic powers that be to build on such natural and communal ground, and Mutwa again is very much of an idiosyncratic figure.

WHAT INHIBITS SUCH GROUNDING FROM EMERGING LOCALLY AND GLOBALLY?

Not Invented Here

While Nelson Mandela is an international icon, and Archbishop Tutu may also have become so, they are not generally recognized specifically for what they draw upon from local 'southern' culture, duly aligned with, and co-evolved through, their 'northern' credentials. The philosophy of *ubuntu*, often associated with Tutu if not Steve Biko as well, while reasonably well acknowledged by 'Africa watchers' is all too often quickly dismissed because of the rampant corruption, if not outright despotism, that is associated with Africa 'for real'.

Moreover, unlike West Africa, which has a rich vein of philosophers, South Africa is not noted for such. Indeed, in Africa as a whole, there are no John Locke's or Adam Smith's, or indeed Karl Marx's, who have laid the philosophical, emergent foundations, like for example the Cosmists in Russia, for political and economic institutions to subsequently navigate (though in Russia the latter has not taken place either). Moreover religion, that other rich source of emergence, as illustrated, say, by the Protestant Reformation in Europe, tends to be hived off from such institutions at large, though there is a rich mix of the indigenous and the exogenous within African religion itself. However, when it comes to politics and economics, such spirituality is relegated to the private realm.

WHY ARE INSTITUTIONS NOT BUILT OUT OF NATURAL GROUNDING AND CULTURE EMERGENCE?

Abstracted Leadership

And now we come to the crunch. If you walk into a good South African bookshop you will find a whole section devoted to Nelson Mandela's own writings, as well as writings about him (a second voluminous biography, further to his *Long Walk to Freedom*, is currently being worked on, as of 2015) but they are all focused on him as an individual. The allusions he himself makes, as we saw in the previous chapter, to organizational (ANC) and social (South African) transformation are somehow by-passed. In fact you have one book after another on Mandela's 'leadership principles', generally abstracted from the nature and culture of the South Africa of which he has been such an intrinsic part, with a view to pursuing integral advantage.

In other words, and with reference to our integral topography (see Chapter 3), the political, and more especially economic, institutional forms, and indeed the ideologies that underpin such, are generally European if not American, and thereby alien to South Africa. Such as I, they emerge from different grounds, primarily Anglo-Saxon (Locke and Smith), if not to a much lesser extent Anglo-German (Marx and Engels). While the new South African constitution is somewhat more eclectic, the actual political process, and above all the business and economic one, is exogenously constituted.

Missed Opportunities: From TRC to Robben Island University

The one glaring exception was the Truth and Reconciliation Commission (TRC), which did build on indigenous *ubuntu* combined with exogenous Christian values, but unfortunately has not been extended and enriched, indeed building on what emerged in the previous chapter, to navigate more broadly based exchange and reconciliation. The other glaring example of unexploited institutional potential is the so called, by Nelson Mandela, *Robben Island University*. Treated generally as a one-off, albeit remarkably as such, born out of unique circumstances, no attempt has been made, other than by ourselves (13) in a modest way, to take on, university-wise, from where it has left off. Interestingly enough then, and in the final analysis, the only institutions which build upon local soils, and emerge from local–global, to come up with their own combinations of 'spiritual navigation' are some of the religious institutions.

WHAT IS THE ULTIMATE SOUTHERN ECONOMIC AND ENTERPRISE EFFECT?

South Africa's Is Not Fit for O'Neil's BRIC Purpose

Jim O'Neil's reluctance to include South Africa, then, as the final one of his BRICS, he claims, is because of the over-dependence of its economy on the mining sector, albeit that the country does also have very strong financial institutions, and a good, overall transport and communications infra-structure. The real problem though, from our integral point of view, is that the economy stands footloose, in its ultimate effect, from the natural and communal grounds, emergent culture and consciousness, as well as technology and society as whole, bereft of any integral polity to establish overall alignment.

Of course, through BEE (Black Economic Empowerment) there has been a sincere attempt to align the social and political aims, of black empowerment, with economic aims, to promote South African enterprise, but all of this has taken place within a conventionally 'western-northern' capitalist dispensation which has benefited, primarily, a tiny black economic elite.

Cashbuild as a Glaring Exception

The glaring exception to this rule has been Cashbuild, in its Koopman heyday, as we have seen, and to this day it remains the one and only such integral ultimately *value sharing* (as opposed to profit maximizing) case, where culture, polity and economy, if not also nature and community, have been aligned, altogether in southern-northern guise. This is absolutely remarkable.

At least some of the fault must lie, then, in the educational sector, at least in higher education, to the extent that none of the South African schools of business or economics, or even of public administration, have picked up and amplified, and thereby further evolved, the Cashbuild model, not to mention even the 'partnership' model developed by Anton Rupert (see opening quote). That is indeed at least one of the reasons why Koopman departed from Southern African shores in favour of Canadian climes, and Remgro (the contemporary of Rupert's original company) is but a shadow, in integral *socio*-economic terms, of its former partnership-oriented self.

We shall be elaborating, then, in our final chapter, on what kind of higher educational institution, what we term as an integral university – as an evolution, in the South African case, of Robben Island University – could play such a role, in enabling, in association with other institutions, a society, like South Africa in this case, to pursue integral advantage. We now turn from Russia, east–west and South Africa north–south, to India in the south-east, thereafter China in the north-east and finally Brazil in the south-west, having already touched based with the conventional western-northern wisdom.

Bibliography

1. Rupert, A. (1981) *Priorities for Co-existence.* Cape Town, Taffelburg.
2. Tutu, D. (2000) *No Future Without Forgiveness.* Cambridge, Perfect Paperback.
3. Biko, S. (2004) *Steve Biko.* London, Picador.
4. Ramphele, M. (2008) *Laying Ghosts to Rest: Dilemmas of Transformation in South Africa.* Cape Town, Tafelburg.
5. Ramphele, M. (2013) *A Passion for Freedom.* Cape Town, Taffelburg.
6. Ramphele, M. (2012) *Conversations with My Sons and Daughters.* Rosebank Johannesburg, Penguin Books.
7. Ramphele, M. (2012) *Conversations with My Sons and Daughters.* Rosebank Johannesburg, Penguin Books.
8. Koopman, A. (1991) *Trans-cultural Management.* Chichester, Wiley-Blackwell.
9. Ramphele, M. (2012) *Conversations with My Sons and Daughters.* Rosebank Johannesburg, Penguin Books.
10. Sections of this chapter have been reproduced from Lessem, R. and Schieffer, A. (2015) *Integral Renewal: A Relational and Renewal Perspective.* Farnham, Gower.
11. Mutwa, V. (2001) *Indaba My Children: African Tribal History, Legends, Customs and Religious Beliefs.* London, Canongate Paperback.
12. Tucker, L. (2001) *Mystery of the White Lions: Children of the Sun God.* London, Hay House Publishing.
13. Schieffer, A. and Lessem, R. (2014) *Integral Development: Realising Transformative Potential of Individuals, Organizations and Societies – chapter 18* – Farnham, Gower.

PART IV

Circumnavigating BRICS: India, China, Brazil

Chapter 12

Integral India: South-East – *Swadeshi* to *Sarvodaya*

The primal law and purpose of a society, community or nation is to seek its own self-fulfilment; it strives rightly to find itself, to become aware within itself of the law and power of its own being and to fulfil it as perfectly as possible, to realise all its potentialities, to live its own self-revealing life. The nation or society, like the individual, has a body, an organic life, a moral and aesthetic temperament, a developing mind and soul for the sake of which it exists. There is only this difference between individual and society, the group-soul is much more complex.

Sri Aurobindo (1), The Human Cycle

12.1 Introduction

SIGNALLING THE DEMISE OF COMMUNISM AND APARTHEID

We now turn from the two BRICS centre-pieces, in our terms, straddling east–west (Russia) and north–south (South Africa), to the circumnavigating ones: India (south-east), China (north-east) and Brazil (south-west), with the US/UK (west-north) setting the initial conventional tone. So we part company from Bulgakov and Gorbachev, Biko and Mandela, so to speak, and embark on our next journey with Aurobindo, Kumar and Gandhi. Of course this runs contrary to the accepted BRICS wisdom, where Brazil, India and China are the three golden boys, of the emerging markets.

SOIL, SOUL AND SOCIETY TO *SARVODAYA*

The first of our circumnavigating BRICS then, occupies pre-eminently the south-east. Yet, as in the two cases of Russia and South Africa that we have already reviewed, we shall once again find, with India, that Effect (economy and enterprise) and Navigation (socio-technical) have not been evolved out

Navigation
Science and Technology
Knowledge Society

Effect
Public, Private
Civic Enterprise
Sarvodaya

Emergence
Culture and
Consciousness
Earth Democracy

Grounding
Nature and Community
Soil, Soul and Society

Figure 12.1 Soil and soul to *Sarvodaya*

of prior Grounding (natural and communal) and Emergence (cultural and spiritual), duly aligned with some form of what we might term an integral Indian polity.

So the all-round release of Indian GENE-ius has been thwarted, notwithstanding its comparative economic success over the last two decades. In our pursuit of integral advantage, India-wise in this case, we shall act as if such differentiation and integration, GENE-wise, has taken place, as in Figure 12.1 above. In that guise we start out by grounding ourselves, naturally and communally, in Satish Kumar's *Soil, Soul and Society.* Thereafter, we emerge, culturally and consciousness-wise, through Vandana Shiva's *Earth Democracy.* For scientific and technological navigation we turn to Singharoy's *Knowledge Society*, and culminate, economy and enterprise-wise, in Sri Lanka's *Sarvodaya* (the very idea of *sarvodaya* – awakening – coming from India's Gandhi).

12.2 Local Grounding in Nature and Community: Soil, Soul and Society

INDIAN TRINITY OF OUR TIME

Liberty, Equality, Fraternity

For India's Satish Kumar (2) now based in England, a former Jain monk, peace activist, ecologist and founder of Schumacher College in the UK, the writers of the American Constitution came up with Life, Liberty and the Pursuit of Happiness, and the French Revolution with Liberty, Equality and Fraternity. In our own time, the New Age movement gathered around the concepts of Mind, Body and Sprit. These trinities have their point and are relevant in their own context – but none of them represents a holistic and ecological worldview in an explicit manner. They are either spiritual or social, but they are mostly anthropocentric and fail to highlight our relationship with nature or the connection between the social and the spiritual.

Yagna, Tapas, Dana

However, Kumar came across three words in an ancient Hindu text, the Bhagavad Gita, that stimulated his thinking on ecology, spirituality and humanity. These three words in Sanskrit are *yagna, tapas, dana. The first one, yagna, informs human/nature relationships; the second, tapas, relates to our inner self, and the third, dana, relates to social relationships.* He has translated this trinity in terms of soil, soul and society.

CARE OF THE SOIL

The Soil is a Metaphor for the Whole Natural System

Kumar puts soil first, because it represents nature and sustains the entire life-system. Everything comes from the soil and returns to the soil. Food which sustains life comes from the soil. Water which nourishes life is held by the soil. The war against nature is driven by our conviction that the function of nature is to fuel the engine of the economy. But the truth of the matter, for Kumar, is that the economy is a wholly owned subsidiary of ecology. If the natural capital is depleted, the natural environment is destroyed, then the economy will come to an end.

According to the principle of *yagna,* we should rather celebrate the beauty, the abundance and the grandeur of nature by replenishing what we have taken from it. If we take five trees to build a home, we must replenish them by planting 50 trees.

CARE OF THE SOUL

Self Knowledge, Selfless Service and the Surrender of the Ego

As we are urged by the Gita to live in harmony with the natural world, soil, we are also guided to create harmony within ourselves. In Sanscrit the word for the individual soul is *atman,* the intimate being, and the word for the universal soul, or *anima mundi,* is *paramatman,* the ultimate being. Similarly the Sanskrit word for the human individual is *nar* and for the universal being (or God) is *narayan*. In Arabic we find a similar formulation – the individual person is called *khud* and the divine being is *khuda* – just by adding an a, the individual is released from his or her narrow identity or ego and is transformed into divine consciousness.

The way to such an enlightened state is through self knowledge, selfless service and the surrender of the ego in favour of understanding that I am part of the whole. I am an organ of the Earth body; I am a member of the Earth community. Like each branch is an integral part of a tree, every creature, human or non-human, is an integral part of the Earth. Therefore the Gita teaches us that there is no need to separate caring for the soil from caring for the soul. We need to do both. Thus through meditation we can connect outer and inner ecologies. Meditation is a preventative medicine to avoid the sickness of the soul and it is a curative medicine for the healing of the wounded soul.

CARE FOR THE SOCIETY

Karma Yogi: Spiritual Warrior

Care for the soil and the soul, for Kumar, needs to be extended to include care for society. So the way of the Gita is the way of the spiritual warrior, a peace warrior and an eco-warrior – what the Gita calls *karma yogi*: one who practices the yoga of action and is engaged constantly for the upliftment and wellbeing of the deprived and dispossessed, but acts without the desiring fruit of his own actions. The Gita says that the tree does not eat its own fruit and the river does not drink its own water, the *karmi yogi* or an activist should not seek any benefit of his or her own action, but should offer their action for the benefit of others. That is *dana*.

We have inherited great architecture: the Pyramids, the Taj Mahal, the great mosques and cathedrals. We are blessed with so much literature, poetry and music and so many paintings. We are enriched by the great teachings of enlightened masters such as the Buddha, Muhammad, Jesus Christ, Lao Tsu and others. We have been endowed with philosophy, science and technology. We are indebted to them. And now it is our turn, Kumar maintains, to contribute to that culture and civilization and ensure that no child in our human family goes without food, no sick person is left unattended, no country or community is afflicted by war, exploitation or torture. He then turns to Gandhi.

BE THE SOIL-FUL, SOULFUL AND SOCIETAL CHANGE

Sarvodaya: Well-Being of All

Mahatma Gandhi played a special role in Kumar's life, starting out from when he read his autobiography, particularly Gandhi's argument that to practice spirituality you did not have to forsake the world and become a monk. The true practice of spirituality, he maintained, has to be in the world, in everyday life, in politics, in business and in domestic life.

What Kumar also understood from Gandhi was that it is the motivation behind your actions that determines the quality of such. If you are in politics for power, fame or money, then it is a politics of pride and materialism. *If your politics is in the service of society or for care of the Earth, or for purification of the soul, then that politics is spiritual, leading to self liberation and the liberation of others.* Since he wanted to learn more about the philosophy and practice of Mahatma, Kumar decided to live in a Gandhian ashram in Bodigaya, where the Buddha had been enlightened while sitting under a tree. It was there that he read Gandhi's book *Sarvodaya* – which means wellbeing of all.

This was in 1956 when Kumar was 20. India was a newly emerging nation, having achieved her independence from the British in 1947. There was much debate about the direction of the country. Some advocated communism; the success of the Soviet Union and China was a beacon of inspiration for young and radical activists of India. Others were advocates of free enterprise, who were looking to the American model of capitalism and industrialism. But Gandhi had a different worldview. He firstly saw the fallacy, the narrowness and the utilitarian foundation upon which socialist, communist and capitalist systems were built, not unlike his counterparts in Russia (Berdyaev) and South Africa (Mandela). In essence there was not a great deal of difference between capitalism (our west-north) and communism (our north-west). They all wanted to exploit and subjugate nature for human benefit. Such systems are not holistic.

Swaraj: Self-Governance

For Gandhi secondly then, if the well-being of all (*sarvodaya)* is the ideal for society, then *swaraj* (self-governance) is the political way to attain it. *Swaraj* is also made of two worlds: *swa* and *raj*, respectively meaning self and to shine. In Gandhi's model, as such, the individual is the centre of an oceanic circle, continually expanding himself to include his family, his neighbourhood, his village, his state, his country. Each self moreover has the capacity to expand outward and to reach out to others, to sacrifice himself or herself for their welfare. So the self in *swaraj* is not a limited but an expanding one – a potentially unlimited self which can stretch to embrace the whole cosmos.

Mahatma Gandhi then took his model of self-governance from nature. As the Earth's systems are self-organizing, self-sustaining and self-maintaining as well as self-governing, so should be human systems. *Swaraj* is possible then only when we embrace the ideal of small cities and small nations. For Gandhi, India would have cultural unity but political diversity and decentralization. On the one hand, we all are world citizens, members of one human family; but on the other we are firmly rooted in our local communities and in our place. In order to establish *swaraj* (self-governance) therefore we need moral education on a massive scale. And the key to success in relation to *swaraj* is appropriate scale of organization, and of community and society.

Swadeshi: Economics of Place

The third key concept developed by Gandhi is that of *swadeshi*, which means economics of place. *Swa* means self and *deshi* means place. It was in this overall context that he introduced the spinning wheel, encouraging people to spin cotton and get it woven locally, rather than in English mills, this bringing livelihood, arts, crafts and community coherence together. *Swadeshi* gives importance to human-scale technology and tools rather than large factories. If technology or a machine aids human hands and makes work light, than that technology is compatible with *swadeshi*; but if technology replaces human hands and makes the workers redundant, then that technology is incompatible with *swadeshi*. When technology and economy become the master and people become the instruments serving the industrial machine, then work becomes soul-destroying, soil-damaging and undermines social harmony.

Sarvodaya, Swaraj and Swadeshi

The philosophy of *sarvodaya* (the wellbeing of all), the politics of *swaraj* (self rule and self-organization) and the economics of *swadeshi* (local self reliance), altogether then, offers a complete programme and a holistic solution, according to Kumar, for most of our contemporary problems such as rising unemployment, depletion of natural resources, climate change, international conflict, global poverty, ill-health and crime. Capitalism instead of *sarvodaya*, centralized politics instead of *swaraj* and global economy instead of *swadeshi* are leading the world toward dangerous environmental degradation, total disregard for spiritual values in the body politic, and complete confusion of purpose in social organizations, making all aspects of society suffer. As socialists have Marx and their philosopher and capitalists have Adam Smith as their guide, Gandhi should be the mentor for the movement for sustainability working towards a just and peaceful future.

We now turn from grounding in nature and community, in soil, soul and society, albeit with an integral overall perspective, to more specific emergence, to begin with through Vandana Shiva's (3) *Earth Democracy.*

12.3 Local–Global Culture and Conscious Emergence via Earth Democracy

AHIMSA

Non-Violent Economics

For Indian physicist, ecologist and social activist Vandana Shiva in fact, taking on from where Satish Kumar has left off, *ahimsa,* or such non-violence for Gandhi, is the basis for many faiths which have emerged on Indian soil, as Kumar has already intimated. Translated into economics, *non-violence means that our systems of production, trade and consumption do not use up the space of other species and other people.* Violence is the result when our dominant economic structures and economic organization usurp and enclose our ecological space of other species or people. The Eurocentric concept of property views capital as the only kind of investment and, hence, treats returns on capital investment as the only kind that need protection. *Non western indigenous communities and cultures recognize that investments can also be of labour or of care and nurturance.* Such cultural systems protect investments beyond capital. They protect the culture of conservation and of caring and sharing.

Ahimsa combines justice and sustainability at a deep level. Not taking more than you need ensures that enough resources are left in the ecosystem for other species and the maintenance of essential ecological processes to ensure sustainability. It also ensures that enough resources are left for the livelihoods of diverse groups of people. Diversity and pluralism, then, are necessary characteristics of an ahimsic economic order. Diversity is intimately linked to the possibility of self-organization. It is therefore the basis of economic and political freedom, that is *swadeshi* and *swaraj,* as we saw above. Living societies then, living ecosystems and living cultures are characterized by three principles:

- the principle of diversity;
- the principle of self-organization, self-regulation and self-renewal;
- the principle of reciprocity between systems, the law of give and take.

EARTH DEMOCRACY

From Cultures of Death to Cultures of Life

The economic, ecological and social crises resulting from corporate globalization, for Shiva (3) then, demand a new way of thinking and living on the planet. They demand a new worldview in which compassion, not greed, is globalized; *a new consciousness in which we are not reduced to consumers of globally traded commodities if we are privileged, or to narrow, fragmented one-dimensional entities based on colour, religion or ethnicity, if we are excluded.* We can and we do experience our lives as planetary beings with planetary consciousness, mindful and aware of what our actions, or consumption, cost other humans, other species and future generations.

Economy shapes culture, culture shapes economy. Earth Democracy reconnects culture to how and what we produce and consume, and to how we govern ourselves. It creates the possibility of strengthening ecological security while improving economic security. And, on these foundations, it makes societies immune to the virus of communal hatred and fear. Earth democracy offers a new way of seeing, one in which everything is not at war with everything else, but through which we can cooperate to create peace, sustainability and justice in our violent and volatile times. Earth democracy provides the context for living creatures – inspired both by the timeless wisdom of ancient worldviews and by the emerging solidarities of new global movements of citizens against globalization, war and tolerance. We are experiencing ourselves as simultaneously local, national and global. This diversity and multiplicity, and the non-violence and inclusiveness it implies, is giving birth to a new living culture of our common humanity and our diversities.

Globalization and Culture Wars

Culture and economy, as we have seen then, are inseparable. The neo-liberal ideology of development and globalization wishes culture away, yet culture dominates and becomes the surrogate for concerns over livelihoods and economic security. Fundamentalist religion, as a reaction against such, becomes, as Marx so aptly observed, the opium of the masses.

Meanwhile, the wars of empire and the economic wars of globalization have morphed into one. Farmer suicides in India are the most tragic and dramatic symptoms of the crisis of survival faced by the country's peasants today. Two factors, for Shiva as of 2005, have transformed agriculture from a positive economy into a negative one for peasants – the rising costs of production and falling prices of farm commodities. Both these factors are rooted in policies of trade liberalization and corporate globalization. The highest rates of suicide are in Andhra Padesh and Punjab, two states with the highest dependence on cash crops, the highest penetration of Monsanto seeds, and the highest level of corporatized agriculture. The states in which farmers are using their own seeds and growing crops for their sustenance and local markets are avoiding the debt trap that forces farmers into despair and hopelessness.

The Trade Metaphor versus Nature's Economy

As the trade metaphor, for Shiva moreover, has come to replace the metaphor of home, the meaning of *value* has been transformed. Value, which means worth, has been redefined in terms of exchange and trade. Unless something is tradable it has no economic value. This assumption that something only has value if it can be exchanged for money has also rendered nature's economy worthless, when, in fact, it is priceless. The marginalization of both women's work and nature's work are linked to perceptions of home as a place where nothing of economic value is produced.

Shiva then turns, together with her German sociology colleague, Maria Mies, who has also spent much of her working life in India, to *Ecofemimism.*

EARTH DEMOCRACY TO ECOFEMINISM

The Culture of the Forest Defines the Culture of India

Whereas Satish Kumar brings a strongly eastern perspective to bear upon his philosophical and spiritual local appreciation of nature and community, Mies and Shiva (4) bring in a local–global south-eastern, natural and philosophical perspective, between them, overall through their *ecofeminism.* To begin with Shiva, like her compatriot Kumar, quotes Rabindranath Tagore, writing at the peak of the independence movement, stating that the distinctiveness of Indian culture consists of its having defined the principles of life in nature as the highest form of cultural evolution:

> *The culture of the forest has fuelled the culture of Indian society … The unifying principle of life in diversity, of democratic pluralism, thus becomes the principle of Indian civilization.*

As a source of life, nature was venerated as sacred, and human evolution was measured in terms of the human capacity to interact in harmony with her rhythms and patterns, intellectually and emotionally. In the final analysis, the ecological crisis is rooted in the mistaken belief that human beings are not part of the democracy of nature's life and that they stand *apart* from and *above* nature.

Soil as Sacred Mother

For communities who derive their sustenance from the soil, in fact, it is not merely a physical property in a Cartesian space; for them the soil is the source of all meaning. Soil and society, the earth and its people are intimately connected. In tribal and peasant societies, cultural and religious identity derive from the soil, which is perceived not as a mere facto of production but as the very soul of society. Desacralization of the soil takes place through the changes in the meaning of space. Sacred space, the universe of all meaning and living, the ecological source of all sustenance, is transformed into a mere site, a location for Cartesian space. When that site is identified for a development project, it is destroyed as an ecological and spiritual home.

Savage Nature

In fact, whenever Europeans discovered the native people of America, Africa or Asia they projected upon them the identity of savages, in need of redemption by a superior race. For Bacon, who is called the father of modern science, nature was no longer Mother Nature but a female nature, to be conquered by an aggressive masculine mind. As America's Carolyn Merchant (5) points out, in her book on *The Death of Nature*:

> *Because nature was now revered as a system of dead, inert particles moved by external, rather than inherent forces, the mechanical framework itself could legitimate the manipulation of nature.*

Need for a New Vision of Life Production

In the final analysis, with increasing ecological destruction in recent decades, it becomes obvious for Mies and Shiva that life production, as they call it, can also show the way out of many of the impasses of the destructive system that for them are the industrial society, market economy or capitalist patriarchy. Some people think that the solution lies in substituting environmentally noxious substances, technologies and commodities with nature-friendly, life-preserving ones. They propose harnessing commodity production and market forces to the service of sustainable development, replacing the production and marketing of destructive goods by eco-marketing.

Instead, from the overall perspective of life production the aim of *economic activity* is not to produce an ever-growing mountain of commodities and money (wages or profit) for an anonymous market, but the creation and re-creation of *life*, thereby *producing use-values.* These economic activities are based on new *relationships*: (a) to *nature*: nature is respected in her richness and diversity, both for her own sake and as a precondition for the survival of all creatures on the planet; and (b) *among people* as man's domination over nature is related to his domination over women. The need for subsistence *security* is satisfied not by trust in one's bank account or a social welfare state, but by trust in the reliability of one's community, thereby based on stable human relations rather than an atomized market economy. This leads to *a reintegration of culture and work*. This also necessitates a reintegration of spirit and matter, a rejection of both mechanical materialism and airy spirituality.

While Kumar then is an ecologist based in the UK, and Mies and Shiva or social activists in India, Debal Singharoy, in focusing as an academic sociologist on new identities emerging in India today, goes on to view India today as moving *Towards a Knowledge Society*, that is, for us, from local grounding and local–global emergence to global navigation, thereby setting India, and its technology and economy particularly, on a world stage.

12.4 Global Navigation through Indian Technology and Society

STRATEGIZING FOR A KNOWLEDGE SOCIETY IN INDIA

Knowledge in Indian Civilization – Restricted to the Few

The processes of generation, accumulation and use of knowledge, according to Singharoy (6), have remained integral parts of Indian society since the very inception of its civilizational journey that started thousands of years ago. However, *a vast body of this knowledge has remained exclusive to a spiritual realm that looks for salvation and discovery of inner truth embodied in nature and in human beings.* Such knowledge has been more closely integrated with cognition, morality and ethics than with economic or societal development. Moreover, such knowledge, especially the process of acquiring and getting access to it, remained more restricted to the limited few. *The journey of India shaped by the inheritance of this vast body of knowledge, is seldom matched by its mass application.*

India has in fact produced *local varieties of wise men and women* in the nooks and crannies of the country with significant command over weather patterns; the land, water and forest; health and indigenous medicine; plant, animal and human being; and strategies for protection against natural disasters. However, they *have never emerged as the scientists in the formal sense of the term due to the lack of systematization, transmission, experimentation and application of knowledge.* Rather, with the prevalence of illiteracy and ignorance, faith in magic and supernatural phenomena among the vast mass of the country, an important part of this knowledge has remained mystified.

Exogenous Knowledge Takes Over

Meanwhile, at least in the nineteenth and first part of the twentieth centuries, English became a tool for British hegemony over colonial India. The English historian T.B. Macaulay, cited by Singaroy (7) was in favour of an elitist education, as expressed in a minute to the Indian parliament in 1835:

> *We must at present do our best to form a class who may be interpreters between us and the millions whom we govern – a class of persons Indian in blood and color, but English in tastes, opinions, morals and intellect. To that class we may leave it to refine the vernacular dialects of the country, to enrich these dialects with terms of science borrowed from the Western nomenclature, and to render them by degrees fit vehicles for conveying knowledge to the great mass of the population. … a single shelf of a good European library is worth the whole native literature of India …*

So, a thin layer of Indian middle class was created in colonial India to take advantage of new venues of employment, to be knowledgeable and to lead the social, economic and political destiny of the country. Immediately after independence, the government of India focused on an education policy to contribute to nation building as a foundation for a modern society.

Technological Transformation: Envisioning an Era of Hope

Independent India inherited a backward technological framework in agriculture, industry and telecommunications from the British. While the Green Revolution in the late 1960s and early 1970s increased productivity in agriculture, its positive impacts, for Singharoy, remained restricted to the upper strata. In many ways, this furthered regional imbalances and class inequality in rural India. It was only in the 1980s, then, that the ICT revolution started reaching the doorsteps of India, more widely. The dramatic acceleration in the development of IT, the enhanced speed of accumulation, dissemination and exchange of knowledge, the emergence of highly qualified manpower and new knowledge-based industries have now become defining features of India's socio-economic mosaic today.

The National Knowledge Commission of India (8) in 2008 signalled that the twenty-first century, in India, should be fashioned to be a century of an emerging knowledge civilization, thereby:

> *Enhancing access to knowledge, reinvigorating institutions where knowledge concepts are imparted, creating a world class environment for the creation of knowledge, promoting applications of knowledge for sustained and inclusive growth, and using such for the efficient delivery of public services.*

The Indian government envisioned such a knowledge society as one whereby its people are empowered and enriched, promoting a learning society committed to innovation, using knowledge to create economic wealth and social good for all, taking an integrated view of life as a fusion of body, mind and spirit. Such a knowledge society would have three key drivers: first, the pursuit of a just and equitable society, second, wealth generation, and third, the promotion of traditional knowledge as well as that generated in modern research laboratories.

Three Separate Knowledge Worlds

India today though, according to Singharoy, stands between two conflicting worlds: one pushes back with the dark influence of illiteracy, incapability, exclusion and inequality and the other tries to push forward with the advancement of education, ICT and other advanced technologies, for integration with knowledge society. More specifically then, *the first world includes only a fortunate few* with access to modern institutions, computers, Internet access and expensive overseas education. *A second world want to maintain the status quo – teachers, administrators, textbook publishers, students* – all have reason to prefer things to remain as they are or change only gradually. *The third world struggles with fundamental issues such as no books, teachers with the wrong commitment, classrooms with hundreds of students, dirty floors and no toilets.* India cannot hope to succeed in the information age, he says, with three separate worlds.

Contemporary India in fact lives in many centuries together with lots of traditional socio-cultural and economic diversities juxtaposing with advanced thoughts and actions of the twenty-first century. The country has inherited a host of cultural, religious and linguistic values, customs, traditions and localized practices. Herein the significance of connectivity – from railways and highways to telephone and Internet – in removing barriers in space and time from social interaction. The process of so-called 'rurbanization' has got a place of prominence in the contemporary development discourse that has been envisioned to bring in rural prosperity through physical and electronic connectivity. For the Knowledge Commission report already cited the intention:

> *is to create an appropriate environment to engage and empower local communities and various other stakeholders and at the same time build effective models of collaboration including public-private partnerships and partnerships between academia, industry and local communities at large to bring about generational changes in our knowledge institutions and infrastructures needed to respond to the opportunities for growth and prosperity in the 21st century for all our people.*

Initiatives for a Knowledge Society: Old Challenges in a New Context

A host of initiatives has been set in motion in India by civil society to enhance the usage of ICT in every domain of activities, for example, the Digital Empowerment Foundation that has been engaged in finding community-based solutions to the digital divide. The Warana Wired Village in Maharashtra is also working to provide facilitation booths in villages, linked to a central computer network. It is now widely acknowledged that the transformation of a predominantly agrarian society into a fully fledged knowledge one is largely dependent on the society's substantive capacity to create, absorb, disseminate, protect and use knowledge for the creation of economic wealth and societal good through the participation of all sections of the population. Though India has achieved 9.4 per cent economic growth in 2006–7, 36 per cent of its population lives below the poverty line.

While the knowledge society in India is presumed to be the latest of societal progressions, the historical experience of developmental initiatives are replete with the evidence of the reinforcement of traditional social divisions and cleavages of caste, class, ethnicity and gender in the new context. This reinforces the points made by ecofeminists Mies and Shiva above.

Emerging Knowledge Society and Cultural Panorama

Overall then, India has seemingly missed the industrial revolution, but has encountered a phenomenal shift from its conventional agrarian setting to a knowledge-based one, being thereby digitally and globally enabled, with an accompanying, diverse intensity. However, the pre-existing political, economic, social and cultural dynamics continue to exist, albeit in modified form.

The emerging India is indeed experiencing a new form of dispersal and fragmentation and also a dark side of development with the advancement of the knowledge society. Economic prosperity and knowledgeability have been accompanied by increasing lust for money and power, corruption and trust-deficit, crime and violence, a break in traditional institutions and practices, lack of morality and ethics in public life, and increasing difference between public discourse and personal action. India today stands at a threshold, which could liberate its citizens through their own strengths, from poverty, domination and isolation, and knowledge society could provide such a platform.

We now turn from technology and society, in general, to public and private, civic and environmental, enterprise specifically, as our culminating global–local effect Indian effect, with a view to realizing its integral advantage.

12.5 Global–Local Effecting Indian Integral Advantage through Enterprise

INFOSYS AND THE AWAKENED COUNTRY

IT Kiosks to Tata Nano Car

Nandan Ninekani (now an Indian politician) as a co-founder (9) of India's famed Infosys, with a $6.4 billion turnover in 2008, through actualizing the next generation of IT and consulting, is a great believer in the free market, as a means of awakening his country. *No plan in India, however visionary he says, was able to achieve what bottom-up economic power and initiative has enabled in the past two decades.* India, recovered then, has proved, for Nilekani, to be young, impatient, vital, awake – a country that might finally be coming close to its early promise.

The problem about being young and vital though, is that you miss out on what has come before, that is the grounding and emergence laid by Gandhi, if not by Tagore's, or Nehru's attempted navigation. To turn then to a form of south-eastern effect that builds authentically on prior local grounding, local–global emergence and global navigation, we need to turn to neighbouring Sri Lanka.

GROUNDED IN THE GANDHIAN *SARVODAYA*

Grounded in Local Traditions

Satish Kumar, to whose work we referred at the beginning, grounding phase of this Indian chapter, when he moved to a Gandhian ashram when he was 20, read Gandhi's book *Sarvodaya*, which meant wellbeing of all. Ironically, and effectively, such has been taken wholeheartedly, not in India, its home ground so to speak, but in neighbouring Sri Lanka. In fact we have picked up on such in several of our previous books, most especially in our (10) *Integral Economics* and in our (11) *Integral Development.*

For founder of Sri Lanka's *sarvodaya* some 50 years ago, A.T. Ariyaratne (12):

> *to enlist popular participation and commitment, development programmes require a value-base that is meaningful to the people, relevant to their perceived needs, and affirmative of their inherent strengths. And where are such values to be found? They are present in indigenous religious traditions, which over centuries have shaped the people's perception of reality and their notions of what is good and true. Principles for the improvement of their present lives can be culled from these traditions, and re-articulated in ways that mobilize the people to take responsibility for social change.*

BUDDHISM, RUSSIAN ORTHODOXY AND THE GUILD TRADITION

Sarvodaya Emerges through Cultural Fusion

Sarvodaya began in 1958 when a 26-year-old science teacher, Ariyaratne, and a group of his 16- and 17-year-old students from Nalanda College, opted to do voluntary work in a downtrodden Sri Lankan village. The prestigious Nalanda Buddhist high school had been founded in Colombo at the turn of the last century by the American theosophist – drawing on the wisdom of Sophia to which we referred in a Russian orthodox context (see Chapter 5) – Colonel *Henry Olcott*. Olcott has in fact been called by Sri Lankans as one of the heroes in the struggle for our independence and a pioneer of the present religious, national and cultural revival. He *was also considered a Buddhist modernist for his efforts to interpret Buddhism through a westernized and scientific lens.*

Revisiting Swaraj and Ahimsa

For Gandhi therefore, in the mid-twentieth century, as for Satish Kumar today (see above) Indian independence was much more than a political issue. Constructive work for him so called, that is home-spun cloth, village industries and local self-reliance (khadi) was at the heart of genuine independence, not just political democracy. In that way he encouraged Indian farmers to grow what they needed themselves.

The same was true for essential village industries. Only when a non-violent social order (ahimsa) was possible; only such a society could attain Truth (satya) and self realization (*swaraj*) grow. This was the composite idea that Ariyaratne drew upon, also acknowledging that this was all in the service of God, or the Lord Buddha in his (13) terms: *I am a part and parcel of the whole and I cannot find Him apart from the rest of humanity.* In his last will and testament, a day before he was assassinated, Ariyaratne affirms, Ghandi wrote: *India has still to attain social, moral and economic independence in terms of its 700,000 villages as distinguished from its cities and towns.*

SARVODAYA'S SOUTH-EASTERN WAY

Beginning with Shramadama – Energy and Caring

The so called Sarvodaya Shramadana Movement, as we have seen, traces its history back to the year 1958, when Ariyaratne took his privileged students to a village in Kanatoluwa, as an attempt to give an urban elite insight into some of their fellow low-caste countrymen in rural areas. A hard core of volunteers, more than 300,000 between 1958 and 1966, with Ariyaratne as the Convernor, started to organize Shramadana camps in downtrodden rural areas over weekends and on school holidays. The volunteers pledged themselves to economic and spiritual regeneration, according to Buddhist values and principles.

In fact, the first shrama (energy) danas (caring) camps organized in 1958 and 1959 were inspired by the youth-work camps organized in post-war Europe by Quakers and other church groups, and brought back to Sri Lanka by Abeysereke, a Rural Development official and close friend of Ariyaratne. The Sri Lankan process began when a village invited *Sarvodaya* volunteers to initiate a programme of activity. As a first step, a worker checked in with the local monk and other key figures, and prompted them to assemble a *paule hamua* or family gathering of local inhabitants, sometimes in the school, but usually in a temple. Here, the initial *Sarvodaya* pitch is given, telling about the awakening that was happening elsewhere in the country, and inviting the villagers to begin to take charge of their own lives by discussing together their common needs.

Gramodaya: Second Village Awakening Stage

After the shramadana camp, embryonic *Sarvodaya* groups coalesce. The youth and mother groups usually form the first, with the children's, farmers' and elders' groups coming later. *With the organizing of these ongoing groups, the village now enters a second stage where the villagers identify their own priorities and initiate their own programmes*, such as planting a garden or conducting a house-to-house survey. The Sarvodaya Movement supplies ideas, contacts, skills and even credit through its now newly formed Gramodaya Centres, and its regional and national facilities. Young people who have demonstrated particular motivation and effectiveness are chosen by their groups to undertake training at the nearest Sarvodaya Institute, in issues, such as agriculture, health or metal-work, which are relevant.

Village Council: Third Participatory Stage

As local efforts take root, the Movement's national and regional network has yet other resources to offer, such as practical skills in organizing local marketing cooperatives and savings schemes, or in creating locally appropriate technology. When a village has reached a point where its various groups – mothers, youth, farmers – are functional, it is ready to incorporate its own Village Awakening Council, which then serves as an autonomous entity designing its own development programme. In guiding this development *Sarvodaya* relies on its identification of the 10 basic needs: water, food, housing, clothing, health, care, communication, fuel, education, a safe, clean, beautiful environment and a spiritual and cultural life. In light of these, and in contrast, all wants are motivated by greed, sloth or ignorance.

The Fourth Stage: From Welfare, to Awakening, of All

Sarvodaya in fact did not talk, from the outset, about welfare. Instead it talked about awakening: awakening of the individual to his highest potential; awakening of human groups to theirs; awakening of the nation to its highest potential. For rural people, such awakening firstly had three components: *first, a political element, in the sense of people having an opportunity to participate in decision making*. Voluntarily, *Sarvodaya* had managed to promote participation initially of over a million people, across 12,000 villages, in such active participation. How then does Ariyaratne propose this state of affairs is continually and successively addressed for him through local, national and global awakening.

LOCAL, NATIONAL AND GLOBAL AWAKENING

Gram Swaraj – Local Awakening

Gram swaraj firstly signifies the liberation of the village through the creation of grassroots economic and social programmes. He argues that the colonial powers destroyed the traditional horizontal axis of village power in order to build up a vertical axis of governmental hierarchy.

For example, today there are 670 *Sarvodaya* village banks, run by the villagers themselves, and 3000 villages with SEED support programmes, providing for economic empowerment and self reliance. Moreover, *Sarvodaya* had recently set up its own Development Bank, serving half a million people with loans and savings. It also has four regional telecentres.

Deshodaya – National Awakening

Sarvodaya envisions a process of political liberation, a community-based participatory democracy, beginning from the grass roots, that parallels and builds upon the economic liberation that has begun with the village banks. *Sarvodaya* established a Deshodaya Organization in 2001 to build up a consensual political culture, devoid of political parties, to enact a new constitution to establish such a system. Moreover, for Ariyaratne, when the present economic system collapses, as was the case with the Berlin wall, the way will be paved for deshodaya.

Vishodaya – World Awakening

Perhaps the most important thing that *sarvodaya* can contribute to the global dialogue today is that of development based on spirituality and spiritual consciousness. Although *sarvodaya* has sought a balanced development that integrates social, economic, political and spiritual elements, the key to its system is the spiritual element. As such, *sarvodaya* is a spiritual movement that seeks social justice and development, a total social revolution. *Sarvodaya* evokes Gandhian and Buddhist values to orient society towards spirituality, equality, simplicity and conservation. These are the alternatives they propose to the violent paradigm of global materialism and consumerism that threatened to undermine cultural values and bring social and environmental chaos to the world.

12.6 Conclusion

Is India Bankrupt of Vision

Three years ago, two Indian environmentalists, Aseem Shrivastava Ashish Kothari A (14) wrote a book they called *Churning the Earth*. In it they raised the question, are Indians so bankrupt in their vision and devoid of cultural self-confidence that they cannot summon an independent vision and imagination to measure their own steps? Are they not forever condemning themselves to playing an unwinnable catch up game with the West, Japan and China? *The shadow of western colonialism on Indian cultures is proving to be the longest, long after the sun of formal colonialism has set.*

The Most Shocking Aspect of the Indian Growth Story

In fact it is interesting that we had to turn to Sri Lanka to find a wide-ranging manifestation of the very *sarvodaya*, or awakening of all, that originally grounded in Gandhi's India, as Satish Kumar had been heard to reveal. Moreover, if we turn to the kind of emerging *earth democracy* that Vandana Shiva envisages, and fully inclusive *knowledge society* that Singharoy envisages, Shrivastava and Kothari (15) believe that:

> *The most shocking aspect of the dazzling Indian growth story is it primary structural feature, unique in the history of the modern world, given the size of India while the wealthy make hay and the top quarter of the population is doing visible better (at least in purely material terms),*

three-quarters of the population of the country has been largely excluded (or rejected) from the processes of prosperity that have unfolded over the past two decades.

Preventing the Robbery of the Soil

The answer, of course, in this south-eastern, integral context, is not for India to become Sri Lanka's rurally-based *sarvodaya* writ large. Rather, and true to our integral colours, it should be nature (Kumar, Shrivastava and Kothari) that takes the lead, in conjunction with culture (Gandhi, Tagore, Shiva) and then science and technology (Nehru and Singharoy), as well as economy and enterprise (Nilekani and Infosys) that follow, altogether contained within an integral Indian Polity.

We now move north-east to China, the truly emergent star, in conventional economic terms.

Bibliography

1. Aurobindo, S. (1950) *The Human Cycle.* Wisconcin, Twin Lakes.
2. Kumar, S. (2013) *Soil, Soul, Society: A New Trinity for our Time.* Lewes, Leaping Hare Press.
3. Shiva, V. (2005) *Earth Democracy: Justice, Sustainability and Peace.* Cambridge, MA, South End Press.
4. Mies, M. and Shiva, V. (2014) *Ecofeminism.* London, Zed Books.
5. Merchant, C. (1980) *The Death of Nature: Women, Ecology and the Scientific Revolution.* New York, Harper One.
6. Singharoy, D. (2014) *Towards a Knowledge Society: New Identities in Emerging India.* New Delhi, Cambridge University Press.
7. Singharoy, D. (2014) *Towards a Knowledge Society: New Identities in Emerging India.* New Delhi, Cambridge University Press.
8. Singharoy, D. (2014) *Towards a Knowledge Society: New Identities in Emerging India.* New Delhi, Cambridge University Press.
9. Nilekani, N. (2008) *Imagining India: The Idea of a Renewed Nation.* Toronto, Penguin.
10. Lessem, R. and Schieffer, A. (2010) *Integral Economics: Releasing the Economic Genius of your Society.* Farnham, Gower.
11. Schieffer, A. and Lessem, R. (2014) *Integral Development: Releasing the Potential of Individuals, Organizations and Societies.* Farnham, Gower.

12. Ariyaratne, A.T. (1996) *Buddhism and Sarvodaya: Sri Lankan Experience.* New Delhi, Sei Satguru Publications.
13. Ariyaratne, A.T. (1996) *Buddhism and Sarvodaya: Sri Lankan Experience.* New Delhi, Sei Satguru Publications.
14. Shrivastava, A. and Kothari, A. (2012) *Churning the Earth: The Making of India.* New Delhi, Penguin.
15. Shrivastava, A.and Kothari, A. (2012) *Churning the Earth: The Making of India.* New Delhi, Penguin.

Chapter 13
Integral China: North-East – Chaxugeju to Guanxi

For the Chinese, reasonableness is placed on a higher plane than reason. For while reason is abstract, analytical, idealistic, and inclined toward logical extremes, the spirit of reasonableness is always more realistic, more human, in closer touch with reality, and more truly understanding and appreciative of the correct situation. This spirit of reason and this religion of common sense have a most important bearing on the Chinese ideal of life, and result in the Doctrine of the Golden Mean.

Lin Yutang (1), My Country and My People

13.1 Introduction

THE CHINESE ECONOMIC MIRACLE

Second Largest Economy in the World

India and China, the two most populous countries in the world, are by far the most pre-eminent of the BRIC countries. Reminding ourselves of what Jim O'Neil (2) had to say in Chapter 2 about the latter: 'There is simply no overstating, China's importance for all of us, not just 1.3 billion Chinese. The entire planet, all 6.5 billion of us, is invested in China's economic success. In 1995 China's economy was worth $500 billion, and it has grown tenfold in fifteen years, averaging 10 per cent annual growth. By 2010 China had overtaken Japan to become the second largest economy in the world'.

And There Are No Slums

Moreover, for the well known Egyptian development economist, Samir Amin (3), Director of the World Social Forum based in Dakar, in a few decades, China has built a productive, industrial urbanization that brings together 600 million human beings, two-thirds of whom were urbanized in two decades. This urbanization has no parallel in what Amin terms the Global South (for us the 'north-east'). *There are certainly 'chic' quarters and others that are not as opulent, but there are no slums, which have continued to expand everywhere in the cities of the Third World.*

But Totalitarianism Reigns

Of course Amin's views are controversial. For many, including ourselves (4) today, China has become even more capitalist than its American counterparts, albeit with local variations on this global 'western-northern' theme. In the developing world, allegedly, China seemingly sides with despotic governments and exploits Africa in particular, in its search for raw materials. Moreover, China in Maoist times was seen to be viciously despotic, and the notorious *cultural revolution* allegedly destroyed the lives, physically or psychologically, of millions, as of course was the case in communist Russia, if not also, albeit to a lesser extent, in apartheid South Africa.

Today, moreover, China's *human rights* record is purportedly dreadful, and the monolithic influence of the so-called communist state is considered by many in the West to be overwhelmingly oppressive, rather than in any shape or form emancipatory.

SOMETHING EMANCIPATORY GOING ON

However, as UK-based political scientist/economist/sociologist Lin Chun's (5) (Associate Professor in Comparative Politics at London School of Economics) reveals, there is indeed something emancipatory going on, in the process of Chinese economic renewal. For one thing we were ourselves taken recently by a throw away remark by one of our Nigerian banking colleagues, and doctoral students, Akeem Oyewale, who claimed that *China was the only country investing in Africa for the long term!* The end 'effect' in this chapter will then bear this out.

We now review China as a whole, as if it were pursuing integral advantage.

Navigation
Technology and Society
Confucian Pragmatism

Effect
Public, Private
Civic Enterprise
Guanxi/Mutual Benefit

Emergence
Culture and
Consciousness
Xiaokang/Moderate Prosperity

Grounding
Nature and Community
Chaxugeju Association

Figure 13.1 Chaxugeju to Guanxi

13.2 Chaxugeju: Chinese Grounding in Nature and Community

THE FOUNDATIONS OF CHINESE SOCIETY

Chaxugeju to Mutual Benefit

We begin, as we have done in all BRICS cases so far (with Russia, South Africa and India), with grounding in nature and community. We now do so from a 'north-eastern' philosophical perspective, that is in terms of what Chinese sociologist Fei Xiaotong has called *Chaxugeju,* the principle of Association. From there we turn to emergence, via political scientist Lin Chun, embodied in contemporary *Xiaokang* (moderation). For navigation we draw on strategist Zhichang Zhu's *Confucian Pragmatism,* effectively ending up with American political scientist, Deborah Brautigam's portrayal of *Guanxi* (see Figure 13.1).

Chaxugeju contrasted against Tuantigeju

We begin then with Fei Xiaotong (6), and his work based on his *From the Soil: The Foundations of Chinese Society.* The main theory that he develops analytically – as one of China's founding sociologists and anthropologists – in the 1940s, to describe Chinese society, depicts the principles of Chinese social organization. 'Soil' is thereby used socially and metaphorically, rather than literally.

Fei's core thesis is that Chinese society is organized through principles different from those prevailing in the west. Organizational principles are for a society what grammar is to a language. The principles provide the structural framework for social action; they are intuitive and taken for granted; they are deeply embedded in people's worldviews, as well as in the society that people re-create every day. He introduces Chinese organizational principles through the concept of *chaxugeju*, the 'differential mode of association'. *Cha* means 'difference' or 'dissimilarity', *xu* means 'order' or 'sequence', and *geju* means 'pattern' or 'framework', that is the patterning of Chinese society through ranked categories of social relationship.

Western society, conversely, is represented, according to Fei, by straws collected to form a haystack, and Chinese society is represented by the ripples flowing from the splash of rock thrown into the water. He says, in effect, that Chinese society cannot be adequately conceptualized in terms of haystacks (that is organizations) nor the west in terms of ripples of water (that is discrete categories of social relationships). Through these metaphors, he argues that in the west individuals produce their society by applying an 'organizational mode of association': *tuantigeju.*

Chinese Modes of Association

Chinese modes of association are composed not of discrete organizations but of overlapping networks of people, which have four features. *First, networks are discontinuous.* They do not link people together in a single systematic way; rather, networks centre on the individual and have a different composition for each person. The western mode of association presupposes the autonomy of individuals, whereas the Chinese mode of association presupposes multiple linkages of self with others and a categorization of those linkages.

Second, each link in a Chinese person's network is defined in terms of a dyadic social tie (*gang*). These *interpersonal ties* are known in Chinese as *guanxi.* Each tie is both normally defined and also strictly personal. Each is normative with regards to requiring a specified ritual *(li)* behaviour, and personal, requiring personal obligations on behalf of each individual: obligations of the child to the parent, wife to the husband, younger to the older, and official to the ruler.

Third, networks have no explicit boundaries. Individuals do not 'sign up' for membership in networks, as they might do in western organizations. Insofar as people uphold their obligations, a network built of strong and weak links can join people separated by considerable social and geographical distance.

Fourth, the moral content of behaviour in a network society is situation specific.

What is considered moral behaviour depends on the situation and the social categories of the actors, rather than on abstract standards. Fei points out, as such, that Chinese society is not group oriented – a view contrary to most interpretations. It is centred on the individual and is built from networks created from relational ties linking the self with other individuals.

Kinship Relations and Family Enterprise

The key example Fei discusses is the family enterprise. *Western families are organizations with fixed members, but Chinese families are networks capable of expanding outward.* These networks are without clear boundaries and consist of differential categories of kinship relations. In the past two centuries, the Chinese have become merchants of the world, because they have been able to create highly efficient, flexible commercial networks on such a family basis. In general moreover, the higher a person's prestige (and perhaps wealth), the more likely that person will have a dense web of horizontal and vertical network ties. Moreover, the more linkages one maintains, the more intensively one is wedged into an existing social order and is committed to the status quo.

THE DIFFERENTIAL MODE OF ASSOCIATION

Chinese Egocentricism

In these elastic networks that make up Chinese society, there is always a self at the centre of each web. But this notion of the self amounts to ego-centricism, not individualism. With individualism, individuals make up organizations in the same way that parts make up wholes. However, in traditional Chinese thought, there is no comparable set of ideas, because, for them, there is only egocentricism. Confucius, in fact, felt that people needed to extend themselves in order to achieve their own interests. But even if one extends as far as possible, one's self is still at the centre.

For Fei then, the Chinese would sacrifice their families for their own interests; their party for their family interests; their country for their party's interests; and the whole world for their country's interests. Indeed in traditional China, the concept of the public was seen as the emperor's family. Hence, the boundary between public and private has never been clear. The state and the public are but additional circles that spread out like waves from the splash of each person's interests. Therefore people must cultivate themselves before they can extend outwards. Therefore our social morality makes sense only in terms of personal connections.

Therefore whenever Confucius wanted to clarify ren, he had to return to the ethical principles in personal relationships: filial piety, fraternal duty, loyalty and sincerity. Similarly, when he tried to clarify tianxia, he had to return to concrete relationships themselves, such as those between fathers and sons, older and younger brothers. In summary then, and in comparing east with now Chinese west, Fei has narrowed the conventional meaning for the term organization, applying it only to groups that have a continuous organizational pattern, accentuating the contrast against those having a Chinese differential mode of association. These groups he calls 'social circles'.

TRADITIONAL SOCIETY AND THE RECONSTRUCTION OF RURAL CHINA

Rural Politics – Founded on Local Consent

Fei was keenly aware that China was experiencing a great historical transformation mid way through the last century. Traditional society had to be reformed to answer the challenges of the time. But unlike many others, who were eager to replace Chinese culture with western values and ideologies, Fei paid close attention to the existing cultural and socioeconomic conditions. As such, to begin with, he envisioned a great transformation of the political system emerging out of traditional Chinese political institutions. For Fei, imperial power would need to change into a central administration responsible to the people; gentry power, into legislative representatives elected by people; bureaucrats, into public servants in an efficient civilian government; factional power, into industrial, commercial and occupational organizations. And *the entire political structure will rest on the foundation provided by local consent power.* Of course this is very different from what has turned out in 'communist' China, as we shall see.

What he called rural industry included the following:

- peasant families participating in industry without giving up farming;
- the location of industries scattered in and around villages;
- such industries belonging to the peasants, as cooperatives;
- the raw material produced by the peasants themselves;
- the profits from the industry directly distributed to the peasants.

In the final analysis: 'I do not suggest we should stop at family production', Fei said, 'but I think this is the most reliable starting point and foundation'. We now turn to contemporary political scientist, Lin Chun, some 70 years later, to reflect on what has actually emerged.

13.3 Xiaokang: Chinese Emergence through Culture and Consciousness

THE TRANSFORMATION OF CHINESE SOCIALISM

China is Intrinsically Plural and always in Flux

Lin Chun, a Chinese political scientist currently based at the London School of Economics, has experienced both the Maoist and Dengist regimes as, hitherto, a Chinese citizen, and thereby the way that China has been co-created so to speak, by its peoples in modern times. From the outset she asks – what does *dzhongguo* or the 'Middle Kingdom', for Lin Chun from the outset, signify? Above all the (self) identity of China, for her (7), unbeknown to most outside observers, is intrinsically plural and always in flux. This is especially so with respect to its more recent history, a history of immensely complicated revolutionary and developmental experiences undergone by *a multi-ethnic, multi-regional, and multi-faceted people transforming one of the world's oldest and largest civilizations or states. China then*, as she perceives, or constructs, it, *is one country of many worlds.*

Centralization and Decentralization

Contrary moreover to a widespread impression, that China is always a highly centralized despotic power, the Chinese state, she says, consistent with what Fei has argued above, has always had a sturdy local dimension and decentralized tendency. Because of its size, uneven-ness, and regional divisions according to coastal-inland, urban-rural, majority-minority and other demarcations, the country's political authorities have customarily been at once centralized and decentralized. In fact sub-national and grass roots power has expanded in the reform era. This expansion was anchored in the phenomenal thriving of township and village enterprises (TVEs) and has been captured in scholarship as 'local-state corporatism'.

Local forces intercepted by global ones routinely by-pass the centre and its rules, regulations and policy instructions, eroding public functions and the state system. Runaway decentralization also leads to corruption.

The Rise of the Social Toward a Communist Moral Economy

The most creative thinking then that emerged from China regarding the invigoration of Chinese socialism rejects conventional modernization and globalization in their prevailing forms. *The new vision is 'local', local national, local social and local communal, as a negation of standard modern markers of relentless industrialization, urbanization, commodification and homogenization.* The ongoing struggles in China to undo privatization of land and strategic industries are intrinsic to the reinvention of the local and national moral economies.

The local, need-oriented and environmentally minded ways of production and consumption, for Lin Chun (8) then, could ultimately support organic and collective webs of life with a fresher, greener, simpler and more economical and energy efficient character. Above all, unlike any pre-capitalist mode of production, the new model, for her, is post-capitalist and fully modern, if not post-modern. It is not an echo of the past but forward looking and conditioned on a socialized political economy sustained by industrial development. *China relies on the socially beneficial progress of science and technology as well as on selected market mechanisms.* In fact such a re-orientation can be traced back, historically, to the 1920s.

The Last Confucian Building on Chinese Foundations

One of China's two pioneering sociologists Liang Shuming then, not himself a communist originally, nevertheless shared with the communist party a vision of the need for 'a great social transformation'. In *Has Man a Future: Dialogues with the Last Confucian* (7) he argued that a backward China could never catch up with advanced nations by copying urban centred industrialization, whether by western-style competition or Soviet state power.

Only an integral movement of peasants and concerned scholars like himself could succeed, since a new society would have to be built from the bottom up through an expanding network of local coops. Fellow sociologist at the time, Fei Xiaotong, as we have now seen, was amongst the most influential spokesmen in the same tradition. Fei *most rigorously advocated 'moderate townships' over grand cities for a distinct developmental strategy to fit the Chinese conditions.*

Human Suffering as Cause and Effect of Communist China

But things did not turn out that way, duly building on local grounds. Instead, as we saw in India, in South Africa and in Russia, the global did not emerge through the local. Instead, communism or capitalism took over. China in the communist Mao years, in particular, suffered from grave institutional defects that often resulted in social and economic destruction. *The Great Leap led to a great famine. The cultural revolution turned into a decade of ideological purification that produced a cultural wasteland.* However, *at the same time, broad social objectives*, side by side with national independence and pride, such as workers' beneficiary status, women's participation, equality of nationalities, universal public education and a government-financed health system leading toward preventive medicine against epidemics, *transformed the country in less than three decades*, that is from the 1940s onwards.

Modernization: Commodification and Casualization of the Precariat

Equally true, though, is that one of the unintended consequences of the communist revolution was its unfulfilled promises in liberty and bureaucracy against hierarchy and bureaucracy, a grave problem exposed foremost by the socialist principles of freedom and equality in themselves. So human suffering, as such, was both a cause and an effect of the Chinese communist revolution.

Today moreover, in the new millennium in China, human suffering continues. In the reformed social and economic structure, most notable is the drastic decline of the state-sector working class caused by de-industrialization of the 'rust belt' of old industrial centres, and especially by the privatization of State Owned Enterprises (SOE). This has been paralleled by the development of a new private sector working class in the 'sun belt' of the coastal south. Catalyzing such is *the sweeping commodification of labour, along with the 'informalization' and 'casualization' of employment followed by inevitable loss of job security.*

Town and Village Enterprises (TVEs)

However, it was in fact the collective organization in the Mao era that enabled fundamental infrastructural improvement of agriculture as well as five small-scale rural industries – iron, tools, cement, fertilizer, water and electricity, and light machinery – producing for local needs. Communal factories also prepared for the TVEs to flourish in the early reform period, allowing absorption of a massive surplus labour in the countryside before what became the largest outflow of rural migration in human history. *TVEs, for example, enjoyed extraordinarily cheap productive factors: direct possession of land and easy supply of low cost labour, as well as credit from previous collective accumulation and friendly financial cooperatives.*

COMMUNITY, CULTURE AND DEMOCRACY IN CHINA

Angang: The Importance of Economic Democracy

Democracy, in China for Chun then is a matter of returning socialism to the social and recapturing the state from within. It is not about fighting a socialist dictatorship to win a capitalist democracy but about mobilizing the resources of socialism to overcome its contradictions and achieve its own democratization. For a Chinese socialist model aspiring to the social power of organization and participation, forms and channels of institutional support should be multifarious: the democratically elected people's and central congress at central and local levels; labour unions and farmers' associations; community and neighbourhood self-managing committees; professional networks.

There can be multiple – old and new, alternative, indigenous and yet to be invented – approaches to achieving representation and accountability. An important dimension of social empowerment is 'economic democracy'. A Chinese example is the Maoist 'Angang constitution'. Endorsing participation of workers in management and of cadres and technicians in shop floor labour, the short lived experiments pioneered a model of combining industrial democracy and post-Fordism; flexible teaming and participatory planning, equal pay for equal work and profit-sharing in management. The reverse course of transition from socialism to a version of capitalism in China may have fuelled growth, but, for Lin Chun, it has also entailed widespread commodification of life processes and resources, including labour, land, nature and bodies.

The rising social forces will have to bring the social and public back in while seeking their re-conceptualization. Even if globalization is the order of the day, downplaying the primary position of the national and local, especially in the cases of geographically and demographically huge and historically uniquely resourceful countries like China, would be a mistake. State roles and responsibilities, for her, cannot yet be evaded anywhere, nor should the power of the people as agents of history be ever forgotten.

The Dystopia of Development

Yet after two and a half decades of spectacular growth, China has awakened to its horrendous cost, Lin Chun maintains, and its ultimate social and natural limits. While some of the predicaments were traditional, for example overpopulation relative to arable land and oversupply of labour, and some were modern, for example industrial pollution, all had been intensified by the market transition.

The country's forested land had been so depleted that it had become one of the world's sparsest (107 out of 140).

Desertification was also at a pace of more than 10,000 square hectares yearly, with desert covering nearly 28 per cent of PRC territory. Water pollution had become such that supplies for 600 million people were now substandard, and two-thirds of Chinese cities were short of water. Finally, China's contribution to greenhouse gases, especially from carbon emissions, was at a level considered appalling.

XIAOKANG SOCIALISM: IN SEARCH OF A VISION

A New Radical Consciousness

That said, and in part resulting from all of such, dialectically so to speak, China is now beginning to embark on the third stage of reform (post Mao and Deng). Some promising changes have already taken place: apart from introducing the notion of a 'green GNP', legal and policy revisions have been sought so as to improve workplace safety, retrieve unpaid wages, cancel agricultural tax, protect migrants, expand social security and cultivate the domestic market. This is altogether part of *a new 'scientific' conception of 'people oriented, comprehensive, coordinated and sustainable development'* which aims at 'all round human development', including high productivity and an affluent life, a sound ecosystem balancing urban and rural development, the development of man and nature, domestic development and opening up to the outside world. This is the radical consciousness the Chinese state purports to promote today.

The new possibilities could be captured in the still-to-be-drawn blueprint of Xiaokang socialism. Xiaokang means literally well-off and moderate prosperity (9) and is a concept bearing distinctive Chinese characteristics. Over 2000 years ago, this word featured one of the Chinese' ideals for a society in which people worked hard for prosperity of their own families, led a well-off life, and enjoyed orderliness of the environment. The idea is in fact as ancient as that of datong or great harmony, cherished in the Book of Rites, incorporating four components: community, security, integrity and democracy. Community then is a core idea not only in various pre-modern traditions in China but also in Maoist socialism, which blends traditional, modern and post-modern. In line with self-management, beyond the ability of central planners, the adjective 'direct' is important in characterizing producers, providers and consumers intimately engaged in socially useful, productive, distributive and service sectors.

Meanwhile, mutual help networked in the neighbourhood and communal settings, with or without market values, could become ever more widespread as a substantive component of a 'caring economy' or a 'solidarity' economy. Universal material security could form a material foundation for a *xiaokang* society, of which the institutional form is yet to be invented. The distant debates in Europe over a guaranteed basic income might one day find themselves learning from the Chinese, who would fashion a form of such an income as an answer to structural unemployment and demographic as well as land pressures. An entire terrain for experiments could thus be opened in which life may not yet be without toil, but will be more humane (as opposed to mechanical), free and ability enhancing.

A Participatory Society as a New Moral Economy

A new moral economy then, as Xiaokang purports to be, drawing on original Confucian (10) origins, could be another case of local, in this case Chinese, contours bearing a universal significance. Its basic assumptions are certainly far broader than such narrow beliefs as the crude 'economic man'. This wholly individualistic doctrine has found difficulty spreading in many cultures and communities. Past and present setbacks notwithstanding, for Lin Chun, China then may strive to lead the way to an imperative global transformation, as the paradigm of capital accumulation has evidently hit a limit. To urgently address climate and environmental crises, for example, is inescapable and hence universal, and is where relevant local knowledge might be normatively constructed. Could not a new kind of 'industrious revolution', this time aimed at both needs and freedom, serve to relax the conceptual and discursive rigidity of capitalist modernity? *A participatory society as a commons, with direct producers as its subjective and realization of human values through united labour as its objective, is within the vision of a grand social model.* We now turn to Confucian Pragmatism (11).

13.4 Confucian Pragmatism: Strategic and Aesthetic Navigation

CONFUCIAN PRAGMATISM

A Better and More Harmonious World

Zhichang Zhu (12), whose formal education was stopped at the age of 16 during the Chinese cultural revolution, is now Reader in Strategy and Management at the University of Hull Business School in the UK. Zhichang in fact has been a Maoist Red Guard, farm labourer, shop assistant, lorry driver, enterprise manager, assistant to the dean of a business school, software engineer, system analyst, IT/IS/business consultant, in China, Singapore and England.

A changing world, he says, together with his Japanese co-author Ikijiro Nonaka (see Chapter 3), in their recent book on *Pragmatic Strategy: Eastern Wisdom, Global Success* demands novel strategies, and strategies are derived from paradigms. Amid the unprecedented, continuing crisis, we need to question the for us 'western-northern' paradigm we have used in the past. We must assess its social, political and intellectual as well as economic consequences, and ask how we could strategize differently, here in 'north-eastern' navigational guise. For bankers still manufacture fat bonuses, governments battle for a 1 per cent debt, consumers fly more often for overseas holidays and companies promote more, not less, consumption. Business has not yet found its Copernicus!

The current economic paradigm, inclusive of O'Neil's (13) BRICs *Growth Map*, for this Chinese and Japanese 'eastern' duo, is chiefly responsible for the crises, calamities and deteriorations we still live with. Facing the dangerous return of business as usual, we need a workable alternative. Beyond the hype of newness, for Nonaka and Zhu, we need enduring wisdom, and, for them, that lies within pragmatism. Such *pragmatism is innovative, ethical and effective, combining moral standing, sound judgement, implementation skill and learning capability*. If then the economic powerhouse is moving eastward, and the world is on course for an Asian century, as many suggest, what unique contributions will Eastern experiences make to strategy? How should people all over the world learn from each other and together make the world better and happier? As such, an inquiry based on Confucian pragmatism, they say, may be a way forward. Overall, and together they say, *let us make the world better and happier (American pragmatist John Dewey) and realize great harmony (Chinese pragmatist Confucius).*

ARISTOTLE MEETS CONFUCIUS

Aristotle's Three Intellectual Virtues – Episteme to Phronesis

The current search for practically wise strategy in the 'West/North', for Zhu and Nonaka as such, has been largely under the flag of Aristotelean ethics, particularly Aristotle's elaboration on *phronesis*.

Aristotle, in effect, conceived of three forms of human intellectual virtues that enable an individual to achieve wellbeing. First, there is the *episteme* (scientific knowledge) which is judgement about things which are universal and necessary. It seeks to discover laws, principles and the essence of things. Then there is *techne* (craft knowledge), which examines how to make things and originates in the maker, not in the things made. Finally there is *phronesis* (practical knowledge), which deals with both universals and particulars; it is about knowing what is good for human beings in general as well as having the ability to apply such knowledge to particular situations. Of the three kinds of knowledge, Aristotle considered *phronesis* the most valuable. While it includes a general awareness of the highest common good, it also involves the appreciation of particular facts; its function is to put into practice the values that the moral virtues provide.

Confucius' Eight Exemplary Doings

Now Zhu and Nonaka turn to Confucius. The way they interpret his pragmatic turn is informed by his eight exemplary doings, formulated into three groups. The *first* two 'wuli' steps – *investigating things and extending knowledge* – are redirected toward the goal of understanding the world. The *second* three 'shili' steps – *making sincere one's intentions, rectifying one's mind, and cultivating or improving one's person* – are directed toward the goal of perfecting oneself from within, so that one can be ready for social and political responsibility to better others. The *third* three 'renli' steps – *regulating a family, governing a state well, and pacifying the world* – are directed toward extending one's virtues among men so that one can be said to realize one's potentiality in the context of relationships.

Walking in the world, the sages coped with flows of *wuli shili* and *renli*. How did they do it? According to Confucius, to act wisely *entails balancing the rational, the creative and the normative in accordance with situated particulars*. This is the quintessence of *shizhong*. In fact the Aristotelian *episteme-techne-phronesis* categorization seems broadly compatible with the Confucian teaching (see Figure 13.2). *Episteme* and *Wuli* pertain to the natural and the technical – what it is; *Techne* and *Shili* concern ways of seeing and making things – how to do; *Phronesis* and *Renli* promote the common good and emphasize value, purpose and morality – why we do it.

What is versus How to Act

While Aristotle studies the *whats*, relying mainly on nouns – episteme, techne and so forth, Confucius looked at the *hows*, using active verbs – extending knowledge, getting it right, and so on. On the one hand, we receive rigorous Aristotelian categories of knowledge, on the other we witness Confucius' appeal to how sages walk the world.

Intellectual Virtues	*Shili* Acting Creatively	
Phronesis	*Shizhong* Timely Balancing	
Techne	*Wuli* Acting Efficiently	*Renli* Acting Ethically
Episteme Aristotelian Hierarchical What	Confucian Circular How	

Figure 13.2 Aristotle meets Confucius

The western 'What' question is usually expressed as something like 'What kinds of things are there?'. The Chinese 'Where' question, on the other hand, leads to a search for the right path, the appropriate model of conduct to lead one along the path, the 'way' that life is to be lived and where to stand. For 'truth-seekers' the question is 'how might I classify or define this and that?', while for 'way-makers' the question is 'How may this or that be brought into the service of our purpose?' The British Chinese scholar Joseph Needham put it this way:

> *Where Western minds asked 'what essentially is it?', Chinese minds asked 'how is it related in its beginnings, functions and endings with everything else, and how ought we react to it?*

Hierarchical versus Circular Knowledge

In contrast to Aristotelian abstraction, logic and reasoning, Confucianism appeals to aesthetic traditions that are expressed through language, music, art, play, rituals, legendary sages and cultural heroes. Knowledge moreover, for Aristotle, is unmistakenly hierarchical. In Aristotle's framework, practical wisdom is clearly the highest intellectual virtue. In Confucian pragmatism, as for John Dewey (14), such a knowledge hierarchy is thoroughly rejected. For Confucius, *wuli, shili, renli* are conceived as a circular, reciprocal flow where no particular *li* is primary, across time or space.

Aristotle then, first split intelligence from morality, the two types of virtues, and then took great pains to reconnect them via the sophisticated category of *phronesis.* This prefigures Weber's antagonism between fact-based scientific knowledge and faith-based moral judgement. Conversely in Confucius, as in the American pragmatists, intelligence and morality are integrated from the outset.

Polarising/Choosing versus Associating/Complementing

Closely linked to categories and hierarchies are the notions in the 'west/north' of contradiction and dichotomy. While Aristotelian polar sensibility usually leads to contradictions and either/or choices, Confucian polar sensibility emphasized interdependence, interpenetration and reciprocity. In the 'west/north', since ancient times, it has been widely accepted that we think with the brain. Not so in Confucianism. 'North-easterners' think with their hearts. While a *brain-mind* tradition emphasizes logical inference, rational analysis, conceptual categories and the separation of subject and object, a *heart-mind* tradition values the tacit, aesthetic and holistic.

Although Zhu is critical of Aristotle's overtly rationalistic style, he does not devalue *episteme* and *logos*. Science, technology, efficiency and the technical rationality behind them are useful insofar as they serve rather than dictate human purpose. In the final analysis, *his purpose is to establish that pragmatism is our best hope for practically wise strategy, and that such 'Confucian' pragmatism is not the exclusive property of the 'north-eastern' Chinese or Japanese.* We now turn to the ultimate economic and business effect of such Chinese communal grounding, societal emergence and strategic navigation.

13.5 Chinese Business and Economic Effect: Mutual Benefit/ Guanxi

THE DRAGON'S GIFT

Principles of Mutual Respect

We choose to focus, in this culminating part of our Chinese chapter, on pursuing such 'north-eastern' integral advantage, via its business and economic impact on Africa, as portrayed by Deborah Brautigam. The reason for doing so is that China's engagement with Africa is perhaps its most noted, or notorious, depending on your viewpoint, illustration of the advantage, or indeed disadvantage, of its economic approach, that it bestows on the world at large. The questions raised then by Brautigam (13), Professor of International Development at the School of International Service at the American University in Washington DC, based on her extensive first hand experience, in *The Dragon's Gift: The Real Story of China in Africa*, are: *what are the Chinese doing in their new wave of aid and economic cooperation across Africa? What will this mean for poverty and development in Africa?*

China's premier Zhou Enlai had originally introduced the 'Five Principles of Peaceful Coexistence' during the 1954 negotiations with India, ironically, given the situation today, over the Tibet issue, that is:

1. Mutual respect for sovereignty and territorial integrity.
2. Mutual non-aggression.
3. Non-interference in each other's internal affairs.
4. Equality and mutual benefit.
5. Peaceful coexistence.

More than half a century later, Chinese leaders will still point to these principles as the bedrock of their foreign policy and their aid strategy.

In fact Chinese delegations visiting Africa in the 1960s also thought they saw a lot of similarities with their own situation. Like China a decade earlier, Africa was emerging from 'a long period of colonial plunder' and needed to produce food, clothing and other daily necessities. They recommended a mix of aid to meet urgent and long term needs, and offered a balance of technical training and modest turn-key projects in industry and agriculture that could been constructed quickly by Chinese experts and handed over, ready for their recipients to just 'turn the key' and start production. They also began sending in medical teams.

Building Self-Reliance – Daquing and Dazhai

In the 1970s then, the west was rethinking its aid programme, moving from a narrow focus on production and infrastructure to direct support for rural development, basic needs and poverty. *Chinese aid* operated in isolation from these trends. It *continued to reflect China's domestic ideas about development: centrally planned interventions to boost production, health and infrastructure.* The Chinese stressed that their aid was *primarily a tool for building self-reliance.*

And most of all it was symbolized by the boosting of two Chinese development models in a slogan that was repeated incessantly: 'in industry learn from Daquing; in agriculture learn from Dazhai'. The massive Daqing oilfields lie in the bleak grasslands of northeast China. Forty thousand Chinese factory workers and engineers converged on Daqing in the dead of winter to prove that the Chinese could produce their own oil. In the northwest Shanxi province, meanwhile, Mao founded a second model, Dazhai. A small production brigade of only 85 families was rapidly promoted as an outstanding example of discipline, sacrifice, cooperation and self-reliance, called upon to 'reshape the mountains, and harness the rivers', building terraces, filling in gullies, channelling streams for irrigation.

Dazhai in Africa: The Tan-Zam Railway

To find China's closest parallel in Africa, we need to look at Tanzania. Tanzanian President Julius Nyerere visited China 13 times. In 1967, inspired by Chinese moves toward collective farming and by his own ideas about African socialist traditions, he established a grand project of social cooperatives – *ujaama* villages – modelled on China's experience. Within two years agricultural production had plummeted and the programme was a disaster, due to the forced resettlement of farmers.

At the height of the chaos of the Cultural Revolution, meanwhile, China's premier Zou Enlai offered to build Africa's longest railway, nearly 2000 kilometres stretching from the copper mines of land-locked Zambia through Tanzania to the sea. The enormous and costly railway project had been envisioned by Cecil Rhodes in the late nineteenth century, and briefly considered by the British colonialists half a decade later. In the lead up to independence, the man who would become Zambia's first President, Kenneth Kaunda, called again for the railway to be built; it was rejected as unfeasible by a World Bank commission.

In 1967, Tanzania, Zambia and China signed off on the project. Construction began in 1970, finishing in 1975, two years ahead of schedule. The enormous railway line, with 10 kilometres of tunnels and 300 bridges, still dwarfs any project to date in China's economic engagement in Africa. The Chinese built railway project continues to represent the pinnacle of the kind of struggle, hardship and 'glorious achievement' pushed by Mao. The language of sacrifice parallels the tales of Daqing and Dazhai. In 2006, China's 'Year of Africa', the Chinese media made sure that the history of the Tan-Zam railway was known in every Chinese home. By 1972, Chinese teams in fact were building close to 100 different turn-key projects around the world. By 1978, 74 countries were receiving aid from China, the largest group of them in Africa.

DENG XIAOPING'S EXPERIMENTS WITH AID

Find Your Way Across the River

In contrast to the approach of the Chinese, the goal of structural adjustment, promoted by the 'Washington Consensus' in the 1970s, according to Brautigam, was primarily about getting prices right, not getting production right. Countries were typically required to impose austerity policies (reduce deficits by cutting public spending) and liberalize markets (cut import tariffs, eliminate price controls and privatize state-owned companies). Shock therapy involved doing all of this at once.

China's turn to the market happened very differently. Cautious about external borrowing and in a region culturally inclined toward high saving rates, Chinese leaders were reluctant to borrow much as they slowly adjusted their own state-led economy. There was no shock therapy, no outside-given conditionality, and *Deng Xiaoping famously urged the country to forget ideological correctness and experiment, but carefully. Find your way across the river,* he said, *but not in one great leap, but by keeping your feet on the ground and cross by feeling the stones.* Arguably, this exemplifies Confucian Pragmatism.

An Ideal Trading Partner

Today, some three and a half decades later, we know China as an industrial powerhouse, the twenty-first-century inheritor of Britain's old label, the workshop of the world. Yet in the 1970s China was primarily an agrarian economy with immense reserves of natural resources – oil, coal, gold, copper – similar in structure to many African countries today. Japan was the earliest to enter the fabled China market, in the 1970s, offering to finance the export of $10 billion of modern plant, industrial technology and materials, and China agreed to reciprocate on a deferred payment basis by exporting the equivalent in crude oil and coal to Japan.

FLYING GEESE, CROUCHING TIGER: CHINA'S CHANGING ROLE

Flying Geese as Industrial Catalysts

China's prowess at manufacturing, in fact, needs little introduction. Africa's feeble economic performance, at least up to now Brautigam adds, is equally well known. Between 1990 and 2005 manufacturing grew by almost 12 per cent annually in China, while sub-Saharan manufacturing grew at a mere 1.5 per cent per annum.

It helps then to have someone experienced leading the way. This can happen in at least four ways. First, if the level of technology is not too advanced, a foreign-owned factory can act as a role model. People can see and decide *yes we can do it too.* Second, skills can 'spill over' from foreign forms when the local employees leave, taking skills they learnt on the job to other companies, or starting their own firms. Third, foreign companies may sub-contract some parts of the work to local firms and help them meet the standards demanded. Finally, competition in local markets can push local companies to invest in new technologies, improving quality, if it does not drive them out of business too fast.

The Chinese then were looking ahead toward their future industrial engagement with Africa. By 1985 China had been seeking to digest, absorb and remould advanced technologies from abroad. Then, over time, China would transfer its production of 'mature' products to developing countries that were just beginning to move into these products. They would be small and medium-sized production projects producing for local needs and supported by local resources; boost demand for Chinese equipment and machinery; and involve 'mature' technologies – those China was already outgrowing. Between 1992 and 2002 at least 93 joint venture loans were received from the joint-venture and cooperation fund worldwide.

Chinese companies for example are a catalyzing presence in Nigeria's automotive spare parts clusters. In South Africa it is the Indians, the Tata Group in this case, who have similarly been catalyzing the development of such industry clusters, with some 350 companies manufacturing vehicle parts, supplying components to the local assembly industry, and even exporting to America. And in the leather industry, for Brautigam, Chinese aid is already helping to create a synergy between a resource many African countries have in abundance – hides and skins – and the needs of an industry Beijing clearly hopes will go global and stay there.

Beijing Consensus Means Experimentation

China's novel approach in Angola, the Congo and elsewhere builds on the system China learned from Japan, using very large credits, at competitive market rates, tied to Chinese machinery, equipment and construction services, with repayment in oil or other resources. This is the essence of the 'win-win' approach. The Chinese say: 'to end poverty, build a road'. *When China launched its own economic development it built roads, ports, rural power plants, modernized agriculture, invited in factories and experimented with different approaches*: special economic zones, for example. *The 'Bejing consensus' was simply*, for Brautigam, *about experimentation,* ironically as such not dissimilar, to 'free trade re-imagined' (see Chapter 2).

13.6 Conclusion

MADE IN CHINA

Dangongmei: Women Factory Workers in a Global Workplace

Inevitably, as in all the cases hitherto, in the pursuit of integral advantage – communal, societal, strategic and economic – in this Chinese instance, we have focused primarily on the positive, integral contribution that the society as a whole could make. At the same time we have pointed out some of the tripping points along the way. However, in concluding, we need, in the interests of comprehensiveness in our coverage, to point out a major Chinese downside, arising out of an authoritarian shadow side, if you like, of a 'north-eastern' culture and society, such as China. For such we turn to Hong Kong-based sociologist Pun Ngai (15), for her recent book *Made in China: Women Factory Workers in a Global Workplace.*

Global capitalism, state socialism and familial patriarchy, for Professor Pun Ngai, work hand in hand in China to exploit labour along class, gender and urban-rural lines. These triple oppressions – political, economic and socio-cultural, reinforce one another as they present new configurations specific to Chinese society at the opening of the socialist system to global production. While these oppressions are still attached to their own cultural and social conditions, they are rapidly shifting and being remade, eagerly looking for new matrices of power and practices to regulate society.

The repositioning of China as a 'world factory' in the new international division of labour is without doubt, for her, a project of global capital, which provides the bedrock for nurturing a new Chinese working class, the *dangongmei*: diligent, well-educated Chinese women workers, invariably from a rural background, willing to toil for 12 hours a day.

> *They are not just fighting against the patriarchal family, but also against an undesirable village life. A deep rural-urban divide existed in China, and nurtured the soil for rural women's struggles between work and family and for the younger generation to live out their desires in the urban areas. There were at least two seductions – effectively a coin with two sides – for this strong dagong desire: one was the womens' struggles between work and family; the other was the great disparity between the countryside and the urban areas, and between the peasantry and the working class. Each step of each work process, at the factory*

where Pun Ngai was employed, was meticulously demonstrated. Each individual occupied only one work position and was adept at only one work process. Moreover, most workers knew nothing about the product they worked on nor the meaning of the English words that appeared on the product itself. But that did not matter. They simply followed the instructions. What the disciplinary machine actually wanted was to produce a body without a mind, a mindless body.

BEYOND CAPITALISM AND SOCIALISM

If we see that individualism as the evil product of western neoliberal capital, and such 'dangongmei' collectivism as the peril of Chinese socialism then we have no choice but to look for a resistance agenda, in Pun Ngai's terms, that can transgress and re-articulate both individuality and community without privileging the former, which serves the logic of capital, and the latter, which could easily fall prey to a political strategy put forward in its name. A worker-subject seeks space in his or her own right, opening up space for a new cartography of transgressions, taking a multiple front, criss-crossing individual and collective levels, and negotiating not only with economic and political factors, but also cultural and psychic experiences.

Of course for us, in China as well as Russia, if not also in India and South Africa, the lack of individual and social integrity to which Pun Ngai alludes arises out of a failure, overall, to pursue integral advantage, drawing purposefully on local as well as global nature, culture, society and economy. We now turn to Brazil for our final, now 'south-western' BRICS case in point.

Bibliography

1. Lin, Y. (1998) *My Country and My People*. Beijing, Foreign Languages Press.
2. O'Neil, J. (2011) *The Growth Map: Economic Opportunity in the BRICS and Beyond.* London, Penguin.
3. Amin, S. (2013) *The Implosion of Contemporary Capitalism.* New York, Monthly Review Press.
4. Lessem, R. with Schieffer, A. (2015) *Integral Renewal: A Relational and Renewal Perspective.* Farnham, Gower.
5. Chun, L. (2006) *The Transformation of Chinese Socialism.* Durham, NC, Duke University Press.
6. Fei, X. (1992) *From the Soil: The Foundations of Chinese Society.* Berkeley, University of California Press.

7. Chun, L. (2006) *The Transformation of Chinese Socialism.* Durham, NC, Duke University Press.
8. Chun, L. (2013) *China and Global Capitalism: Reflections on Marxism, History and Contemporary Politics.* New York, Palgrave Macmillan.
9. Xianchun, X. (2009) *The System of Xiaokang Indicators: A Framework to Measure China's Progress.* Busan, Korea, Conference Address.
10. Liang, S. et al. (2013) *Has Man a Future: Dialogues with the Last Confucian.* New York, Springer.
11. Sections of this chapter have been reproduced from Lessem, R. and Schieffer, A. (2015) *Integral Renewal: A Relational and Renewal Perspective.* Farnham, Gower.
12. Nonaka, I. and Zhu, Z. (2012) *Pragmatic Strategy: Eastern Wisdom, Global Success.* Cambridge, Cambridge University Press.
13. O'Neil, J. (2011) *The Growth Map: Economic Opportunity in the BRICS and Beyond.* London, Penguin.
14. Brautigam, D. (2011) *The Dragon's Gift: The Real Story of China in Africa.* Oxford, Oxford University Press.
15. Pun, N. (2005) *Made in China: Women Factory Workers in a Global Workplace.* Durham, NC, Duke University Press.

Chapter 14

Integral Brazil: South-West – Eco-Services to Free Trade Re-Imagined

Increasingly the notion of 'ecosystem services' is being promoted as one of great importance. For it succinctly sums up the wide range of benefits that people derive from properly functioning natural systems. In many respects the advantages provided by nature are like those of giant utilities, and indeed include services that are instantly recognizable, as such, for example the provision and purification of water. Rain clouds in fact, generated by the Amazon rainforest, help to water crops across a wide swathe of South America, including the vast grain lands of Brazil. Some of this moisture also falls on the prairies of North America, and even reaches across to North Africa and Southern Europe. It is like a system of 'flying rivers' that move moisture across the skies, all driven ultimately by the rain-forests themselves.

HRH Prince Charles, Juniper and Skelly Harmony (1),
New Way of Looking at Our World

14.1 Introduction

REMAKING BRAZIL

Taking the World by Surprise

The final case of pursuing, as we do in this chapter, 'south-western' integral advantage, is that of Brazil, whereby nature and community (southern), embodied in *Eco-Services*, and economics and enterprise (western), thereby 'trade re-imagined' as we shall see, come to the fore. Brazil is in fact a suitable culmination to our integral endeavours, prior to an overall concluding chapter, because, in a sense, it is the BRICS ultimate 'surprise package'. While China and India have been BRIC frontrunners, as emerging markets, for a good two decades now, and Russia and South Africa have recently faltered, at least in economic guise, it is Brazil that had seemingly taken the world by surprise in the new millennium.

In fact, following in the footsteps of Chinese overall state power, it is interesting to see *The Economist's* Americas editor, between 1999 and 2013, Michael Reid (2) saying in his book *Brazil: The Trouble Rise of a Global Power*, in 2014:

> *Overall then, and for almost the first time in history, Brazilians are now demanding to remake their country from the bottom up, as a country of equal citizens rather than patrimonial privilege. That has placed the corporate state on the defensive. It gives grounds to hope that the achievements of the past two decades will be built upon and extended in a new phase in the Brazilian story.*

BRAZIL AND THE OTHER BRICS

Bringing BRICS Together

Similarly, for Director of the Western Hemisphere Studies Centre at John Hopkins University in the USA, Riordan Roett (3), *The New Brazil* has been the most active in bringing all the BRICS together:

> *As part of its broader vision to boost its vision on the world stage, Brazil has reached beyond South America to strengthen ties with the other BRICS, as well as with other members of the developing world. A leading example is IBSA, a dialogue forum between India, Brazil and South Africa. Annual IBSA meetings since 2003 have emphasized stronger trade relations, support for democracy and human rights, peace and development. The goal in such developments is for the three countries to act as a counterweight to the industrial countries by using 'soft power', instead of acting as a rival hegemon.*

Under President Lula's leadership (Roett was writing in 2010), Brazil (now under the Presidency of a Lula disciple, Dilma Roussef) has become the most significant regional actor in South America – a voice for mediation and integration. At the international level, Brazil is now a respected player with both the emerging-market countries and the industrial states. South-south diplomacy has proven to be an effective mechanism for furthering Brazilian political and security interests and for building new diplomatic relations with other emerging actors, especially Russia, China and India.

14.2 South-Western Natural Grounding towards Economic Effect

THE RAINFOREST WAS HER PEOPLE'S LIFE

Defending Rainforests to Overcoming False Necessity

We shall start this penultimate chapter then, naturally and communally, by grounding ourselves in Marina Silva's defence of rainforests, or what Britain's Prince Charles (see opening quotation above) has called Amazonia's *Ecosystem Services.* Silva as an indigenous Brazilian recently, and remarkably, stood for Brazilian president.

We then turn culturally and societally, to the unique Gilberto Freyre, to his emergent *social theory in the tropics.* For navigation, thirdly, we move to a rare breed, an academic sociologist who became Brazil's democratic president in the 1990s, focused on what he termed the *social solidarity,* Fernando Cardoso. For overall social and economic effect, ultimately there can be nobody better than the Brazilian polymath Roberto Mangabeira Unger (see also Chapter 2), effectively *re-imagining free trade* (see Figure 14.1).

Trees as Friends and Relatives

Marina Silva, 2014 Presidential candidate in Brazil, as described in the book by her American follower, Ziporah Hildebrandt (4), had originally grown up in the *seringal,* the rubber-tapping region of Amazonia. The rainforest was her people's life. They loved their trees as friends and relatives. *Marina,* already as a young child, *dreamed that her people would be recognized for their character and their knowledge of the forest, rather than scorned for their poverty and illiteracy.* Forest people and communities would then control their own

Navigation
Technology and Society
Social Solidarity

Effect
Public, Private
Civic Enterprise
Trade Re-Imagined

Emergence
Culture and
Consciousness
Luso-Tropicology

Grounding
Nature and Community
Ecosystem Services

Figure 14.1 Eco-services to re-imagined trade

lives rather than suffering under the brutal power of wealthy ranchers, business people and politicians.

LARGEST RAINFOREST ON EARTH

How to Take from the Forest without Destroying It

The state of Acre where Silva was born and raised is in Amazonia, the largest remaining rainforest on earth. When Brazil's military government decided to build new roads, in the 1960s, to make new human settlement possible, settlers and ranchers burned thousands of miles of forest to make farms and pasture therein. But the soil was thin and poor. Crops failed. Farmers gave up and moved west to cleared land.

The government then imposed its own exogenous ideas on how people would make a living from this newly cleared Amazonian forest. Yet *indigenous people had lived there for tens of thousands of years. They understood what the government did not, how to take from the forest without destroying it.*

LEARNING LESSONS FROM THE TREES

Of Afro-Brazilian Heritage

Maria Osmarina Marina da Silva Vaz de Lima then, called Marina Silva, was one of 11 children, the second oldest of eight who are still alive. She was born in the rainy season in 1958, in Serengal Bagaco, 70 kms east of Rio Banco, the capital city of the state of Acre, in the far west of Brazil's Amazon region. *Marina's parents were of Afro-Brazilian parentage, descended of European colonists and enslaved Africans.*

Take Only What You Need

As for the original indigenous people of Amazonia, recent estimates put its population before the arrival of Columbus close to 20 million. First contacts with Europeans brought epidemics – diseases which indigenous peoples had not seen and could not treat – may have killed 90 per cent of the population. Now there are only some 250,000 left. Yet they form 215 groups that speak about 170 languages.

To Marina, it is their stories and beliefs that taught the lessons of the forest: take only what you need, so that others may live and life may continue.

The rubber tree teaches the same lesson: cut only so deep, or the tree will die; don't cut every day, or the tree will grow tired. It is a lesson that the government of Brazil – and the world – is learning too slowly. The rainforest gives life only when it is healthy and whole. Once damaged it means death. Until recently this powerful value system guided the forest people's lives and sustained their livelihood. Yet Marina was very aware then, even when young, of the precariousness of her family's existence.

AVIAMENTO – HOLDING POWER OF LIFE OVER YOU

Back to the Generals

Aviamento came from Brazil's colonial days, according to Hildebrandt, when the plantation owner held the power of life and death over his family and slaves. The attitudes this created in both rich and poor people are deeply ingrained in Brazilian society. The wealthy look down on physical labour and consider it their right to take what they want and order people around.

In 1964, when Marina was six, the democratically elected president was forced from office. The military took over, with support from the US. They chose a general to be the next president. In the next few years, the regime ruled by terror, and murdered, exiled or imprisoned anyone they did not trust. On a map Amazonia looked blank to the generals. They saw an area almost as large as Europe but with no roads at all, and just a few cities and towns. *The regime thought that Amazonia's empty spaces might be developed and turned into farms, factories and iron and gold mines to make money, pay off the country's debts, and make Brazil a world power.*

Forced Out of Their Land

In 1970, the government began building the highways into Amazonia. It also started a huge project to move farmers and their families, called settlers, into Rondonia, the state east of Acre. Once bulldozers pushed down trees, the settlers came, then business people, ranchers and those buying and selling the land for quick profit. The main highway BR-364 into Acre, though unpaved, brought thousands of settlers to Acre looking for land. Millions of poor farming families were forced from their land, making way for electric power plants, for mines and for giant farms growing food for sale. As many as 7,000 families a week crowded into buses to go to Amazonia, having been promised farms by the government, together with tools and seeds.

Local Heritage Lost

The strength of guns, bulldozers, planes, radios and antibiotics can make traditions look weak. When a people lose faith in their traditions, for Hildebrandt, they can lose the will to live, and illness, depression and addiction as well as suicide strikes. Cultural heritage and expert knowledge of land, plants and animals are lost, along with unique ways of viewing the world and solving human problems.

Five epidemics hit Brazil's Amazonia in the 1960s, killing Marina's three-year-old sister, Deusilene. Then Maria Rosilene, six months old, died. The next epidemic was meningitis, a serious infection that affects the brain and spinal cord. Marina's mother ultimately contracted such and died. Marina then had to care for six children, the house and the garden. Soon she was not well herself, and contracted hepatitis, which she luckily survived. *Was this her destiny, she asked herself, to cling onto an existence of work, disease and death. Instead she longed to become a nun.* Surely a Catholic school would support such an escape route?

JOINING THE BRAZILIAN LITERACY MOVEMENT

Beginning to Discover Life's Possibilities

Marina was just 16 when her whole life changed. Securing her father's permission she moved to the big city, Rio Branco, to join an evening programme run by the Brazilian Literacy Movement. In two weeks she learnt to read and write. She was then sent on to a special programme, where it was possible to complete four years of primary schooling in one year. At the age of 19, after finishing sixth grade, Marina was beginning to discover life's possibilities. She had acquired a strong feeling for justice, and let go of her youthful desire to become a nun, to pursue a different social cause, in support of which she was to join a Christian Base Community.

Paulo Freire's Liberation Theology

Just as many trees make a forest, for Silva, many people make a movement. All over Brazil people joined movements, most especially Christian Base Communities (CBCs) to create change. There were over 80,000 CBCs in Brazil. Workers formed unions to demand fair treatment. Priests, nuns and union activists organized landless farmers to claim unused land. In Acre, the actions called *empates* (meaning 'standoff' – seeking social justice) were organized by *seringueiros* (rubber tappers) to save their land.

Marina was in fact one of the first women to join the *empates*. More then followed. So Marina was at school, while at the same time having joined the *empates* and movements for social justice. Also involved with the CBCs she learned about both liberation theology and the educational methods of Paulo Freire. *Libration theology showed Marina how her burning need to understand God, herself and the world, could build on her grandmother's simple morals, and expand into a vision of justice and equality*. Historical figures like St Frances of Assisi and Gandhi (see Chapter 12) became her role models.

Seeking Some Answers at University

In Sao Paulo, she saw a truly modern city for the first time, the third largest in the world. *A stone's throw from the skyscrapers, millions suffered in favelas.* Only four years earlier she could not read and write, and now she would enter the Federal College of History in Rio Branco.

All her life Marina asked questions, and at the university she found some answers. To her delight, she discovered books by people who thought as she did about freedom and equality for all.

Meanwhile after generations of believing they had no rights, *seringueiros* finally formed their own Rural Workers' Union. Marina at the same time acted in a theatre group that drew attention to oppression. She also joined a student group opposed to the military regime, PT, the Workers' Party, Partido does Trabalhadores. When the regime legalized political parties, many sprang up. But only the PT welcomed *seringueiros*, landless people, landless farmers and other excluded from power and opportunity. It required 30 per cent to be women.

CARRYING THE DREAM TO THE GOVERNMENT

Marina as 'the Tip of the Iceberg'

In 1990 Marina was ultimately elected representative to Acre's state congress. She was incredibly popular with the poor of Acre. There was nobody like her, for Hildebrandt: a rubber tapper, born poor as they were, with a university degree. More miraculous was the fact that Marina had not forgotten her good fortune. She helped them get more schools and health clinics.

She in fact called herself 'the tip of the iceberg', in that 'I am the voice and fight of so many who are against the destruction of the Amazon, but who are in favor of developing it with sensitivity to its eco-structure and awareness of its impact on so many lives. This is why I became a senator'. Marina supported new ways of farming that don't destroy the rainforest. Agro-forestry mixes fast-growing crops with slower-growing coffee and trees. Amazonia's diversity is too valuable to lose. Europe, much of the US, and coastal Brazil were once heavily forested. When the forest disappears so does biodiversity. 'We are not going to suffer from the devastation that Europe and the US experienced', Marina said.

Amazonia: Not as a Place to Exploit, but as a Resource to Care for

Once she was in the senate, Marina Silva's mission was to change how Brazil – and the world – thought about Amazonia: not as a place to exploit, but as a resource to care for; not as an empty space, but as home to millions of people and to the species of a priceless ecosystem. Over 70 per cent of drugs derived from plants, for example, come from Amazonia. Researchers believe that cures for diseases like cancer, AIDS and heart disease are hidden in tropical forests. Yet indigenous nations, Marina argued now with her newly acquired political status, get none of the profits. 'One fungus, one plant or insect could produce a product worth millions or billions of dollars. A portion of that money, returned to rainforest communities, would support sustainable development in Amazonia'.

Nature and Spirit

'When I really dream I think we should come up with solutions to show the world', Marina says. With its vast rainforest, traditional peoples, and high technology Brazil could become a world leader by showing a new vision of society working with nature. Just as Marina was healed first as a child, she fights now to heal Brazil, as if you like Bishop Tutu (see Chapter 10), a fellow 'Christian southerner' has fought to heal South Africa. We now turn to Gilbert Freyre to take the Brazilian natural and communal local story now culturally and societally, via historians Peter Burke (5) and Maria Lucia Pallares Burke, both based at Cambridge University in England, locally–globally on.

14.3 Luso-Tropicology: Local–Global Emergent Brazilian Hybrid

RACE, CULTURE AND HYBRIDITY

Mixing Ingredients Improves Life

Gilberto Freyre was born in Recife – as indeed his namesake Paulo Freire was – in the Brazilian North-East in 1900 (he died in 1987), travelled around Europe and America in his young adulthood, and became a veritable polymath: historian, anthropologist, sociologist, politician and journalist over the rest of his twentieth-century life. In his (6) best-known work on *Masters and Slaves* written in the 1950s, *instead of equating the mixture of races with deterioration, he associated such,* harking back to Kropotkin if not also to a latter day Darwin, *with the improvement of species.*

Combining History, Sociology and Psychology

Although Freyre preferred the anthropological approach, as such, with its emphasis on the direct observation and the details of everyday life, he was more involved with sociology, a subject on which he was to write a textbook. He regularly used terms from sociology, such a 'sub-culture', or 'social cohesion' or the idea of a 'complex'. In fact he was a sociologist at a time when fellow sociologists in Europe or the United States were more generally concerned with politics rather than with culture and society at large. *Still more unusual was his attempt to combine history with sociology and psychology, using such terms as 'masochism' and 'libido', and describing the Amerindians as 'introverts' and the Africans as 'extraverts'.*

A central theme of *Masters and Slaves*, moreover, was the way in which the violent actions of the Portuguese colonizers and plantation owners, taking and sometimes raping indigenous and African women, led to a miscegenation that would lead to a situation of relative racial harmony. In other words, the reader is offered *a complex story about unintended consequences, the dominant trope being that of synecdoche, where the part stands for the whole, the Big House for the plantation system and even for patriarchal civilization across Brazil.*

THE TROPICAL SOCIAL THEORIST

Freyre's Discourse on Polytheist Method

For the Burkes, associated with his critique of pretentions to objectivity is *Freyre's* 'southern' *polemic,* not unlike the Russian 'eastern' Slavophiles, *against abstraction and quantitative methods, to which he prefers impressionistic descriptions packed with concrete and sensuous details.* He used to recommend students of sociology to begin by observing everyday life in the street in which they lived, the number of houses and their inhabitants, the lighting, the paving, the hygiene, the security and so on.

As for the critique of sociological 'purity', Freyre began by emphasizing what he called the 'insufficiency of sociological methods'. *Sociology,* he maintained, *should by 'polytheist' rather than 'monotheist'. 'It has to be mixed and amphibious concerned with natures and cultures'.* Sociology, for him, depends on its neighbours: anthropology, ecology, social history, folklore, psychoanalysis, biology and other disciplines. People on the margins of the profession, for example journalists and historians, had a fundamental contribution to make.

Mestizo Logic: Polarities and Mediations

Freyre, moreover, was fascinated by the effects of cultural encounters, not only between Portugal and Brazil, Europe and America, or the Orient and Occident, but also between past and present, republic and empire, order and progress, town and country, authoritarian and democratic regimes. He thereby emphasized the importance not only of the mestizo or mulatto as an agent of mediation, but also that of the nanny or the street. His own writings are an attempt to mediate, then, between art and science, sociology and literature, insider and outsider, involvement and attachment, intuition and analysis, of, if you like, a 'mestizo logic'.

Social Democratization: Laboratory of Civilization

The most famous kind of mixing discussed in Freyre's work is *the ethnic and cultural mixing presented in Masters and Slaves, which he considered to be central to Brazilian identity.* As a kind of shorthand for the positive social consequences of miscegenation, he used the expression 'social democratization' from the outset. Later, according to the Burkes, especially when writing for North American readers, he referred to 'ethnic democracy' or to 'racial democracy', contrasting such with, say, the merely 'political democracy' of the English. *What was distinctive about Brazil was the 'democratization of personal relations' in the sense of a fraternal tendency*, not so much liberty and equality as fraternity.

Luso-Tropicalism: Instituto Nabuco

According to Freyre therefore, it was easier for the Portuguese than for the British or Dutch to survive in the tropics because so far as climate is concerned, *Portugal 'is more Africa than Europe'*. This 'acclimatability' was accompanied by an adaptability to local customs. 'Tropicalism', for him then, is worth taking seriously. It describes a project intended to combat what Freyre calls 'the persistent notion that everything tropical is the negation of the refinement of civilization'.

'Southern-Western' Tropics Lead and the 'West-North' Follows

At a more general level, for the Burke's, *Freyre* suggested that Brazil might become a leader in the process of making 'civilized man in cold regions' aware of the aesthetic values of the tropics. He *predicted a movement that might be described as cultural imperialism in reverse, with the tropics leading and Europe following, not least because Brazil was a pioneer in racial mixing that was become characteristic of the word in the twentieth century.*

He offered a critique of European reason and modernity from a tropical point of view. His main point, frequently reiterated, was that the tropical way of life was better adapted than the 'western' way to the demands of post-industrial and post-modern society. His own brand of tropical sociology or anthropology, as such, came to be known as *tropicology*.

Tropicology: New Models for Humanity – Instituto Nabuca

He viewed tropical societies then as the new models for humanity. By 1975 he was calling it a new science that drew on ecology, anthropology, sociology, history and other disciplines, employing a comparative approach to discover common futures in tropical societies and cultures, their food, clothes, mentalities and so on. Transnational and regional studies – in which a political or national criterion is replaced by an ecological or cultural one – help solve the problem, he said, of bringing peoples together and opening up ways of common understanding and communication between them. As an example Freyre had in mind the transnational scientific study of 'pan-Latin American' problems carried but by people of different disciplines and nations.

He opposed a narrow nationalist Brazilian sociology as much as he opposed a narrow nationalist German one. On the other hand, he supported a broadly based tropical sociology that would reveal the insufficiencies of a study of society based on western European and North American experiences alone, thus contributing to what he called a ecumenical sociology. The new science of tropicology found a home in the institute Freyre helped to found, the *Instituto Nabuco* in Recife. How then might Freyre be viewed in an international context?

Tropical Syncretic Culture

Four analogies or affinities, finally for the Burke's, between the ideas of Freyre, and those of post-colonial theorists are particularly worth noting, even if we allow for differences in both emphasis and application:

- *first* there is Freyre's lifelong *concern with the subaltern* as well as the dominant, with slaves as well as masters, with men, women and children;
- *second* is his *interest in cultural identity;*
- *third* place comes the *preoccupation with hybridity,* cultural as well as biological, and especially with the two-way process called trans-culturation;
- *fourth* is his *critique of Eurocentricism.*

In the speech that Gilberto Gil gave, on being appointed by President Lula's Minister of Culture in 2003, he spoke of 'cultural multiplicity' and 'tropical syncretic culture' affirming that 'we are a mixed people'. Freyre then had suggested at a UNESCO conference in 1948, that *while political and military history pursued a national style, often driving people apart, 'the study of social and cultural history' is or might be a way 'to bring peoples together'*, and 'open ways of understanding an communication between them'. We now turn from Freyre to Brazil's president, and fellow sociologist, Fernando Cardoso.

14.4 Social Solidarity: Political and Economic Navigation via Social Science

CHARTING A NEW COURSE

French Social Scientists Craft a New Era

Mauricio Font is the Director of the Bildner Centre for Western Hemisphere Studies at Cuny University, New York, and editor of *Charting a New Course* based on the work of Fernando Cardoso (7). Cardoso was unique in transforming himself from an academic sociologist into Brazil's President, in the 1990s, without losing touch with his sociological roots.

Already in the 1920s, Sao Paulo, where Cardoso was based (born in 1931 and became President in 1995), had become the main locus of Brazilian industrialization, economic development and modernization. But the revolution of 1930, heralding the demise of the old republic and the onset of the Vargas military dictatorship, put into question the state's preeminence.

A new, modern university though would prepare a new intellectual elite to help face this challenge. A contingent of French social scientists helped launch the social science programme of the University of Sao Paulo, amongst those being the anthropologist Claude Levi-Strauss and the historian Fernand Braudel. The key founding figure in what would be known as the Paulista school of sociology was Fernandes Florestan, Cardoso's mentor.

Focus on Dependency in Development

Cardoso's doctoral thesis, *Capitalism and Slavery in Southern Brazil*, provided an analysis of the rise and demise of the slavery system in the nineteenth century in the southern-most state in Brazil. His thesis approached the subject using a dense dialectical approach inspired by Karl Marx. By 1962 he had been named director of the Center for Industrial Labor Sociology (CESIT). But the 1964 military coup disrupted the centre's plans, and he fled to Chile. *Exile turned out to be a godsend.* In the social sciences and in economic thought, *Santiago in Chile may have been the intellectual capital of Latin America at the time. It provided access to a rich theoretical and comparative Latin American context* and developed frameworks through which to probe ideas about development. While in Chile, Cardoso recast and renamed 'sub-capitalism' the concept earlier developed in Sao Paulo, as the 'dependent development' model. He elaborated such in his (8) book on *Dependency and Development in Latin America.* It was at this time that

Cardoso met the leading American development economist Albert Hirschman, who would become a close colleague and perhaps his main influence in the US.

In 1968 he decided to return to Brazil, but the fateful second denial of his academic career by the military brought Cardoso closer to the path that would eventually lead him to the presidency. *The response to this setback was to launch CEBRAP: the Brazilian Centre for Analysis and Planning in 1969, drawing support from international foundations as well as from national sources.*

Embedded in the Social Sciences

Cardoso and associates emerged as significant players in the gradual process of political reopening that began in 1973. The Brazilian Democratic Movement (MDB) was the main political organization demanding the return of democracy in the 1970s. A CEBRAP task force played a distinguished supporting role in the MDB struggle. Its very success in creating space to study alternative views about Brazilian society turned the research centre and its leaders into actors in the democratic movement.

Embedded in an academic and intellectual trajectory, the Cardosian worldview accepted the leading economic role of the market, while maintaining that it does not address all needs, creates problems of its own and tends to dissolve human solidarity. So the state needed to play a fundamental role in reducing inequality, poverty and other social problems. The state and market, however, and as Mangabeira Unger will elaborate further (see below) are not the only choices. Community and civil society also play important roles. Yet at the dawn of the twenty-first century, Brazil remained a country of high inequality and poverty, notwithstanding the fact that between 1994 and 1998, approximately 280,000 families acquired land through an agrarian reform programme.

DEPENDENCY AND DEVELOPMENT IN LATIN AMERICA

The Politics and Economics of Exclusion

In his Dependency and Development in Latin America, Cardoso reconsidered the problems of economic development through an interpretation emphasizing the political character of the processes of economic transformation. The formulation of the relation between economic process, structural conditions and historical situations made clear, for him, that theoretical schemes concerning the formation of capitalist societies were of little use in understanding the situation in Latin American countries. Not only the historical moment, but also the structural conditions of development and society were different. Recognizing these differences, Cardoso went on to criticize the concepts of underdevelopment and economic periphery and to stress both the economic aspects of underdevelopment and the political processes by which some countries dominated others. It was thereby necessary to determine the way in which state, class and production are related in each basic situation of dependence.

To sum up then, studies of dependency continue a live tradition in Latin American thought, reinvigorated in the 1960s in opposition to the theory of modernization, and of predetermined stages of development, something to which the Russian Slavophiles were also very resistant (see Chapter 4). The *protests* of American blacks, the Vietnam War and opposition to it, the counterculture, the student movement, the feminist movement, all *demanded paradigms that were more sensitive to the historical process, to social struggles and to the transformation of the systems of domination.*

Academia and Politics

In the evolution of social thought in Brazil then – and for Cardoso the same could be said of other countries – there has been an opposition between a purely academic outlook (based on scientific rigour and research) and a mindset more engaged in the transformation of social structures (where the political project of social change was the priority, and where scientific rigour took a back seat). Arguably our own work at Trans4m, through CARE-ing-4-Society (see next chapter) serves to bridge that divide. Overall then for Cardoso:

- Is it possible to reconcile scientific rigour and politics? What role does the rigour of learning play in the political project?
- Is it possible to know objectively which policy will be the best for a given set of historical circumstances? Does knowledge predetermine policy?

SOLIDARITY SOFT POWER

Brazilians are a Solidarity People

In Cardoso's inaugural speech as President, in contrast with what the conventional BRICS wisdom implies (see Chapter 2), he said the development of a country is not measured by what it produces. *True development is measured by the quality of attention the country gives to its people and its culture.* In a world of instantaneous global communication where people fragment and specialize, *cultural identity is rooted in nations.*

Brazilians, as Freyre has said, are people of great cultural heterogeneity, born from a 'south-western' combination of occidental Portuguese tradition with African and indigenous Indian traditions. The collective support for the country is moved, moreover, by sentiment, and this sentiment has a name: solidarity. It lets the country break free from small circles of particular interests so that it helps its neighbour, colleague, or compatriot, near or far. *Brazilians, for Cardoso, are a solidarity people.*

Pursuing Soft Power as Distinct Identities

Cardoso as President in fact, in a diplomatic visit to South Africa in the mid 1990s, made the point that *globalization is too narrow a framework to explain what is behind concrete and specific cases.* Disregarding this, or the importance of a country's history, makes any analysis incomplete, and flawed. *The interaction between what is universal and what is specific is lost, as is the possibility of identifying opportunities for integration,* since these opportunities will only be discernible if they are based, he says, on a national perspective of the globalization process.

Real differences, then, at the beginning of the negotiating table, have to do, primarily, with different stages of development and features of social and political structures. In a word, with each country's history, distinctions can hardly be explained by the forces that promote uniformity. What Cardoso describes as 'soft power', in fact, involves the ability to collect and process information, the power to create and disseminate worldwide cultural and social patterns, as well as international prestige and diplomatic influence. *Paradoxically, then, globalization forces us to have a greater and keener awareness of our respective identities. It is based on our specific individuality that we will seek to integrate our economies into the processes of globalization.*

Providing a Human Dimension to Development

Moreover, we are in effect experiencing changes, for Cardoso, that will reorganize the policies and economies of the twenty-first century. The task of providing a human dimension to development in the era of globalization has become a major challenge, since all of us have to deal not only with a radically new reality, but especially with the ethical vacuum which the idolatry of the marketplace has caused and which the demise of the revolutionary utopias have exacerbated.

If, through globalization, the economy becomes the conditioning factor in the realm of production and management, the same does not apply to the realm of values.

It is necessary to separate the concrete facts ushered in by globalization from a pseudo-ideology which is building up around the phenomenon, with nuances which range from the uncritical preaching and celebration of the 'virtues' of the emerging system, to the affirmation of the inevitability of the loss of the nation state. *How then can we reinvent the sense of community on an international plane, so as to avoid social exclusion and segregation?*

A New Renaissance

Why then does Cardoso allude to a 'New Renaissance'? The Renaissance has numerous philosophical and historical implications. One of the most fundamental was to give to individuals the notion that they could control their own fate. The Renaissance Man came to feel, on the one hand, abandoned, since he was missing the certainty of hierarchies created by religion; on the other hand, he came to feel stronger despite this, because in the end he was master of his own destiny. Nothing expresses this better than the transformations in the modes of scientific investigation, the liberation of politics from religious constraints, and above all changes in the visual arts.

In sum, *man today lives with the possibilities of 'rebirth', a new liberty to reinvent models of social existence.* The models are still in the process of being defined, and in the present stage point more to the limits to what should not be done than to positive patterns. *Another contemporary phenomenon engendered by technical progress that reinforces the thesis of the 'new Renaissance' is that of globalization, which is producing a new consciousness of the dimensions of the world.* The Renaissance established the individual as subject, and with the retreat of religious interference in politics left the terrain open for the definition of a new model of social organization, the sovereign state. Now the advance of globalization designates 'humanity as a new subject', and in a certain way, that every same state is obliged to adapt to its new circumstances. *This powerful notion of 'global community' is altering our worldview.*

Solidarity, for Cardoso, is becoming an exigency that does not result only from the conscience of peoples. Conceptually, then, we are prepared, he says, to make a qualitative leap, in terms of one of the central problems of humanity, which is social justice. His compatriot, and fellow social scientist, Mangabeira Unger, from whom we have already heard in Chapter 2, takes the story on from here, towards its ultimate 'south-western', experiential and experimental, effect.

14.5 Re-imagine Trade: Southern Cooperation/ Western Experimentation

WHERE ART AND SCIENCE, RELIGION AND ACTIVISM MEET

Coming from a Political Family

Brazilian polymath Roberto Mangabeira Unger, based today at Harvard Law School in the US, remains politically active to this day in Brazil. His maternal grandfather, Octávio Mangabeira, was the last of eight children of Augusta Mangabeira and Francisco Cavalcanti Mangabeira, a poor pharmacist living in the Brazilian state of Bahia, like Silva and Freyre in the Brazilian north-east. Octávio's brother João Mangabeira founded the Brazilian Socialist Party. His sister Maria Mangabeira founded a religious order. Octávio became professor of astronomy at the Escola Politécnica in Bahia and gained popularity after delivering an inspired public lecture in 1910 on Halley's Comet, which propelled him into a career in politics. He served as Brazil's minister of foreign affairs in the late 1920s before the dictatorship subjected him to a series of imprisonments and exiles in Europe and the United States.

His mother, Edyla Mangabeira, was a Brazilian poet and journalist. She published numerous books of poetry, and a memoir of her experiences in social activism in Brazil entitled *Três exílios e uma guerra*.

FALSE NECESSITY: OVERCOMING FATE

Confining a Type to an Overall System

For Mangabeira Unger (9), in his seminal work on *False Necessity: Anti-Necessarian Social Theory in the Service of Radical Democracy*, two types of fatalism have dominated our understanding of society. One of these types is rooted in the tradition of classical European social theory from Montesquieu to Durkheim to Weber. *Marxism*, as we saw in both Russian and Chinese cases, has been its most relentless and influential exponent. The other type of fatalism is represented by the contemporary *positive social sciences* particularly as they have come to be practiced in the universities in the United States, and has been reflected in empiricism and in rationalism generally, and free markets and in capitalism specifically.

Such theories recognize the importance of institutions and beliefs of society. However, they *present each such formative context as an example of a general type, like capitalism or the market economy*. They see the type as an invisible system: all its elements stand or fall together. According to such a view then, *our deliberate action is the largely unwitting agent and accessory of a historical script we are unable to rewrite.* A market economy, for Mangabeira Unger rather, can be *effective in many different ways,* with radically different consequences for social life. This fact was the most important discovery, for him as a legal scholar, made by legal theory over the last 150 years. Yet it never fully penetrated into economics. To rather see the arrangements of the market, like other economic institutions, as a solution to problems of production and efficiency, separate from the rest of social life, as O'Neil has done, is to misunderstand all of them.

Once we free ourselves from the impulse to see contemporary institutions as the outcome of a narrowing funnel of possibilities, we can begin to find in our institutional history, as Unger puts it, hidden resources for reconstruction.

GLOBALIZATION HAS BECOME A EUPHEMISM FOR AMERICANIZATION

Emancipated from Self Reliance

False necessity then develops a set of ideas that makes it easier to distinguish the democratic and experimentalist commitment to enlightenment, emancipation and empowerment, from this spiritual perversion of self reliance. If our chains are the institutions of society and our songs are the achievements of the spirit, as Mangabeira Unger puts it, we are left to sing in our chains. Will the new practice of permanent innovation be confined to islands of privilege, or will it be opened up to a broader part of humanity? The study of emergent forms of flexible production may reveal opportunities to reconcile these interests. It cannot, however, generate the institutional content of ways of organizing markets, democracies and civil societies that would move us toward such goals.

Educational Endowment to High Energy Democracy

We must rather recognize one another as the radical originals, the context-transcending individuals that we know ourselves ultimately to be. This recognition, premised on the capacity to imagine other people becomes an act of love. We must give practical reality to the bond between the ideas of love and spirit, connection and transcendence. It is the most important link, for Mangabeira Unger, between the concerns that have driven the Near-Eastern salvation religions of Judaism, Christianity and Islam, and the ideals lying at the centre of the democratic creed. How might such institutionally, and transitionally, arise?

The *first* element in such an institutionally oriented programme of transition is to ensure the government *develops the human and financial resources with which to lift up ordinary people.* Such a government grants people the educational and economic means for independent self-development and cooperation. It helps them to free themselves from drudgery and repetition. It makes it possible for them to develop forms of life that are suited to spirit – towering over its station in life. *The second major platform in the transitional programme is to strengthen the educational and economic endowment of the ordinary worker and citizen.* By giving the ordinary person a state in the social order and a chance for greater mastery over his immediate circumstance, they give greater practical effect to democracy. *This includes* the *organization of politics and civil society in ways that make it easier to identify, challenge and change, piece by piece and step by step, the established institutions and practices.*

The *third* axis of the institutionally oriented transition programme is the effort to *democratize the market.* The working assumption here is that we can and should reorganize the market economy rather than merely regulating or compensating for its unequalizing results. The crucial conceptual assumption is that *the market economy, like representative democracy or another other abstract institutional conception, is institutionally indeterminate: it lacks a natural or necessary institutional form.* In the transition programme, Mangabeira Unger tries to prevent the turn to the market from meaning the dictatorship of a minority who hold the keys to the market that the majority do not. We attempt to do generally what the Americans did for a decentralized agriculture and banking in the nineteenth century.

The fourth element of the institutionally laden transition programme is the commitment to high-energy democracy: one that invites a greater expression of popular political energy and encourages a more repeated practice of basic reform than now exists in the sleepy democracies of Europe and North America. To have a transformative force, changing institutional arrangements and ideological assumptions, *politics must rise in temperature, and find the institutions that can perpetuate such intensity.* To diminish the dependence of transformation on crisis and radicalize democratic experimentation, we must energize politics. To energize politics, we must adopt arrangements that keep society at a higher level of organized civic engagement, and favour repeated structural reform in government.

The Uniqueness of Each Nation State

A high energy democracy, for Mangabeira Unger moreover as for us, *imagines itself in the great theatre of the nation-states of the world,* as already intimated in Chapter 2, from whence, from our perspective here overall, integral advantage comes. It envisages society-wide experimentation in the development of different forms of life, as well as experiments in the lives of individuals and groups. It refuses to treat the largest setting – the setting of the nation-state or of the world as a whole – as a dim low energy background, meant to ensure the enabling conditions for creating the new through the initiatives of individuals and groups.

In fact, for him, among the evils supported by the ideas sustaining the doctrine of institutional convergence is the weakening of national diversity. *We can know and develop ourselves only through contradiction. A mark of a higher civilization, in fact, is the collective ability to experience contradiction without war.* Strong difference, difference capable of alternative forms of humanity, requires the marriage of spirit and institution in the organized life of a people. The idea of the many ways is that a progressive alternative can best arise through the combination of local heresies with elements of the established economic and political orthodoxy. Such heresies must be inspired by each country and culture. The organizations of the Bretton Woods system then must not be allowed to continue operating as a long arm of a dominant neoliberal programme. Their job should be to assist national experiments.

EFFECTIVELY REMAKING INSTITUTIONAL ARRANGEMENTS

The Rescue of Petty Commodity Production

Mangabeira Unger then sets out a programme for reconstructing the large-scale institutional structure of society in the here and now: the constitution of government, the organization of the economy and the system of legal rights. This 'south-western' institutional programme, for us as it were, is extended by *a programme for the making of the fine texture of social life – the style of direct, person to person relations.* His argument also suggested that many of the deviations that took root, and an even larger portion of those that did not, represented variations *on the theme of small-scale, relatively equal producers, like the medieval guilds, operating through a variable mix of cooperative organization and independent activity.*

Many of the economy's most technologically advanced as well as its most technologically retrograde sectors depart from the model presented by mass-production industry and display features of petty commodity production, as highlighted in Chapter 1 by Kropotkin. Nevertheless, as a principle for organization of the economy, the programme spearheaded by the artisanal classes and by the 'utopian' propagandists of cooperation has been repeatedly defeated in the course of modern western history. *The alliance of central governments with pre-existing and emergent elites generally sufficed to ensure that the dominant style of economic organization won out. This 'something-like-capitalism', dominated by large-scale economic organization, was the result.*

Reinventing the Institutional Frameworks of Markets and Democracies

The dilemma of concentration, Unger goes on to argue, can be broken only by a method of market organization that makes it possible to pool capital, technologies and manpower without disturbing permanent and unqualified rights to their use. Claims upon the divisible portions of social capital have to be made temporary and limited; temporary, to prevent the ongoing accumulation of economic power in particular hands; limited, to stop accumulated capital in some enterprises or to reduce large numbers of property-less workers to wage-dependent status.

Thus, the attempt to give the repressed alternative form of industrial organizations a chance requires nothing less than the reinvention of the institutional framework of markets and democracies. The acceptance of decentralized forms of production and exchange, then, saves the popular state from having to wage war against its petty bourgeoisie and aspiring working classes. It therefore also prevents the economic disruption and governmental authoritarianism that such brings to its wake, as the Soviet post-war experience has dramatically illustrated.

Experimentation and Cooperation

Two great constructive forces, for Mangabeira Unger in the final analysis, work upon social – including political, economic and cultural – life. *One force is restless experimentation with institutions, ideas and techniques for the sake of enhancing our practical capabilities. This search for worldly power shades into a quest for a second, less tangible empowerment: the ability to question and revise our shared institutional and imaginative assumptions* as we go about the business of life. It is the opportunity to join social engagement ('southern') with self-consciousness ('western'), and to avoid the choice between alienation and stupefaction, to act confidently within a society or a culture without becoming its puppets. All of such, of course, is dependent on the state of our moral development.

14.6 Conclusion

THE COURSE OF LIFE – LOVE AND HIGHER FORMS OF COOPERATION

In Mangabeira Unger's (10) most recent book on *The Religion of the Future* he cites the axis of moral development that advances the course of our lives as a whole, ultimately reaching towards *love, in our most intimate experience*, thereby involving a sense of *community based on reciprocal engagement and recognized difference*, rather than upon similarity or sameness. From there moreover, and this is key for him, it extends to *reform of the division of labour in the spirit of the higher forms of cooperation*, as we have witnessed in South Africa (Chapter 11) in the Cashbuild *value-sharing* case.

The defining attribute of love, for him then, is the recognition and embrace of the beloved as a completion and affirmation of one's own existence, as illustrated by Albert Koopman. The distinguishing mark of the better form of community is that it can withstand difference, turning conflict into sources of union. These higher forms of cooperation then involve the ability to connect people regardless of their position in the social hierarchy; the weakening of any contrast between the definition and implementation of tasks; and the use of machines to save our time for the activities we have not yet learned to repeat.

In the final analysis, and here we see a 'southern' connection between Brazil and South Africa (see Chapter 10), the three instances of reconciliation – love, community and cooperation – lie on the same continuum of moral experience. All three of them rest on the same double requirement. The first requirement is the acceptance of heightened vulnerability to other people: both to those loved of other members of a community of difference, and also to those with whom one cooperates when such cooperation can no longer conform to an invariant and hierarchical scheme. The second requirement is the cultivation of our ability to imagine alien experience, the experience of those whose otherness we discovered when we underwent painful de-centring. This harks back to the 'uses of the Eurasian other', to which we alluded in the Russian context.

THE NEW FRONTIER: BUILDING A GREEN CATHEDRAL – MISSING GROUNDS

In the final analysis, then, what we see effectively being played out, through overcoming 'false necessity', is the revisiting of the social solidarity, as Cardoso's means of Brazilian navigation, on the one hand, and the accommodation of difference which is such a strong theme of Freyre's emergent orientation toward hybridity, and tropicality on the other. However, there is little harking back to origins, or standing on the grounds, as it were, of Amazonian nature, if not also local community, as per Marina Silva. Such eco-services somehow get left behind, while Brazil remains one of the most unequal – though less so than hitherto – societies on earth, as well as being one of the most environmentally destructive (of the Amazonian rainforest). American environmentalist Juan de Onis (11), made the point, some 20 years ago:

> *The waste of wood, natural forest products, and unique genetic resources through extensive land clearing is incalculable. The loss of potentially recoverable gold and tin, in the way these minerals are mined in Amazonia, is worth billions of dollars. Experience has shown that tropical commodities, such as coffee and cacao, carry high risks in international markets, and bulk grains are uncompetitive without a reduction of freight costs through heavy investment in agro-industrial processing in the region and a railroad system that replaces trucks. In consequence, the forests and the mineral resources must be the foundations for a new strategy of economic development of Amazonia based on productive activities that are profitable, socially stabilizing and compatible with the life-sustaining ecosystems that are Amazonia's most valuable natural resources.*

To that extent, Marina Silva, in defending the rainforest and its communities, and indeed, beyond such, drawing on both as the very grounds of Brazil's pursuit of integral advantage, has a long way to go. Perhaps she needs to become the nation's next President! Can there then be a way whereby the BRICS between them combine forces, not forgetting also the 'north-west' (Washington Consensus) as part of an overall integral process, serving to bring together a Eurasian 'east–west', a South African 'north–south', and Indian 'south–east', a Chinese 'north–east' with Brazil's 'south-west' to pursue such, with her? Indeed for Mangabeira Unger (12), in his *Democracy Realized: The Progressive Alternative*:

> *The organizations of the Bretton Woods system (Washington consensus) then must not be allowed to continue operating as a long arm of a dominant neoliberal program. Their job should be to assist national experiments.*

This brings us to our concluding chapter.

Bibliography

1. HRH Prince Charles, Tony Juniper and Ian Skelly (2010) *Harmony: A New Way of Looking at Our World.* London, Harper Collins and Blue Books.
2. Reid, M. (2014) *Brazil: The Troubled Rise of a Global Power.* New Haven, Yale University Press.
3. Roett, R. (2011) *The New Brazil.* Washington DC, Brookings Institution Press.
4. Hildebrandt, Z. (2001) *Marina Silva: Defending Rainforest Communities in Brazil.* New York, Feminist Press of City University.
5. Burke, P. and Pallares-Burke, M. (2006) *Gilberto Freyre: Social Theory in the Tropics.* Witney, Oxfordshire, Peter Lang.
6. Freyre, G. (1974) *The Gilbert Freyre Reader.* New York, Random House.
7. Cardoso, F. (2001) *Charting a New Course: The Politic of Globalization and Social Transformation.* New York, Rowman and Littlefield.
8. Cardoso, F. (1992) *Dependency and Development in Latin America.* Berkeley, CA, University of California Press.
9. Mangabeira Unger, R. (2004) *False Necessity: Anti-Necessarian Social Theory in the Service of Radical Democracy.* London, Verso.
10. Mangabeira Unger, R (2014) *The Future of Religion.* Cambridge, Harvard University Press.
11. De Onis, J (1992) *Green Cathedral: Sustainable Development of Amazonia.* Oxford. Oxford University Press.
12. Mangabeira Unger, R. (1998) *Democracy Realized: The Progressive Alternative.* London, Pluto Press.

Chapter 15

Reconstituting the BRICS: Comparative to Integral Advantage

unrestricted exchange between countries will increase total world output if each country specializes in those goods it can produce at a ***relatively*** *lower cost compared to its potential trading partners. Each country will then trade some of its lower-cost goods for others that can be produced elsewhere more cheaply than at home. With free trade among nations, all countries will find that their consumption possibilities have been expanded by such specialization and trade beyond that what would have been possible from their domestic production possibilities alone. Because of this compelling argument, economists tend to favor free trade, since it is presumed to be 'welfare enhancing' in that the aggregate level of world income is increased ...*

Roberto Mangabeira Unger (1), Free Trade Re-imagined

15.1 Introduction

AMERICA STILL RULES AT A META-ECONOMIC LEVEL

In this concluding chapter, in moving from comparative to integral advantage, we want to review where the conventional wisdom on the BRICS stands now, and how we might proceed with an integral BRICS in the future (see Table 15.1 below). In fact our opening argument is that the dominance of the Anglo-Saxon world ('west-north') continues, despite the rise of China, India and the emerging markets, because such 'meta-institutions', as the 'free market', 'global finance', the 'Washington Consensus' (IMF, World Bank and WTO) and the American-style Business School continue to rule the overall, global economic roost. In other words, while China may be imposing an alternative 'Beijing Consensus' (see Chapter 13) in experimental state-market combination, on at least parts of the 'developing world', the free market, global finance and the business schools remain alive and well, the last with its standardized management curriculum.

Table 15.1 Comparative to integral advantage

	GROUNDING	**E**MERGENCE	**N**AVIGATION	**E**FFECT
CARE 4 SOCIETY	COMMUNITY **A**CTIVATION	**C**ATALYSE DEVELOPMENT	**R**ESEARCH and INNOVATION	TRANSFORMMATIVE **E**DUCATION/AND ENTERPRISE
RUSSIA East/West	*Mutual Aid* Kropotkin	*Cosmism* Fedorov	*Anthropoecology* *ISRICA*/Bugakov	*Zemstvo* Evtuhov
SOUTH AFRICA North/ South	*Earth Jurisprudence* Cullinan	*Future Primal* Herman	*Ubuntu/TRC* *Tutu*/Mandela	*Value Sharing* Koopman
INDIA South/East	*Swadeshi (Economics of Place)* Gandhi	*Earth Democracy* Vandana Shiva	*Knowledge Society* Singharoy	*Sarovodaya/Awakening of All* A.T. Ariyaratne
CHINA North/ East	*Chaxugeju (Association)* Fei Xiaotong	*Xiaokang (Moderation)* Shu Ming Liang	*Confucian Pragmatism* Zhichang Zhu	*Guanxi/ Mutual Benefit* Zhou En Lai
US/UK West/ North	***Natural Law*** **Free Trade**	***Emerging Markets*** **Global Finance**	***Comparative Advantage*** **Washington Consensus**	***Leadership/ Management*** **Multinationals/ Business Schools**
BRAZIL South/ West	*Eco-Services* Marina Silva	*Tropicology* Freyre	*Solidarity Society* Cardoso	*Re-Imagined Trade* Mangabeira Unger

So, contrary to popular opinion, for us little has changed substantively across the world's economic stage. Indeed, cutting across that stage, overall, as we revealed in our opening chapter, is a newly networked economy controlled by the youthful, Silicon Valley based, 'western-northern' Internet oligarchs. As Andrew Keen observes, as such, they are taking CARE of themselves much more wholeheartedly than they are looking after ourselves, as a whole.

15.2 CARE for Silicon Valley to CARE-4-Society

COMPARATIVE TO INTEGRAL ADVANTAGE

In concluding our pursuit of integral advantage, then, we turn from the 'western-northern' globalizing Washington Consensus to our integral means of taking CARE (2), as we shall see, for each particular society as a local–global whole. To begin with as such, we remind ourselves of the theory of *comparative advantage* (see Chapter 2), originated by David Ricardo in the nineteenth century, that underlies today's conventional wisdom on 'emerging markets', as per the so called BRICS in the twenty-first century, altogether aligned with economic growth:

and then we paraphrase the above, as if we were pursuing *integral* advantage, thereby CARE (see bold lettering below)-ing-4-Society as a whole:

> *exchange and reconciliation within and between countries will increase local and global wellbeing if each country pursues its natural, cultural, social and economic advantage thereby exchanging knowledge and value with its potential trading partners, thus re-imagining free trade. With such exchange and reconciliation among nations, all countries, as a whole, will co-evolve by* **C***atalysing development within and between each other, whereby specific local communities are* **A***ctivated, innovation driven technological and social* **R***esearch is duly institutionalized, and transformative* **E***ducation instituted within and across each. Through such each country will actualize its individual societal uniqueness and thereby contribute to the integrated potential of the global whole. We favor as such the pursuit of each country's integral advantage, since it is presumed to be 'welfare enhancing' in that the aggregate level of local and global wellbeing is thereby increased.*

TAKING CARE: TOWARDS AN INTEGRAL UNIVERSITY

As we have articulated in our (2) previous work on *Integral Development*, such a process of taking CARE, needs to be fostered, middle-up-down-across so to speak, by a developmental agency, such as a duly reconceived *integral* university, together with other environmental, civic, public and private enterprises, to altogether pursue integral advantage. Four CARE-ing functions are required as such, in each case, as we shall see below, taking on from where a conventional university leaves off, for each and every one of the BRICS in turn:

Function 1 – Individual Thought Leadership to Catalyze Collective Development

Catalyzing Development, in relation to a society as a whole, be it for example South Africa through a purposeful evolution of Robben Island University, involves partnerships between all stakeholders, catalyzed by a developmental agency (such as an integral university). It supplants the more limited role of an individual 'guru', be he a Mahatma Gandhi in India (cited in Chapter 12 with no university base) or a Michael Porter (cited in Chapter 3 at Harvard Business School) in America. The aim is to further enhance the knowledge and value-creating potential of a society, such as South Africa, as a whole, thereby transcending artificial (but yet often very real) borders between academia, business, politics, civil society, local communities and the environmental sector.

Here such a catalytic function occupies an in between, middle-up-down-across position so to speak, thereby interconnecting nature, culture, society and economy. Thus it seeks to not only align experience and imagination, theory and practice, but also to emancipate the interdependent stakeholders concerned from the intellectual and ideological forces that independently hold them back, thereby serving to realize their own individual and collective potential. This catalytic function then interconnects with all three others, as we shall see, aligned with transformative education, innovative institutional research and communal activation to contribute to the development of society as a whole.

Function 2 – Project Outreach to Community Activation

Community-based Activation transcends conventional project-based university outreach, in that it seeks to sustainably, and collectively, develop a particular community's potential, drawing on its specific nature. Such community activation is therefore profoundly lodged within the particular reality (worldview) of the community, and has a particular emphasis on the integral impact of the agency's engagement with community. It addresses the calling, so to speak, of that community, or province as we saw in the Russian case (Chapter 7) by activating the community's particular gifts or capacities. It also serves to build up on on going capacity for learning, within the community or province as a whole, building on such approaches to communal and societal learning as are becoming common currency in certain NGO, if not university, circles today.

*Function 3 – Theme-Based to Innovation based Institutionalized **R**esearch*

Innovation-driven **R**esearch, in the social as well as the natural sciences, while potentially having a strong 'transformational' orientation, is virtually non-existent in the world at large, because technology-based research, based on the natural sciences, predominates. Probably the best-known example of such innovative social research, in recent times, was the Chicago School of Economics, home of neo-liberal economics. Yet its influence has arguably been more negative than positive. Such social research, integrally for us, draws on the full transformational rhythm underlying this book, from origination to transformation, drawing out a particular society's genius (as we shall see below for each of the BRICS distilled in turn) and geared toward bringing about social as well as technological innovation. Such innovative projects require fundamental research on the one hand, that serve to interlink social science and society, and result, on the other hand, in transformative impact on the ground.

They thereby profoundly differ from much of today's highly individualized research, the latter engaging students or practitioners in doing social research-as-data processors. By way of contrast, institutionalized, innovation-driven research involves going beyond the notion of the 'individual researcher', leading to the establishment of research communities. Such research groups are not only much better equipped to deal with the complexity of any given issue, but they are also much more likely to establish long-term, sustainable processes of collective knowledge and value creation, leading on to transformative education and enterprise.

*Function 4 – Taught Courses to Transformative **E**ducation and Enterprise*

Much of today's higher educational offerings or professional training, worldwide, are highly standardized and 'productized' in individual courses, all too often modelled on western European or American curricula or 'training courses'. Invariably moreover, local contextualization and also a global interconnecting framework are missing, leaving students or practitioners with large bits of fragmented knowledge. Many then leave universities, or their workplaces, bereft of indigenous-and-exogenous knowledge and context, also without having a sense for the real-life problems within their specific field, and how to creatively engage with them. Moreover, the all important task of linking Chinese or Indian, Russian, Brazilian or Southern African (B R I C S-wise) indigenous knowledge with the exogenous Anglo-Saxon mainstream is seldom if ever undertaken.

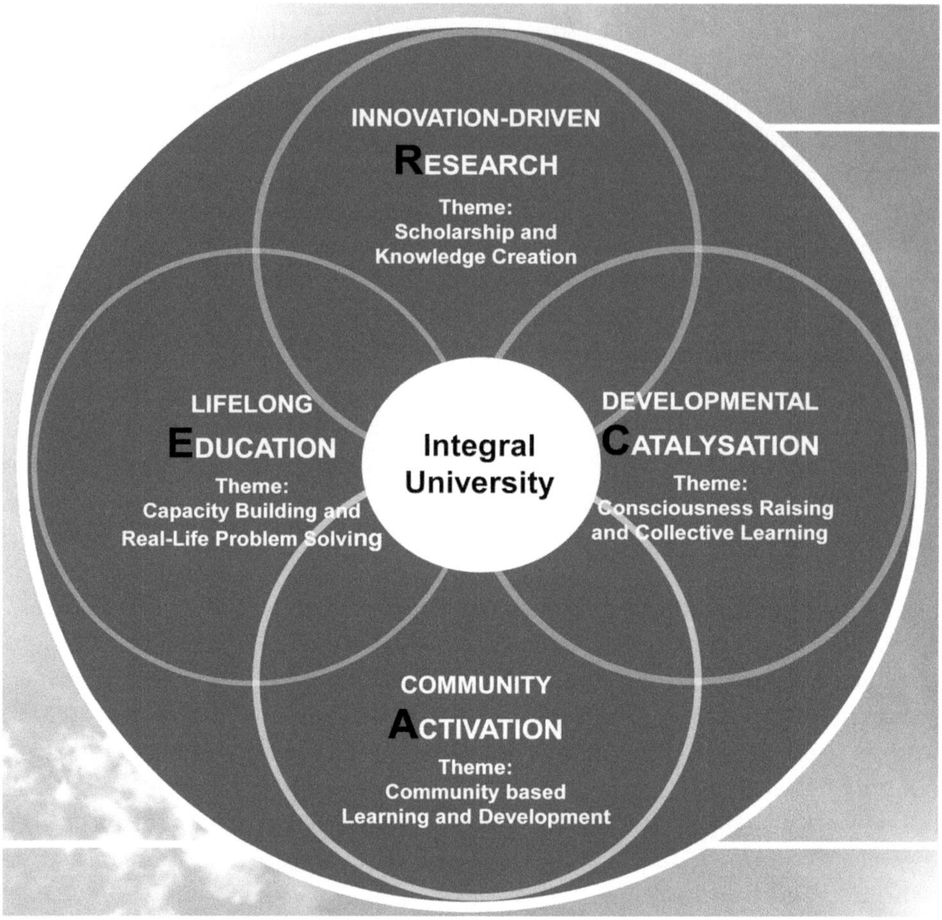

Figure 15.1 The integral university – Overview

Transformative education and learning turns such standardized courses – from short courses to PhDs – into integral educational journeys, that build capacities and skills in relation to real-life problems in particular societal contexts, drawing on local as well as global knowledge in combination (see Figure 15.1). Thereby, the initial focus on 'individual students' is equally transcended, by connecting such students to organizational, communal and societal contexts with which they ultimately need to build upon. Thereby, such a new approach to education has a particular 'trans-personal' emphasis, equally emphasizing the *rounded* development of individual, organization, community and society.

So much for the overall CARE process (see Table 15.2). We now turn to the release of GENE-ius, as we have termed it (see Chapter 3) for each BRICS society in turn.

Table 15.2 Pursuing integral advantage in the west/north: CARE 4 America

US/UK ***West/ North***	*Natural Law/ Free Trade* Free Market **A**ctivate Community *Grounding*	*Emerging Markets* Global Finance **C**atalyse Development *Emergence*	*Comparative Advantage* Washington Consensus Innovation Driven **R**esearch *Navigation*	*Entrepreneur, Leader, Manager* Multinationals/ Business Schools Transformative **E**ducation *Effect*

GROUNDING: ACTIVATING COMMUNITY – LAWS OF NATURE/ FREE TRADE

We start with the conventional wisdom underlying the originally constituted BRICS, in this initial Goldman Sachs instigated case (see Chapter 2), implicitly if not explicitly, *CARE-ing for America*. The US and the UK, in the business and economic arena, today increasingly infiltrate societies worldwide, as the international standard bearer, thereby inhibiting other countries from pursuing their own integral advantage, albeit they have much to learn from the 'west-north', at the same time as they ground themselves in their own soils.

As such, in the UK and thereafter in the US, from the eighteenth century onwards, *laws of nature*, as per Adam Smith and David Ricardo as we have seen, historically overtook nature itself. Thereby the free market, free association, freedom of contract and free enterprise ruled the economic roost from hereon, at least for those becoming 'developed'. To that extent, at a community level, and increasingly today since the ascendancy of neo-liberalism, *entrepreneurship and enterprise, whether economic or social in nature and scope, is seen to be the community-cure all*, the infallible route to poverty alleviation, employment creation or indeed economic growth. Such promotion of enterprise through free trade follows, as night follows day, as a 'law of nature' so to speak. The market, economically as such, has replaced the 'marketplace' as a social entity, and laws of *nature* have duly departed from the 'self-organizing' processes that characterize the natural environment.

EMERGENCE: CATALYZING SOCIETAL DEVELOPMENT – GLOBAL FINANCE-AND-MARKETS

The catalytic agency that makes the world go round, according to today's conventional wisdom, is the 'global' (for *global* read 'western-northern') financial market. As we know 'the markets' can wreak havoc on countries ranging from Thailand historically or Greece currently, or they can indeed facilitate international trade, investment and development. Goldman Sachs then, from which the notion of BRICs originally emerged (see Chapter 2), lies at the heart of such global finance. In fact its noted, or notorious CEO, Lloyd Blankfein, had brazenly declared himself some five years ago in 2009, as quoted in the American financial press, to be *doing God's work.*

As for the emerging markets, if we genuinely wish to pull more people out of poverty, according to O'Neil (3), into the middle class and facilitate greater trade and wealth creation, then we need to think hard about overcoming the obstacles which still hinder the free flow of commerce. International economic governance is no longer just a subject to excite economists, he says, as an embodiment of such conventional wisdom, it is a vital element of the way the world works today, and one that affects us all.

NAVIGATION: INNOVATION DRIVEN INSTITUTIONAL RESEARCH – WASHINGTON CONSENSUS

The World Bank, the IMF (International Monetary Fund) and the WTO (World Trade Organization), between them, supplementary to the markets then, provide the global navigation for the world economy. Moreover, their operational role, jointly, is accompanied by major social and economic institutionalized research activity supportive of these global institutions. 'Social' and economic research is complementary to much larger scale, technology-based research and innovation, conducted by multinational companies in America, Western Europe and Japan, if not also now China and India.

Universities then, in relation to such technology-based research, often play a prominent role, but, in the social sciences and humanities, that is much less likely to be the case, where 'social innovation', as an offshoot of such, is very thin on the ground. While hugely innovative individuals, like Mangabeira Unger (Chapters 2 and 14) are a product of, for example in his case, Harvard Law School, his approach to 're-imagining trade' is an individual rather than an institutional research activity. We finally now turn to the 'west-north' effect.

EFFECT: TRANSFORMATIVE EDUCATION – BUSINESS SCHOOLS AND MULTINATIONAL COMPANIES

At the turn of the last century, according to Harvard Business School's Rakesh Khurana (4): For the institutional entrepreneurs who invented the university business school, the primary purpose of the new institution was to legitimate and institutionalize the new occupation of management.

Management at the time, early in the twentieth century, was a veritable social innovation, a product of psychology, sociology, political science and economics, with Austro-American social scientist Peter Drucker (5) almost singlehandedly paving the way, in the first half of the last century, for the business schools to follow. However, in the latter part of the century, as Khurana goes on to say: The two institutions of management and business education have reciprocally defined the ultimate ends of the corporation and shaped the means whereby management seeks to achieve them. They have given rise to the contemporary understanding that *the purpose of management is to maximize shareholder value, thereby legitimizing practices such as the liberal granting of stock options and a focus on share price …*

The standard MBA product of the business schools around the world then, encompassing marketing and human resources, operations, finance and strategy, whether in Brussels or Beijing, Boston or Bermuda, has remained substantially unchanged, over the past half century. However, its ultimate purpose has been transformed, over the course of that time, as identified by Harvard's own Khurana above, from legitimizing management to maximizing profit. Now the stock in trade of the world's multinationals, it serves as the culminating effect of such western-northern conventional business wisdom, geared ever more to short-term profit maximization. We now turn from the capitalist 'west-north' establishment to the 'ex-communist' one, albeit with an 'east–west' difference.

Table 15.3 Pursuing integral advantage in the east/west: CARE 4 Russia

RUSSIA ***East/West***	*Mutual Aid* Kropotkin Activate Community *Grounding*	*Cosmism* Fedorov Catalyze Development *Emergence*	*ISRICA/Anthropoecology* Bugakov Innovation Driven Research *Navigation*	*Zemstvo* Evtuhov Transformative Education *Effect*

GROUNDING: ACTIVATING COMMUNITY – MUTUAL AID, ARTEL/OBSHCHINA

Russia, as we have argued in this book, was by no means inevitably drawn to communism, or indeed neither now to its currently oligarchic version of capitalism (see Table 15.3). Going back in time, the medieval European cities, for Kropotkin (6), in the eleventh and twelfth centuries, had rendered an immense service to European civilization in general, and to Russia, via the Eurasian *artel* – urban guild – or *obshchina* – rural commune, in particular. Such mutual aid prevented feudal states from drifting into theocracies and despotic entities of old; *endowing Europe with the variety, self reliance, force of initiative and immense intellectual and material energies it now possesses.*

Why then was Europe seized with senile debility, in Kropotkin's terms, by the sixteenth century? For one thing, he maintains, mutual aid cannot be limited to small local associations. It must spread to its surroundings (in our terms from local grounding to local–global emergence), or else the global surroundings will absorb the local association. Trade then in the Middle Ages, formally communal, became the privilege of the merchant and artisan 'families' and the next step – that of becoming individual – seemed unavoidable. For us then, at least in the Russian case, there was a failure to purposefully pursue integral advantage, whereby the activation of local provincial community would further emerge, through the catalyzation of overall provincial-societal development.

EMERGENCE: CATALYZING DEVELOPMENT – FEDEROV'S DELO TO RUSSIAN COSMISM

So there has been nothing institutionally equivalent, for example, to global financial markets, to catalyze, locally–globally, to further, societal emergence of mutual aid. In fact for Federov (7) his 'projectivism', the bridge between the 'world as it is', and 'the world as could be' was *delo* in Russian, a word that can mean 'business', 'affairs', 'matter', or 'activity' (not emerging into the contemporary business curriculum). For him (see Chapter 5), it is *delo* – the common task – applied to fields of knowledge that will transform everyday current *-ology* into *-urgy. Orthodox Christianity assumes the radically active cosmic project of resurrecting the common task (delo), as a Christian alternative to Marxism.*

But how is this to take place? The overall 'cosmist' approach to world problems, of which Federov was an originator, was that of *seeking unity, wholeness and universality by facing and attempting to overcome a multitude of apparent contradictions*. In fact, communism – as opposed to cosmism – ducked that very issue by its overly simplistic, ultimately despotic approach, a distortion of the 'north-west' (Marxism) and a negation of the 'east–west', cosmism. Bulgakov at least made an attempt to take on from where his fellow cosmist, Federov, left off. But there was no institutional support, no business school, in contemporary American guise to take this intrinsically Russian emergence further on, except, albeit tenuously, through Siberia's 'far out' ISCRA.

NAVIGATION: RESEARCH AND INNOVATION – ISCRA, ANTHROPOECOLOGY

Already in the 1870s, fellow Slavophile philosopher, Vladmir Soloviev, perceived a 'crisis in Western philosophy', and specifically such a crisis of positivism vis à vis his integrality (thought, feeling and will), 20 years before it erupted on the European scene. Following their German Romantic predecessors, he and his fellow Slavophile philosophers argued against the 'rationalism' of western philosophy. Bulgakov's (8) *Philosophy of Economy* was premised on an interaction of two major disciplines. He believed that *philosophy and political economy existed in artificial isolation and that insights from each discipline could be productively brought to bear on the other*. In fact *khoziaistvo* in Russian, means both economy and household. The discipline of *anthropoecology*, as per ISCRA constituted in Siberia, took on such cosmic proportions.

Bulgakov then, like many of his predecessors, was concerned above all with constructing a worldview that addressed the real concerns, as per world-as-household, of our life in the world, that treated human beings as active creatures, thereby economic, interacting with the world around them. What he termed an interaction of the disciplines of philosophy and economy was a restatement of Russian philosophy's preoccupation with life. *Bringing the concerns of political economy to philosophy was a means of introducing the realities of labour, wealth and poverty into an otherwise meaningless abstract intellectual exercise*. Out of such was born ISCRA (9), the International Scientific Research Institute of Cosmic *Anthropoecology* based in Siberia, lodged in the far-eastern Russian outreach, a long way, too long a way from American business school heatlands.

EFFECT: TRANSFORMATIVE EDUCATION – THE ZEMSTVO AND THE NATIONAL ENLIGHTENMENT

We finally turn to the Russian zemstvo for effect. The separation between city and countryside in Russia, for historian Catherine Evtuhov, remained partial even up to the early nineteenth century. *Life in the province* she cited

Niznhii Novogrod, in the heart of Russia, *pulsed to the rhythms of the surrounding countryside, as well as to the rhythms of commercial enterprise and those created by the religious calendar.* Two points, for Evtuhov (10), are critical here: the *multiplicity and diversity of emerging economic structures and activities on the territory of this single province, and the constant, active interchange and motion within such.* What mediated between the two, catalytically, was the self-governing zemstvo, as the local polity as it were.

Economic historians take more or less for granted the basic distinctions between *agriculture, industry, trade and commerce. In the Russian experience,* particularly in the world of the nineteenth-century province, these manifestly different forms of activity *intersected, forming, if not a coherent unity, at least an infinitely connected continuity*. Indeed *an entire network of zemstvo-run schools was created under the jurisdiction of the Ministry of National Enlightenment.* All of such, ultimately, was by-passed by the 'north-western' communist establishment, and the opportunity to pursue integral advantage, in Russia 'east–west' was missed. The same applies when we turn 'north–south' to South Africa (see Table 15.4).

Table 15.4 Pursuing integral advantage in the north/south: CARE 4 South Africa

SOUTH AFRICA *North/ South*	*Earth Jurisprudence* Van der Post Activating Community *Grounding*	*Future Primal* Herman Catalyzing Development *Emergence*	*Ubuntu:Truth and Reconciliation* Tutu/Mandela Innovation-driven Research *Navigation*	*Value Sharing* Koopman Transformative Education *Effect*

GROUNDING: ACTIVATING COMMUNITY – WILD LAW TO EARTH JURISPRUDENCE

The South African 'wilderness' movement, the most notable member of which was Laurens Van der Post (11), provided a distinctive natural grounding, subsequently further evolved by South African environmental lawyer Cormack Cullinan (12) in terms of Earth Jurisprudence. It recognizes and embodies the qualities of the Earth system upon which his South Africa is grounded. His approach then *seeks both to foster passionate and intimate connections between people and nature, and to deepen their connection with the wild aspect of our natures.* It tends to focus more on relationships and on the processes by which they can be strengthened, than on end points and 'things' such as property. It protects wilderness and the freedom of communities of life to self regulate. It aims to encourage creative diversity rather than impose uniformity.

For Cullinan then, the dominant cultures of the twenty-first century could learn important principles and techniques from the systems of governance of those indigenous people, for whom such 'wild law' came naturally. Such would be useful in developing more Earth-centred structures for our times. Three good reasons for taking a closer look at indigenous cultures are: firstly, certain cultures did manage to evolve laws and other means of regulating human conduct that enabled them to live successfully over long periods of time as part of a wider community of living and non-living beings. Second, there is a dearth of plausible new ideas about how to govern ourselves in a manner that will improve our relationship with the rest of the Earth Community. The fundamental issue we are dealing with here, our relationship with the Earth, is as old as humanity itself. We would be foolish indeed not to consult the fantastic library of different techniques of human governance that have succeeded over thousands of years. Third, after being in the stifling, virtual monoculture of governance thinking for so long, it is inspiring to be exposed to worldviews outside of it.

EMERGENCE: CATALYZING DEVELOPMENT – FUTURE PRIMAL

South African political scientist now based in Hawaii, Louis Herman (13), takes on from where Van der Post and Cullinan leave off. Even if we wanted to he says, we have lost the vast expanse of unspoiled, game-filled country to which the latter alludes, needed to keep more than a handful of humans alive. But we can recognize the complexity of his so called 'primal politics', according to Herman, as ubiquitous within us all. Our wilderness origins fashioned our creative self-consciousness, which is both expanded and balanced by following the primal dynamic:

> *face-to-face communication within a caring community of individuals, passionate for living and learning in a mutually enhancing resonance with the natural world.*

This is the 'truth quest', he says, and it is our primal inheritance. We can ignore it and repress it, or we can cultivate it in all our endeavours and bring it into a creative engagement with the reality we find ourselves caught up in: a civilization rushing to self destruction while displaying tantalizing possibilities of a more beautiful, joyful way of life. What then enables us, in pursuing integral advantage in South Africa, to navigate such?

NAVIGATION: INNOVATIVE RESEARCH – *UBUNTU*/ TRUTH-AND-RECONCILIATION

For South African theologian and academic, John De Gruchy (14), the Greek words translated in the New Testament by 'reconciliation' or 'reconcile' are compounds of the Greek 'to exchange', and this in turn is derived from the word meaning 'the other'. The words thus carry with them the sense of exchanging places with 'the other' and therefore being in solidarity with them.

This was born out, to the greatest possible degree, in what became known as Robben Island University. For Nelson Mandela (15) the university grew up partly out of necessity. As young men came to the island, he realized that they knew very little about the history of the ANC (African National Congress). Walter Sisulu, perhaps the greatest living historian of the ANC, began to tell them about the organization in its early days. Gradually this informal history grew into a full course of study, which became known as Syllabus A, involving two years of lectures on the ANC and the liberation struggle. It also included a course on 'A History of the Indian Struggle'. Another comrade added a history of the Coloured people. Mac Maharaj, who had studied in the German Democratic Republic, added a course on Marxism. *The community formed was intimate. The Big Picture before them was that of their African Liberation. The style of teaching was Socratic. The focus was on Individuation. The Long Walk to Freedom was their truth quest.*

EFFECT: TRANSFORMATIVE EDUCATION/ENTERPRISE – BUILT THROUGH VALUE SHARING

There are distinct parallels between Robben Island University and South African manager extraordinaire, Albert Koopman's (16) Cashbuild *Worker Democracy*. Cashbuild was started as a wholesaler in 1978 and became a very successful business in a short space of time. Situated predominantly in the rural areas of South Africa and focusing on the black housing market, our staff complement consisted of 84 per cent black, 13 per cent white and 3 per cent Indian. However, by mid 1982, with 12 outlets, profits started sliding. Everything 'northern' was in place – systems, procedures, technology, combined with a booming market – but something was going wrong and Koopman did not know enough about the south, at that point, to recognize where to start looking.

Key questions went through Koopman's mind. Why do the workers actually work? What is their social or Divine Will? What went wrong in Cashbuild with respect to capital and labour? What were we actually trying to achieve as a business organism? *How do we bring together the rights of people, their spiritually-based humanity and the economic process as represented in the workplace?* He had to turn his thinking about people upside down and look at his business totally differently. The perception of capitalist exploitation at Cashbuild had to be changed. This change needed to be achieved not merely through some superficial 'western' programme of empowerment, but through an active 'northern' restructuring of the hierarchy, to liberate the work ethic. *He had to design an organization that was truly free so that the cooperation between all individuals in fact became its own 'ubuntu-like' value-sharing form.* We can now compare and contrast this veritable 'north–south' with India in the 'south-east' (see Table 15.5).

Table 15.5 Pursuing integral advantage in the south/east: CARE 4 India

INDIA ***South/East***	*Swadeshi* *(Economics of Place)* Gandhi	*Earth* *Democracy* Vandana Shiva	*Knowledge* *Society* Singharoy	*Sarvodaya/* *Awakening of All* A.T. Ariyaratne

GROUNDING: ACTIVATING COMMUNITY – SWADESHI, ECONOMICS OF PLACE

Having turned, as such, for initial grounding, and community activation, from Anglo-Saxon natural law (west-north) and Russian-style mutual aid (east–west) onto South African earth jurisprudence (north–south) we come onto Indian economics of place (south-east), that is Gandhi's 'swadeshi'. *Swadeshi,* according to Kumar (17), as per *Soil, Soul and Society* gives importance to human-scale technology and tools rather than large factories.

If technology or a machine aids human hands and makes work light, then that technology is compatible with swadeshi; but if technology replaces human hands and makes the workers redundant, as for example is the Silicon Valley instigated case (see Chapter 1) then that technology is incompatible with such. When technology and economy become the master and people become the instruments serving the industrial machine, then work becomes soul-destroying, soil-damaging and undermines social harmony.

EMERGENCE: CATALYZING SOCIETAL DEVELOPMENT – EARTH DEMOCRACY

Economy then shapes culture, culture shapes economy. Earth Democracy reconnects culture to how and what we produce and consume, and to how we govern ourselves. It creates the possibility, for Indian eco-feminist Vandana Shiva (18), of strengthening ecological security while improving economic security. And, on these foundations, it makes societies immune to the virus of communal hatred and fear. Earth democracy offers a new way of seeing, one in which everything is not at war with everything else, but through which we can cooperate to create peace, sustainability and justice in our violent and volatile times. Earth democracy provides the context for living creatures – inspired both by the timeless wisdom of ancient worldviews and by the emerging solidarities of new global movements of citizens against globalization, war and tolerance.

NAVIGATION: INNOVATION DRIVEN INSTITUTIONALIZED RESEARCH – KNOWLEDGE SOCIETY

Meanwhile the processes of generation, accumulation and use of knowledge, according to Indian sociologist Singharoy (19), have remained integral parts of Indian society since the very inception of its civilizational journey that started thousands of years ago. However, *a vast body of this knowledge has remained exclusive to a spiritual realm that looks for salvation and discovery of inner truth embodied in nature and in human beings.* Such knowledge has been more closely integrated with cognition, morality and ethics than with economic or societal development. Moreover such knowledge, especially the process of acquiring and getting access to it, remained more restricted to the limited few. *The journey of India shaped by the inheritance of this vast body of knowledge, is seldom matched by its mass application.* The National Knowledge Commission of India in 2008 signalled that the twenty-first century, in India, should be fashioned to be a century of an emerging 'knowledge civilization', thereby:

> *Enhancing access to knowledge, reinvigorating institutions where knowledge concepts are imparted, creating a world class environment for the creation of knowledge, promoting applications of knowledge for sustained and inclusive growth, and using such for the efficient delivery of public services.*

The Indian government envisioned such a knowledge society as one whereby its people are empowered and enriched, promoting a learning society committed to innovation, using knowledge to create economic wealth and social good for all, taking an integrated view of life as a fusion of body, mind and spirit. Such a knowledge society would have three key drivers: first, the pursuit of a just and equitable society, second, wealth generation, and, third, the promotion of traditional knowledge as well as that generated in modern research laboratories.

India today though, according to Singharoy, stands between two conflicting worlds: one pushes back with the dark influence of illiteracy, incapability, exclusion and inequality and the other tries to push forward with the advancement of education, ICT and other advanced technologies, for integration with knowledge society. In Sri Lanka we find a more integral case in point.

EFFECT: TRANSFORMATIVE EDUCATION – *SARVODAYA*, AWAKENING OF ALL

For founder of Sri Lanka's *Sarvodaya* 50 years ago, school physics teacher and social philosopher and activist A.T. Ariyaratne (20), contrary to the Indian Knowledge Commission cited above, in his case duly aligning the spiritual and economic:

> *I sought to enlist popular participation and commitment, requiring a value-base that is meaningful to the people, relevant to their perceived needs, and affirmative of their inherent strengths. And where are such values to be found?* They are present in indigenous religious traditions, which over centuries have shaped the people's perception of reality and their notions of what is good and true. *Principles for the improvement of their present lives can be culled from these traditions, and re-articulated in ways that mobilize people to take responsibility for social change.*

Gram swaraj as such, that is first, *Local Awakening* signifies the liberation of the village through the creation of *grassroots economic and social programmes*. Second, through Deshodaya – *National Awakening, Sarvodaya* envisions a process of political liberation, a *community-based participatory democracy.* Third, Vishodaya – *World Awakening,* perhaps the most important that *Sarvodaya* can contribute to the global dialogue today, is that of *development based on spirituality and spiritual consciousness.* Although *Sarvodaya* has sought a balanced development that integrates social, economic, political and spiritual elements, the key to its system is the spiritual element. As such, *Sarvodaya* is a spiritual movement that seeks social justice and development, a total social revolution, involving some 15,000 villages in Sri Lanka today.

We now turn to China (see Table 15.6), where the pursuit of 'north-eastern' integral advantage is very different, starting out from *laws of association: chaxugeju*.

Table 15.6 Pursuing integral advantage in the north/east: CARE 4 China

CHINA *North/East*	*Chaxugeju* *(Association)* Fei Xiaotong	*Xiaokang* *(Moderation)* Shu Ming Liang	*Confucian* *Pragmatism* Zhichang Zhu	*Guanxi/* *Mutual Benefit* Zhou En Lai

GROUNDING: ACTIVATING COMMUNITY THROUGH PROMOTING ASSOCIATION – CHAXUGEJU

Whereas (north)-western families are organizations with fixed members, Chinese families, for indigenous sociologist Fei Xiaotong (21), are networks capable of expanding outward. These networks are without clear boundaries and consist of differential categories of kinship relations. In the past two centuries, the Chinese have become merchants of the world, because they have been able to create highly efficient, flexible commercial networks on such a family basis. In general, moreover, the higher a person's prestige (and perhaps wealth), the more likely that person will have a dense web of horizontal and vertical network ties. Moreover, the more linkages one maintains, the more intensively one is wedged into an existing social order and is committed to the status quo.

EMERGENCE: CATALYZING SOCIETAL DEVELOPMENT THROUGH PROMOTING XIAOKANG

Building upon such, in the new millennium, as a response to the social and environmental destructiveness of current economic policies, a new moral economic approach, that is Xiaokang (the Chinese communist party pursuing moderation), purporting to be drawing on original Confucian origins, could be another case of local, in this case Chinese, contours bearing global significance. Its basic 'north-eastern' assumptions, for Chinese political scientist based at the London School of Economics, Lin Chun (22), are certainly far broader than such narrow beliefs as the crude 'economic man', born and bred in the 'west-north'.

Past and present setbacks notwithstanding, for Lin Chun, China then may strive to lead the way to a twenty-first-century global transformation, as the paradigm of capital accumulation has evidently hit a limit. The need to urgently address climate and environmental crises, for example, is inescapable and hence universal, and is where relevant local knowledge might be normatively constructed. Could not a new kind of 'industrious revolution', this time aimed at both needs and freedom, serve to relax the conceptual and discursive rigidity of capitalist modernity? *A participatory society as a commons, with direct producers as its subjective and realization of human values through united labour as its objective, is within the vision of a grand social model.*

NAVIGATION: INNOVATION DRIVEN RESEARCH – CONFUCIAN PRAGMATISM

In explicit, institutional pursuit of such, if then the economic powerhouse is moving north-eastward, and the world is on course for an Asian century, as many suggest, what might be the navigational result? How should people all over the world learn from each other and together make the world better and happier? As such, an inquiry based on Confucian pragmatism, for Chinese management scientist Zhichang Zhu (23), may be a way forward. Overall he says *let us make the world better and happier (American pragmatist John Dewey) and realize great harmony (Chinese pragmatist Confucius).*

Zhu then specifically turns to Confucius. The way Zhu interprets the sage's pragmatic turn (see Figure 15.2 below) is informed by his eight exemplary doings, formulated into three groups. The *first* two 'wuli' steps – *investigating things and extending knowledge* – are redirected toward the goal of understanding the world. The *second* three 'shili' steps – *making sincere one's intentions, rectifying one's mind and cultivating or improving one's person* – are directed toward the goal of perfecting oneself from within, so that one can be ready for social and political responsibility to better others. The *third* three 'renli' steps – *regulating a family, governing a state well, and pacifying the world* – are directed toward extending one's virtues among men so that one can be said to realize one's potentiality in relationships.

How is this ultimately reflected practically speaking, as it were?

EFFECT: TRANSFORMATIVE EDUCATION – MUTUAL BENEFIT

According to American development economist Deborah Brautigam (24), in *The Dragon's Gift: The Real Story of China in Africa*, China's premier Zhou Enlai had originally introduced the 'Five Principles of Peaceful Coexistence' during the 1954 negotiations with India, ironically, given the situation today, over the Tibet issue, that is:

1. Mutual respect for sovereignty and territorial integrity.
2. Mutual non-aggression.
3. Non-interference in each other's internal affairs.
4. Equality and mutual benefit.
5. Peaceful coexistence.

More than half a century later, Chinese leaders will still point to these principles as the bedrock of their foreign policy and their development strategy.

Between 1990 and 2005 manufacturing grew by almost 12 per cent annually in China, while sub-Saharan manufacturing grew at a mere 1.5 per cent per annum. It helps then to have someone experienced leading the way toward mutual benefit. This can happen in at least four ways. First, if the level of technology is not too advanced, a foreign-owned factory can act as a role model. People can see and decide *yes we can do it too.* Second, skills can 'spill over' from foreign firms when the local employees leave, taking skills they learnt on the job to other companies, or starting their own firms. Third, foreign companies may sub-contract some parts of the work to local firms and help them meet the standards demanded. Fourth, competition in local markets can push local companies to invest in new technologies, improving quality, if it does not drive them out of business too fast.

We now finally turn from 'north-east' to 'south-west', that is to Brazil (see Table 15.7).

Table 15.7 Pursuing integral advantage in the south/west: CARE 4 Brazil

BRAZIL ***South/West***	*Ecosystem Services* Marina Silva	*Tropicology* Gilberto Freyre	*Solidarity Society* Cardoso	*Re-imagined Trade* Unger

GROUNDING ECOSYSTEM SERVICES: ACTIVATING AMAZONIAN COMMUNITY

Marina Silva's (25) mission, as we saw in the last chapter, was to change how Brazil – and the world – thought about Amazonia: not as a place to exploit, but as a resource to care for; not as an empty space, but as home to millions of people and to the species of a priceless ecosystem.

Over 70 per cent of drugs derived from plants, for example, come from Amazonia. Researchers believe that cures for diseases like cancer, AIDS and heart disease are hidden in tropical forests. Yet indigenous nations, Silva argued, get none of the profits. *'One fungus, one plant or insect could produce a product worth millions or billions of dollars. A portion of that money, returned to rainforest communities, would support sustainable development in Amazonia'.*

'When I really dream I think we should come up with solutions to show the world', Marina says. With its vast rainforest, traditional peoples and high technology Brazil could become a world leader by showing a new vision of society working with nature. Just as Marina healed the first as a child, she fights now to heal Brazil. Freyre's approach to such is more cultural than ecological.

EMERGING TROPICOLOGY: CATALYZING SOCIETAL DEVELOPMENT

Brazilian anthropologist and sociologist Gilberto Freyre (26) has then suggested that his country might become a leader in the process of making 'civilized man in cold regions' aware of the aesthetic values of the tropics. He *predicted a movement that might be described as cultural imperialism in reverse, with the tropics leading and Europe following, not least because Brazil was a pioneer in racial mixing that was become characteristic of the world in the twentieth century.* He offered a critique of European reason and modernity from a tropical point of view. His main point, frequently reiterated, was that the tropical way of life was better adapted than the 'western' way to the demands of post-industrial and post-modern society. His own brand of tropical sociology or anthropology, as such, came to be known as *tropicology.*

He viewed tropical societies then as the new models for humanity. By 1975 he was calling it a new science that drew on ecology, anthropology, sociology, history and other disciplines, employing a comparative approach to discover common futures in tropical societies and cultures.

NAVIGATING SOCIAL SOLIDARITY: INNOVATION DRIVEN INSTITUTIONALIZED RESEARCH

In the evolution of social thought in Brazil then – academic sociologist and national President Fernando Cardoso (27) argued there has been an opposition between a purely academic outlook (based on scientific rigour and research) and a mindset more engaged in the transformation of social structures (where the political project of social change was the priority, and where scientific rigour took a back seat). Overall then:

- Is it possible to reconcile scientific rigor and politics? What role does the rigour of learning play in the political project?
- Is it possible to know objectively which policy will be the best for a given set of historical circumstances? Does knowledge predetermine policy?

In Cardoso's inaugural speech as President, he said the development of a country is not measured by what it produces. *True development is measured by the quality of attention the country gives to its people and its culture.* In a world of instantaneous global communication where people fragment and specialize, *cultural identity is rooted in nations.* Brazilians are people of great cultural heterogeneity, born from a combination of occidental Portuguese tradition with Africa and Indian traditions. The collective support for the country is moved, moreover, by sentiment, and this sentiment has a name: solidarity. It lets the country break free from small circles of particular interests and help neighbour, colleague, compatriot, near or far. *Brazilians, for Cardoso, are a solidarity people.*

We leave the climax of Brazil's integral argument to the Unger effect!

UNGER EFFECT: RE/IMAGINED TRADE – TRANSFORMATIVE EDUCATION

For Brazilian polymath, and Harvard Law School Professor Roberto Mangabeira Unger (28), once we free ourselves from the impulse to see contemporary institutions as the outcome of a narrowing funnel of possibilities, we can begin to find in our institutional history, as Unger puts it, hidden resources for reconstruction.

The **first** element in such an institutionally oriented programme of transition is to ensure the government *develops the human and financial resources with which to lift up ordinary people.* The **second** major platform is *to strengthen the educational and economic endowment of the ordinary worker and citizen.* The **third** axis of the institutionally oriented transition programme is the effort to *democratize the market.* The **fourth** element of the institutionally laden transition programme is *the commitment to high-energy democracy*: one that invites a greater expression of popular political energy and encourages a more repeated practice of basic reform than now exists in the sleepy democracies of Europe and North America. *A high energy democracy,* moreover, *imagines itself in the great theatre of the nation-states of the world,* from whence, from our perspective here overall, integral advantage comes. This brings us towards our final conclusion.

15.3 Conclusion

COMPARATIVE TO INTEGRAL ADVANTAGE

In the final analysis, through this book, we have traced a path from comparative advantage, underpinning free trade and conventional BRICS, to a complementary set of altogether integral paths, leading to re-imagined trade, in which each one of the BRICS has its on unique story to tell. For the conventional (see Figure 15.2 below in bold lettering) 'western-northern' wisdom, *free trade* (grounding) underpins now the *emerging markets* (emergence) and hitherto economic development in general, while the *Washington Consensus* (navigation) occupies institutional pride of place, and ultimately the American-style *Business Schools* (effecting) ensure that such business and economic conventions are maintained.

What we have proposed here is that such a 'one-size-fits-all' solution is replaced by a 'unity-in-variety', that is the pursuit of integral advantage, whereby each individual economy-and-society, in the BRICS case Brazil, Russia, India, China and South Africa, plays its varied part in an integral and thereby unified whole.

We now turn, in conclusion, from the picture of integral advantage as a whole to each of its five BRICS parts.

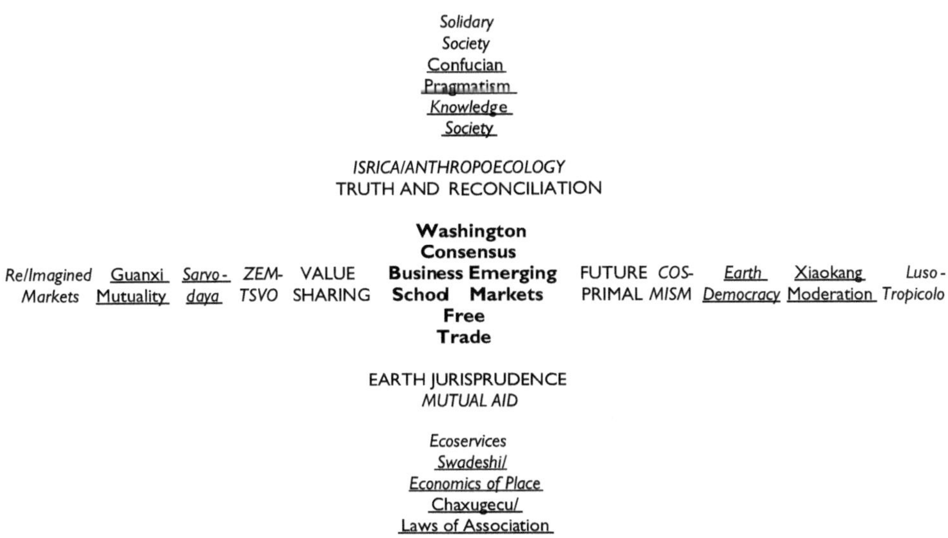

Figure 15.2 Comparative to integral advantage

NAVIGATE
TRC/Truth and Reconciliation
ISRICA /Anthropoecology
(Washington Consensus)

EFFECT Value Sharing
Local Self Government
(MBA – Business School)

Future Primal *EMERGE*
Cosmism
(Emerging Markets)

Earth Jurisprudence
Mutual Aid
(Free Trade)
GROUND

Figure 15.3 Integral underlying advantage

INTEGRAL ADVANTAGE AT CORE: RUSSIA EAST–WEST/SOUTHERN AFRICA NORTH–SOUTH

To begin with then, at core, we can see, in the combined Russian (east–west) and South African (north–south) integral cases, from grounding to effect (see Figure 15.3 above) there is a complete transformation of the status quo. Navigation-wise, for example, instead of the Washington Consensus (IMF, World Bank and WTO) we have, in duly institutionalized guise, anthropo-ecology, instead of neo-liberal economics, and social as well as economic reconciliation instead of simply commercial exchange. As a result, and in effect, local self government (zemstvo) and worker democracy replaces business administration writ large.

N
Knowledge Society
Confucian Pragmatism
Solidary Society

E *Re/Imagined Free Trade* Guanxi Mutuality *Sarvodaya Awakening*

Earth Democracy Xiaokang Moderation *Luso Tropicology* E

Swadeshi/ Economics of Place
Chaxugecu/ Laws of Association
Eco-services
G

Figure 15.4 Integral overarching advantage

We now turn from underlying to overarching BRICS. As such we turn from the underlying 'east–west' (Russia) and 'north–south' (South Africa) polarities, to the overarching 'south-eastern' (India) and 'north-eastern' (China), as well as the 'south-western' (Brazil) circumnavigation.

CIRCUMNAVIGATING INTEGRAL ADVANTAGE: INDIA/CHINA/BRAZIL/ AMERICA

As such the focus (see Figure 15.4 above) now turns to the Knowledge Society (India), Confucian Pragmatism (China) as well as Solidarity Society (Brazil), with a view to Indian *Awakening*, Chinese *Guanxi* and a Brazilian version of *Re-imagined Trade*, as articulated above by Unger:

> *every country, richer or poorer (mist) avoid lasting confinement to a particular place in the international division of labor and to the styles of production, the strategies of development, and institutions that may exert this confining influence.*

BRICS PARADISE LOST AND FOUND

As we survey the BRICS world today, and take note of the fact that Putin's Russia is under fire, South Africa has lost the Mandela touch, and President Rousseff's Brazil seems not to be now, politically and economically, what it was in the Lula glory days, we need not be surprised. Even China and India, as of 2015, are not growing, economically, at least the way they had been before, that is over the course of the last decade. Why all of this is hardly surprising, then, is that none of the BRICS is pursuing its integral advantage, as illustrated above, in any overall, purposeful way. Let us hope, if and when the integral penny drops, in Brazil and Russia, India and China, South Africa and of course America, as well as wherever else in the world you happen to be based, it will be all integral change.

Bibliography

1. Mangabeira Unger, R. (2007) *Free Trade Re-imagined: The World Division of Labor and the Method of Economics.* Princeton, Princeton University Press.
2. Schieffer, A. and Lessem, R. (2014) *Integral Development: Realizing the Transformative Potential of Individual, Organization and Society.* Farnham, Gower.

3. O'Neil, J. (2011) *The Growth Map: Economic Opportunity in the BRICS and Beyond.* London, Penguin.
4. Khurana, R. (2007) *From Higher Aims to Hired Hands: The Social Transformation of the American Business Schools and the Unfulfilled Promise of Management as a Profession.* New Jersey, Princeton University Press.
5. Drucker, P. (1973) *Management: Tasks, Responsibilities and Practices.* London, Heinemann.
6. Kropotkin, P. (1914) *Mutual Aid: A Factor of Evolution.* New York, Dover Publications.
7. Young, G. (2011) *The Russian Cosmists: The Esoteric Futurism of Nikolai Federov and his Followers.* Oxford, Oxford University Press.
8. Bulgakov, S. (2000) *Philosophy of Economy: The World as Household.* New Haven, Yale University Press.
9. Young, G. (2011) *The Russian Cosmists: The Esoteric Futurism of Nikolai Federov and his Followers.* Oxford, Oxford University Press.
10. Evtuhov, C. (2011) *Portrait of a Russian Province: Economy, Society and Civilization in Nineteenth Century Nizhnii Novgorod.* Pittsburg, Pittsburg University Press.
11. Van der Post, L. (1955) *The Dark Eye of Africa.* Cape Town, Lowry Press.
12. Cullinan, C. (2004) *Wild Law: A Manifesto for Earth Justice.* Totnes, Green Books.
13. Herman, L. (2013) *Future Primal: How Our Wilderness Origins Show Us the Way Forward.* Novato, CA, New World Library.
14. De Gruchy, J. (2000) *Reconciliation – Restoring Justice.* Cape Town, SCM Press.
15. Mandela, N. (1994) *The Long Walk to Freedom.* London, Abacus.
16. Koopman, A. (1991) *Trans-cultural Management.* Chichester, Wiley-Blackwell.
17. Kumar, S. (2013) *Soil, Soul, Society: A New Trinity for our Time.* Lewes, Leaping Hare Press.
18. Shiva, V. (2005) *Earth Democracy: Justice, Sustainability and Peace.* Cambridge, MA, South End Press.
19. Singharoy, D. (2014) *Towards a Knowledge Society: New Identities in Emerging India.* New Delhi, Cambridge University Press.
20. Ariyaratne, A.T. (1996) *Buddhism and Sarvodaya: Sri Lankan Experience.* New Delhi, Sei Satguru Publications.
21. Fei, X. (1992) *From the Soil: The Foundations of Chinese Society.* Berkeley, University of California Press.
22. Chun, L. (2006) *The Transformation of Chinese Socialism.* Durham, NC., Duke University Press.

23. Nonaka, I. and Zhu, Z. (2012) *Pragmatic Strategy: Eastern Wisdom, Global Success.* Cambridge, Cambridge University Press.
24. Brautigam, D. (2011) *The Dragon's Gift: The Real Story of China in Africa.* Oxford, Oxford University Press.
25. Hildebrandt, Z. (2001) *Marina Silva: Defending Rainforest Communities in Brazil.* New York, Feminist Press of City University.
26. Burke, P. and Pallares-Burke, M. (2006) *Gilberto Freyre: Social Theory in the Tropics.* Witney. Oxfordshire, Peter Lang.
27. Cardoso, F. (2001) *Charting a New Course: The Politic of Globalization and Social Transformation.* New York, Rowman and Littlefield.
28. Mangabeira Unger, R. (2004) *False Necessity: Anti-Necessarian Social Theory in the Service of Radical Democracy.* London, Verso.

Index

Page numbers in **bold** refer to figures and tables.